Fab Four FAQ

Fab Four FAQ

Everything Left to Know About the Beatles . . . and More!

By Stuart Shea and Robert Rodriguez

HAL•LEONARD®

Published in 2007 by Hal Leonard Books
An Imprint of Hal Leonard Corporation
19 West 21st Street, New York, NY 10010

Printed in United States of America

All memorabilia in this book are from the private collections of the authors unless otherwise noted.

Book design by Snow Creative Services

Library of Congress Cataloging-in-Publication Data
Shea, Stuart.
    Fab Four FAQ : everything left to know about the Beatles– and more! / by Stuart Shea and Robert Rodriguez.
       p. cm.
    ISBN-13: 978-1-4234-2138-2
    ISBN-10: 1-4234-2138-8
    1. Beatles–Miscellanea. I. Rodriguez, Robert, 1961– II. Title. III. Title: Fab Four frequently asked questions.
    ML421.B4S25 2007
    782.42166092'2–dc22
    [B]
                                                              2007019752

www.halleonard.com

This book is respectfully dedicated

to Arthur Hegewisch, who, in 1962,

invented the Close and Play phonograph.

Contents

Foreword by Chris Hillman

Sunday night, February 9, 1964.

It was just a little over two months since that tragic Friday morning in Dallas, Texas.

But a great healing wind blew through America, for this was the night we all met the Beatles, "live," on the *Ed Sullivan Show*.

Full of fire, the Beatles lit up our lives with an energy and hope we all thought that we had lost forever.

I remember that night so well. I was in Los Angeles, visiting my mom, and though I had heard about this new rock-and-roll band from England, I really hadn't given them too much attention . . . that is, until I heard the first note of "I Want to Hold Your Hand."

It hit a nerve inside me that ultimately changed my whole life forever.

Paul became my bass teacher, John my singer/songwriter coach, George my guitar teacher, and Ringo made it all swing with a smile.

What an incredible time! I observed, I learned, I was swept away into a world I never knew existed.

Eventually, I did get to meet and hang out with the Beatles . . . although I was so shy back then I was sort of in the shadows, watching David Crosby and Roger McGuinn jockey for position to win the Beatles' favor. Meanwhile, Michael Clarke, Gene Clark, and I were sort of in "observation mode."

But I was there!

Chris Hillman
May 2007

An original member of the Byrds, Chris Hillman played bass and sang on seven of their albums and wrote many classic songs, including "So You Want to Be a Rock & Roll Star," "Have You Seen Her Face," and "Time Between." Since his time with the Byrds, he's also played in several other legendary ensembles, including the Flying Burrito Brothers, Manassas, and the enormously successful Desert Rose Band. He is a highly rated mandolin player, guitarist, and singer/songwriter, as well as one of rock's most admired bassists. Please check in with what Chris is up to at www.chrishillman.com.

Introduction

The Sea of Time

Don't let anyone fool you. A book is as much a process of discovery for the writer as it is for the reader. And we discovered plenty of new things about the Fab Four as we wrote this book—some facts that others knew, some previously little-known spins on history, and some concepts we formulated that we hadn't considered before.

Our goal was to write a book for Beatles fans that told them some things they didn't know, and to further illuminate and interpret things they *did* know. Of course, the most fanatical of Beatle-ologists may know most, or all, of what's in here—one thing you discover as you go about your business in the world is that there's always someone who knows more about a given subject than you do.

But this book celebrates the fact that there's still *so much* to know about the Beatles, so many facts to tease out, so much interpretation yet to come. The Beatles, with their effect on pop culture, politics, fashion, the entertainment business—and, of course, the structure of rock and roll—are one of those phenomena through which one can examine the entire spectrum of the 1960s. And the fact that their rise coincided with the advent of color television, more affordable color photography, and new techniques in film and audio recording makes the evidence brighter, splashier, more vivid to us today in a way that vintage black-and-white film of the equally revolutionary Elvis Presley is not.

One can look at Beatles history in so many ways: for example, the way they affected the future of recorded music through their production tricks, new instruments, complicated arrangements, and the like. Or through their "competition" on the pop charts. Or through the prism of live performances, their films, their wives, girlfriends, and children. How did they grow and change through their experiences, their work, their *lives*?

The Beatles existed as four human beings, and as a popular phenomenon. They made the news; they changed society. They expanded the borders of what a pop group could stand for—which not everyone necessarily thinks is a good idea. They suffered tragedies, gained unimaginable triumphs.

And how fascinating it is to explore how the group unfolded. The Beatles' narrative takes in equal parts talent, drive, luck, and divine (!) providence, existing in a hermetically sealed time and space called the 1960s, one that the Beatles, as much as anyone else, helped move from grainy black-and-white to blinding color.

But despite time's fleeting nature—and surely the one great lesson of the '60s is that all things must pass away—the promise, optimism, and positive energy of the Beatles continue to penetrate the circles of music, culture, and social history. Through a concrete body of musical work, this energy captivates new fans every year even though (or perhaps *because*) we know how painfully the Beatles' story ended. Their story combines perfectly the innocence of a time and the hard-won experience of its youth . . . a time of poets in the marketplace, popular musicians aspiring to higher things, and a total lack of a road map.

Because all of this was a first. The Beatles set the entire template for rock and roll bands as we know them—for an attempt at band democracies, for giving the drummer a song, for a cute one and a quiet one and one who would say the right thing and one who would say the wrong thing.

Despite all the words already written about the Beatles, there were still new things we wanted to read, old things we wanted to better understand, classic things we wanted interpreted. But we also wanted to see a book aimed at the general reader that gave real, interesting history and analysis about the Beatles. Many Beatles books are either ridiculously simple or ridiculously complicated. We wanted to bring the knowledge in an entertaining and provocative way. We hope we succeeded at giving you a raft with which to sail down the Sea of Time.

Do You Want to Know a Secret?

The need for a book like this became clear when we realized that there is still information out there, truly critical for those who like the Beatles, that not that many people know. And we realized how much *we* didn't know . . . until we started digging around, learning more, listening more, and listening differently, and really *thinking*, in various ways we hadn't previously, about the Beatles and their music.

For example . . . how weird is it that very early pressings of mono copies of *Revolver* had a different version of the album's last song?

Yes, the mix of "Tomorrow Never Knows" heard on those select few early-on mono British pressings is *completely different* from any other version; it's more in-your-face, because the volume is higher, less reverberation has been added, and sound effects fade in and out at different places and levels.

Yet who, besides some bootleggers who have put this version out on unauthorized CDs, even knows about this? Why wasn't this alternate mix on *Anthology 2*? Why hasn't it been released as a twelve-inch dance single, for

God's sake? (DJs play "Tomorrow Never Knows" at clubs anyway, and John's groundbreaking psychedelic epic fits in with techno and house as well as it does with 1966 rock.)

The point is not that we're brilliant for telling you this . . . but that there is still a lot left to learn, explain, interpret, discuss about the Beatles. And if you're crazy about the band, you'll know that it's worth it.

Another example?

Did you know that there are 78-rpm Beatles records?

Yes, 78-rpm records, the only kinds of records available commercially for much of the twentieth century, which went out of fashion in America and England by the mid-1950s with the advent of the 45 and the rise of the album . . . but in other parts of the world, 78-rpm records were still printed into the 1960s. For example, in India, several Beatles titles were pressed in the ten-inch 78 format.

And what about the different versions of "She's Leaving Home" on the mono and stereo versions of *Sgt. Pepper*? The mixes of the song aren't different, but the *speed* of the recording is. The version currently available on compact disc—the only one commercially available, in fact, since mono albums went out of print in the late 1960s—is at the "correct" speed, somewhere between E and E-flat. The mono mix, however, was intentionally "sped up," most likely to make Paul's lead vocal sound more youthful, and rests in the key of F. Hard to tell why one version was faster than the other, but this *was* 1967.

And guess what: research by writer Steve Turner indicates the song was written about a real-life girl, Melanie Coe, whose adventure about running away from home was on the front pages of the *Daily Mirror*. And, amazingly, *Paul McCartney had met her before*—judging her to be the winner of a lip-synch "miming" contest to Brenda Lee's "Let's Jump the Broomstick" on an early 1964 appearance on the television program *Ready Steady Go!*

Finally, another little bit of trivia: on the photos accompanying the *Sgt. Pepper's* release, two Beatles are shown sporting their MBE's (George and Paul), while Ringo and John are wearing a cluster of medals. It is long assumed that, five years earlier, when drummer Pete Best was handed his walking papers, that the break was complete and irrevocable. Not so. In 1967, John called up Pete's mother, Mona, and asked to borrow the medals belonging to her father, Major Tom Shaw, who'd been awarded them for service in the Bengal Lancers during the Second Anglo-Afghan War back in the late nineteenth century. John had seen them many a time at the Best home during the band's dates at the Casbah. He remembered them, and Mona happily complied.

These little tidbits are known to many Beatles fans, but not all . . . and we offer them as a bonus to those people who actually go to the trouble of reading book introductions.

P.S. I Love You

This book is, in a way, our love letter to the Beatles, an attempt to thank them for all the pleasure they've given.

But we have others—many others—to acknowledge as well. One thing we've both realized is how big a role music, Beatles music in particular, has played in our family lives—and what a good thing that's been.

Stu would like to thank the following:

Starting at the top, I wish to honor my darling wife, lifemate, and partner in crime, Cecilia, with whom I've enjoyed everything Beatle virtually from the day we met. I still want to hold your hand, after all these years. Thank you for being the sunshine, the moon, the everything. I love you, yeah, yeah, yeah!

Thanks also to Agustin and Carolina Garibay for raising Cecilia, and for blessing the world with her siblings, Adrian, Maria, and Liz.

My angelic nephew Marco Garibay, at age five, proudly declared one night as *Please Please Me* played, "That's *my* kind of music." Meanwhile, his younger sister Carolina's first viewing of *Help!* proved she's been raised well; during the film, in a scene when the Fabs are enjoying cigarettes, she turned and asked her older brother with righteous indignation, "Why are they *smoking?*"

Mark Caro and Bob Purse have shared the Fabs' music with me for more than three decades. I love both of you guys dearly. Thank you for being such great friends.

Other friends who've shared this music with me include the Fiendish Thingies (Sheila, Shannon, Kathy, Carroll, Jimmy, Suz, Lynn, Karen, Pam, Annette, Craig, Naughty Sam, Sheri, Laura, and Cherrie), Rick and Rita, Carlos, Ted, Phillip, Jennifer, Lisa, Helen, the CBO, Dan, Bubs, James R., Clark Besch, Paul Hippensteel, Kristie, Jonathan, Doug Tonks, Scotts Bennett and Smoller, Eric Colin, Dan and Carole, Dog, Joe, Amy, DD, Terri, Mary D., MLD, and all at RAS. I have been blessed by your friendship. Bouquets also to the Hungerdungers: Lou, Jim, James, Pat, and Gordon. Your support means a lot. And to Leigh . . . many thanks.

Buzzy Linhart, thanks for just being you. Mark and Carol Lapidos, thanks for throwing the Fest for Beatles Fans!

And I happily thank Marion Claire Smith Shea-Light and John S. Shea II for introducing their sons to the Beatles in the late 1960s. And to my brothers John and Tom, a personal note: the few times we've sung three-part harmony to Beatles music are among the happiest moments of my life.

Rob's turn:

The true measure of the things we love is the pleasure realized when we share them with people dear to us. Strangely, it has been my good fortune in this life to be surrounded with a good many people whose introduction to the Beatles came through *me*. Right place at the right time, I guess.

First in my heart is my wife, Kathryn. Not only did I have the exquisite joy of introducing the Beatles' music and story to her, but I had the added satisfaction of watching the ripples spread outward as she passed it along to her folk (most notably to Amii, but to Val and Bill Holcomb as well). Darling, I love you.

Zane and Zoe Rodriguez are no less precious. For all of the sacrifice that comes with being a parent, there is reward a thousandfold when the lives that you have brought into being show their delight in the environment you've provided them, and throw it back to you.

One example would be little Zane, sitting in his car seat at the age of one, singing, "Know, know, know . . ." and "Love, love, love . . ." along with the Beatles' BBC rendition of the Teddy Bears' hit "To Know Him is to Love Him."

Another would be baby Zoe, a nearly a one-year-old herself (four years later), bopping along to the strains of the newly-released Beatles' *Love* album. It is my hope that my children's earliest memories of Beatles music will be inextricably intertwined with feelings of well-being, comfort, and love.

(In fact, Beatles music has literally been a part of their lives since each emerged from the womb: Zane to the sound of "Here Comes The Sun," Zoe to George's "I'd Have You Anytime." Okay, technically, that last one isn't a Beatles tune, but if things had broken differently, it *could* have been!) Kids: Love is all, Love is you.

I have been equally blessed with a family that has shared my pursuits with responses ranging from tolerance to equal fervor. My sister Zanny really ran with the whole thing, as did (to varying degrees of enthusiasm) Missy, Amy, and Russ. Big brother Rick unwittingly laid the seeds for collecting, with his intriguing collection of 45s that contained both orange-and-yellow swirl labels and ones sporting green Apples—sliced and unsliced. My love to you all.

But full credit for shaping my most fortunate life must go to Richard and Shirley Rodriguez. Each contributed mightily in complementary ways to the richness of my early surroundings, providing a home full of music and books while nurturing curiosity—no small accomplishment. My thanks, eternal gratitude, and love.

Further thanks to Doug Brooks, *who was there* (and knew it)! Also to David J. Hogan and Jim Slate for their well-attuned Jacque eyes, and the rest of the PIL ACQ gang, plus Rebecky. A toast to The Ring: Sharon, Philip, Kim, Kathy, Rob and Shannon, Maria, Lauren, and Sharon. "Trolls forever!"

Thanks to Chicago's very own Bob Stroud, Dick Biondi, and Terri Hemmert.

Our special thanks to Jackie Lomax and Chris Hillman.

Also to Frank Daniels and Mitch McGeary: you guys are lifesavers!

And Craig would like to thank Suzy and Joe would love to thank Debbie.

And thanx, Dogbro.

Robert Rodriguez and Stuart Shea have been friends for more than fifteen years, playing together in bands, hanging out, sharing Indian buffet, and, now, cowriting this book. It's been a joy, and we hope it's the first of many collaborations.

The two of us wish to thank John Cerullo of Hal Leonard for taking a chance on this book! Belinda Yong, Carol Flannery, Sarah Gallogly, Jenna Young, and Mary Vandenberg, and the sales and production staffs at Hal Leonard and Amadeus, also deserve our heartfelt appreciation.

S: Peace, love, and thanks, brother.
R: And to you, too.

Finally, thanks to the Beatles and to all who sail with them.

Fab Four FAQ

In the Beginning

Some History

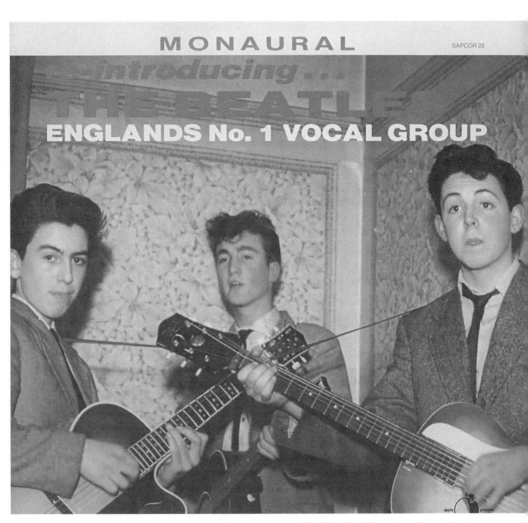

The nucleus of the Quarry Men is seen here in mid-1958. This bootleg release depicts the core around which a succession of transient members orbited.

When I Was a Boy

The Beatles' 1950s Roots

While the phenomenon that was the Beatles didn't arrive until the 1960s were in full bloom, the roots of future fabdom lay in the previous decade. The series of occurrences that added up to a cultural tsunami unfolded this way:

Lonnie Donegan Kicks Off the Skiffle Craze in England, January 1956

Born Anthony Donegan in Glasgow, this itinerant musician had been playing in Chris Barber's Jazz Band since the early 1950s. While Barber's band was essentially an instrumental outfit, Donegan (renamed Lonnie in honor of the bluesman Lonnie Johnson) often performed American folk, country, and blues chestnuts between sets, sometimes accompanied by a washboard for rhythm.

When the group recorded an album in late 1955, Barber asked Donegan to sing a couple of his between-sets tunes to round out the release. "Rock Island Line," an old Leadbelly warhorse, was released as a single from the LP. Credited to "Lonnie Donegan and His Skiffle Group," the song amazed everyone by rocketing up the charts. Even more astounding was the song's performance in America, where it went Top 20. Overnight, Donegan was a sensation, a Brit presenting a unique hybrid of American styles.

"Skiffle" was a term for "party" that Donegan claimed to have copped from an American record sleeve. Like punk twenty years later, the music—devoid of pretension or artifice—represented a triumph of spirit and energy over virtuosity. Suddenly stardom didn't seem beyond reach; anyone with a cheap guitar or household objects (a washboard, a tea chest, a washtub) could make music.

The standard repertoire tended to be happy and fun rather than depressing or overtly bluesy. As Donegan's follow-ups began charting ("Lost John," "Does Your Chewing Gum Lose Its Flavor," "My Old Man's a Dustman"), an

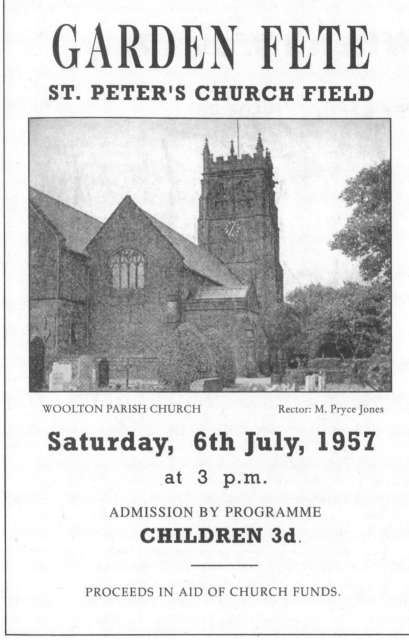

GARDEN FETE

ST. PETER'S CHURCH FIELD

WOOLTON PARISH CHURCH   Rector: M. Pryce Jones

Saturday, 6th July, 1957

at 3 p.m.

ADMISSION BY PROGRAMME

CHILDREN 3d.

PROCEEDS IN AID OF CHURCH FUNDS.

At this churchyard summer celebration, the roots of Beatlemania were planted.

entire generation of young kids was inspired to take up instruments. Literally to a man, everyone who was anyone during the '60s British Invasion credited Donegan's music with giving him a direction.

Paul McCartney Attends a Lonnie Donegan Show, November 11, 1956

Among those feeling the influence was fourteen-year-old Liverpudlian James Paul McCartney. The son of an ex-bandleader, the bright but conservative adolescent was still feeling around for a creative outlet when skiffle hit. Until then, his musical bent had leaned more toward the trumpet, an appealing instrument that had the drawback of prohibiting singing (so long as he played it with his mouth).

Coinciding with the arrival of Elvis and rock and roll, the rise of skiffle portended guitar as the next step, suggesting a path at a time when Paul was most susceptible. He attended a Donegan show one Sunday, a week to the day after he had buried his mother. The two events are not unrelated; as his brother Michael would say years later, "You lose your parent but you gain a guitar."

Doubtless seeking inspiration, Paul caught a glimpse that evening of what stardom looked like in the flesh. The workaholic tendencies that would define his career years were established when the grieving boy channeled his loss into a musical obsession, taking the instrument everywhere, including the bath and the toilet. At night, he would listen to radio under the covers, learning the words to songs and later attempting to figure out the chords on his instrument. Vague stirrings were now given form as the innately musical lad was at last finding his way.

The Cavern Club Opens in Liverpool, January 16, 1957

Alan Sytner, the son of a Liverpool physician, was a jazz fanatic and entrepreneur. Already the owner of two jazz venues in the city, he wanted the third to be something special.

Traveling to Paris for inspiration led him to discover clubs in the jazz district that were actually built in caves. No doubt his finely tuned ears appreciated the way the acoustics affected the sound. Upon his return, knowing that no actual caves were available, he scoured the city looking for the next best thing.

Over on Mathew Street (more of an alley by American standards), he found just the site: a storage cellar, belonging to a fruit warehouse, that had been used as a bomb shelter during the war. With its distinctive arches, long vaults, and damp, dank atmosphere, it promised grand possibilities.

Named after Le Caveau in Paris, the Cavern opened for business headlined by the Merseysippi Jazz Band. Homegrown rock and roll (or "Beat music" as it was known locally) was strictly *verboten*. It would take new ownership, and writing on the wall, for the situation to change four years later.

The Quarry Men Are Formed, March 1957

Sixteen-year-old John Lennon was a natural leader. While clearly gifted in a witty, artistic way, he caused much exasperation in his school instructors; it seemed that this exceptionally bright youth was more interested in provoking people and playing the fool than in getting down to academic business.

A habitual risk taker, he was surrounded by a group of like-minded subversives who probably possessed less daring than he—but every leader needs followers. Rock and roll entered his life full force, first with Bill Haley's "Rock Around the Clock," then with Elvis.

With skiffle's arrival, young John suddenly knew what he wanted. Instinctively seeking entry into a forbidden world, he cajoled his caretaker, Aunt Mimi (his mother's sister, Mary Smith), into springing for a secondhand guitar. Frowning on rebellion but keen to please her beloved nephew, she acquiesced. The keys to the kingdom were now in his hand.

Though not terribly musically inclined, John's fellows were also eager to get on the skiffle bandwagon. Initial lineups were somewhat nebulous, but the "classic" grouping included Eric Griffiths and Len Garry on guitar and bass respectively. Classmate Rod Davis had managed to get his hands on a real banjo, so he was in. Another fellow student, Colin Hanton, acquired a real drum kit, so he was *definitely* in. John's best friend, Pete Shotton, completely devoid of musical ability, was assigned the washboard.

As it happened, John's mother, Julia Lennon, had a bit of a musical background. Delighted to be a source of inspiration to her son, she taught him what she knew: the fingerings to banjo chords. (It would take some time for John to be completely de-programmed from using the wrong chord shapes.)

The ensemble would initially call themselves the Black Jacks, after the black jeans they favored, but found more relevant inspiration from their school song at Quarry Bank High School, which contained the line, "Quarry men, strong before our birth." John found the words sardonically irresistible.

John and Paul Meet, July 6, 1957

With four months of experience, the group's opportunities to perform were limited mostly to parties and church halls. But in early summer, they somehow finagled an invitation to perform twice at what for them would have been a prestigious event: the annual Summer Garden Fête sponsored by Saint Peter's Church in Woolton.

During the afternoon, the group performed outdoors on a makeshift stage. Among the onlookers was a schoolmate of John's named Ivan Vaughan. He'd brought along his musically inclined mate, Paul McCartney, to witness the Quarry Men's performance. Already fancying himself an old hand at performing, Paul was unimpressed by most of what he saw.

What did raise his eyebrows was the group's frontman. Although clearly playing ridiculous chords and unburdened by knowledge of the actual words to the songs he sang, John was striking in his ability to make up his *own* lyrics, apparently on the spot. Also, this guy was an undeniably dynamic performer.

There would be some time to kill before the band set up in the church hall for the evening's performance, and Ivan was keen to introduce his friend Paul to John. In the interim, Paul rode his bike home to retrieve his guitar (strung left-handed, as ordinary guitars were useless to him) while John got his hands on some alcohol and partook.

When the actual meeting came, the two youths remained outwardly unmoved by each other. But Paul saw that he had something to contribute to this band. Unlike any of its members, for example, he knew how to tune a guitar. (The Quarry Men had been in the practice of *paying* someone to do the tuning.)

He also knew the actual words to rock-and-roll songs, and, to John at least, seemed to possess a bottomless repertoire of material. What John saw was someone who could reinforce his own rock-and-roll aspirations within the band. (The other members tended more toward pure skiffle or folk. Playing rock had the tendency to limit their venues.) Also, Paul obviously had some useful know-how: after wowing John with a performance of Eddie Cochran's "Twenty Flight Rock," he obligingly wrote down the words.

John's dilemma was whether to admit someone into the group who might challenge his authority. Dominance was easy with fellows so demonstrably beneath him in talent; was strengthening the group worth diminishing his supremacy? He mulled it over for a couple of days, then sent emissary Ivan back to Paul with the word: "Fancy joining me group?" A musical force had been ignited.

The Quarry Men (Minus Paul) Debut at the Cavern Club, August 7, 1957

Paul's acquiescence definitely improved the Quarry Men's possibilities, but tangible forward movement would have to wait, as Paul was committed to a two-month stint at scout's camp over summer. Nonetheless, the boys got a foot in the door at the wildly successful Cavern Club.

Owner Sytner had sought to expand his club's clientele by offering lunchtime sessions, bringing in the student crowd during nondrinking hours. Since few young people were jazz aficionados, skiffle would be the draw.

It is not recorded how well the group went over on this occasion. What is known is that John would bait the crowd at other venues by dropping "beat" numbers into the set, raising the ire of some of his bandmates—not because they hated the music but because they feared for their personal safety from outraged patrons. As Rod Davis recalled, it was like playing heavy metal for a New Romantic crowd.

John further inflamed the situation by pretending notes passed up to the stage from the club manager demanding they "knock off the bloody rock!" were actually requests, allowing him to steer the band in any direction he fancied.

By 1959, Alan Sytner had sold his club to Ray McFall, an accountant who hated beat music. But falling revenues and increased competition from other clubs forced the bitter pill of rock and roll on him. Initially turned over to beat one night a week, then two, then at lunchtime as well, by 1961 the club gained a second life as the jazz attractions thinned out.

The Beatles would debut in March of 1961, essentially becoming the house band between Hamburg stints. The increased demands on their schedule in the wake of recording success would at last force them to bow out in August 1963 (following the release of their fourth single, "She Loves You") after nearly three hundred performances.

The Quarry Men Record "That'll Be the Day," Summer 1958

The ever-evolving Quarry Men lineup at last acquired some stability with the addition of a promising lead guitarist. Though more than two years John's junior, fifteen-year-old George Harrison, a protégé of Paul's, had undeniable chops.

John's initial reservations were overcome by George's ability to pull off the tricky instrumental "Raunchy," as well as by his Aunt Mimi's utter contempt for the youth's lower-class coarseness.

The new addition brought the band a quantum leap forward in terms of musicality and support. The former came with young George's almost masochistic drive to master his instrument, and the latter with the unconditional encouragement the boys got from Mrs. Harrison, one of the few adults around who "got it."

Filled with renewed confidence (as well as nourishment from her kitchen), the band ventured boldly into a makeshift recording studio in Liverpool to stake their claim to vinyl greatness. The Quarry Men pooled their resources and, for less than a pound apiece, cut a shellac disc featuring Buddy Holly's hit from the previous September on one side and a composition of their own on the flip.

Their rendition of "Day" features John on lead vocals, with creative vocal support from Paul and George. The lead guitar work is suitably impressive, but the percussion is virtually nonexistent. (Paul at this point still contributed second guitar. He would not assume full-time bass duties for another three years.)

The flip side is an interesting study in group dynamics. "In Spite of All the Danger," an Elvis/Everly Brothers–inspired ballad, would be the only song in the Beatles' canon credited to McCartney-Harrison. Curiously, it too features lead vocals from John!

During the Beatles years, a song's authorship could be divined, with rare exceptions, by who sang lead. At this time, the Lennon-McCartney songwriting partnership had yet to gel. Though Paul was already writing on his own, George had not yet been frozen out of the process. He and John would pen an instrumental in 1961 ("Cry for a Shadow"), but once the primary team was established, it would be a long time before George found encourage-

ROCK 'N' ROLL   SKIFFLE

The Quarry Men

                                        MANAGER
OPEN FOR ENGAGEMENTS   GATEACRE 1715

As evidence of their burgeoning professional aspirations, by 1958, the Quarry Men were prepared to hand out their business card to would-be employers.

ment from his bandmates to write, and only then capriciously. (During the post-*Anthology* thaw in relations, Paul often speculated about the possibility of writing with his former mate. The by-then terminally ill George would respond, "Why now?")

Julia Lennon Is Killed, July 15, 1958

Though living comfortably with his aunt, John's relations with his own parents were somewhat unconventional. When the two fell out, he became separated from both. At age five, having spent a glorious holiday with his long-at-sea father, John was literally placed between his parents and asked to choose whom he would live with. He chose his father—but at the sight of his mother walking away in tears, the young boy's heart immediately melted, and he reversed his decision.

Recognizing the limitations that her free-spirited life would offer, and desiring stability for the boy, Julia quickly ensconced him with her sister and brother-in-law. As a result, John would enjoy the most materially well-off upbringing of all the future Beatles, growing up in a strict but loving environment.

By adolescence, his bohemian, fun-loving mother had resurfaced as a force in his life. The two shared a great love of nonconformity and challenging the status quo at every turn. She encouraged his rebellion and influenced his comedic tastes. His only formal musical education, limited though it was, came at her knee.

Having re-established a relationship with his mother at this key stage of his emotional development would have lasting effects on John, his band, and by extension popular culture. Years later he would sing, "I've got a chip on my shoulder that's bigger than my feet." The roots of that anger can certainly be traced in part to the traumatic events of July 15, 1958.

On that summer evening, Julia had paid her son a visit, as she'd recently been in the habit of doing. Upon leaving, she had to walk up the block, then cross the street to reach the bus stop. A blind turn occurs near where she crossed. She apparently never saw a speeding car driven by a drunken, off-duty policeman. John heard nothing; it was not until police showed up at the door that he realized he'd once again lost his mother, this time forever.

Richard Starkey Debuts with Rory Storm and the Hurricanes, March 25, 1959

As an only child raised by a single mother, eighteen-year-old Ritchie had already seen more than his share of squalor. Growing up in Dingle, one of

Liverpool's toughest neighborhoods, the boy had suffered inordinate health problems, requiring constant hospitalization throughout his childhood.

Formal education was the first casualty of his periodic illnesses; after losing so much class time, there could be no catching up. The children's ward, however, where he was a regular, provided rudimentary band instruction. The opportunity to learn an instrument proved a worthy diversion; here the youth discovered a love of percussion. With few prospects other than life on the dole, music gave him something to look forward to.

School career finished by age thirteen, young Ritchie worked as a messenger and apprentice engineer. Seeking greener pastures, he filled his head with visions of an idyllic life in the Old West and dreamed of emigrating to America. The Houston Chamber of Commerce responded to his query with a stack of paperwork that proved too daunting.

But by now his stepfather had gathered enough funds from his relatives to gift the happy-go-lucky lad with a secondhand set, and Ritchie soon found his services behind a drum kit in demand. He worked his way up through the skiffle circuit until joining forces with an outfit fronted by one Alan Caldwell.

Formerly of a group called the Texans, Caldwell now called himself Rory Storm and his backing band the Hurricanes. With their common love of all things Western and American, it proved a good fit. Now going pro, the young drummer also acquired a stage name: befitting his cowboy culture fixation and love of hand jewelry, he became Ringo Starr.

The Quarry Men Re-form at the Casbah Club, August 29, 1959

In the months following Julia Lennon's death, the Quarry Men fell on hard times. Bookings dried up as the skiffle craze seemed to play itself out. In early 1959, drummer Colin Hanton quit after a drunken free-for-all following a gig. Even the ever-steadfast George began making time with another group, the Les Stewart Quartet. For all intents and purposes, the Quarry Men no longer existed as a performing entity.

During this fallow period, the Lennon-McCartney musical partnership formally began. John and Paul would eventually fill a schoolboy's notebook with songs, most of which the Beatles would never play. A rare handful would eventually make the cut, resurrected in the absence of stronger material. Among these were "One After 909," "I Call Your Name," "I'll Follow the Sun," and "Love Me Do."

Fate conspired to bring the core band back together. Mona Best, wife of boxing promoter Johnny Best, had recently decided to open up a juice bar with live entertainment in the cellar of her home in West Derby. With help from son Peter, an aspiring drummer, and some friends, the Casbah was set to open on that Saturday night with the Les Stewart Quartet.

That very day, a violent fight broke out between the band's frontman and bassist Ken Brown. The quartet in disarray, Brown was frantic not to lose the job and incur Mona's wrath. He asked George if he knew anyone who might want to fill in. John and Paul were contacted and jumped at the chance to get a gig.

That night, the Quarry Men were reconstituted and given a residency that would last for seven weeks. Following a dispute with Brown over money, John, Paul, and George withdrew from the booking, only returning to the Casbah in August 1960 as the Silver Beatles.

In the Town Where I Was Born

The Liverpool of Beatle Legend

T o truly appreciate the achievement that was the Beatles' success story, one has to know two things: first, compared to life in these United States, English society was (and remains, to a lesser degree) very class-structured. Whatever level of society you were born into, you could expect to remain there for the rest of your life. Not for the Brits is the "American Dream" mythology of upward mobility, the truth of which is less important than the fact that it is widely believed.

Second, the greater U.K. perception of Liverpool in the early 1960s was roughly akin to how Americans think of, say, Port Arthur, Texas. The 'pool was Hicksville writ large, a stagnant backwater utterly bereft of sophistication and culture. Outsiders mocked the local accent, while the different Liverpool neighborhoods, in a strange sort of caste system, mocked each other's pronunciation in turn.

Against this setting, one must therefore appreciate the odds against achieving any sort of national renown, much less worldwide stardom. But, like everyone, the Beatles had to start somewhere. The following ten locales (all popular tourist attractions today) take the reader back to where they once belonged.

"Mendips," 251 Menlove Avenue

Once the Beatles became established in public consciousness, the legend of their rise to success from the slums took hold; yet only Ringo really came from a background depressed enough to qualify as "squalor." John, on the other hand—"working class hero" nonsense notwithstanding—enjoyed the most prosperous upbringing of any of the Fabs.

Following his mother Julia's understandable (given her bohemian lifestyle) decision to forego raising her son, John, aged five, was brought to

"Mendips" to live. Middle-class custom of the day mandated the naming of one's home, and the owners previous to John's Aunt Mary (a.k.a. "Mimi") and Uncle George Smith named their well-appointed house after the Mendip Hills of Somerset, England.

Julia, as well as Paul and eventually George Harrison, whose lower-strata crudity earned Mimi's disdain, were all frequent visitors at Mendips. Though the group never rehearsed at this house, many a song later recorded by the Fabs would be written here, either by John alone or with Paul.

George and Mimi were otherwise childless, so John was raised as an only child (though he had three half-sisters through Julia and, eventually, two half-brothers through his father). After George died, Mimi took in boarders at Mendips to supplement the household income.

The house's location in Liverpool's Woolton placed it close to Brian Epstein's family home as well as a pair of sites that became well known to Fab aficionados in coming years: St. Peter's Church and the Strawberry Field orphanage.

Though Mendips was still considered home, in 1960 John moved in with Stuart Sutcliffe for a spell at Gambier Terrace, a communal residence near the art college both attended. Following his 1963 wedding to Cynthia Powell, John left Mimi's home for good. Two years later, he purchased a home for her in Dorset.

Though years later the National Trust inexplicably declined to purchase the house for preservation (despite having bought Paul's childhood home), Yoko Ono bought the property and donated it to the state. After full restoration to its 1950s splendor, it opened to the public in 2003.

The McCartney Residence, 20 Forthlin Road

In 1956, the McCartney family—Jim, wife Mary, and sons Paul and Michael—moved into this council house in Liverpool's Allerton district. Not long after moving in, Mary took ill with cancer and died. Jim mitigated the sadness that threatened to engulf the family with steadfast care for his sons. Music became the preferred escape from their heartache, as sing-alongs around the family's upright piano (purchased at North End Music Store, or NEMS, from the father of the Beatles' future manager) filled their evenings.

Though his background as a bandleader certainly made the elder McCartney receptive to his son's growing interest, he believed music should take second place to Paul's school responsibilities. But the teen would frequently "sag off" his classes to make time for songwriting sessions with John at the house on Forthlin Road while Jim was away at work.

Unimaginative in design, but built with large rooms for maximum functionality, the McCartney residence typified the council, or public, housing that had sprung up all over England after the war, replacing destroyed homes while clearing slums. The housing council imposed strict limitations on residents regarding décor and maintenance, as the homes were intended as temporary residences, pending improvements in the occupants' fortunes.

But on Jim's cotton salesman salary, chances for upward mobility were remote. Paul would live at Forthlin Road until moving to London in 1964. Meanwhile Michael, later a famous musician in his own right (as Mike McGear) in the Scaffold, began honing a talent for photography while in his teens. It is through his photographs that Beatle fans would one day gain insight into the Quarry Men's formative years.

The Harrison Residence, 12 Arnold Grove

The McCartney digs on Forthlin were positively palatial compared with the crowded Harrison home where George was born on February 24 (not 25, as many sources report), 1943. A classic "two up, two down" (referring to the number of rooms per floor), the Wavertree home's six residents (Mr. and Mrs. Harrison, sister Louise, brothers Harry, Peter, and George) shared an outdoor toilet, a tiny cookstove, and a coal-burning fire for heat. Though living conditions were abysmal by almost any standard, the Harrisons were a tight-knit, loving family.

George's parents, Harold and Louise, had moved to the house after their 1930 wedding. Nearly twenty years later, the Harrisons moved to much more appropriate housing located at 25 Uptown Green in Speke. It was there in 1958 that the Quarry Men functioned as the wedding band for brother Harry's nuptials. The Harrisons resided at the Speke address until 1962, just as George was on the cusp of fame.

The Arnold Grove residence is still in existence and still draws the interest of tourists, though apparently its current occupant finds the attention most unwelcome. The National Trust has so far not seen fit to designate either property a landmark.

The Starkey Residence, 9 Madryn Street

Of all the Beatle childhood neighborhoods, the Dingle, where Richard Starkey Jr. entered the world on July 7, 1940, takes top prize for being the most unsavory and dangerous.

Born past his due date, Ritchie would endure shaky health for most of his childhood. At the age of three, his parents split up, with his mother, Elsie, leaving young Ritchie in the care of his paternal grandparents while she worked. The two eventually moved to a two up, two down at 10 Admiral Grove. Here, a neighbor girl named Marie Maguire home-schooled the education-deprived boy.

In time, Elsie married again, to Londoner Harry Graves. The three would live at Admiral Grove until 1963, when the Beatles broke big. (George and Ringo then shared a flat in London before buying their first homes.) A mere twenty yards from their doorstep was a local pub, the site of many an evening's socializing. The Empress, as it was called, years later graced the cover of Ringo's first solo album, *Sentimental Journey*.

As for Madryn Street, Ringo's birthplace was the subject of much spirited debate throughout 2005 and 2006. City planners came under fire for announcing their intent to raze the home, along with thousands of others, in an attempt to clear the way for new development. As fans around the world protested the move, Ringo himself weighed in, questioning the wisdom of displacing families unable to afford better for themselves.

Strawberry Field Children's Home

A foretaste of the *Sgt. Pepper's* album came with the February 1967 release of the double A-side single "Penny Lane" / "Strawberry Fields Forever." John and Paul's differing perspectives of their Liverpool background sparked this remarkable pair of tunes. While the latter chose (unsurprisingly) a rather literal invocation of childhood vignettes for "Penny Lane," John simply tapped the rich imagery evoked by the *name* of a familiar locale from his past and built upon it.

The Salvation Army orphanage located just around the corner from Mendips occupied a picturesque Victorian mansion. Opened in 1936, the home hosted an annual carnival, where John and his friends, when not partaking in the festivities, sold bottles of lemonade for a penny apiece.

This idyllic milieu manifested itself in 1966 when John, alone in Spain for the filming of *How I Won the War*, added an "s" to the name and created one of the best loved compositions in the Beatles' catalog (though, it must be noted, it was also the group's first single since "Love Me Do" to stall short of the number one slot on the charts, blocked by, of all things, crooner Engelbert Humperdinck's "Release Me").

Naturally, the record's success gave Liverpool an added attraction for traveling Beatle tourists. Most were satisfied to be photographed in front of the ornate red gates denoting the famous name. The decrepit old

With the demise of the Casbah Coffee Club in 1962, the Cavern became *the* place to catch the city's hottest bands. Lunchtimes, evenings, and weekends, the club was always jumping. *Photo by Max Scheler/Redferns*

manor was razed in 1977, replaced by a nondescript structure dubbed John Lennon Hall.

In 1984, the orphanage came perilously close to being shuttered, but an eleventh-hour infusion of cash from Yoko Ono kept the facility operating for another two decades. But in early 2005, Beatles fans the world over were saddened by the news that Strawberry Field would be closed for good, its three remaining residents dispatched to foster homes.

Just as legions of Lennon's followers prepared to accept the passing of a beloved landmark, an unexpected twist occurred: the property, famed gates intact, would be preserved and reopened as a Christian prayer center affiliated with "Boiler Rooms—Millennium Three Monasteries." Here visitors can book a "prayer slot" or even one of eight prayer meeting rooms, 24/7.

Penny Lane

Paul's composition—musically, if not quite lyrically, as brilliant as John's— presented a roll call of sites familiar to anyone of his age who had grown up in Woolton. While Penny Lane itself is a main drag, heavy with bus traffic, the name connotated the area, not merely the thoroughfare.

The district's denizens are called out by profession—barber, banker, fireman, nurse—while Paul describes both rain and sunshine in pleasant suburbia. That such a mundane locale could be made to sound so charming and picturesque is a tribute to Paul's gift for detail.

All the sites enumerated in the song can be found throughout the area today: the barbershop, fire station, several banks, and of course the round-about. The latter serves as a focal point for tourists wishing to experience the song's sites and sounds for themselves.

Predictably, souvenir hunters quickly made street signs extinct (as they would later at Los Angeles's Blue Jay Way and at Abbey Road in St. John's Wood), raising the ire of the local authorities. But such notoriety cuts both ways, as locals quickly capitalized on the attention. Sgt. Pepper's Café, for instance, anchors a former bus depot in the roundabout.

Penny Lane drew less desirable scrutiny in 2006 during a wave of politically corrective revisionism. The country's unsavory past surfaced when city officials discovered that the road had been named in "honor" of eighteenth-century slave trader James Penny. Public outcry over a potential name change caused city officials to recognize that whatever the origins, the connotations of Penny Lane today have long since superseded its ugly past.

St. Peter's Church

Located in Woolton near Mendips, St. Peter's Church was the site of the historic meeting of John and Paul on July 6, 1957. Built in 1887, it is one of the most impressive houses of worship in the Liverpool area, boasting a ninety-foot bell tower and a magnificent pipe organ unusual for a parish church of its size.

While George and Mimi were members of the Anglican congregation, John was not, although he did apparently sing with the choir on occasion and participated in the church-sponsored youth group.

The key connection with the church came when John scored two gigs for the Quarry Men for St. Peter's summer fête in 1957. The first took place outside on a makeshift stage, the second at an evening dance inside the church hall. Paul, who had come primarily to scout out pretty girls, would, in meeting John, set events into motion that fulfilled that summer day's goal beyond his wildest dreams.

A small graveyard adjoins the church. Here John's beloved Uncle George is buried, although his mother is not; Julia was laid to rest in Allerton Cemetery, in an all but unmarked grave.

Another familiar name can be found lurking among the gravestones: Eleanor Rigby. By all accounts, Paul made up the name, melding the name of a business he spotted in Bristol with that of *Help!* costar Eleanor Bron. Yet here lies a formerly flesh-and-blood woman, mere yards away from the spot where the seeds of the Beatles first germinated. Eerily, she passed away at the age of forty-four on October 10, 1939, exactly 365 days before John Lennon entered the material world.

The Jacaranda

Always on the lookout for opportunities to improve his lot, Liverpool plumber Allan Williams spotted a vacant watch repair shop on Slater Street in the summer of 1958. Recognizing the possibilities, in September he opened the Jacaranda Club as an attempt to cash in on the growing coffee bar craze.

The Royal Caribbean Steel Band, fronted by his friend Harold Phillips ("Lord Woodbine," so named in tribute to his favorite cheap cigarette), became the club's chief draw. But with students and teens at night outnumbering the professional clientele who came at lunch, Williams accommodated the prevailing demographic by adding skiffle and beat groups to the evening schedule.

John Lennon and Stuart Sutcliffe, students at the nearby Liverpool College of Art, soon began haunting the Jac. Eventually, they managed to charm Allan into letting their band, the Quarry Men, rehearse in the club's basement.

Though unimpressed with their sound, Williams found his largesse repaid when Stu and John painted murals in the club. By May of 1960, Williams judged that the boys were ready to go public. Following the Johnny Gentle tour of Scotland that month, the Silver Beatles officially turned pro when they began appearing regularly at the Jacaranda.

While largely overshadowed by the Cavern in Beatle mythology, the Jacaranda experience was essential to the band's future success, affording a public platform where they could hone their act on a regular basis. More importantly, the Williams connection set them on the road to Hamburg, where their entertaining skills were perfected.

Shuttered for many years, the Jacaranda reopened in 1996, though without Allan Williams. Today, it is highly regarded as both a historical site and a popular pub/entertainment venue.

The Casbah

Another often-overlooked link in the Beatles' development was their stint at the Casbah Coffee Club, located in the cellar of a nineteenth-century home in West Derby, Liverpool. Here the Quarry Men reconstituted after having all but disintegrated; the Casbah was also the site of their first Liverpool appearance after learning to "mach schau" in Hamburg.

The proprietor was the remarkable Mona Best, the very embodiment of what is today called a "Type A" personality. A television program featuring a story on the growing coffee bar phenomenon sparked her to open one in the voluminous cellars beneath her home. (Family legend holds that the house was bought with the winnings Mona scored after pawning her jewelry and betting on a 33-to-1 dark horse.)

Putting sons Rory and Randolph (better known by his middle name, Pete) to work, Mona soon had the cavernous underground facility cleared of storage. Helping out was Pete's friend Ken Brown, who played in an outfit called the Les Stewart Quartet. The band was booked to open the club on August 29, 1959, but a row (over, ironically, Ken missing rehearsals to help get the club ready) led to an immediate breakup. The group's lead guitarist, George Harrison, formerly of the Quarry Men, contacted Paul and John to salvage the gig, and the rest is history.

As they had done at the Jac, Stuart and John, along with Paul, and John's future wife, Cynthia Powell, set the club up by painting murals throughout the facility. (The boys would also volunteer to work the coffee bar itself, recognizing an opportunity to chat up girls.)

The Casbah Coffee Club was an immediate success, eventually booking the top bands of Liverpool. In August of 1960, Pete joined the Beatles for the first Hamburg stint; upon their return, the band regularly played the Casbah. Meanwhile, following a falling out with Allan Williams over a booking fee the Beatles neglected to pony up, Mona began taking an active interest in her son's band, securing them some prestigious bookings in Liverpool. After Brian Epstein entered the picture, Mona, with Pete as the conduit, offered helpful advice to the novice manager, whether desired or not.

Just on the verge of their Parlophone recording deal, the Beatles played a final gig at the Casbah. Shortly afterward, despite its success, Mona closed the club, following her unexpected pregnancy under somewhat scandalous circumstances. (Unlike virtually every other important Liverpool Beatles venue, however, the Casbah was simply closed and not destroyed.) The loss of the club accelerated the ascendancy of the Cavern, which hadn't fully embraced rock acts until that time.

Though he had already penned an autobiography (*Beatle! The Pete Best Story*), Pete also published *The Beatles: The True Beginnings* in 2003. This coffee-table book, replete with photos and memorabilia, attempts to restore both the Casbah and Mona Best to their proper place in Beatle history.

Lest the point be missed, in 2004 the Casbah Coffee Club opened to the public for the first time in over forty years. Today visitors can see for themselves this virtual time capsule of cultural significance, complete with the preserved paintings done by the group and the stage on which they performed.

The Cavern

The legendary site of some 292 Beatle performances, the Cavern also hosted an array of acts that embodied the so-called "Mersey Sound." Gerry and the Pacemakers, the Searchers, and the Swingin' Blue Jeans all experienced chart success as part of the 1964 "British Invasion."

Future British showbiz institution Cilla Black worked at the Cavern as a hatcheck girl under her given name, Priscilla White. (As "Swingin' Cilla," she often sat in with the club's many acts, drawing attention for her innate star quality as well as for her big voice.) As local promoters began flexing their muscle, some big name acts performed at the club, notably bona fide legend Gene "Be Bop a-Lula" Vincent.

In the wake of the Beatles' success, Liverpool's vibrant music scene drew notice from all over the country. Such attention naturally gravitated toward their Cavern stomping grounds, and in 1964, a program called *Sunday Night at the Cavern* began airing on radio.

George Martin considered recording the Beatles' Parlophone LP debut at the Cavern, but his reservations over the technical logistics ruled it out. Local powerhouse the Big Three, however, did issue an EP recorded on-site.

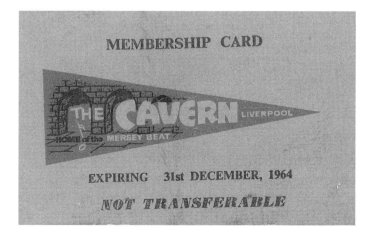

A Cavern Club member in good standing was guaranteed admittance to the frequently overcrowded club, though by 1964 they'd missed any chance of seeing the Beatles perform there.

Changing musical tastes and bad management led to hard times for the club, which closed in 1966. Though a grassroots campaign to reopen the Cavern that same year included a show of support from Prime Minister Harold Wilson (!), the ensuing seven years merely postponed the inevitable. A city council decision to condemn the property to make way for a subway ventilation shaft in 1973 sealed its fate.

But destiny wasn't finished with the Cavern. The ventilation shaft was never built. Following John Lennon's 1980 murder, a movement to reopen the club as a sort of living memorial gained footing, resulting in the Cavern's 1984 resurrection. At first a venue for spinning records, the club brought live music into the mix in the 1990s.

1999 hosted a homecoming for one of the Cavern's most famous alumni; in support of his *Run Devil Run* release, Paul McCartney performed at 10 Mathew Street for the first time since 1963. Macca's band included guitarists David Gilmour (Pink Floyd) and Mick Green (Johnny Kidd and the Pirates); drummer Ian Paice (Deep Purple); and keyboardsman Pete Wingfield ("Eighteen with a Bullet"). McCartney eventually released the show on DVD.

Contrary to popular belief, the current Cavern in fact occupies seventy-five percent of the site, rebuilt with original bricks more or less to its original specs (although thirty steps now lead down to the premises where there once were eighteen). The Cavern remains a city landmark as well as a popular entertainment venue.

Then There Was Music

The Road to Fabdom

The fortunes of the young band, such as it was, rose to the next level by the end of 1960 after a series of developments that included their first stint in Hamburg. This journey proved to be the key element in transforming the former Quarry Men from inspired hobbyists into a viable rock-and-roll outfit. With the addition of an imaginative manager to the mix, suddenly a record contract and stardom seemed within reach.

The Johnny Gentle Tour: May 1960

The year began with the boys adding Stuart Sutcliffe, John's art school pal, to the band as bass player. (Paul was still playing rhythm guitar, having fumbled an opportunity on lead some time before.) Though largely ignorant of rock and roll and possessing no discernable ability on his instrument, Sutcliffe did possess a James Dean–like cool, in contrast to the over-the-top Elvis moves of John and Paul.

Connecting with Welsh Liverpudlian Allan Williams gave the boys a big break. A colorful character who knew a thing or two, Williams was an entrepreneur on the fringes of big-time show business, operating a coffee bar called the Jacaranda. Despite their demonstrable lack of polish, Williams saw potential in the group, who now called themselves the Silver Beatles. (This followed a short-lived stint as Johnny and the Moondogs.)

Williams was keen on getting some recognition for Liverpool's rock scene (and, incidentally, himself) by hitching his wagon to the biggest homegrown star of the day, Billy Fury. Fury was an Elvis-like singer managed by the pugnacious Larry Parnes, who promoted a stable of singers sporting equally dramatic handles: Tommy Steele, Vince Eager, Dickie Pride, and Johnny Gentle.

Williams somehow talked Parnes and Fury into agreeing to audition some local talent to back the singers on tour, with Fury being the biggest prize. The dressed-down, rough-edged Silver Beatles—who had been honing their act in the Jac's basement—stood out from a crowd of hopefuls that included Gerry and the Pacemakers and Derry and the Seniors.

After a brief Silver Beatles set, Fury and Parnes were intrigued enough to ask the boys to run through another number, minus their painfully ham-fisted bass player. Lennon refused and the matter was dropped. Though they lost out on the chance to back Fury, the Silver Beatles accepted the consolation prize of backing Johnny Gentle on a weeklong tour of Scotland.

Though rather a low rung on the showbiz ladder, the gig had tremendous ramifications. It gave the group its first taste of touring, an experience on which the Fabs would burn out in exactly six years. For the first time, they faced audiences outside their hometown, a challenge that would be instrumental in forging their talents as entertainers. Lastly, it meant a tangible commitment to turning pro. John and Stu ditched college for the adventure; Paul inveigled his dad into believing that school had granted a two-week pre-exam holiday; and George, his academic career already over, skipped out on his apprentice electrician job.

Their drummer at this time was a thirty-six-year-old laborer by the name of Tommy Moore. Though remembered by George as the best drummer he ever played with (!), Moore found himself on the receiving end of John's cruel wit one time too many. Following a vehicular mishap during the tour that resulted in the loss of his front teeth, Moore quit the Silver Beatles, returning to his job driving a forklift.

The First Hamburg Trip: August–December 1960

Harold Phillips, an Allan Williams sidekick, is known in Beatle mythology as "Lord Woodbine." The Trinidad native, who performed in a calypso band, unwittingly abetted the future greatness of the Fabs by setting them on the course to Hamburg, Germany.

Growing restless with the Liverpool club scene, Woody's Caribbean Steel Band slipped away for greener pastures one day without notice. Williams soon received a letter, postmarked Hamburg, from his friend, advising him to check out the nightlife possibilities in this wild, untamed town. Intrigued, Williams ventured out, only to discover the wretched quality of what passed for rock and roll in Germany.

Sensing opportunity, he struck a deal with local club owner Bruno Koschmider to send some "authentic" English rockers their way, beginning with Derry Wilkie and the Seniors. The gamble paid off, and soon Koschmider was demanding more.

Meanwhile, the Beatles, reduced to backing a stripper named Jan at Williams's Blue Angel club in Liverpool, clamored for the opportunity to expand their horizons. The reluctant Williams agreed to send them to Hamburg on the condition that they find themselves a steady drummer.

Enter Pete Best. The son of Casbah club owner Mona Best was playing in their house band, the Black Jacks, when the offer arrived. Hardly one to turn down such an exciting break, he quickly assented. The Silver Beatles were good to go.

News of the Beatles' pending arrival did not sit well with Derry Wilkie, who begged Williams to reconsider lest the rough-and-tumble Beatles "ruin" the now-thriving scene. But Wilkie hadn't seen their act recently, which had vastly improved despite the low-rent gigs they'd played since the Johnny Gentle tour. The harmonies were sharper, the lead guitar more focused. Even Stu was coming along on bass, no longer routinely playing notes a half step flat.

The Fab Five arrived at an enclave called the Reeperbahn in August of 1960, with sex and sin on open display. Coming of age in such an environment was bound to be life-changing, especially when contrasted with the blue suburban skies back home.

Though the group's music was steadily evolving, the real value of the Hamburg experience lay in challenging the boys as a stage act. With Koschmider exhorting them to "Mach schau!!" ("Make show"), the anarchic atmosphere further loosened the boys' already relaxed inhibitions, giving them leave to enact any distasteful impulse they fancied.

Playing eight hours at a stretch spurred creativity and resourcefulness, forcing the band to keep themselves as well as their audience interested. Fueled by alcohol and amphetamines, they learned to pull out the stops and engage the attention of drunks seeking a spectacle.

This first trip ended ignominiously with George deported (for being underage), Paul and Pete arrested (for arson), and John left to return home alone (Stu having decided to stay behind). But their worth as a band had improved tremendously. Having established a fan base, they headed back to Hamburg the following spring.

The Tony Sheridan Sessions: June 1961

Now a known quantity, the group (with the name shortened to Beatles) mixed it up regularly with their peers, including Rory Storm and the Hurricanes, newly arrived in Hamburg. Another act that bonded with them was singer/guitarist Tony Sheridan. Though only a few months older than John, he seemed to possess years more experience and polish. The Beatles looked upon him as a mentor, with George actually learning guitar licks from him.

Signed to a recording contract with Polydor in Germany, Sheridan tapped the Beatles as his backing band. (Recognizing his limitations, Stu deferred bass duties to Paul for the session.) Several tracks were recorded, notably "My Bonnie," issued as the single, while another old chestnut, "Ain't She Sweet," featured John on lead vocals. It is believed that the future Fabs cut eight songs with Sheridan; all would be reissued in countless variations and packages after the band hit big in 1964.

As the name "Beatles" was a little too close to German slang for "penis," the record was issued in Germany under the name "Tony Sheridan and the Beat Brothers." Though not *quite* a Beatles record, this first commercial release did extremely well for a debut act, making it to #5 on the local German pop chart.

Though unissued in England at the time, the single played a huge part in the band's success. Liverpool fans soon learned of its existence through steady rotation by Cavern Club DJ Bob Wooler and from the boys themselves.

Brian Epstein Signs On: December 1961

Soon enough, requests for the record began to filter into the local record retailer, an adjunct to a family-owned furniture business called North End Music Store (NEMS). Featuring a listening booth for would-be buyers to try out potential purchases, NEMS's main outlet was a popular hangout for students and club visitors.

Brian Epstein, the owner's eldest son, managed NEMS. At twenty-seven, Brian was at loose ends. Having had a brief army career and an equally fleeting episode at the Royal Academy of Dramatic Art, Brian had yet to find a satisfying outlet for his creative impulses.

Though not particularly a rock-and-roll fan, he prided himself on the ability to keep abreast of current trends and stock any record a customer might desire. That was what made the requests for "My Bonnie" so frustrating; a cursory search for the elusive disc came up dry. Eventually, he discovered that the record was a foreign release and ordered a hundred imported copies, which quickly sold out.

Brian's 1964 autobiography, *A Cellarful of Noise* (ghosted by Beatle publicist Derek Taylor), describes how he learned that the very band whose mystery disc he'd been seeking was playing daily at the nearby Cavern Club. Much of this account must be taken with a massive helping of salt; Brian could not have been *entirely* ignorant of the Beatles' existence, since not only did he write a review column in the *Mersey Beat* music paper, which splashed the band throughout every issue, but the Beatles themselves were frequent visitors to NEMS, habitually listening to records without ever buying them.

On November 9, Brian, accompanied by assistant Alistair Taylor, paid a visit to the Cavern during the Beatles' lunchtime session. The culture shock he experienced was superseded by the attraction he felt toward the band. Crude, noisy, and impolite though they were, Brian felt that these Beatles could, with a little shaping, become bigger than Elvis. In this, at least, his delusions of grandeur matched theirs.

After a whirlwind courtship and assurance that Brian would not meddle with their sound, the boys were ready to commit. An agreement was struck: Brian would play all the cards he possessed to get the group a record deal; they, in return, acceded to his wishes to present them in a polished, professional manner. No more leather gear and no more swearing or tomfoolery onstage; precision and smart suits would be the order of the day. Alistair Taylor was witness to four Beatle signatures; conspicuously absent was Brian's.

The Decca Audition: January 1, 1962

As a record seller, Brian Epstein possessed nine stores' worth of leverage. In initiating talks with Decca to secure an audition for his clients, he was not shy about playing the retailer card, intimating that failure to get a hearing for his boys might not be good for business.

On New Year's Day 1962 (not a U.K. holiday at the time), the band arrived at Decca's London facilities, having made the long trek down from Liverpool the day before. At 11:00 A.M., they were escorted into the studio, where they were told that they needn't have bothered lugging their tatty gear—they would use the studio's equipment instead.

In slightly less than an hour, the band tore through fifteen songs handpicked by Brian to show off its versatility. Songs ranged from promising originals ("Hello Little Girl," "Love of the Loved") and contemporary hits ("Take Good Care of My Baby") to pop standards ("September in the Rain," "Till There Was You") and inexplicably bizarre novelty numbers ("Three Cool Cats," The Sheik of Araby"). In hindsight, Epstein did the Fabs no favors by masking their chief strength—songwriting—in favor of an "all-around entertainer" angle.

Years later, Decca A&R (Artists and Repertoire) man Dick Rowe was pilloried for passing on the Beatles, but one can hardly fault his decision under the circumstances. The group was in less than top form, probably due to nerves, coming off as a bunch of enthusiastic amateurs with much to learn in terms of commerciality and sorely in need of discipline.

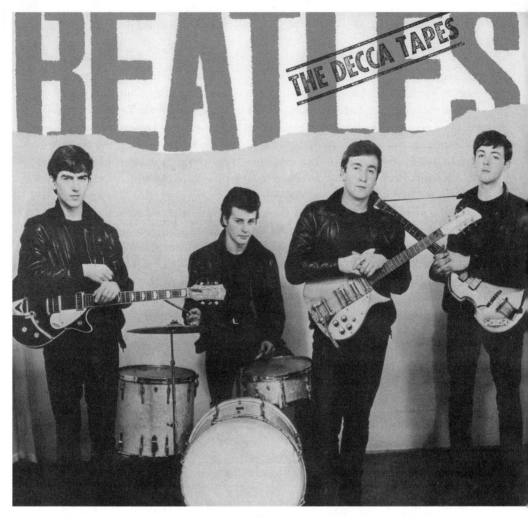

This quasi-legal issue of the Decca audition tapes proves why the Dick Rowe was blameless in turning down nothing less than a shaky novelty act, hamstrung by a hopelessly rudimentary drummer.

It would be another month before Decca officially turned them down, though they sweetened the bitter pill by offering Brian the use of their facilities to record a proper demo tape for the boys. Brian rejected their offer with a petulant "You'll be sorry!" Meanwhile, Pete Best was the last to hear the news; foreshadowing later events, the other three simply couldn't be bothered to keep him in the loop.

Pete Best Is Fired: August 16, 1962

Stung by Decca's rejection, Brian at least salvaged the recordings from the debacle, having them pressed as a demonstration disc to shop around to other labels. But over the next several months, each record company that Epstein approached snorted with derision at the idea that anything of value could come out of Liverpool.

While Brian busied himself with letter writing and phone calls, the Beatles themselves kept moving. In March, they made their BBC radio debut on "Teenager's Turn (Here We Go)." The following month saw their first return to Hamburg following the advent of Brian Epstein and their new look. But their arrival was met with tragedy; Stu had died suddenly from a cerebral hemorrhage just days before.

Though he'd left the group the previous year to study art in Germany and marry Astrid Kirchherr, Stu was hardly out of their lives, and his loss hit hard. Swallowing their grief, the boys soldiered on. Their heartache was mitigated later that month when Brian sent a telegram announcing that EMI—well, Parlophone—had requested an audition.

Virtually every English record company had by this time passed on them, including three other divisions of EMI. Parlophone represented the end of the line. Heretofore, it had been mostly an outlet for jazz and comedy records, but it did boast one essential asset: a house producer/A&R named George Martin.

Struck by their personalities rather than their act, Martin recognized that the John-Paul songwriting team was an asset that could be developed, though he at first harbored doubts that their tunes were up to standard. Martin tried to suss out which member could be the focal point before concluding that the group dynamic worked quite well. It is a credit to George Martin that, unlike most record producers of the time, he did not attempt to bend the Beatles to his will.

The one point he would not accommodate was their drummer. Though recognizing that whatever happened onstage was not his business, he would not countenance wasting studio time on a member who lacked the fundamental skills to play on a record. Getting people to dance in a club was one thing, but the skill needed for transfer to a turntable was another. Martin let Brian know that Pete would be spelled by a professional in the studio.

This development dovetailed with John, Paul, and George's unspoken reservations about their drummer. Their time with Pete had begun as a marriage of convenience, one that had lasted two years and through a world of changes. Now, on the cusp of realizing their dream, they were not about to let sentimentality get in the way.

Though much debated through the years, George Martin's professional assessment seems simply to have been the icing on the cake. (Assertions that Best was a better drummer than Ringo are easily dispelled by *Anthology 1*.)

In addition, the other Beatles' disquiet regarding their drummer may have been rooted in his individualist tendencies.

Pete would not (or could not) adopt the others' trademark hairstyle. Rather than cutting up like the others, he projected a simmering moodiness that came off as unsettling alongside three comedians. Rather than share the other three's hedonistic pursuits, Pete went off on his own during downtime.

In addition, there is the question of jealousy. Revisiting contemporary accounts of the band, one is immediately struck by how often Pete was given top billing or premium coverage. Fan demand dictated his solo singing spot during sets, often on the song "Peppermint Twist." Beyond a doubt, his smoldering good looks accounted for a good percentage of the band's popularity. A desire for someone with less individual star power may have dictated the Beatles' choice of replacement.

Brian Epstein was called upon to do the dirty work. After he had confirmed that the group's old pal Ringo Starr—contractually bound to the Hurricanes during a stint at Butlin's Holiday Camp—was willing to forego his commitments, Pete was summarily dismissed.

But Pete's fans were not about to take the news lightly. While dozens maintained a vigil outside the Best home, others directed their outrage at the perpetrators. Brian's car was vandalized, while George was given a black eye outside the Cavern by some disgruntled followers.

All of this activity came on the eve of the Beatles' Parlophone recording debut. A television film crew showed up at the Cavern a week after the firing to document their act; following (ironically enough) "Some Other Guy," one partisan yelled, "We want Pete!"

Meanwhile, John's marriage to an already expecting Cynthia Powell presented yet another potential firestorm. Not wishing to aggravate the existing Pete backlash, the Beatles kept John's wedding under wraps, lest female fans chafe at John's presumed unavailability.

"Love Me Do" Is Released: October 5, 1962

The Beatles invited Ringo to join the group while he was working at Butlin's Holiday Camp in Skegness. The Nose had to overcome some reservations; though quite close with the boys socially (arguably closer than Pete), Starr had misgivings about leaving Rory Storm high and dry. What ultimately tipped the decision toward the Beatles was the fact that they were willing to offer him more money. Lennon ordered Ringo to shave his beard but allowed him to keep his "sideboards."

Drummer Johnny Hutch from the Big Three filled in for three shows until Ringo arrived. When Starr joined the Beatles, he gamely weathered a storm of irate fans while looking forward to their planned recording session with EMI.

Ringo already had some recording experience with John, Paul, and George at a one-off session in Hamburg on October 15, 1960. The Hurricanes had a second singer, known as Wally, whom Allan Williams was keen to record. Williams, who was paying for the session, directed that the ad hoc Beatles record the show tune "Summertime." ("Fever" and "September Song" may also have been taped.) This most mysterious of recordings is probably lost forever; none of the six discs cut appear to have survived.

George Martin met Ringo for the first time on September 4. It is commonly believed that Martin decided to take no chances for the Beatles' debut recording session, securing the services of studio pro Andy White in advance. This is not so; Ringo was actually allowed to perform on this date. However, when the song was remade a week later, the hapless Ringo was demoted to tambourine and maraca duty.

Listening to the first version of "Love Me Do," it is obvious why Martin requested a new recording. Ringo's performance, while competent, lacks the energy and punch that he would later be known for. It is Paul, however, who really botches the take. Newly assigned to singing the song's tag, "Love me do-oo" (in place of John, who now had to play harmonica), Paul sounds nervous and tentative. Curiously, it was the Ringo-on-drums version that Parlophone issued as the single, while Andy White's superior take was relegated to the album (and all subsequent reissues).

The fact that an original tune, and not even one of their best, was chosen as the Beatles' first 45 demonstrates the considerable leap of faith that Martin was making. All along, he had been pushing a trifle titled "How Do You Do It," composed by professional tunesmith Mitch Murray, for their first release.

With little recourse, the Beatles went through the motions of recording the song, but with little spirit and less heart. Recognizing that forcing the issue was futile, Martin acquiesced to their wishes to debut with a tune of their own. ("How Do You Do It" did not go to waste, instead premiering as Gerry and the Pacemakers' debut release. Fulfilling Martin's prediction, it went to #1.)

With modest promotion, the Beatles' debut single reached #17 on the charts. As records go, this was impressive; as a trailblazer, putting the English pop world on notice that a band from the sticks could successfully compete on the national stage (with a self-penned tune, no less), "Love Me Do" was a stunning achievement.

Please Please Me Album Is Released: March 22, 1963

Hoping the Beatles weren't a one-trick pony, Parlophone agreed to release a follow-up single. On November 26, 1962, the band revisited a number they'd attempted at the tail end of the "Love Me Do" session ten weeks earlier.

At that time, "Please Please Me" was slower and more subdued, in the Roy Orbison style. While feeling that the composition had merit, George Martin wasn't happy with the arrangement and said so.

So the Beatles retooled the song, accelerating the tempo and adding tight harmonies. The climactic ascending call-and-response vocal and harmonica riff added the final pieces to a thoroughly exciting performance. No one second-guessed Ringo's dynamic, assertive drumming on this one. Indeed, so good were the vibes that Martin chimed in over the studio's intercom system, "Boys, you've just made your first #1."

Some would quibble over the accuracy of that prediction; in most U.K. music charts of the day, the song indeed reached the top, but in *Record Retailer*, nowadays recognized as the most authoritative chart, "Please Please Me" peaked at #2, thereby robbing the song decades later of a slot on *Beatles 1*. (Keeping it from #1 was Frank Ifield's long-forgotten "Wayward Wind.")

Hairsplitting aside, the Beatles' undeniable success made them *the* up-and-comers to watch. Their style, their hair, their charm, and their wit all attracted notice throughout the U.K. Parlophone wanted to strike while the iron was hot and get a long-player into the stores.

Exactly one month after the "Please Please Me" single was issued, the group convened at EMI studios to essentially commit their stage act to tape. With Brian Epstein wisely staying out of the selection process, Martin and the group chose ten songs to go with the two singles' A- and B-sides for a total of fourteen tracks.

The songs, including cabaret ("A Taste of Honey"), percolating rockers ("I Saw Her Standing There"), and potential singles material ("Do You Want to Know a Secret"), showcased the Beatles' blend of originals and covers to good advantage. Each Beatle was afforded a vocal showcase, with Ringo's take on the Shirelles' "Boys" a particular stand-out.

Possibly the most productive day in the history of rock and roll ended with John's famous one-take performance of the throat-shredding "Twist and Shout." Plagued by a cold, he only had one shot at nailing the vocal before potentially rupturing his larynx; years of stage experience and a fistful of Zubes cough drops did the trick.

It took a mere eight weeks after release for the *Please Please Me* LP to knock Cliff Richard's *Summer Holiday* from the #1 spot. The Beatles' long-playing debut topped the charts for a U.K. record-breaking thirty straight weeks, giving way in December to *With the Beatles.*

Beatlemania Officially Erupts: October 13, 1963

Events were now unfolding at a dizzying pace. From spring through autumn, the Beatles were in perpetual motion, touring, recording, and playing television and radio shows. Brian Epstein carefully crafted the band's image, presenting them as four cheeky but benign mop-tops that even a mother could love. That the reality didn't match the image was irrelevant.

The four drank, smoked, gobbled pills, enjoyed an endless stream of female companionship, and strayed not one iota from their characteristically scatological means of expressing themselves. Given the mounting demands and pressures placed on them, the real wonder is that the Fab Four stayed as sane and productive as they did.

Even more miraculous was the quality of their releases. Deviating only slightly from the established formula, "From Me to You" followed "Please Please Me" onto the charts, this time undisputedly reaching the top spot. "She Loves You" took over at #1 in late summer 1963, featuring the "yeah yeah yeah" refrain that helped define the group's sound. Between the two releases, Epstein protégé Billy J. Kramer also reached #1 by recording "Do You Want to Know a Secret," further validating the McCartney-Lennon (as it was known then) songwriting team.

While gratified by the success and accolades, Brian had bigger fish to fry. All agreed that America would be the ultimate triumph . . . but that going there without a hit record would be pointless. Corporate resistance to the Fabs' charms (despite a personal entreaty from Brian) at Capitol, EMI/Parlophone's subsidiary in the U.S., had meant releasing their singles on small, anemic labels in the States, with little muscle to secure airplay. Therefore, conquest of the New World would have to wait.

In the meantime, the Beatles busied themselves touring throughout the U.K., appearing with such hit-makers as Chris Montez ("Let's Dance"), Tommy Roe ("Sheila" was a staple of the Beatles' set), and, eventually, Sun Records legend and future Traveling Wilbury Roy Orbison. Seeing the writing on the wall, headliners Montez and Roe generously offered to let the Beatles close the show.

They scarcely could have done otherwise. The screaming, hysterical audiences that defined "Beatlemania" first made their appearance this year. The term gained a foothold when the national press sat up and took notice, following the band's appearance on *Sunday Night at the London Palladium,* a variety program roughly akin to America's *Ed Sullivan Show.*

The Beatles' appearance on the show (hosted by comedian Norman Vaughan) drew notice for events inside the West End venue and out. Thousands of out-of-control fans, mostly female, rushed the theater, necessitating a cordon of bobbies to maintain order. Inside, the Beatles performed "From Me to You," "I'll Get You," "She Loves You," and "Twist and Shout," setting off well-documented pandemonium; fifteen million Britons saw the evening's broadcast.

Suddenly awakened to the possibilities of the band as a phenomenon, the national press had a field day with every angle of the story, both report-

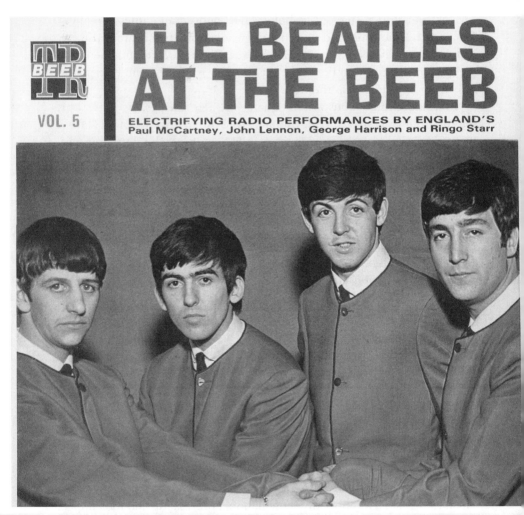

THE BEATLES AT THE BEEB

VOL. 5

ELECTRIFYING RADIO PERFORMANCES BY ENGLAND'S
Paul McCartney, John Lennon, George Harrison and Ringo Starr

The Beatles, shown here in 1963, wear their Pierre Cardin–inspired grey collarless suits to good effect on this bootleg release.

ing on and adding to the whole phenomenon. By week's end, no one in England, rock fan or not, was ignorant of the Beatles' existence. Events had now officially taken on a life of their own.

The Beatles were slated to play the Royal Variety Performance on November 4, 1963, before an audience well stocked with Royals and the Queen herself. It was on this occasion that John famously suggested, in setting up "Twist and Shout," that the people in the cheaper seats clap their hands, and that everyone else just rattle their jewelry. The irreverent zinger established the Beatles in general, and John in particular, as cheeky iconoclasts.

The First American Visit: February 7, 1964

Just four days before the Royal Variety Performance broadcast, the Beatles returned from Sweden after concluding their first non-U.K. tour. Also at the airport was American impresario Ed Sullivan, who observed the pandemonium caused by the thousands of fans waiting for the Fabs to land. (Later he would note that the commotion was reminiscent of Elvis's early days.) When Brian flew to America on November 5 with Billy J. Kramer in tow, a meeting with Ed Sullivan was part of the agenda.

The deal with Sullivan called for three consecutive top-billed appearances in February in exchange for somewhat less than the top rate. The transaction was a calculated risk, since the Beatles had yet to score a hit of any kind in America. As Brian knew, the band did not want to suffer the ignominy of other English pop acts that ended up supporting third-rate Americans like Fabian.

Though Sullivan's deal was intended as an exclusive, his own network jumped the gun. On December 10, 1963, the *CBS Evening News with Walter Cronkite* ran a piece on the growing spectacle, illustrated with footage from the band's November 16 Bournemouth show. (A brief version of the report had run on CBS's *Morning News* on Friday, November 22, 1963; the day's tragic events in Dallas postponed the extended piece for two and a half weeks.)

The story's tone was slightly condescending, but the clip of "She Loves You" was enough to engage the attention of fifteen-year-old Marsha Albert, who wrote a letter to her local rock-and-roll radio station, Washington, D.C.'s WWDC, demanding to know why such music wasn't given airplay. WWDC DJ Carroll James had been wondering the same thing. Albert's letter set into motion forces that forced Capitol to rush-release "I Want to Hold Your Hand."

One week after the CBS report aired, James began spinning an imported copy of the Beatles' newest U.K. single on WWDC. At first annoyed at the "unauthorized" premature airing, Capitol gave in to positive listener reaction by kicking the pressing plants into high gear, getting the disc into shops the day after Christmas, two and a half weeks ahead of the original date.

To reinforce their commitment, the label, prodded by Epstein, spent some $40,000 to launch the group, an expenditure that included stickers sent to radio stations announcing "The Beatles Are Coming!" (Meanwhile, Sullivan was scooped again on January 3 when *Tonight Show* host Jack Paar ran a clip from the Bournemouth show, aping CBS's mocking tone.)

It took only until February 1 for "Hand" to top the American charts. And on February 7, the Beatles first collectively set foot on American soil. With thousands of fans greeting them at Kennedy Airport, no one could have scripted a better coalescence of many seemingly unrelated events.

Two days later, 73 million American lives changed forever when the Beatles launched into "All My Loving" live on *Ed Sullivan*. The band then underscored their triumph with concerts at the Washington Coliseum in D.C. and Carnegie Hall in New York before returning to England. In little more than two years, Brian had succeeded beyond anyone's wildest dreams, making the Beatles bigger than Elvis.

Yes, I'm Gonna Be a Star

Beatlemania

LIFE

THE BEATLES
They're here again
and what a ruckus!

AUGUST 28 · 1964 · 25¢

Six months after their American debut on *The Ed Sullivan Show*, Beatlemania had officially taken root worldwide as Britain's former colony welcomed them back.

Off to the Jukebox Man

The Beatles' Record Labels

The Beatles had plenty of trouble getting a record deal in the first place, suffering rejection even before Brian Epstein could secure an audition. When they ended up on Parlophone—a second-rate division of EMI—they eventually turned the U.K. recording industry upside down.

Despite enjoying hits in the U.K., the band found little immediate success in America. Capitol (parent company of EMI and Parlophone) turned down the Fabs until agreeing to release "I Want to Hold Your Hand" in late 1963.

Capitol's reluctance to issue the band's work in early 1963 allowed rights for their early singles to go to any company that wanted to release them—which eventually led, in 1964, to six different labels releasing various Beatles recordings as the group became the hottest thing in showbiz.

These record labels put out Beatles product in the U.S., the U.K., and Canada. Going into record labels around the world would necessitate a book of its own.

Parlophone

In 1896, German Carl Lindstrom founded the Parlophone record company, which became a British EMI subsidiary in 1923 and had been doing business in England since then. By the early '60s, though, Parlophone wasn't doing much business anywhere. That made it easier for a fairly successful producer like George Martin to put his weight behind the signing of an unknown band.

Martin, born in 1926, heard something he liked in the Beatles' raw charm, and following a June 6, 1962 audition, had the Fab Four inked to a conditional deal with Parlophone to release their first 45, "Love Me Do." The rest is hysteria.

Prior to the Beatles, the label had focused on comedy and international music; the biggest Parlophone artists in 1962 were the Goons (Peter Sellers, Harry Secombe, and Spike Milligan), actor Bernard Cribbins, musical funnymen Flanders and Swann, and Irish singer Jimmy Shand.

Once the Beatles broke big on Parlophone, the company gained a lot of prestige in the pop world, inking Cilla Black, the Hollies, the Fourmost, and the Easybeats. In the '70s and '80s, Queen represented the Parlophone label. Today the company hosts, among others, Blur, Radiohead, Kylie Minogue, the Beastie Boys, and the Redwalls.

In the same year the Beatles released *Revolver*, yet another repackaging of their Tony Sheridan material appeared on the market, this time on MGM's Metro subsidiary.

Incidentally, what looks like a pound sterling symbol on the Parlophone label (£) actually denotes the name of Lindstrom.

All U.K. Beatles records were issued on Parlophone until Apple debuted with "Hey Jude" in September 1968.

Decca

In the early 1960s, Decca was a successful record company, boasting among its artists Brenda Lee, Peggy Lee, and Ricky Nelson. The label also had a substantial interest in international music. When the German-based American singer Tony Sheridan landed a conditional recording deal with the German Polydor label, owned by Decca, he laid down eight songs in Hamburg in 1961 with his backing band—the Beatles.

Given the company's international focus, it made sense for Decca to release a Tony Sheridan record—especially since Bert Kaempfert, Decca's European A&R director and himself a successful Decca recording artist, whose "Wonderland by Night" was an American #1 and a worldwide smash in 1960, produced the session himself.

"My Bonnie," backed with "The Saints," came out in Germany on Polydor in April 1962, with the artists billed as Tony Sheridan and the Beat Brothers. Decca released the 45 in America around the same time; this was therefore the first American record to feature the Beatles.

Decca management heard little positive feedback from disc jockeys on its promotional copies of the disc, however, and therefore pressed only a few commercial copies. Decca's commercial release of "My Bonnie" is now arguably the rarest of all Beatles collectibles; only twenty or so copies are known to exist.

Vee-Jay

Capitol Records had the first option on releasing the Beatles' records in America, but declined the opportunity to put out "Love Me Do," "Please Please Me," or "From Me to You."

When "Please Please Me" shot to the top of the British charts, American label Vee-Jay, a rhythm and blues label based in Chicago, released the 45 —unfortunately with the band's name spelled "Beattles."

Vee-Jay executive Calvin Carter claims that the Beatles were a throw-in from EMI, which, through its American agent, Transglobal Music, had offered yodeling singer Frank Ifield's "I Remember You" to Vee-Jay if they'd take on the Beatles as well.

"Please Please Me" was a hit in Chicago in spring 1963, hoisted onto the local charts by DJ Dick Biondi, who then went to Los Angeles and, in the early summer, helped make Vee-Jay's follow-up, "From Me to You," something of a hit in California.

The company at this point had an option to release the fourteen tracks from the British *Please Please Me* LP, and prepared a twelve-song package, *Introducing the Beatles*. The Vee-Jay record was scheduled for release in late summer 1963, but did not hit the shops.

Meanwhile, Vee-Jay was struggling financially, largely due to managerial misconduct, and failed to make royalty payments to EMI for the (fairly small) sales of the two 45s, thereby forfeiting rights to any further Beatles recordings. Only in early 1964, when "I Want to Hold Your Hand" became a smash for Capitol, did Vee-Jay recognize its folly.

But the company did still have rights to the earlier singles, and re-released "Please Please Me," backed with "From Me to You," in late January 1964. The single, this time with the band's name spelled properly, reached #3 on *Billboard*. Vee-Jay at this time also rush-released the *Introducing the Beatles* album, even though their legal right to do so was shaky at best.

Capitol and Vee-Jay spent January throwing lawsuits at each other, while the smaller company continued to put out Beatle product, with "Do You Want to Know a Secret" reaching #2 in April 1964.

Capitol could afford more and better lawyers, and the two record labels eventually hammered out an agreement allowing Vee-Jay to continue to release its fourteen Beatles songs through mid-October 1964. Vee-Jay set about maximizing its investment, endlessly repackaging the same songs in different combinations for several more months (and churning out an interview LP titled *Hear the Beatles Tell All*). The label finally crashed and burned in 1966; one of their last-ever 45s was by a group called the Manchesters, titled, curiously enough, "I Don't Come from England."

Swan

Founded in 1957 in Philadelphia, Swan (and its subsidiary label, Lawn) mostly released teen-oriented music, which at that time meant R&B, early rock, and novelty songs. The label's top artist was Freddie "Boom Boom" Cannon, a big-beat rock-and-roll shouter famous for "Palisades Park," "Way Down Yonder in New Orleans," and "Tallahassee Lassie," as well as a fistful of smaller hits.

Some of Swan's artists sounded as if they were *parodies* of rock groups: Billy and Lillie, Dickey Doo and the Don'ts, and the Gay Charmers, for example.

On September 16, 1963, Swan took a chance on issuing "She Loves You" (backed with "I'll Get You"). The record did nothing on release, and quickly moved to the back of the pile of Swan's priorities; after all, the company had new records by Azie Mortimer, Sammy Stevens, and the Vespers to promote.

But in early 1964, when Capitol released and promoted "I Want to Hold Your Hand," "She Loves You" became a hot property and entered the *Billboard* charts on January 25—just one week after "Hand." The Swan 45 eventually hit #1 on *Billboard* for two weeks.

Swan found out that it also owned the rights to the band's German-language recording of the hit, so on May 21, 1964, the label also issued "Sie Liebe Dich," which scraped onto the *Billboard* charts at #97 for one week. The label's right to issue Beatle product ran out later in 1964.

Beyond the Beatles, though, Swan wasn't having many hits by the mid-'60s, instead dividing their 45s between groups past their prime (Link Wray and the Raymen, the Rockin' Rebels), before their prime (the Three Degrees, a twenty-one-year-old Ronnie James Dio), or quick cash-ins guaranteed to sputter (the Guys from U.N.C.L.E., Mr. Miller, and a group called John and Paul, which obviously had no relation to Lennon and McCartney). Swan folded in 1967.

Capitol

In 1963, Capitol Records—owned by EMI, who also owned Parlophone in the U.K.—was home to Al Martino, Bobby Darin, the Kingston Trio, and the Beach Boys, America's top rock group. They declined to pick up the option on the Beatles' new single, "Please Please Me." Rock and roll from England? Who'd buy it in America? Cliff Richard, the U.K.'s biggest star, had already flopped in the U.S.

So Capitol passed on the record (as well as on "From Me to You" and "She Loves You"). EMI assigned the rights of the song to their American agent, New York's Transglobal Music Company, and asked it to find an American label for the Beatles ASAP. Transglobal called Vee-Jay and did the deal.

Capitol of Canada, on the other hand—perhaps still feeling loyal to the British Commonwealth—was much more enthusiastic, jumping on "Love Me Do" in January 1963. Sales, however, did not justify the label's confidence, at least until "She Loves You" in September 1963. Several months before American kids went gaga for JPG&R, Canadian teenagers, especially those in Toronto, made "She Loves You" a hit.

This led to two Canadian Beatles 45s, "Roll Over Beethoven" and "All My Loving," reaching the American charts in spring 1964 through import orders alone.

By then, of course, Capitol in America had jumped on the band—inspired by a gutsy Brian Epstein move.

According to author Bruce Spizer, Epstein, angered that Capitol's A&R, Dave Dexter Jr., had turned down "I Want to Hold Your Hand," called Alan Livingston, president of Capitol, himself, in November 1963 and convinced Livingston to 1) listen to the record himself, 2) release it, and 3) spend a huge chunk of money promoting it.

Not afraid to take chances, Livingston had his marketing department devise an ingenious "The Beatles Are Coming" campaign, which spread the word about the group's upcoming American single by going right to the kids with high-school newspaper advertising, record-store displays, and promos for radio disc jockeys.

Beatlemania in England was now a big enough story to inspire news pieces in *Time*, *Newsweek*, and *Life*, even before "I Want to Hold Your Hand" was released in the United States. Pieces concerning Beatlemania also ran on NBC and CBS news programs in November 1963.

The record itself was pretty fair, too. When Washington-area DJ Carroll James, spurred by local listener Marsha Albert, had a copy of the British 45 delivered to him in December, WWDC became, on December 17, the first station in the U.S. to play "I Want to Hold Your Hand." The demand for the record forced Capitol to rush-release it on December 26.

From that point, Beatlemania was on its way. Primed by the marketing campaign, and quite probably needing some sort of joy following the death of John F. Kennedy on November 22, American teenagers went Beatle-mad in January 1964.

From "I Want to Hold Your Hand" through "Lady Madonna," Capitol released nineteen Beatles singles, thirteen of which climbed to #1.

The *Meet the Beatles!* LP, containing "I Want to Hold Your Hand," "This Boy," and ten more songs cherry-picked from their first two albums, sold more than 3.5 million in two months. It was the first of ten original Capitol Beatles album to reach the top spot in America; only two, which not so coincidentally featured previously released material (*The Early Beatles* and the somewhat deceptively titled *Something New*), did not.

Tollie

Vee-Jay, working hard to repackage its fourteen Beatles tracks in as many ways as possible, believed that customers (and disc jockeys) might be more likely to look at "new" Beatles records if they were printed on a "new" label.

So the company created a new imprint, Tollie (named after Vee-Jay executive Calvin Carter's son), which pressed two more early Beatles 45s. "Twist and Shout" was the #2 record in America for four weeks during the spring of 1964, while "Love Me Do," released in April, made #1 in May.

Prior to losing its license to sell Beatles material in October 1964, Vee-Jay also released four Beatles singles on the custom-created "Oldies" label, which allowed the records to be stocked in stores all over again.

MGM

The stodgy MGM label, which stumbled through the 1960s trying to catch up with what was happening in music, bought the rights to Tony Sheridan's 1961 Germany recordings, in which he was backed by the Beatles. Two of them, "My Bonnie" and "The Saints," had already seen the light of day back in 1962 on Decca.

Dutifully, MGM pressed new copies of "My Bonnie," which due to the mania for all things Beatle actually climbed to #26 on the American charts in March despite the Fabs only being heard as instrumentalists and, briefly, as background singers. A Sheridan-sung follow-up, "Why," hit the *Billboard* rolls for just one week, at #88, on April 18.

What is not widely known is that the MGM version of "My Bonnie" features drum overdubs by sessioneer Bernard "Pretty" Purdie. Pete Best's original drumming was found unsatisfactory, and MGM hired Purdie to make the overall sound that much sharper. In later years, a possibly nutty Purdie began to claim a much greater role on the Beatles' records than the truth warranted. (See chapter 12 for more information.)

Atco

This subsidiary of Atlantic Records acquired rights to four Sheridan-era tracks, and in June 1964 put out a single of "Sweet Georgia Brown" and "Take Out Some Insurance on Me, Baby," both featuring Sheridan's lead vocal. The record didn't even reach the *Billboard* Hot 100.

Atco's second Beatles release, however, did. "Ain't She Sweet," a track sung by Lennon recorded at the Tony Sheridan sessions, actually broke into the Top 20 in August 1964, becoming the last 45 rpm record issued by a competitor of Capitol to reach the American charts. It is not clear why Atco waited to release the Lennon vocal; perhaps "Ain't She Sweet" was the ace in the hole.

Apple

The Beatles had been told in 1967 that they had to find some way to shelter their finances or risk losing a huge amount to the tax man ("Should five percent appear too small / Be thankful I don't take it all"). The group and its advisers kicked around several strategies, finally settling on a record/film/electronics company.

The Fabs unveiled the new corporation, named Apple both for the fruit's purity and in tribute to artist Rene Magritte's iconic images, in early 1968. The "Apple" production company name, however, had first been seen in the liner notes to the *Sgt. Pepper* album.

Conceived as a company where young talent would not have to beg just to be signed, Apple had music publishing, film, and electronics divisions as well as a record division. But while songwriters were signed, avant-garde music and poetry recorded, films made, a clothing boutique opened, and electronic toys designed, Apple from the very beginning was first and foremost a record label—and first and foremost focused on the Beatles' own discs.

"Hey Jude" was Apple's first Beatles 45 and the last of the Fabs' singles released in mono. Of the six Beatles singles released from 1968–70 on Apple, five (all but "The Ballad of John and Yoko") reached the #1 spot in America. Albums *The Beatles, Yellow Submarine, Abbey Road, Hey Jude,* and *Let It Be* fed the world's appetite for new Fab Four music.

The Apple story has been told many times; suffice it to say that ambition outran competence. While the Beatles' records sold well, and a few other groups and artists (Mary Hopkin, Badfinger) found some success, Apple's original dreams dissolved in the reality of the marketplace. By 1969, the boutique had been shuttered, the films division gutted, the electronics department shut off, and much of the staff fired by newly hired *enfant terrible* Allen Klein.

Following Klein's ascension, Apple ceased to be anything but a record label. When the group split, all four Beatles released solo product on Apple, but by 1975, the label was essentially defunct.

Zapple

One of Apple's more ambitious notions was Zapple, a sub-label conceived as a low-priced imprint to be used exclusively for avant-garde releases. The Beatles talked of recording albums with poets Roger McGough and Allan Ginsberg and the American group the Fugs, and of undertaking various non-Beatles projects. The group hired Barry Miles, a denizen of London's underground, to run the project.

As it turned out, the only two records issued on Zapple were Beatle solo projects. Both were released May 26, 1969.

George Harrison—usually uncomfortable with the avant-garde—for some reason put out an album of synthesizer bleeps called *Electronic Sound*. One side was recorded by Harrison himself in Esher in 1969, and the other was done in California in 1968 with electronic music pioneer Bernie Krause. (For some reason, probably nefarious, Krause's name is almost completely obscured on the album cover.)

The other Zapple LP belongs to John Lennon and Yoko Ono: *Unfinished Music 2: Life with the Lions*. With one side a live concert recording and the other documenting Yoko's heartrending miscarriage in a British hospital, *Lions* certainly met the "documentary" brief.

The Beatles' appeal was truly universal in scope, with this release in particular (from Uruguay) crossing cultural boundaries.

Allen Klein, brought in by three Beatles (save Paul) to make Apple's finances more stable, chose to shutter the whole avant-garde project. A third Zapple LP, a spoken-word piece by American poet Richard Brautigan, was just *that* close to being released when Klein pulled the plug.

Lingasong

During the mid-1970s, Beatles fans read news items that a tape of the group playing in Hamburg, Germany, would be released. Finally, in June 1977, the small Lingasong label released *The Beatles! Live at the Star Club Hamburg, 1962.*

The original tapes, recorded by Adrian Barber at the request of Ted "Kingsize" Taylor, a Liverpool musician, were thought initially to feature the group—with amazing prescience—on a night when Ringo Starr was sitting in for an absent Pete Best. The tapes sat in a cellar for several years; neither George Martin nor Brian Epstein saw much potential in the admittedly primitive recording.

Former Beatles manager Allan Williams discovered the tapes in 1972 and scraped together several thousand pounds to have the original reel-to-reels transferred to twenty-four-track tape and cleaned up. The remastering process couldn't remove all the tape hiss, crowd whistles, whoops, catcalls, and ambient noise, but did make the tapes suitable for release.

On copies of the original album, no exact concert date is given. Since the LP's 1977 release, it has become known that the recording dates from December 31, 1962, the last gig the Fab Four would ever play at the famous German club. By this time, Ringo was a full member of the Beatles.

Lingasong's U.K. release led to an American release several months later on Atlantic (parent of Atco). The Atlantic release deleted four songs from the German LP and inserted four new ones that Lingasong had left off its release, thus forcing any Beatle completist who had already bought the album to buy the Atlantic release as well.

While the fidelity of the two-album set left much to be desired, even after an expensive remastering and clean-up process, *Star Club* is an amazing audio document—the only one, really—of the Beatles' Hamburg experience. Tearing through classic rock-and-roll material, standards, and some of their own compositions, the Beatles "mach schau" for their rowdy and rip-roaring listeners.

Sure, they curse, and drink onstage, and sometimes have to dodge flying bottles. A German waiter sings two songs. It doesn't matter. If you want to hear what it was like when John Lennon said the Beatles were truly at their peak, this is the record to get.

Move Over Once

Ten Acts Knocked from the #1 Spot by the Beatles

The Beatles registered a staggering twenty #1 songs on the *Billboard* magazine charts between 1964 and 1970. Among the acts the Fab Four knocked from the top spot on the national survey are some of the biggest names in pop music history, along with others not so big, and some who saw their ride at the top halted forever with the advent of a new Fabs 45.

Bobby Vinton: "There! I've Said It Again," Knocked Out February 1, 1964

Nothing seemed to symbolize the change from the popular music of 1963 to that of the "new order" more than the #1 records of the first two weeks of February '64: the first recorded by American balladeer Bobby Vinton and the second by the Beatles.

Vinton's remake of the 1945 Vaughn Monroe ballad was the third chart-topper of his saccharine-laced career, racing up the *Billboard* survey and holding the #1 position for four weeks.

But the rush-release in late 1963 of "I Want to Hold Your Hand" brought about a sea change in popular music; Vinton soon dropped unceremoniously from the top spot when the Beatles' first Capitol 45 leapt from #43 to #1 in just its third week on the chart.

Already twenty-nine when the Beatles made it in America, Vinton had another #1 in 1965 with "Mr. Lonely," but his time as a teen hit-maker had essentially passed as rock and roll regained the airwaves. Vinton only enjoyed three more Top 10 records in his career as he concentrated on cultivating a more adult audience.

The Four Seasons: "Rag Doll," Knocked Out August 1, 1964

In 1964, the biggest British pop group in the world and, arguably, the biggest such American group were labelmates on Vee-Jay, a Chicago R&B imprint.

Vee-Jay Records was riding high with the Four Seasons and the Beatles; the Seasons registered nine Top 40 hits for the label. Meanwhile, Vee-Jay and its sister labels Tollie and Oldies managed, during 1964–65, to squeeze four albums, an extended-play 45, and *ten* singles out of the twelve Beatle tracks they had acquired the rights to when Capitol passed on them in 1963.

One of these Vee-Jay LPs, titled *The Beatles Versus the Four Seasons,* was a double album "pitting" the two acts against one another ("Each group delivering their greatest vocal punches"). The release was so limited, sold so poorly, and was so hard to keep in good shape due to a gatefold cover, that even copies in just "good" condition can bring over $300 today on the open market. A pristine copy sold on eBay in 2005 for more than $1,400.

By the time of "Rag Doll," which spent two weeks at the top of the charts, the Seasons had left Vee-Jay for a new record label, Phillips. The loss of the Four Seasons, litigation costs accrued while battling Capitol over Beatles issues, and misappropriated funds to cover gambling debts of top management effectively ended Vee-Jay.

The deposing of "Rag Doll" at the hands of "A Hard Day's Night," which, like "I Want to Hold Your Hand," jumped to #1 in its third chart week, proved to be a symbolic and pivotal point in the career of the Four Seasons, who had previously enjoyed four #1 hits but would not reach the top spot again until releasing the disco-fied "December '63 (Oh, What a Night)" in late 1975.

The Supremes: "Come See About Me," Knocked Out December 26, 1964; "Love Is Here and Now You're Gone," Knocked Out March 18, 1967

Twice the Fab Four ousted the Supremes from the top spot, first with "I Feel Fine," which took a whole month to get to #1, and second with "Penny Lane," which took only three weeks.

The Beatles, themselves huge fans of the Motown sound, were also responsible for pushing a second Detroit act, the Temptations, from the top in January 1965. "My Girl," the first of four #1 songs by the Temps, removed "I Feel Fine" from the top spot on January 11, but the Beatles retook the #1 position the following week.

Not even the Beatles could claim the kind of overpowering chart success enjoyed by the Supremes in the mid-1960s. "Come See About Me" was the third of *five* straight #1 singles on the Motown label; the Beatles never had that many consecutive number ones. The winsome threesome would enjoy seven more chart-toppers by the time the '60s had ended and Diana Ross had finished her Berry Gordy Customized Star-Grooming Course.

Herman's Hermits: "Mrs. Brown, You've Got a Lovely Daughter," Knocked Out May 22, 1965

Of the many acts to cash in on the British Beat Boom in the states, Peter "Herman" Noone of Herman's Hermits was the only one with the kind of across-the-board teen appeal enjoyed by any of the individual Beatles.

Noone, not even seventeen at the time of the band's first American hit in 1964 ("I'm Into Something Good"), had a toothy grin and a goofy charm, as well as a winning way with a song. The Hermits notched eleven Top 10 songs in just over two years, but just two of them ("Mrs. Brown" and "I'm Henry VIII, I Am") got to the top. Such was the competition during those heady years.

"Mrs. Brown," a mawkish ballad reminiscent of 1920s British music halls, held down the #1 spot for three weeks before dropping out, thanks to John Lennon's infinitely superior "Ticket to Ride," which, due to its proto-metal drums, chiming guitars, and double-time countryish ending, sounded unlike anything ever previously recorded.

Simon and Garfunkel: "The Sound of Silence," Knocked Out January 8, 1966; "Bridge over Troubled Water," Knocked Out April 11, 1970

Already favorites of coffeehouses and the folk circuit, Simon and Garfunkel proved a tremendous chart duo as well after producer Tom Wilson grafted folk-rock instruments onto the previously spare "The Sound of Silence" in late 1965.

After two weeks at the top of the chart, though, the New Yorkers gave way to the Beatles' "We Can Work It Out," an expansion on the folk-rock form that featured classic Lennon-McCartney harmonies and song structure as well as the innovative use of the drone-producing harmonium keyboard.

Four years later, Simon and Garfunkel had their third and last chart-topper with a heartfelt gospel number destined to become a classic. "Bridge over Troubled Water" seized the #1 spot and held on for six weeks in the late winter and early spring of 1970, to be followed by . . . a heartfelt gospel

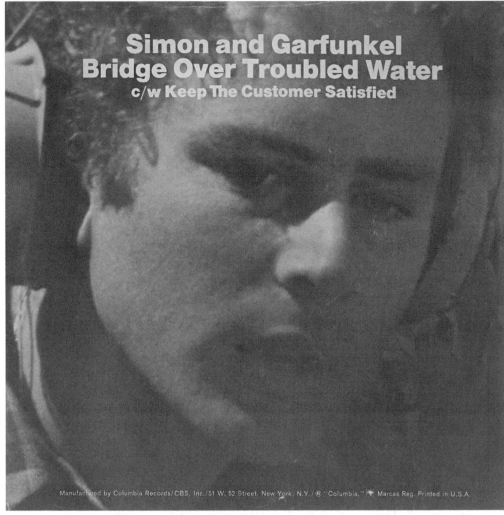

Simon and Garfunkel
Bridge Over Troubled Water
c/w Keep The Customer Satisfied

Manufactured by Columbia Records/CBS, Inc./51 W, 52 Street, New York, N.Y./® "Columbia," ℗ Marcas Reg. Printed in U.S.A.

Probably Art Garfunkel's finest moment as a vocalist came on this single, the title track to the duo's final album. Roy Halee's majestic production provided a fine climax to their string of chart successes.

number destined to become a classic: Paul McCartney's "Let It Be," featuring churchy organ and a knockout George Harrison solo.

The Rolling Stones: "Paint It, Black," Knocked Out
June 25, 1966

Friends of the Beatles as well as their natural rivals, the Rolling Stones played harder blues, sang slower country, and posed for creepier pictures than their Liverpool brethren. The Stones' "dirtier than you" approach, as well as some fine songwriting and ensemble playing, led to a slew of controversial hit records in the mid-1960s.

"Paint It, Black" added the in-vogue Eastern touches of sitar and whirl-ing-dervish rhythm to a driving beat and a lyric about mourning a dead girlfriend. Only in the 1960s could such a song be a number one, and the Stones held the top spot for two weeks—that is, until "Paperback Writer" leapt to the top in just its third week out of the chute.

While "Paint It, Black" was Eastern to the core, "Paperback Writer" featured atypically jagged George Harrison guitar in addition to backing vocals paying homage to that most American of bands, the Beach Boys. By early 1966, Harrison and Stones guitarist Keith Richards were sporting the same hairstyles, sunglasses, and fashion sense—but would grow easier to distinguish in the coming years.

The Monkees: "Daydream Believer," Knocked Out December 30, 1967

Plenty of Beatles fans can't stand the Monkees, believing the TV-created foursome to be disposable bubblegum pap. The Beatles themselves, how-ever, found the Monkees to be friendly and capable fellow musicians as well as outstanding comic actors. Michael Nesmith attended the "A Day in the Life" orchestral session and bunked with the Lennons; Micky Dolenz hung with and got high with Paul McCartney; George Harrison asked Peter Tork to play banjo on *Wonderwall Music*.

The groups also had chart interactions. "Daydream Believer," which fell from the top spot less than a month after "Hello Goodbye" was released, was the Monkees' third and last #1 song in America. Though nobody knew it at the time, the Prefab Four's time as hit-makers was nearing an end. "Valleri," released in March 1968, was the Monkees' sixth and final gold record, and by late 1968, they were struggling just to get a record into the Top 60 on the *Billboard* charts.

Oddly, "Hello Goodbye" may be the most overtly bubblegum Beatles single, one that John Lennon disliked, saying, "Smells a mile away, doesn't it?"

Jeannie C. Riley: "Harper Valley P.T.A.," Knocked Out September 28, 1968

"Harper Valley P.T.A.," the only Top 40 hit enjoyed by country songstress Jeannie C. Riley, featured Tom T. Hall's witty and wicked lyrics exposing the hypocritical nature of certain small-town do-gooders. Ms. Riley, just twenty-two, sounded far more mature than her years, and the record ran a quick path to #1 in August 1968.

The "Prefab Four," as would-be wits were likely to call the Monkees, certainly gave the Fabs a run for their money in 1967 with a string of fine pop-rock releases.

But "Harper Valley P.T.A." was no match for "Hey Jude," which took just two weeks on the charts to rocket to the top spot. Paul's triumphant ode to perseverance in the face of trials knocked out Ms. Riley's 45 after one week at the top, then remained #1 for nine weeks that fall, dropping from the top spot for good only after Thanksgiving.

The flip of the 45, Lennon's stinging "Revolution," became the Beatles' final B-side to make the Top 20 (it reached #12) before *Billboard*, in 1969, decided to stop computing B-side positions separately. "Revolution" surely was the first-ever pop hit to offer both a name-check and a smackdown of Chinese premier Mao Tse-Tung.

The Fifth Dimension: "Aquarius / Let the Sunshine In," Knocked Out May 24, 1969; "Wedding Bell Blues," Knocked Out November 29, 1969

Moving beyond their early status as Johnny Rivers's protégés and blossoming into one of the pop scene's hottest groups, the Fifth Dimension and their "California Soul" sound were big stuff in the late 1960s and early 1970s.

Both of the group's #1 records came in 1969, and both of them were ejected from the top spot by the Beatles.

"Aquarius / Let the Sunshine In" was by far the biggest hit song from the musical *Hair*; several groups and artists enjoyed major successes with various tunes from the popular Broadway show. The Fifth Dimension's catchy, gospel-tinged reading was #1 for six weeks, then fell from the top spot when the Beatles' "as nature intended" 45, "Get Back," leapt up the charts, needing only two weeks to take over at #1 and remaining there for five weeks.

Later in the year, "Wedding Bell Blues," Marilyn McCoo's paean to Billy Davis Jr. (the two soon married) was a three-week number one after a surprisingly slow run up the charts. But the record's time at the top ended when the double A-side of "Come Together" and "Something" made the #1 spot just after Thanksgiving. Oddly, this power-packed 45 remained atop the *Billboard* survey for just one week.

Ray Stevens: "Everything Is Beautiful," Knocked Out June 13, 1970

Heretofore known for cornball comedy disks ("Ahab, the Arab," "Harry the Hairy Ape," "Gitarzan"), Georgia pianist/singer/arranger Ray Stevens surprised in early 1970 with the out-of-left-field anthem "Everything Is Beautiful," a song so overtly earnest and syrupy that radio stations nearly forty years later can barely be persuaded to play it.

Stevens's record has some significance outside of its own chart-topping status. "Everything Is Beautiful" is also the last 45-rpm record to be knocked out of the #1 spot by the Beatles, whose swan song, "The Long and Winding Road," climbed to the top in its fourth week on the charts. What the chart music of the early '70s was quickly becoming is perfectly summed up by these two string-laden, treacly hits.

Ray Stevens' other #1 smash came in 1974, and served as a return to novelty form. Remember "The Streak"?

I Read the News Today, Oh Boy

Grabbing the Headlines

When they weren't making music, the Beatles were making the news on a regular basis. Beyond the standard teen tabloid fodder, the Fabs periodically cropped up on the covers of the major mainstream magazines of the day (*Time, Life, Look, The Saturday Evening Post*, etc.), thereby penetrating the consciousness of even non-rock fans.

While pop-rock acts tended to be ignored by non-music press, the Beatles' appeal, import, and news-making ability were such that most any event involving the quartet was certain to provoke a reaction. The following selection of stories runs the gamut from trifling to weighty, showing that no matter what they did, the Beatles were never boring.

The Beatles Conquer America: December 1963–January 1964

The world had never seen anything like it. Sure, Valentino, Sinatra, and Elvis had taken America, and some of the rest of the world, by storm, but the multimedia explosion of the 1960s made the Beatles the first modern entertainment bonanza—and indicated that youth had taken hold of the popular culture machine, and wouldn't be giving it back.

Rebuffed by Capitol Records, the American cohort of British EMI, on the band's first three singles, Brian Epstein finally convinced Capitol to release a Beatles 45, calling label president Alan Livingston personally to plead the case for "I Want to Hold Your Hand."

Livingston not only bit on the record, he also agreed to an unheard-of $40,000 promotional campaign.

By the time the promo work ("The Beatles Are Coming!") started in late 1963, the news about a wild-haired rock-and-roll group from England had permeated some television news outlets. NBC aired a story about the Beatles, in slightly mocking tones, on their nightly news program on November 17, while *Tonight Show* host Jack Paar ran some performance footage, drawing laughter from his studio audience.

But the Beatles were about to make inroads where it really counted—pop radio. Carroll James of WWDC had a friend send one over from England posthaste, began playing the track, still unreleased in America, and watched his phones ring off the hook with calls from excited listeners.

Word spread among other DJs around the country—some of whom were already familiar with the Beatles from their smaller hits ("Please Please Me" and "From Me to You") in Chicago and L.A. earlier that year—and the demand for "Hand" forced Capitol to rush-release it in America lest they lose this precious momentum.

By the time the record hit the stores in late December 1963, the record-buying public was primed for Beatlemania. The high quality of the record, the novelty of the band's appearance, the Capitol promotional campaign, and precious radio and TV exposure had laid the groundwork for the Beatles' American takeover.

The MBEs: Summer 1965

How does the hottest act in show business achieve validation from the establishment? In England, it's through a multi-tiered honor called the Order of the British Empire (or OBE). Established in 1917, the awards are theoretically chosen by the monarch, but in practice, the Prime Minister in power and/or his people do the actual nominating.

At the highest end, the OBE confers knighthood upon recipients. The bottom end, commonly bestowed upon those with shining military careers, is called the MBE (or, to be veddy proper, the Member of the Most Excellent Order of the British Empire). It was at this level that the Beatles became recipients in June 1965.

The unprecedented move to honor the Fabs—rock and rollers were heretofore unrepresented in the MBE rolls—was a shrewd political calculation by Prime Minister Harold Wilson. Anxious to align himself with anything popular and youthful, Wilson only needed to point at the millions of dollars in cash the Beatles were generating, supporting the British welfare state with its punitive taxation (which George railed against mightily the following year in "Taxman"), to justify his decision.

While the Beatles were flattered by the recognition (if privately holding some reservations, wondering why their manager wasn't included), some members of the order were outraged at the elevating of "vulgar nincompoops" to their level, a handful going so far as to return their medals.

John, typically, was unmoved, pointing out that the malcontents had won theirs "for killing people" while the Beatles had been recognized for their professional success—making music and entertaining. "I'd say we deserved ours more," he mused.

Though Lennon's comments only added to the controversy, the Fabs accepted their medals at Buckingham Palace with good grace. The October 1965 investiture drew thousands of screaming fans to the palace. Scarcely aware of the members individually, Queen Elizabeth asked Ringo if he was the one who had started it all. "No ma'am," he responded. "I'm just the little fellow."

Their medals themselves would eventually accessorize the psychedelic military outfits on the *Sgt. Pepper*'s sleeve. Only Ringo ever actually used his newly acquired title (albeit cheekily), on his eponymous 1973 solo album. Conversely, John returned his medal in 1969 as an "event," not realizing that the honor remains whether one possesses the "gong" or not.

Paul was officially knighted in 1997—a year after George Martin—while George Harrison, surely deserving recognition for his charitable efforts on behalf of Bangladesh in 1971, went to his grave as an MBE (knighthoods cannot be bestowed posthumously).

On Tour in Asia: June–July 1966

For the first and only time, the Beatles' 1966 road show included stops in the Far East. With the Fabs' popularity in Japan particularly strong, EMI saw personal appearances as a just reward to the fans for robust sales. The Beatles themselves, laboring under the weight of fatigue and boredom, saw this leg of the tour as a way to keep themselves interested, at least for a while.

The trip to Japan was not without controversy. First, a Japanese Nationalist group claimed it would administer haircuts to the boys upon their arrival. Taken slightly more seriously was the perception that the Fabs' concerts at the Nippon Budokan, an arena used mostly for sumo wrestling, would be something akin to blasphemy.

The facility, first opened for the 1964 Olympics, was considered a shrine in a land where martial arts are equated with godliness. In later years, though, Budokan gained worldwide renown as a prestigious rock venue, hosting Cheap Trick, Bob Dylan, and others; the Beatles, as usual, led the way.

To protect the band during their concerts, authorities packed the ten-thousand-seat stadium with *three thousand* security personnel. Moreover, safety concerns forced the Fabs to remain in their hotel suite for the duration of their stay. (Some enterprising merchants were allowed to bring in their wares for the Beatles' shopping convenience.)

The professional film crew that recorded the concerts captured some of the most listless, indifferent performances of the Beatles' career. Just as *Let It Be* documented a recording band going through the motions, the Tokyo concerts showcased four musicians who couldn't care less, running out the clock on their touring career.

From Tokyo, the Beatles flew to Manila. With tens of thousands of fans turning out to greet them, the entourage breathed a collective sigh of relief at escaping Tokyo's stifling atmosphere. Before long, however, events in the Philippines' capital had them pining for Japan's controlled chaos.

With two scheduled performances (one of which was second only to Shea Stadium as the band's biggest crowd ever), the Fabs looked forward to resting during their down time. Unbeknownst to them, however, Imelda Marcos, wife of the country's strong-arm dictator, Ferdinand, had invited the Beatles to a "reception" at Malacañang Palace. In turning down what he believed to be a simple meet-and-greet, Brian Epstein unwittingly ignited a firestorm.

The Beatles, in fact, were expected to headline a full-blown media event, with three hundred children present and live television coverage. When they failed to arrive as billed, government functionaries placed a series of increasingly shrill phone calls to their hotel, and Epstein soon discovered the makings of a public relations disaster.

Taking to the airwaves, Brian issued a mea culpa for any misunderstanding, but "technical difficulties" mysteriously disrupted the transmission. Meanwhile, the seeds for a riot were none-too-subtly sown by headlines blaring "Imelda stood up!"

Trouble began as the band left their hotel. All prior security arrangements had been rescinded, forcing the Fabs to exit amid hundreds of incensed Filipinos jeering, kicking, and spitting upon the party. At the airport, baggage handlers went absent and power to the escalators was cut, forcing the group and crew to lug their suitcases and gear up and down staircases.

Meanwhile, Filipino tax officials moved in, demanding (and getting) the equivalent of $18,000 as surety against taxes owed on the band's earnings—which promoters elected not to pay anyway following the perceived "snub" of the first family.

The ugliness continued on the runway as government officials grounded the Beatles' plane, harassing the entourage over supposed discrepancies in their paperwork. After stalling for nearly an hour, officials gave the go-ahead, and the band was allowed to leave, never to return.

In the wake of the fiasco, concerts by Cilla Black, Sounds Incorporated, and Freddie and the Dreamers were canceled in the Philippines. Once back in England, asked about the Beatles' immediate plans, George replied that they were headed stateside to get "beaten up by Americans." His words proved more prescient than anyone realized.

"Bigger Than Jesus": Summer 1966

Maureen Cleave, a journalist with London's *Evening Standard*, was friendly with the Beatles, especially John. This closeness translated into more candid exchanges than might otherwise have been possible. In March 1966, she profiled him in an article titled "How Does a Beatle Live?" The piece was the typical "day in the life of a celebrity" fodder, albeit more thoughtful than most.

Buried within its 2,200 words was an aside made in response to a query about his current reading. Dr. Hugh Schonfield, a Biblical scholar, had penned a controversial best-seller, *The Passover Plot*, which argued that a scheme by the historic Jesus to stage his own death by crucifixion had been inadvertently bungled. The book deeply influenced Lennon's religious thinking to his dying day.

John remarked, in passing, that given the current state of Christianity, it wasn't surprising that the Beatles held more sway with young people than did the Bible ("We're more popular than Jesus now"). The remark was intended as irony, rather than arrogance, with John noting that organized religion, disseminated by mere "thick and ordinary" humans, had so twisted the Master's message that it was ruined for him. Long accustomed to Lennon's provocative tongue, the English citizenry let the story go by without a ripple.

On the eve of the Beatles' American tour, however, the quote "I don't know which will go first: Christianity or rock and roll" was stripped of its context and rerun on the cover of *Datebook* magazine (which featured, oddly enough, a photo of Paul). Included amid cherry-picked excerpts from the original article, this manufactured bombshell achieved its intent—to stir up controversy and ignite a backlash, particularly in the Bible Belt, which had been looking for an excuse to brand the Beatles "subversives" from day one.

Almost overnight, radio stations began to ban Beatles records from their airwaves while organizing boycotts and bonfires worthy of Hitler's SA. Condemnation of the band generally, and Lennon in particular, emanated from pulpits around the country. The few voices in support of his point struggled to be heard.

In an attempt to defuse the stunningly incendiary reaction, Brian Epstein left his sickbed to fly to the States in advance of his charges and gave a news

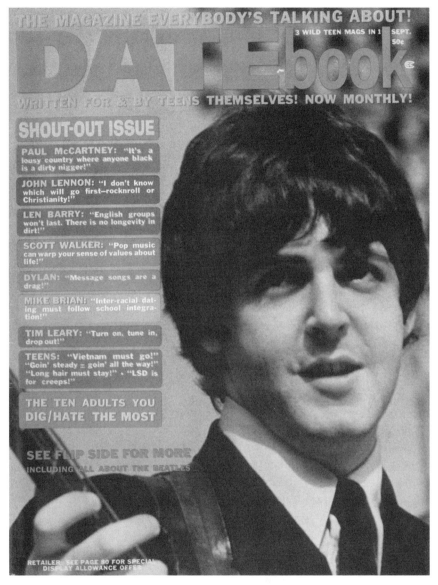

Datebook's July 1966 issue (dated September) was guaranteed to spark controversy. Amazingly, Paul's equally inflammatory indictment of American racism stirred nary a ripple.

conference, correctly noting that John's observations had been taken out of context. But so inflamed were the media that nothing short of a very public—and humiliating—apology would do.

On August 12 in Chicago, an uncharacteristically chastened Lennon appeared before reporters in a display that was equal parts defensive explanation and contrite regret. This seemed to satisfy the gathered press, who appeared nearly gleeful to be delivering a comeuppance to the Fabs. (Asked one: "Do you think you're being crucified?")

After the disastrous swing through the Pacific, the table was set for putting an end to touring once and for all. With death threats plaguing the American tour at several stops, and crowds thinner in some cities than in the previous two years, the Beatles recognized at the end of their two weeks in America that the string had been played out. Having had a bellyful of all that performing had to offer, and a taste of the recording studio's possibilities with *Revolver*, the summer of '66 ended this phase of their career with a resounding thud.

Our World Broadcast: June 25, 1967

In one of his last managerial acts, Brian Epstein pledged the Beatles to represent Great Britain in *Our World*, a two-hour television special. The historic event was the first live-by-satellite worldwide broadcast, with twenty-six nations contributing content for an audience of some four hundred million.

Initially, the Fabs were slightly put out at the commitment, feeling that a role in a "pageant" was beneath them. But after Brian impressed upon them the opportunity the broadcast presented to reach the world with a message of their choosing, the boys couldn't resist the challenge.

Both John and Paul set to work on fulfilling Epstein's brief: to compose something "stirring." Unfortunately for Paul, his tendency to crumble under the pressure of writing to order under deadline (demonstrated earlier by his inability to write title songs for the Beatles' first two films) manifested itself. McCartney again choked, ceding the spotlight to John by concocting the less than anthemic "Your Mother Should Know."

John, on the other hand, after procrastinating until a little over a week before the event, demonstrated the grasp of musical sloganeering that would soon become his trademark. Building upon the message of "The Word" from *Rubber Soul*, "All You Need Is Love" perfectly encapsulated the Summer of Love's gestalt, being at once deceptively simple and apparently weighty.

Though billed as a live event, the Beatles' portion of the broadcast didn't entirely fit this description. The backing track had been laid down in advance, so that only the bass, orchestration, lead vocal (later recut), and backing vocals were played and recorded live.

With only the sketchiest of rehearsals, the logistically daunting broadcast went off without a hitch (although, comically, the show went live almost a minute early, catching George Martin and engineer Geoff Emerick in the control booth nervously sharing a bottle of Scotch).

A number of celebrity friends, invited on short notice, added vocals and presence to the festivities. Among those seen at the Fabs' feet, clapping and joining in the chorus, were Mick Jagger and Keith Richards, Keith Moon of the Who, Graham Nash of the Hollies, Eric Clapton, Jane Asher and assorted Beatle wives, and Mike McCartney, who sent streamers sailing and provided cue cards ("Come Back Milly").

Coming on the heels of *Sgt. Pepper*, the Beatles' most acclaimed album to date, "All You Need Is Love" provided a fitting coda to a work that contained, after all, no love songs and no hit singles. It amplified the notion that in 1967 the band was all about the Big Statement, while the broadcast's in-person element provided a glimmer of hope to the faithful that perhaps the Fabs weren't entirely finished with live appearances. In many ways, the *Our World* broadcast was the high-water mark of Beatlemania.

Apple Is Launched: December 1967

The first faint rumbling of the Beatles' foray into big business came with a tiny blurb on the back of the *Sgt. Pepper's* album cover, offering part credit to "The Apple." At the time, little existed of "The Apple" beyond grandiose dreams of a multimedia empire, anchored by record and music publishing divisions.

The band's accountants precipitated the notion of the Beatles becoming businessmen, recognizing that the musicians' earnings—while somewhat reduced by Epstein's financial missteps—were in peril of being absorbed by Inland Revenue (i.e., the "Taxman"). Therefore, a productive means of divesting Fab earnings became necessary.

The first tangible Apple enterprise came in the form of a boutique, located on Baker Street near EMI House. Described by Paul as "a beautiful place where you could buy beautiful things," the shop was stocked with garish threads, largely designed by a spare-no-expense Dutch collective called the Fool.

Opened amid much fanfare in December 1967, the store was notable less for its contents than for its four-story-high psychedelic mural commissioned by the Fool, with the Fabs' blessing. Though the cosmic Day-Glo rendering was unexceptional by Summer of Love standards, local businesses complained long and loud about the wall detracting from the neighborhood and drawing unwelcome gawkers who clogged traffic flow. The Beatles whitewashed over the mural three months later.

Typifying what would be an ongoing pattern, the group showed remarkably poor judgment in staffing their investment. Though Lennon pal and former Quarry Man Pete Shotton managed the venture (assisted by George's sister-in-law, Jenny Boyd), other employees—including the Fool—recognized the bounty they were amidst, and plundered the store blind.

Seven months after opening the shop and running it at a loss, the Beatles decided that they were tired of being shopkeepers and chose to liquidate. This they did initially by informing customers that they needn't pay for their items. A full-blown giveaway was announced for the next day, July 31, 1968. (The night before, the Fabs, save Ringo, who lamented that nothing was in his size, picked over the remaining stock themselves.)

Slightly more successful was Apple Films, run by movie producer Dennis ("You Know My Name") O'Dell. Credited on *Magical Mystery Tour*, *Yellow Submarine*, and *Let It Be*, the film division served little purpose beyond Beatles product, though 1972's T-Rex documentary, *Born to Boogie*, marked Ringo's directorial debut.

Each Beatle had pet projects that he envisioned Apple would bring to fruition, but collectively they made at least one spectacularly naïve gesture to recruit unknown talent. An ad depicting Apple director Alistair Taylor garbed as a one-man band ran in the trade papers, announcing that due to his having sent a demo tape in to Apple, he now owned a Bentley. This open invitation to every quack and wannabe resulted in thousands of tapes flooding in, blindsiding no one *except* the Fabs. Eventually, nearly all the unheard submissions were quietly disposed of.

Equally doomed was Apple Electronics. Headed by Lennon hanger-on "Magic" Alex Mardas, a self-styled "inventor" of dubious veracity, the company promised a line of astounding electronic gear. Instead, over one hundred patents applied for by the division were rejected, because they were merely minor alterations of existing products.

Mardas's long-overdue dismissal finally came in the wake of his failure to equip Apple Studios with the seventy-two-track recording facility he had promised, at a time when the norm was eight tracks.

Apple, predicated upon the notion of "Western Communism" and the belief that no one with a good idea (or song or film treatment or invention) should have to beg for funding, was the embodiment of the hippie dream. A complete disconnect from the rigors of disciplined business practices and a lack of insight into basic human nature ultimately led to the company's downfall. In addition, the Apple nightmare fed the band's internal discontent.

The Trip to Rishikesh: February–April 1968

Of all of those within the Beatles' inner circle, the least likely source sparked an awareness of Transcendental Meditation. Pattie Harrison, who, one might charitably say, was not usually associated with weighty issues, actually took a deep interest in spiritual matters. Her husband's infatuation with Indian music eventually merged with and expanded on her own philosophical pursuits.

By 1967, George's sway with his fellow Beatles was cresting. Given their recent LSD experimentation, it wasn't a stretch to look beyond the chemical and seek a more durable path to expanded consciousness and peace of mind. Maharishi Mahesh Yogi's arrival on the British scene coincided with the Beatles' growing philosophical appetite.

The Maharishi, as he was commonly known, advanced a brand of TM that drew upon the teachings of Adi Shankara, believed to be a descendent of the Hindu god Shiva. What the former Mahesh Prasad Varma brought to the table was a fundamental understanding of marketing, razor-sharp financial acumen, and showmanship.

In August 1967, the Beatles and their wives traveled to Bangor, Wales, to attend a TM seminar with the Maharishi. (Portentously, Cynthia Lennon missed the train and was left behind at the station.)

While in Bangor, word reached the party that Brian Epstein had accidentally fatally overdosed. The stunned group was comforted by the yogi, who informed them that thoughts of Brian should be kept happy, since they would travel to him. Besides, Brian wasn't "really" dead anyway.

With world-famous, trendsetting musicians as pupils, the influence the Maharishi could wield was enormous. Thus, though the yogi had been accustomed to spreading the word via traveling road shows, at last the mountain had come to Mohammed.

Once the *Magical Mystery Tour* film project was out of the way, the Beatles cleared their schedules to undertake a three-month meditation course in Rishikesh, India, under the Maharishi's tutelage. Completion of the study would officially certify them as "gurus."

Several other celebrity students, including actress Mia Farrow (newly divorced from singer Frank Sinatra) and her sister, Prudence, Mike Love of the Beach Boys, and Donovan, joined the Fabs and their mates on the trip. Isolated from fans, the media, and nearly all communication with the outside world, the Beatles were at last afforded a break from stardom.

Almost immediately, earthly concerns interrupted. Ringo, with a history of digestive problems, feared that the spicy Indian meals would be problematic and had filled an entire suitcase with cans of baked beans. After two weeks, his wife, Maureen, had reached her absolute limit with the flies. The couple departed, blaming the food.

Jane Asher and Paul were the next to go, after a month. (George would later complain bitterly that the two "never got it.") Before Paul left, however, he, John, and George wrote a passel of tunes—nearly a double album's worth. Strikingly, the isolation (as well as fingerpicking lessons from Donovan) sparked a torrent of creativity.

Macca's departure left two Beatles: George, who maintained his studies in earnest, and John. It was the latter whose expectations were the highest. (As Yoko would observe later, John, always on the lookout for a "Daddy" figure, seemed doomed to self-fulfilling disillusionment.)

Lennon, fed innuendo by the credibility-challenged "Magic" Alex (who had come along for the ride but was fearful of losing sway with John), was incensed to hear that the Holy Man's attentions toward some of the women, including Mia, might have been something less than spiritual.

An ugly confrontation led to John and George's hasty departure. While George had doubts (and years later apologized to the Maharishi), John very publicly denounced the guru. At first channeling his bile into a musical diatribe called "Maharishi," he eventually softened somewhat, changing the song's name to the less inflammatory "Sexy Sadie."

Unfinished Music No. 1: Two Virgins: Recorded May 1968

Since their meeting at London's Indica Art Gallery in November 1966, John Lennon and Yoko Ono had maintained a discreet, if active, correspondence. Deluging the bored Beatle with unfathomable missives and impenetrable poetry, she alternately exhilarated and confounded him.

With his marriage to Cynthia running on fumes by early 1968, John found himself increasingly smitten with the professional provocateur. He had considered bringing Yoko to Rishikesh for the meditation camp, but ultimately opted to take this last trip with Cyn while corresponding almost daily with Ms. Ono.

Back in England, John occupied himself with the launch of Apple while pondering his next move. That move turned out to be on Yoko; with Cynthia out of town, John took the opportunity to conduct an all-night sonic free-for-all by inviting over his new love interest.

Given their common interest in avant-garde sound, it was natural for the two to occupy themselves by playing around with John's tape machines. After John demonstrated a few of his experimental loops, Yoko suggested that they make one together. While she supplied her characteristic squawks and warblings, John provided a backdrop of various instruments and electronic effects. Their "date" climaxed with the consummation of their union—which occurred out of microphone range.

The two decided to commit the recording session to wax. Had they limited their artistic statement to the album's title and contents, *Two Virgins* could have remained a footnote, drawing little attention and causing even less of a stir. But John's insistence on letting it all hang out extended to full frontal nudity on the record's sleeve, mortifying the public as well as his fellow Beatles.

Between the album's creation in May and its eventual release in November, John argued forcefully to win even nominal approval from both his band and the head of EMI. The firm's chairman, Sir Joseph Lockwood, offered that if a bare-naked man was necessary, why not use Paul? "He's much prettier." (McCartney, present at the exchange, was said to have blushed.)

EMI and Capitol refused to distribute the offending disc. Arrangements were made in England with Track, home to Jimi Hendrix and the Who; in America, Tetragrammaton, a Warner Brothers offshoot, did the honors. *Two Virgins* became Apple's second album release, following George's soundtrack for the film *Wonderwall.*

Though packaged in a mock brown-paper wrapper, replete with a quote from Scripture ("They were both naked, the man and his wife, and were not ashamed," Genesis 2:25), the album soon became one of those things people talked about more than actually heard.

As far as the media were concerned, JOHNANDYOKO had handed them a defining brand, marking themselves as ripe for salacious parody while inevitably becoming the butt of innumerable punch lines. (*Private Eye*, an English satirical rag, lampooned John's partner as "Okay Yoni," referring to a Sanskrit word for the female pudendum.)

Less than impressed with the attention garnered by the album, Ringo best articulated the feelings of his fellow Fabs. "But John," he told Lennon, "*we* have to answer for this!" "You only have to answer the phone," was John's inscrutable response.

The Drug Busts: October 18, 1968, and March 12, 1969

In June 1966, Donovan became the first high-profile English pop singer to be busted by police for drug possession. Though this was big news at the time, the drug squad was just getting started.

Detective Sergeant Norman Pilcher, who had headed the raid, very quickly garnered a reputation as a "head-hunting cop" (in Lennon's words), pursuing the biggest names in rock. Abetted by the weekly scandal sheet

News of the World, Pilcher was soon privy to the private goings-on within the rock community and targeted his subjects accordingly.

In 1967, the Redlands home of Rolling Stones guitarist Keith Richards was raided during a party. Richards and Mick Jagger were arrested and subjected to a drawn-out judicial proceeding; this was Pilcher's biggest score to date.

'NO COMMENT' — GEORGE MARTIN
UNFINISHED MUSIC NO. 2: LIFE WITH THE LIONS
JOHN LENNON/YOKO ONO   APPLE RECORDS
MADE IN MERRIE ENGLAND. NOV. '68

As shown on the back cover to their *Two Virgins'* follow-up, *Life with the Lions*, John and Yoko's drug arrest was unnecessarily traumatic and heavy-handed.

Rumor has it to this day that police refrained from swooping down until George and Pattie Harrison, guests at Richards's home at the time, left the scene. Word was that Brian Epstein had worked out an "understanding" with authorities that would leave the Beatles (and him) untouched.

But by fall 1968, Brian was dead and the Beatles were vulnerable. Having vacated his marital home, John was temporarily ensconced with Yoko at Ringo's rental property, a basement flat in Montague Square and a popular lodging for rock's elite.

Three weeks before the hammer came down, a reporter tipped John off that his name was on Pilcher's hit list. No fools they, John and Yoko—realizing that Jimi Hendrix had been the last resident of the flat—went over every inch of the dwelling. Assured that the property was clean, and not using at the time, the couple went about their business.

The expected knock came while the couple was in bed, but not sleeping, on October 18. Seven cops, including one matron, and a pair of dogs (named Yogi and Boo-Boo) cooled their heels outside for thirty minutes before John finally let them in. As police ransacked the premises, the Apple office learned of the raid via John's phone call to Neil Aspinall: "Imagine your worst paranoia, 'cause it's here now."

Four months with child, Yoko had a history of troubled pregnancies. The trauma of the arrest took its toll; on November 21, she miscarried a baby boy. Wishing to spare her further distress, John copped a plea in court one week later, accepting a £150 fine.

(The implications of that deal became clearer during John's U.S. residency in the early '70s. Fearing the prospect of an activist Lennon swaying newly enfranchised youth against him, Richard Nixon's administration used the bust as a weapon to initiate deportation proceedings. The full extent of the illegal campaign would be revealed after Nixon's downfall.)

Four months after John's arrest, Pilcher's platoon swooped down again, this time in Esher. At the same moment that Paul and Linda were getting married in Marylebone, Pattie Harrison answered a knock on the door to discover the sergeant and company. As the Harrisons later recounted, the police uncovered a small amount of hashish that they'd brought with them while overlooking the couple's actual stash.

The raid had been timed to hit a presumably empty house, so as not to repeat the charge of overkill that had been leveled after the earlier Beatles bust. But the law hadn't counted on Paul's bandmates being absent from his nuptials. George was furious at the way the cops trashed the place, saying that he would have led police to his supply had they bothered to ask.

Coming at this point in their careers, the arrests did John and George little harm professionally (if anything, being busted enhanced their outlaw bona fides). Times being what they were, an event that might have been ruinous in 1966 was hardly earth-shattering in 1969.

As for Pilcher, his habit of securing convictions by ensuring that drugs would be found caught up with him in 1972, when he was sent to prison for four years on a perjury charge. In the end, Pilcher served more jail time than all of his victims added together.

Paul Announces He Is Leaving the Beatles: April 10, 1970

In the months following John Lennon's statement that he wanted a "divorce," Paul McCartney kept his distance from the other Beatles. Though largely absent from the Apple office, he stealthily journeyed into London from his Scottish retreat, recording at the Beatles' Abbey Road stomping grounds under the name of "Billy Martin" (confident that no one in the U.K. would associate him with the recently fired manager of the Minnesota Twins).

Still dealing with the trauma of John's declaration, and with no particular intent other than to put a newly purchased Studer four-track machine through its paces, Paul began laying down tracks to what would eventually become his solo debut.

Some tunes, like "Junk" and "Teddy Boy," were "Get Back" session castoffs; others, new compositions such as "Every Night" and "Maybe I'm Amazed," showed considerable care in arrangement and production. The remainder of the album apparently began as improvisation, fleshed out through overdubbing to rise to the level of "half-baked."

Once word leaked out to Paul's fellow Beatles that a solo LP was in the works, trouble began—not because of any perceived disloyalty to a band that had ceased to exist, but rather due to a scheduling clash with a raft of Apple albums penciled in for spring release.

The much-delayed *Let It Be* soundtrack, uppermost in everyone's mind, clearly needed all the support it could get. The release of *McCartney* could conceivably have strangled it in its cradle in terms of sales.

Following Ringo's thankless efforts as peace broker, John and George acquiesced to Paul's demand that *McCartney* be released per his wishes, without delay. But Paul had another card to play. Stung by the untidy way in which his former partners were willing to let the Beatles be, as it were, Macca ensured that no ambiguity resulted from *his* first public statement on the band's future.

A press release, with a series of queries penned by Paul himself, accompanied British promotional copies of the album. The pointedly sharp responses left little doubt of the anger and hurt that the band's disintegration had wrought on him. By announcing the start of *his* solo career, Paul had managed to spin *his* departure from the Beatles as their end.

Asking himself if he had ever missed the others while making the album, Paul assured fans that not only did he not miss his fellow Beatles, but he also was having a better time with his family. Still, he appeared to hedge his bets by refusing to declare the break permanent.

The "interview" came as a bombshell to the millions who had no idea of how fragmented the Beatles had become. Despite the Fabs' ever-longer breaks between projects since retiring from touring, the constant stream of solo issues only seemed to mark time between group efforts.

Paul's declaration of independence, dripping with defensiveness, if not arrogance, laid the seeds for defining him as the instigator of the Beatles' break-up, simultaneously earning the enmity of the fans generally and John Lennon in particular. Stung by Paul's headline-grabbing announcement, which he felt was intended to sell the *McCartney* album, Lennon told English music journalist Ray Coleman, "Paul hasn't left. I sacked him."

Interestingly, news of the Beatles' demise received bigger play in England than in America. In the States, millions of loyal fans took Paul's pronouncement with a grain of salt, doubting that the Beatles had truly disbanded forever. The notion of *no more Beatles* seemed even more bizarre than Paul's reported death.

John's iconoclastic *Rolling Stone* interview, deconstructing the Beatle myth, coincided with Paul's legal action against the other three at the end of 1970. Together, the two events rather conclusively ended the public's wishful thinking. The process of acceptance proved just as drawn out for the public as it was for the band members themselves, with a glimmer of hope lingering on for exactly one decade longer.

We All Want to Change Your Head

The Beatles in Politics

Early in the Beatles' careers, everyone—from fading entertainers to marketers to politicians—wanted to associate themselves with the Fab Four, the most dynamic act in show business.

Soon, however, like a few other entertainers of the day—Eartha Kitt, Bob Dylan, and James Brown come to mind—the Beatles began to turn the tables on the media, making their own pronouncements about war, lifestyle issues, revolution, and politics in order to get *their* message across.

While some of what the Beatles said and did seems childish now, they were the first rock-and-roll act that tried to use their time at the top to change the world. That in itself deserves respect.

Oxfam's 1963 Charity Relief Effort

By late 1963, the Beatles were already tiring of legions of screaming girls, reporters, and—for some reason—legions of the physically disabled ("cripples," in the PI lingo of the time). To give the group some peace, Brian Epstein refused all charitable organizations that wished to gain the Fabs' imprimatur, fearing that if he allowed one, they'd all get in.

But with Epstein otherwise occupied in America, Jeffrey Archer, an ambitious young man running Oxfam's anti-hunger campaign, got backstage for a December 7, 1963, Beatles show in Liverpool and arranged a quick photo. The Fabs, looking as if they knew they'd been ambushed, held up an Oxfam banner and collection cans as a smiling Archer posed with the biggest entertainers in the country. The group had signed autographs in June 1963 for the benefit of Oxfam, but this was another thing entirely.

The photo helped leverage Archer's power within the organization and led to other government figures and celebrities becoming involved. But what did the Beatles think? Writer Sheridan Morley told *Mojo* magazine in 2002 that Ringo had described Archer to him as "the kind of bloke who would bottle your piss and sell it."

Labour Embraces the Beatles

The Variety Club of Great Britain held its annual luncheon on March 19, 1964. The Beatles were presented that day with an award honoring them as "Show Business Personalities of 1963."

Somehow, Labour Party Senior MP Harold Wilson snagged the opportunity to present them with the award. This was a real coup for Labour, whose members wanted to be associated with all things young and hip (fast forward nearly forty years to Tony Blair's trendy embrace of Britpop after *his* election as Prime Minister).

But the Beatles, apolitical at this time, made fun of the whole process. Noting the color and shape of the awards, Lennon sardonically quipped, "Thanks for the purple hearts, Harold," certain that Wilson and the assembled throng were quite unaware that in the Beatles' world, "purple hearts" were amphetamines.

Later that year, Labour, under Wilson's aegis, was elected to majority rule in Britain for the first time since 1951. A couple of years later, George Harrison's lyrics to "Taxman" specifically skewered Prime Minister Wilson as well as Conservative leader Edward "Ted" Heath.

The Beatles and the Royals

Invited to perform at the 1963 Royal Command Performance variety show, John Lennon—in a jokey comment that showed some contempt for the rich—directed those in the cheap seats to clap along, and "the rest of you, just rattle your jewelry."

But the Beatles did their dutiful part, smiling and shaking hands with the Queen, Princess Margaret, the Queen Mother, and other dignitaries. Leery of being sucked into "state entertainer" status, however, the already anti-establishment foursome declined further invitations to play the royal variety show.

On June 12, 1965, the establishment continued its efforts to embrace the Beatles. Harold Wilson, as Prime Minister, nominated the four musicians to receive medals making them Members of the Order of the British Empire, ostensibly for their contributions to the country's economy. The MBE medals caused consternation among many old-guard soldiers and industrialists, who felt their award was tarnished by association with a mere pop group.

The Beatles, especially Lennon, weren't too crazy about it, either (according to an apocryphal story, the boys smoked marijuana in the men's room of Buckingham Palace prior to the ceremony). Named John Winston Lennon in honor of Winston Churchill, the "rhythm guitar and mouth organ" Beatle was nevertheless suspicious of politicians and their eagerness to exploit the group for their own ends.

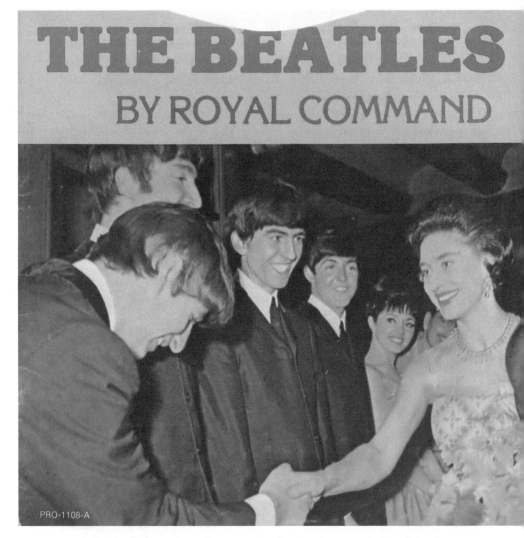

Not necessarily fans of royalty generally, the Beatles nonetheless did enjoy warm relations with the jet-setting Princess Margaret. (Years later at a party, however, she turned down the chance to share a joint with them.)

War

While in the early days of the Beatles' international success, press conference questions tended to be of the "What do you think of American girls?" variety, things got tough pretty quickly.

At the dawn of "protest music" in 1965, Lennon, asked if the Beatles would be writing antiwar songs, declared that "All our songs are antiwar songs," and later said that the grotesque pop-art cover of 1966's *Yesterday . . . and Today* compilation was "as relevant as Vietnam."

Always more comfortable speaking out in England, Lennon had told interviewer Maureen Cleave in 1965 that the group was "more popular than Jesus now." He did raise some legitimate points about Christianity, but when his remarks were reprinted the next year in an American magazine, *Datebook,* some rabid anti-Beatle ministers and disc jockeys twisted the comments into a statement of "blasphemy."

The ensuing controversy, which blew up as the group began its summer 1966 tour, made the four, especially Lennon, even more suspicious of the American hype machine, and helped them feel even more empowered to speak out.

Asked on August 21 in New York to comment on the Vietnam War, Lennon simply said, "We don't like it." Harrison chimed in, to applause, that "War is wrong, and it's obvious it's wrong. And that's all that needs to be said about it."

From that point, the gloves were off—the Beatles were against America's official policy. It's probably no coincidence that the group never returned, in full, to the United States following the end of the 1966 tour.

That the Beatles were among the first entertainers to come out against the conflict did not escape the eyes and ears of their fans, or of the press, or of the group's more virulent opponents. As concert promoter Sid Bernstein told *Time* magazine in September 1967, "Only Hitler ever duplicated [the Beatles'] power over crowds. . . . When the Beatles talk—about drugs, the war in Vietnam, religion—millions listen."

Drug Legalization

When Paul McCartney embraced the bohemian lifestyle of mid-1960s London's underground community, he wasn't just being fashionable. Macca was a committed presence in the underground, helping fund and build the Indica bookstore, attending concerts at the Roundhouse and UFO club, and giving interviews urging tolerance and understanding of what the psychedelic community was trying to do.

McCartney's ITN television interview on June 19, 1967, in which he admitted he had tried LSD four times (a revelation already published in *Life*), caused a furor all over England. While Brian Epstein worried, and more conservative members of society tsk-tsked, McCartney—who should have known better—claimed in the wake of the interview that the notorious British tabloids were partially at fault for fanning the flames (which they surely did).

But the group didn't stop there. On July 24, all four Beatles signed a newspaper ad in the *London Times* calling for the legalization of marijuana. Among sixty-one other signers were authors Graham Greene and Kenneth Tynan, artists Richard Hamilton and David Hockney, Brian Epstein, and two members of Parliament. The ad claimed that British anti-pot laws were "immoral in principle and unworkable in practice."

The group's drug use was documented in Hunter Davies's *The Beatles: An Authorized Biography*. Eventually both George Harrison and John Lennon were busted for possession, both under circumstances casting more than a little doubt on the legitimacy of the police's methods.

Be at Les(Lo)

During a wide-open and acid-addled 1967, the Beatles entertained some wild ideas. Make a movie with no script? Fine. Write a song and record it almost overnight for a worldwide TV broadcast? Sure. Buy an island? Why not?

John had decided that a communal hideaway would be good for the Fabs' marriages as well as for the group dynamic. In addition, by 1967 it had become evident that the Beatles would need to invest some of their money—preferably in an offshore venture—in order to avoid paying the high tariffs demanded by Britain's tax man.

Alex Mardas, a rock scene hanger-on who had befriended Lennon with electronic gizmos and flattery, claimed to have government connections that could help the Beatles buy a small isle, called Leslo, off the Greek coast.

So on July 20, 1967, the four Beatles and their significant others (save a pregnant Maureen), Mardas, Neil Aspinall, Mal Evans, and a few more took off for a communal vacation. Ringo and Neil returned after just one day, but the rest remained.

A three-general military junta had seized power in Greece on April 21. The Fabs quickly realized that they would be welcomed into Greece largely as a distraction, to put a happy face on a brutal and repressive dictatorship; this disgusted everyone involved.

Mardas was obviously trying to improve the image of his home country, and brokered a deal that would allow the Beatles to enter the country unmolested and unsearched in exchange for the group posing for promotional photos with various government ministers. He also alerted the press to the traveling party's every move, thus guaranteeing that crowds and hubbub greeted the Fabs and their friends and relations at every stop.

While their Leslo jaunt was, at times, a perfectly fine vacation, the group eventually returned to England and never again considered purchasing the island.

You Say You Want a (Counter) Revolution?

Except for a brief period of rabble-rousing and New York–radical-inspired talk of overthrowing the U.S. government in the early '70s, John Lennon was generally more interested in building political systems than in tearing them down. An often violent person by nature, he was also drawn to more peaceful solutions.

Hence his 1968 "Revolution," recorded in different versions for the "Hey Jude" 45 and the *Beatles* LP, urged everyone on the left to tone down the rhetoric and stop talking about bloodshed.

While showing empathy for those tired of the same old political drivel, Lennon also gave a thumbs-down to Mao-inspired violence. Despite his jokey "When you talk about destruction / don't you know that you can count me out (in)" on the album version, the message of "Revolution" was clear: just be cool. It's gonna be all right. In classic Lennon irony, the hard-rocking version released on 45 had the more pacifist lyric.

"No Pakistanis"

Right-wing British politician Enoch Powell found a lot of support in the late '60s for his anti-immigration positions; shooting at easy targets always seems productive during tough times. Powell's 1968 "Rivers of Blood" speech, in which he fulminated about Britain's imminent destruction—which he felt could only be stopped by stemming the tide of immigration—made quite an impact in Britain.

Paul McCartney, drawing inspiration from the headlines, thought it would be funny to satirize Powell's views, and those of conservative Brits, during the back-to-the-basics sessions the Beatles began in January 1969.

The group began jamming on a simple song called "Commonwealth," in which John and Paul, lampooning the more out-of-touch British, urged the immigrant poor to return overseas, "back to the Commonwealth homes." This eventually turned into a faux-racist screed called "Get Back," in which McCartney sang that he "don't dig no Pakistanis takin' all the peoples' jobs."

McCartney eventually expanded the lyrics of "Get Back" to include Jo-Jo and Sweet Loretta Martin, eventually choosing to chop the entire third verse of the song, which concerned the Pakistani issue. Perhaps this was for the best—there often stands a very thin line between satire and insult.

John and Yoko's Year of Peace

While Lennon had always been antiwar, his burgeoning romance with Yoko Ono—artist, actress, freethinker—pushed him toward out-and-out activism. In 1969, John and Yoko became JOHNANDYOKO, a multi-headed, media-friendly beast intent on using Beatle fame and fortune to bring about world peace.

Foolish as it may have been to think that two artists could themselves change the world, Lennon and Ono did as much as anyone in their generation to turn rock and roll into a true community, something more world-changing and relevant than just the latest Top 10 record. They helped nurture a generation of peace activists.

And the reaction of both those on the right (who excoriated the "godless" duo for their radical views) and the far left (who wanted J&Y to be *more* radical, or even violent) just showed how much the Beatles had become a screen onto which people of many persuasions projected their own private insecurities and passions.

After enduring several weeks of suffocating "Get Back" sessions, John and Yoko took off to get married on the Isle of Gibraltar on March 20. They then decided to fly to Amsterdam for their honeymoon, and from March 25–31 at the Hilton Hotel held their first of two "Bed-Ins" for peace. While the more salacious among the press hoped for an open physical consummation of the marriage, the Lennons were more interested in giving interviews and talking peace—which at least got the cause onto the front pages.

J&Y held their second "Bed-In" from May 26 through June 2 at Montreal's Queen Elizabeth Motel. During this event, they and a couple of dozen guests recorded "Give Peace a Chance."

The Lennons found a lot of sympathy for their cause in Canada, and visited twice more in 1969. First, on September 13, they played a concert in Toronto with a pickup band including Eric Clapton, Klaus Voormann, and Alan White (said concert produced an LP released as *Live Peace in Toronto*).

They returned in December, where they spent most of the 23rd in Ottawa meeting with Canadian Prime Minister Pierre Trudeau. While Trudeau professed little understanding of Yoko's more artistic ways of trying to bring about peace, such as planting acorns, Trudeau—one of the

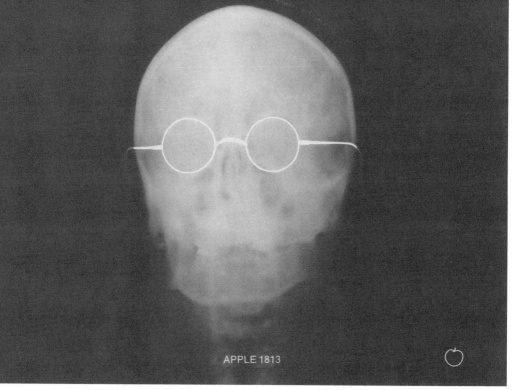

Though his provocative politics caused many a bewildered fan to wonder what was going on inside John Lennon's head, the "Cold Turkey" sleeve offered little insight.

first "hip" Western politicians of the time—enjoyed hobnobbing with the famous couple.

John Returns His MBE

In late November 1969, Lennon acted on his latent anti-establishment feelings and decided to return his MBE medal, which he had received in 1965, to Queen Elizabeth.

Some time earlier, John had given the medal to his Auntie Mimi, who proudly displayed it on top of her television set. But Lennon sent his chauffeur around to Mimi's house in Dorset, ostensibly to "borrow" the award (clearly, Lennon was too chicken to face his beloved aunt himself), but really to take it permanently.

On November 25, Lennon returned the MBE to Buckingham Palace in protest against Britain's support of the United States' involvement in the Vietnam War, against Britain's support of Nigeria against the secessionist state of Biafra, and, in Lennon's words, against his new solo single "Cold Turkey" "slipping down the charts."

Lennon added the bit about "Cold Turkey" to lighten the mood, but it didn't really work. While John and Yoko got their antiwar headlines, and gave scores of interviews about their controversial decision to a hungry press, they also convinced some more old-fashioned Britons that they had been right about this ungrateful rock-and-roll creep all the time.

Not that Lennon cared too much about that.

We Hope You Have Enjoyed the Show

Ten Immortal Performances

I t is for their records that the Beatles are rightly remembered today. Sure, they had the look, and the wit, and the films, and the personality, and so much else going for them, but in the end, it is the songs they wrote and performed that built their reputation.

Having said that, it's also critical to note that during their career, much renown came from the Beatles' capacity for working an audience. Though they weren't the most virtuosic of musicians, a discernible synergy was at work on those occasions when the band was firing on all cylinders. The excitement that they generated was legendary, and contributed mightily to their appeal.

Eventually, of course, nonstop activity would take its toll. A certain amount of fatigue, coupled with the impossibility of hearing themselves over the screams of their fans, led to the decay of their skills. But, especially in the early days, given a challenge and an audience, the Fabs seemed to be able to summon up an inexpressible dynamic at will, making them a musical powerhouse (or as Paul put it, "a good little band").

Here are ten auspicious occasions tracing their development as a musical force.

December 27, 1960: Litherland Town Hall, Liverpool

Though their first trip to Hamburg ended with the band in disarray, the Beatles pulled themselves together back in Liverpool, recognizing that they wanted to carry on. The first order of business was to find a new bass player, as Stuart Sutcliffe had decided to stay behind in Germany with his girlfriend, Astrid Kirchherr.

Chas Newby, from Pete Best's former group, the Blackjacks, agreed to interrupt his winter school break to fill in for the time being. (Not only was he a lefty like Paul, he even shared Paul's birthday.)

Next, they needed bookings. Allan Williams's newest nightspot, the Top Ten, had burned down shortly after its opening. But the defunct club's manager (and future Cavern compère) Bob Wooler was available, and offered to find the boys some work. Pulling some strings, he was able to get them booked at the Litherland Town Hall, a cut above their normal Liverpool haunts.

At the last minute, the Beatles' name was hastily added to posters advertising the gig. Someone, whether to be cute or out of ignorance, described them as "Direct from Hamburg." To north Liverpool audiences, who had never heard of the Beatles, the novelty of a German rock band was hard to resist.

As has been chronicled, time away had utterly transformed the Beatles' act. Instead of the ragtag group of wannabes who had left for the continent months before, an alien apparition clad in leather and cowboy boots took

By 1962, the Beatles had reached the top of Hamburg's nightclub ladder with stints at the newly opened Star Club (shown here). Furthermore, Brian Epstein's managerial skills had considerably upped their fee.   *Photo by K&K Ulf Kruger Ohg/Redferns*

the stage, accompanied by an unearthly din. Even those who knew the Beatles from their previous incarnation were shocked by the makeover.

At every level, their musicality had grown by leaps and bounds. Even their drummer, at best a reliable timekeeper, pounded a primitive but steady four-on-the-floor bass drum rhythm that mesmerized the crowd. (It even acquired a name: the "Atom Beat.")

Beyond the tightened harmonies and razor-sharp guitar licks, another new aspect appeared: a worldly, couldn't-care-less attitude. Coupling exuberant energy with studied indifference, the Fab Five showed their hometown crowd something it hadn't seen—and the audience loved it. As revelers rushed the stage, the Beatles, for the first time, found themselves mobbed.

Though the gig was over after thirty minutes, the electrifying performance left an impression on both sides. (Those sticking around to chat afterwards complimented the Beatles on their command of English.) As for the band, they had tangible evidence, for the first time, of their powers over an audience. Their dreams of stardom were finally taking shape.

December 18–31, 1962: The Star Club, Hamburg

This holiday season gig at the Reeperbahn's newest and most prestigious venue was perhaps the only Hamburg stint the Beatles entered into reluctantly. Their reticence stemmed less from a wish to avoid returning to the land where sin flowed freely than from concern over their budding recording career.

"Love Me Do" had begun its ascent up the charts before the Beatles left Liverpool, peaking on December 20. The follow-up, "Please Please Me," was in the can, awaiting release. The Fabs were understandably nervous about losing momentum by leaving the country just when things were about to take off.

Still, for the sake of history, the real value of this gig (which the band was contractually obliged to play) was that "King Size" Ted Taylor of the Dominos arranged to have another musician, Adrian Barber, record the Beatles' set on a reel-to-reel recorder. This fascinating document encapsulates the only audio evidence of the group's Hamburg club days—albeit at the tail end of their German experience.

The recordings publicly surfaced in the '70s and the subject of much speculation (not to mention lawsuits), memories having grown foggy through the years. Initially thought to have been recorded earlier in 1962, the tapes eventually were ascertained to have been produced during that final Hamburg stint, with Ringo safely aboard and an EMI recording contract in the group's collective pocket.

While quite coarse upon first listening, the tapes do manage to capture the band's last vestiges of rough edges. Between bursts of aural assault, plenty of between-songs tomfoolery is apparent. Most revealing is how few of the band's original tunes were recorded. Though on the verge of taking the world by storm with their own compositions, the Beatles played a cover-heavy set showcasing astoundingly catholic tastes, with songs chosen to please themselves as much as their audience.

Though the album's original packaging suggested that the Fabs were still in their leather gear at the Star Club, they had in fact been smartened up by Brian by this time. That aside, the looseness and evident sloppiness in the performances is somehow endearing. "Bum notes," as writers Roy Carr and Tony Tyler put it, "flew like beer bottles."

August 3, 1963: The Cavern, Liverpool

After hosting their debut as "the Beatles" in March 1961, the Cavern quickly became a sort of band residence. It was at this smoky, sweat-drenched subterranean venue that the boys truly felt at home, rehearsing during off hours and playing to their peers.

In return, the Cavern cultivated its most hard-core fan base. Regulars would drop in for the Beatles' popular lunchtime sessions during school hours; other times, the punters turned out to see the boys share the stage with the likes of Rory Storm and the Big Three.

By today's standards, the Cavern would likely be shut down for overcrowding, nonexistent ventilation, and appalling toilet facilities. Such close quarters, however, put the performers eyeball to eyeball with their audience. Here the Beatles learned, close up, exactly how to engage an audience and how to project their own personalities.

As they progressed, the Beatles carefully maintained their Cavern ties. It was here that they returned to play between Hamburg sojourns; here that Brian Epstein first observed them in action on November 9, 1961; here that they were first filmed for television broadcast, during a lunchtime session on August 22, 1962; and here that Ringo met Maureen Cox, who would become his wife.

But as their recording career began to blossom, the band found themselves increasingly on the road, extending their fan base to the south. Cavern loyalists found themselves dreading the day that their "boys" would grow too big for Liverpool and cut their ties to the club that had nurtured them.

That day came in August 1963. Now mushrooming into a national phenomenon, the success of "She Loves You" and the *Please Please Me* album (topping the charts since May) insured that performing at the tiny club was foolhardy and even dangerous.

The band played their last lunchtime session in February, and in late July the club announced what everyone expected to be the Beatles' farewell performance. Tickets sold out within thirty minutes. For one last time (the 292nd, to be exact), the foursome mounted the rickety, two-foot-high wooden stage, as compère Bob Wooler announced, "Here they are: the Beatles!"

Tears were undoubtedly shed on this night—likely on both sides. Though Brian Epstein kept the door open for a future Cavern engagement, fate decided otherwise. The Beatles would perform in Liverpool only four more times; in 1973, the original Cavern was shut down, taking with it untold emotions and history.

November 4, 1963: Royal Command (Variety) Performance, London

Coming on the heels of their career-making performance on *Sunday Night at the London Palladium*, the Beatles' appearance before the royals just two weeks later solidified their status as media darlings. Lest anyone in England miss the import of the Palladium show, the Royal Variety Performance sealed the Fabs' ascent to stardom.

The event was the latest in an annual series that had commenced in 1912, coming more or less annually, contingent upon whether Britain was at war or not. (The first such Royal Command Performance was to have occurred in 1911, but a fire destroyed the venue and inflicted fatalities.)

Traditionally, only the most rock-ribbed, establishment acts were chosen to entertain the royal family; this honor was reserved for very few, and suffice to say in 1963 no rockers needed apply. The Beatles owed their invitation to the foresight of one Bernard Delfont, a former entertainer himself and eventually one of England's top entertainment moguls.

Showcasing homegrown acts was something of a trademark for Delfont, but in 1963 he had no idea who the Beatles were. Heavy lobbying by his daughter soon brought him up to speed. Having ascertained months ahead of time that the Beatles were indeed doing bang-up business, he booked them as the seventh of nineteen acts. As it happened, no one could have scripted a more fortuitous time for maximum exposure.

Everyone recalls this occasion for John's invitation to the commoners to clap along, while advising the upper crust—including the royal family—to "rattle their jewelry." Those who had heard his more intemperate paraphrasing of the line backstage worried that such pointed impudence might backfire, but as always, the Beatles managed to charm even the most blasé.

According to observers, the Windsors appeared to enjoy the Fabs' four-song set, with the Queen Mother even clapping along (on the offbeat). Meeting the band after the show, she drew chuckles with some offhand chit-chat, inquiring where the Beatles were appearing next. Hearing "Slough," located close to Windsor Castle, she remarked, "Oh, that's by us."

Somewhat less captivated that night by the Fabs' performance was top-billed German actress/singer Marlene Dietrich. In a tableau reminiscent of *A Star Is Born*, the show-biz professional, her own star in eclipse, recognized that she was being upstaged by the "long-haired boys." Craftily, she handled it by squeezing in close to the Beatles when news photographers were present.

For the Beatles, this appearance at the Royal Command Variety show—the culmination of many a career—went against tradition: their best was yet to come. Though repeat invitations came, both the Fabs and Brian Epstein took an attitude of "been there, done that" and never returned.

February 11, 1964: Washington Coliseum, Washington, D.C.

Beatlemania in Britain's former colony truly began with the band's first *Ed Sullivan Show* appearance on February 9. Two days after charming America, the boys traveled by train from New York to the nation's capital to perform their first U.S. concert.

By this time, the Fabs were at the center of a full-blown media frenzy, with a coterie of reporters and filmmakers following them everywhere. Albert and David Maysles, renowned for cinéma vérité documentaries later in the decade like *Don't Look Back* and *Gimme Shelter*, were on hand to document events as they unfolded.

The Washington Coliseum (later called Uline Arena) had sold out its entire allotment of seats. For the princely sum of $4, one could sit ringside to witness up close a supporting bill including the also-British Caravelles ("You Don't Have to Be a Baby to Cry"); Tommy Roe (who had headlined with the Beatles in England the year before); and the Chiffons, whose hit "He's So Fine" would cause untold grief for George in years to come. Over eight thousand screaming fans saw the performance live, while thousands more paid to see it in theaters around the country via a closed-circuit feed.

The Coliseum in its previous life had been skating rink—and it showed. The Beatles were placed in what amounted to a boxing ring, turning the performance into theater in the round. Ringo, situated precariously atop a shaky two-foot riser, had to dismount every third song, as Mal Evans and a stagehand physically rotated the platform one-quarter turn, so that the Beatles could then face another segment of the paying audience.

Technical snafus were to be expected, such as George's dead mic at the start of the set for "Roll Over Beethoven." But overall, the set was a supercharged version of their American network debut two days earlier. The performances had a pronounced edge to them, with Ringo being especially hard-hitting on "I Saw Her Standing There." "This Boy" offered a preview of their upcoming *Ed Sullivan Show* appearance in Miami, with its crowd-pleasing three-on-a-mic staging.

A film of the concert was released as a DVD in 2003, but omits the last song and a half. "Twist and Shout" is presented in incomplete form, while set-closer "Long Tall Sally" is missing altogether. Despite speculation that the film ran out, complete versions exist.

Overall, the concert represented a genuine high point in the Beatles' American touring experience. Gushed Ringo: "What an audience! I could have played for them all night."

August 23, 1964: The Hollywood Bowl, Los Angeles

In August, the Beatles returned to North America for a month-long sweep across the U.S. and Canada. Meanwhile, their American record label, Capitol, had not yet given up on milking additional dollars out of the Fabs by issuing a live album. An attempt to record their Carnegie Hall show in February that year had been thwarted by union interference, but six months later, these issues had been resolved.

The Hollywood Bowl, Los Angeles's premium outdoor concert venue, seemed ideally suited for a live recording. Its location in the city where Capitol was headquartered meant access to offered recording equipment and engineers that were second to none. The thousands of screaming fans that attended every Beatles concert had until now been perceived to be an insurmountable impediment to recording clarity, but recording outdoors was expected to neutralize this obstacle.

The seventeen thousand faithful proved otherwise. Utilizing a three-track (!) recording console, Capitol's engineers did their best to capture the Fabs' electrifying performance. Ultimately, however, the prospect of separating the full-throated din from the music seemed daunting, and the less-than-enthusiastic support for such a release by the Beatles and their management caused the project to be shelved. A similar attempt to chronicle their two shows at the Bowl a year later went similarly unused.

The tapes sat neglected in Capitol's vaults until the mid-'70s, when public demand for some live product from the Beatles (and the bedeviling effects of extra-legal recordings, which were doing brisk underground trade) prompted EMI to take a second listen. George Martin was duly recruited to make what he could of the tapes. Ultimately, he tapped tapes of both the 1964 and 1965 shows, assembling an excellent facsimile of Beatlemania in action.

Interestingly, the Beatles would likely never have played the Hollywood Bowl at all but for the efforts of one man. L.A. DJ Bob Eubanks went to considerable personal effort and expense to make the booking happen, going so far as to mortgage his home to the tune of $25,000 to book the facility.

Employed at the time by rock-and-roll powerhouse KRLA, Eubanks is best known today as the host of the long-running *Newlywed Game*. Few today realize that it's his voice heard at the start of the Hollywood Bowl album, announcing, "And now . . . here they are! The BEATLES!" (Though personally netting a mere $1,000 for his show-booking efforts, Eubanks did parlay his gamble into a 1965 Plymouth Barracuda, simply by getting the Beatles photographed in one.)

August 15, 1965: Shea Stadium, Queens, New York City

The "arena rock" era began in 1965 when promoter Sid Bernstein contracted the Beatles to play at the biggest venue he could book. Shea Stadium, home of the fledgling New York Mets, was the site of rock's grandest concert to date, with over 55,600 screaming fans in attendance.

Bernstein deserves credit for recognizing the Beatles' potential before virtually anyone else in America. Being a bit of an Anglophile, he regularly scanned the English dailies. Early coverage of their rising popularity and its attendant hysteria led him to personally track down Brian Epstein and call him at home in Liverpool.

Though Brian was loath to send the boys to America before they'd scored a hit, Bernstein's persistence eventually paid off when he was given leave to book them to play Carnegie Hall in New York one day after their debut concert in Washington.

For Bernstein, the experience conclusively reinforced the Beatles' drawing power. Perpetually striving to outdo himself, he drew on an imagination teeming with possibilities. No one, in early 1964, had ever booked a rock band in a baseball stadium, but given the evidence of the Fabs' popularity, and with no end to it in sight, Bernstein was prepared to think big.

Though Epstein was wary of the possibility that Beatles couldn't fill Carnegie Hall, Bernstein had no such qualms, and proceeded to sell out the venue *by word of mouth*. Suitably impressed, the Beatles and their entourage made Shea the first stop of the 1965 tour.

A television crew was on hand to document the event for a network "behind-the-scenes" documentary. Opening acts included Brenda Holloway, whose composition "You've Made Me So Very Happy" was later a smash for Blood, Sweat, and Tears; Cannibal and the Headhunters, of "Land of a Thousand Dances" fame; and saxophonist King Curtis, whose final gig before his tragic 1971 murder in the streets of New York would be on John Lennon's *Imagine* album.

In musical terms, the show was something of a mirage, with the acts being seen—just barely—on a stage set up near second base (placing the musicians, as some wits suggested, farther than the Mets had gotten all season). The sound was virtually nonexistent, with the stadium's tiny speakers drowned out by crowd noise. But as an event, the concert *killed*. The sheer number of bodies gathered in one spot (including future Beatle spouses Linda Eastman and Barbara Bach) was a sight to behold.

Following a warm introduction by Ed Sullivan, the Beatles sprinted onto the stage, amid thousands of popping flashbulbs and vocal wattage that their Vox amps had no chance of besting. Clad in matching military-styled jackets (each with a Wells Fargo security badge), they tore right into "Twist and Shout," barely pausing for breath between numbers.

That they were able to function in the face of such an overwhelming onslaught of adoration without a trace of nerves demonstrates either the Beatles' sheer comfort with their position or the level of detachment they forced themselves to adopt in order to survive.

All the Beatles were in rare form, clearly delighted at their reception. An ever-hyper John clowned throughout the show, culminating with a manic Jerry Lee Lewis–style turn on the organ for set-closer "I'm Down." Later he would say of the experience to Sid Bernstein, "I . . . (have seen) the top of the mountain."

August 29, 1966: Candlestick Park, San Francisco

If Shea was the top of the mountain, then events of the following year represented the depths of the valley. Between their scourging in the Far East, the "bigger than Jesus" debacle, and the controversy in America over the *Yesterday . . . and Today* album's "butcher cover," the bloom had gone off the Beatles for many, including some of their biggest fans.

In 1966, Shea, like other stops on the tour, was not the sellout it had been a year earlier. Though the hits records continued, weariness of touring—from fans as well as the band—had been nagging for some time. George, increasingly enthralled by all things Indian, was especially ready for change. Ringo and John leaned toward at least curtailing their roadwork, absent more compelling duties. But Paul, as always, remained addicted to the smell of the crowd and the roar of the sawdust.

McCartney's tipping point came toward the end of their American dates. Beyond the sporadic protests and empty seats seen at some venues, one incident proved especially portentous. In a scene straight out of their cartoon likeness, an armored car used in L.A. as their transport for security

The Beatles' final U.K. gig came at the head of an amazing bill, with acts including the Yardbirds, the Who, Spencer Davis, the Small Faces, and the Rolling Stones.

reasons became stuck within the confines of the venue due to a locked gate. The Beatles spent two hours cooling their heels inside while out-of-control fans pounded on the walls. At last Paul, too, was ready to cut the string.

On a cool, damp San Francisco evening, Paul pulled publicist Tony Barrow aside and asked him to tape-record the band's gig. While the recording reveals George and John's less than full engagement in the proceedings, Paul opted to go out with gusto, ending his Beatles performing career with a rip-roaring "Long Tall Sally" before twenty-five thousand fans.

Just before leaving the stage, John picked out the opening guitar line to "In My Life." Moments later, sinking into his seat aboard a chartered plane, George announced, "Well, that's it. I'm not a Beatle anymore."

It is hard to imagine today, but in the 1960s, a musical act pulling the plug on live performances was essentially announcing its retirement. No precedent had been set for a rock-and-roll act to survive purely on the strength of their recorded output (save perhaps Elvis, whose records had become incidental to his film career).

But the Beatles' success afforded them the leverage to write their own ticket. Excited at the prospect of breaking free of the limitations imposed by composing purely for the concert stage, they were ready to embrace the risk.

January 30, 1969: 3 Savile Row, London

The Beatles next reconvened to perform, semi-publicly, in the least likely of settings. What eventually became known as the *Let It Be* sessions began with the aim of documenting, on film, the group at work on new material, shaping and honing it before the cameras. A live concert at an intriguing locale would conclude the mission.

What happened between the original conception and the final product has provided fodder for countless articles (entire books, in fact) ever since. Suffice it to say that the Beatles picked exactly the wrong moment of their career to embark on such a demanding project.

Strains within the group that had first aired openly during the "White Album" sessions were now exacerbated by the early shooting schedule, the cold environs of Twickenham studio, and the uncertainty of the band's ultimate destination. But most defeating of all was the collective disaffection evident from everyone—save McCartney, who overcompensated for the apathy of the others by pushing just a little too hard.

The inability to arrive at a group consensus on where to conclude their film epitomized the disparate views of each Beatle. Early ideas included a Roman amphitheater, but Ringo flatly refused to travel out of the country.

A plan to film aboard a ship was kiboshed by George. Yoko suggested an empty auditorium, while John asserted that an asylum was not out of the question.

Fittingly, Paul at last offered that they simply lug their gear up to their Apple headquarters rooftop and have done with it. Film director Michael Lindsay-Hogg quickly seconded the idea.

With the band's instruments in the basement, and the roof four floors above, Mal Evans had his work cut out for him. But with the logistics settled, the four, accompanied by Billy Preston and assorted assistants, wives, and girlfriends, assembled on the roof. The windy January noon hour was less than ideal for an outdoor recital, but something once again transformed the Beatles once they committed to performing.

Slightly ragged initially, they soon found their groove, though their audience was largely unseen. Typically, John flubbed the words to "Don't Let Me Down" (shrewdly, he had an assistant hold up a cheat sheet for the free-associating lyrics to "Dig a Pony") but otherwise had shaken off the lethargy characterizing his recent output.

As the Fabs proceeded, their performances gained verve and spirit (though the band was, of course, oblivious to the street-level reaction). Indeed, despite countless takes in the studio of "I've Got a Feeling," "One After 909," and "Dig a Pony," the rooftop versions were chosen for inclusion on the subsequent album.

Though George had withdrawn his rather mellow recent compositions from live consideration, his sonic contributions to the set were impeccable. His leads were fluid, focused, and memorable, as was Ringo's drumming under less than ideal conditions. Though John is heard noting the challenge of playing in the chill ("Me hands are getting too cold to play chords!"), his vocals more than made up for any playing shortcomings. And Paul, as usual, was the spark plug, whooping it up and keeping things moving.

The rooftop set, as seen in the film (with second takes and a "God Save the Queen" interlude edited out) provided exactly the bit of lift needed in an otherwise dreary film. It also showed the innate professionalism the Beatles were capable of when not distracted by extra-musical issues.

December 15, 1969: The Lyceum, London

This list ends not with a true Beatles performance, but rather with two Beatles sharing a stage for the last time in the group's lifetime. In the nearly dozen years and thousands of gigs played since John and George had joined forces with Paul, they had changed the world. Now the Beatles' guitarists were preparing to leave the group identity behind as they began charting their courses as individuals.

Beginning with "Give Peace a Chance" earlier that summer, John applied the "Plastic Ono Band" moniker to anyone he happened to be playing with outside of the Beatles. Members had included Ringo on "Cold Turkey" and Klaus Voormann, Eric Clapton, and Alan White at the September 1969 Toronto Rock and Roll Revival gig. Pointedly excluded was Paul, because (at least per "The Ballad of John and Yoko") his presence with John constituted "Beatles."

Having first played without his familiar bandmates in the Rolling Stones' *Rock and Roll Circus* in December 1968, and again more recently in Toronto, John found his interest in appearing before an audience being reawakened.

George, the first Beatle to tire of touring, had been performing alongside Eric Clapton throughout Europe in late 1969 as a sideman to American soulsters Delaney and Bonnie. Reveling in relative anonymity, he found he could enjoy audiences if he wasn't expected to do the heavy lifting.

"Peace for Christmas," a benefit for UNICEF, brought the two all but officially ex-Beatles together. Also appearing that night were Desmond Dekker ("Israelites"), the Rascals, and Delaney and Bonnie. (A D&B live album, scheduled for release on Apple, was later dropped.) John also used the occasion to launch his "War Is Over (If You Want It)" campaign.

This time, the Plastic Ono Supergroup included John, Yoko, George, Eric Clapton, Delaney and Bonnie Bramlett, Klaus Voormann, drummers Jim Gordon, Alan White, and the Who's Keith Moon, horn players Bobby Keyes and Jim Price, and Billy Preston. (Billy's organ part was somehow lost on the resulting tape, and keyboardist Nicky Hopkins later replaced it in the studio with electric piano.)

The band's set consisted of just "Cold Turkey" and Yoko's "Don't Worry Kyoko"—but the two songs together ran about the length of an average Beatles concert. Despite the assembled musicians producing a Spector-esque wall of sound, John's intense, anguished vocal still cut through.

The occasion marked the last time John and George would share a stage, though they came close in 1971 and 1974. It was also John's last live appearance in England. With the Beatles in the final winter of their discontent, they simply could not pull in the same direction, even though alliances still existed within the group. The weight of living up to the expectations of being "Beatles" had simply become insupportable.

I Saw the Photograph

Ten Notable Beatles Photo Sessions

A s unquestionably the most photographed rock band in history, the Beatles certainly had access to the world's finest photographic talent. It is not surprising, then, that so many images captured during their career have come down to us as something approaching iconic. In examining these photos, taken by more than a dozen different photographers, one is immediately struck by a demonstrable "it" factor at work, as every one of the following shoots produced imagery that would burn itself into the memory cells of multiple generations.

1960–61: The Hamburg Photos (Astrid Kirchherr and Jurgen Vollmer)

Well before anyone could divine their future greatness, the Beatles drew the attention of photographers, many of them quite gifted. (It is striking how incredibly well-documented was this scruffy group of Liverpool amateurs.) Oft-told legend records their 1960 discovery in Hamburg's seedy nightclub scene by Klaus Voormann, an aspiring artist removed from the world of rock and roll. Not long after catching their act, he dragged along his soon-to-be ex-girlfriend, Astrid Kirchherr, and the equally artsy Jurgen Vollmer to experience the group. All three were well versed in the visual arts; and, struck by the seamy tableau before them, each felt the same compulsion to chronicle its noisy purveyors.

Astrid moved first. In late 1960, having established a rapport with the band (and a love affair with Stuart Sutcliffe), she took a series of pictures around Hamburg's desolate fairgrounds. These gritty images are familiar to anyone who has ever picked up a Beatles book; she lost an untold fortune before reclaiming the rights to the photos decades later. One classic shot shows the five of them, instruments in hand, leather-clad and moody—only Pete and George acknowledging the camera—an almost anti-stardom vision. Another familiar series depicts George, John, and Stu perched on a truck.

Afterward, Astrid composed individual studies of both John and Paul, each featuring an out-of-focus Stuart in the background. These, and others of Stu alone, sporting dark shades, contributed mightily to the bassist's growing mystique.

Jurgen Vollmer had a similarly dark vision of the rockers. His first session with the boys, taken during their second German stint in April 1961 at the Top Ten Club, produced documentation of the band in full performance mode, minus an audience (the unpredictable rough-and-tumble atmosphere of an actual gig entailed a risk of bodily harm). In his photos, he captured what John would later describe as the band's "beauty, and . . . spirit." He depicted the core threesome front line, Stu only in passing, and Pete not so much. George warranted some solo attention, shot on the empty stage, seated, holding John's Rickenbacker, and later outdoors in leather.

Some time later, Jurgen set up a series centering on John. Framed in a dockside doorway, he stands immobile, the archetypical rocker, as the blurred figures of Paul, George, and Stu stroll by. Notwithstanding the eventual fame of the camera's subjects, the photos reek of atmosphere, a striking encapsulation of a time and place long gone. John himself clearly recognized this, choosing one of the photos to grace the sleeve of his '50s covers album, *Rock and Roll*, fourteen years later.

March 5, 1963: The *Please Please Me* Cover (Angus McBean)

For their inaugural LP release, George Martin displayed a literal-minded creativity rivaling Paul's, whose initial design of a Beatles logo resulted in scripted letters on the front of Ringo's kick drum, with the letter "B" sporting antennae. (Get it? This idea was abandoned by mid-1963.) The producer had looked into getting the boys photographed in front of the Insect House at the Royal Zoological Gardens, but permission was thankfully denied.

More fruitful input came with the suggestion of photographer Angus McBean, with whom Martin was familiar from past collaborations on comedy productions. This protégé of Cecil Beaton was widely considered to be one of the greatest British photographers of the era, specializing in portraiture of stage and screen personalities; his shot of an unknown Audrey Hepburn for a beauty advertisement led directly to a Hollywood screen test. When not working on theatrical projects, McBean did good business in record sleeve photography. The fact that he was contracted to shoot the Beatles' debut album cover speaks volumes for the prestige EMI attached to the project.

One idea considered for the cover involved posing the group on the steps of the Abbey Road recording facilities; indeed, several Dezo Hoffman photos taken at that time ended up as publicity shots. But McBean instead opted to photograph the Beatles on the balcony of the visually striking stairwell located inside the entrance to EMI House in Manchester Square.

Lying on the floor, he posed them peering down from several floors above, capturing the fresh look of a band poised on the edge of greatness. (Conspicuously, Ringo's do hadn't yet grown into the Beatle mop despite some six months in their employ.) McBean also photographed the boys downstairs in the building, posed around a grand wooden chair. (One from this series ended up as the cover of their American debut, *Introducing the Beatles*, in early 1964—printed in reverse. Shown correctly, it graced the cover of the U.K. EP *The Beatles' Hits.*)

The resulting cover, with artist and title copy printed boldly in three colors, did the Beatles justice by heralding the LP's dynamic contents without resorting to clichés. Wisely, they chose a title capitalizing on their first number one single to announce their arrival in the marketplace. (The ever-helpful Martin had a title suggestion: *Off the Beatle Track*. He may have thought his attempt at wordplay would score points with the hypercritical Lennon, but he was wrong. Still, he resurrected it a year later with his own album of Beatle instrumentals.)

A postscript came six years (and a world of changes) later. On May 13, 1969, McBean was again summoned to Manchester Square, this time to document a rapidly disintegrating foursome. Planned as a perverse re-creation of the *Please Please Me* sleeve for the sketchy "Get Back" project, the shoot went unused until 1973, when a frame from the series ended up gracing the *1967–1970* compilation LP (better known as the *Blue Album*).

July 1963: The "Collarless Suit" Session (Dezo Hoffman)

Slovakian expatriate photojournalist Dezider (Dezo) Hoffman had seen a lot of twentieth-century history up close. Present at Mussolini's Abyssinian invasion of 1936, he soon found his services in demand covering the Spanish Civil War, rubbing shoulders with legendary war photographer Bob Capa and an American scrivener named Hemingway. Years after recovering from his war wounds, he settled in London, accepting a position at music weekly *Record Mirror*. In 1962, at age fifty, a chance assignment to cover some up-and-coming rock and rollers from Liverpool initiated an association that lasted for several years.

Dezo documented Ringo's EMI debut, the infamous "Love Me Do" session that saw the hapless Pete Best sidelined (and George sporting a black eye). More jobs followed, as he became "photographer of choice" in fulfilling an increasing demand for pictures. A summer of '63 shoot, coinciding with the recording of "She Loves You," forever enshrined his work in Fabdom.

A series depicting the group in collarless gray suits became, for many, an introduction to the newly minted stars. (It is a print of the classic pose from this set that Paul's "grandfather" covets in *A Hard Day's Night*.) In America, pictures from the session would grace sleeves to five singles: "She Loves You," "I Want to Hold Your Hand," "Can't Buy Me Love," "I'm Happy Just to Dance with You," and "And I Love Her."

Hoffman's work ranged from the casual (images of the foursome at the beach in old-fashioned striped outfits) to the artistic. His images soon graced all manner of product, from metal trays to postcards and more. Though Hoffman never shot an original album cover, an archived 1963 shot was chosen to grace the *Live at the BBC* release in 1994.

August 22, 1963: The *With the Beatles* Cover (Robert Freeman)

Symptomatic of the whirlwind that their lives had fast become (soon to be dramatized in *A Hard Day's Night*), the cover to the Fabs' second album was shot at Southampton's Palace Court Hotel while the band was touring.

Photographer Robert Freeman had made a name for himself in England, notably on the first Pirelli calendar, but his moody, atmospheric 1960 shots of jazz saxophonist John Coltrane first drew the Beatles' attention. Summoned to meet the boys in Bournemouth, Freeman was given little time to conceptualize an album sleeve, but as often was the case with the Beatles, serendipity ruled the day.

The photographer improvised a studio backdrop with a heavy maroon curtain in a hotel dining room with large windows to one side. His subjects arrived clad in matching black polo-neck sweaters, following what had been their offstage bent at least since the Hamburg days. To Freeman, this look strongly suggested shooting in black and white, a look with the added benefit of standing out among a current crop of color-splashed pop record sleeves.

He posed the boys perpendicular to the windows, creating a half-lit effect. (Interestingly, this theme echoed a series of shots taken by Astrid of John and George in her loft just after Stu died.) Though to the casual eye the finished photo looks like a montage, this was not the case: Freeman shot them grouped just as you see them, with Ringo slightly stooped to fit the square format, using a telephoto lens to compress the depth of field, giving the boys equal focus and roughly the same space. Alternate shots exist, including one that switches John and Paul and features all four sporting incongruous grins. But the serious pose became the obvious choice—and EMI paid Freeman *twice* their normal outlay for such work.

It proved the beginning of a prestigious professional relationship between the foursome and Freeman, who went on to shoot their next four album sleeves—*A Hard Day's Night, Beatles for Sale, Help!*, and *Rubber Soul*—an unmatched record (so to speak). In addition, he did prolific documentary photo work on their film sets and in the studio. His pictures, culled from souvenir tour booklets, made up the collage assembled by Klaus Voormann for the *Revolver* sleeve.

March 25, 1966: The "Butcher Cover" Session (Robert Whitaker)

A chance encounter between Brian Epstein and Robert Whitaker ultimately led to the most infamous album jacket in Beatles lore (unless you count *Two Virgins*, which isn't really the same thing).

Brian hired Whitaker to act as house photographer for his NEMS management company, giving him duties that included taking publicity shots for all the acts in their corporate stable, including the Fabs. Whitaker was deadly serious about his art, and by 1966 was prepared to issue a Grand Statement. This coincided with the Beatles' own boredom with the typical starmaking machinations to which they had been subjugated.

A happily cooperative band, then, acquiesced to Whitaker's concept for a series of photos that intended to show the world that despite being the most adored group on the planet, they really were just four human beings, the same as everyone else (or something like that).

The first shot of the intended triptych, intended to convey that the Beatles were not gods and were born unto a woman just like the rest of us, depicted the foursome facing the camera, linked to a young adult female (whose back is to the viewer) by a chain of sausages symbolizing an umbilical cord. (No, really.) The second showed George preparing to pound some rather large nails into the head of an unconcerned John. This, assured Whitaker, illustrated that the Beatles are as ordinary as pieces of wood.

But the tableau's centerpiece, titled "A Somnambulant Adventure," got all the attention when, inexplicably, it was shipped to the States in response to Capitol's request for a cover shot for the *Yesterday . . . and Today* album, a hastily assembled collection of singles and tracks harvested from British albums.

The four Beatles, clad in white butcher's smocks, were seated among an assortment of meat cuts and decapitated dolls. Though George would later go on record describing the session as "sick," he, in the most famous shot, held aloft a doll's head while sporting an expression best likened to bloodlust. As cardiac-arrest-inducing as the photo must have seemed at the time, the outtakes from the session are even more grisly, with assorted limbs and even glass eyeballs being presented for your approval by the band.

In Whitaker's defense, it should be noted that the picture was never intended as an album cover. In fact, the image as reproduced was not even finished, as far as the concept goes. Silver halos were intended to be painted in surrounding the Beatles' heads, as well as a gold backdrop, giving the scene a deliberately iconic flavor. But before the post-production artwork was completed, the picture was pulled for use, appearing first in U.K. print ads for the "Paperback Writer" 45, with an alternate shot coming a week later on the cover of *Disc* magazine above the caption "What a carve-up!"

Nary a complaint was heard in Merrie Olde England, but when advance copies of *Yesterday . . . and Today* shipped in America, DJs and reviewers went apoplectic, beseeching Capitol president Alan Livingston to "do something." John, for his part, declared the whole issue "as relevant as Vietnam."

March 30, 1967: The *Sgt. Pepper* Cover (Michael Cooper)

The groundbreaking effort that went into the making of this album (and its jacket) has been well chronicled, but to omit a mention would be unthinkable. Though Cooper is responsible for shooting this landmark release's cover, credit for the concept itself must be shared between Paul McCartney, artist Peter Blake, and gallery owner Robert Fraser.

Originally, the Fool (a Dutch cadre of designers/hangers-on/con artists) created an unremarkable psychedelic landscape that the group, particularly Paul, was keen to use for the cover. When they shared that notion with Fraser, the latter took great pains to argue that such an album deserved better than a transient piece of low-rent ephemera.

Pop artist Peter Blake, pulled into the project by Fraser, was, with wife Jann Haworth, the primary architect of the finished product. (As for the Fool, an abstract doodle of theirs was given inner sleeve placement for the first pressings as a consolation prize.)

Brainstorming, the three conceived of an old-fashioned band-in-the-park tableau, with an audience surrounding the musicians after a concert. From there, the idea grew to building the "crowd" with images of people that they admired. Despite considerable misgivings from their record company and their manager, the Beatles' idea grew legs and the rest is history. The personas depicted were chosen by John, Paul, George (who apparently limited his choices to Indian gurus), and Blake. Ringo cheerfully left the decision-making to the others.

John, ever the provocateur, suggested both Jesus and Hitler, while actor Leo "Bowery Boys" Gorcey's demands for compensation precluded his involvement. EMI head Sir Joseph Lockwood requested that Gandhi be removed, lest sales in the former colony be affected. (An outtake photo depicting an Elvis Presley mannequin suggests he was pulled at the last minute.)

With the Fabs sporting colorful quasi-military suits tailored by a theatrical costumer, Cooper recorded, in three hours' time, all the shots he needed of what John recalled later as two Beatles "flying" and two not. Little did anyone foresee the implications of decisions made that day that, two years on, would offer "proof" of a death within the ranks.

So iconic was the cover image gracing the *Sgt. Pepper's* sleeve that it's hard to imagine it any other way. The outtake shown on this bootleg depicts what might have been.

August 11, 1967: The *Look* Shoot (Richard Avedon)

The end of the Beatles' touring days gave photographers limited access to the group. This, coupled with their ever-changing looks and a general youth-culture paradigm shift, meant that by 1967, up-to-date images were in order. Fashion/celebrity photographer Richard Avedon was contracted to shoot group and individual photos.

Avedon had been making a name for himself with his work with artists like Joan Baez, Simon and Garfunkel, and the Fugs. Applying Day-Glo colors to his groundbreaking "solarization" process resulted in a series of Beatle portraits that fully embodied 1967's "Summer of Love" gestalt. The images were then mass-marketed through *Look* magazine in the States, the *Daily Express* in the U.K., and West Germany's *Stern* throughout Europe.

Each individual portrait played up a singular characteristic: as the group's "mystic," George was revealed gazing beatifically upward, palm raised as if bestowing a blessing. Paul, as the "pretty" Beatle, posed with orchids. Ringo, the Everyman, holds a dove, while John is depicted in bold yellow and red, the lenses on his glasses swirling with "psychedelic" patterns. This image graced *Look*'s cover on January 9, 1968.

Also in that issue was Avedon's stark group shot, mainly a study of the musicians' faces. Compositionally, John's mug looms the largest, with Ringo's second, Paul's third, and George's least of all. (Interestingly, ten years on, when Capitol Records wanted desperately to re-sign Paul's Wings, the company used the group shot for the gatefold and promotional material of the compilation *Love Songs*. The Avedon shot was reconfigured: Paul was swapped with Ringo and enlarged to equal size with John, with Ringo's image, characteristically, shunted aside and reduced. George, by then associated with Warner Brothers, remained condensed. Paul signed with Columbia anyway.)

Today, Avedon's Fab Four work still reaches millions via its inclusion in the packaging of *The Beatles 1*.

July 28, 1968: "Mad Day Out" (Tom Murray, Don McCullin, and Others)

On this summer Sunday, the Beatles interrupted their "White Album" sessions to spend a day posing for photos. The scope of the shooting entailed multiple locales (chosen by Paul's then-girlfriend Francie Schwartz) and several changes of outfit, recording in the process a swath of images so diverse as to serve a variety of purposes for six months. Among the images recorded that day were shots of a bare-chested Paul sporting chains, Ringo with a parrot on his shoulder, a helmeted George blowing a bugle, and John on the ground, playing dead.

The variance in tone throughout the images indicates that the Beatles were attempting to cover a lot of ground, just as they were in their recording project. Many are playful or silly (the boys in mock fisticuffs or spitting water), while others are somewhat somber. Several shots feature Paul in a lavender suit; one from this series would grace the cover of *Life* magazine's September 13, 1968, issue. Others show John wearing Yoko's fur coat, the same one he later immortalized in the *Let It Be* rooftop performance. Yoko, along with Ms. Schwartz and Mal Evans's six-year-old son, Gary, was present all day.

After mingling with the crowd that had gathered behind an iron fence near St. Pancras Church (a shot of this moment appears on the inner gatefold to the Red and Blue compilations), the Beatles retired to Paul's home on Cavendish in St. John's Wood. There the final images were recorded, with the group lounging beneath a geodesic dome with Martha, Paul's sheepdog. Two days later, recording would resume with the epic "Hey Jude."

August 8, 1969: The *Abbey Road* Cover (Iain MacMillan)

Just as their "Get Back" (a.k.a. *Let It Be*) sessions earlier that year had been rife with fanciful but impractical notions, discussions on what to name their last recorded album spawned similarly outlandish suggestions. A favorite title well into the final hour was *Everest*, in honor of the cigarettes chain-smoked by engineer Geoff Emerick. To that end, arrangements began being made to fly the foursome to the foot of the Himalayas for a cover shot. But this plan died, as they say, in committee.

Someone—usually Paul is credited—finally suggested that the group just step outside, shoot a picture in the street, and call the release *Abbey Road*. While it is not recorded whether or not he asked, "Why don't we do it in the road?" it is documented that he sketched out on paper an almost precise likeness of the eventual cover shot.

Per John's recommendation, Scottish photographer Iain MacMillan was tabbed for the cameraman role that day. (Also present and shooting was Paul's bride, Linda, who documented the periphery of the morning's events.) MacMillan had first worked with Yoko three years previously and later documented her and John's burgeoning peace activism.

After consulting with Paul on the concept, MacMillan mounted a ten-foot stepladder as police brought traffic to a halt. In ten minutes, he recorded six images; one frame was the obvious choice, with the Beatles' legs forming perfect inverted Vs. Following the shoot, a nearby tile street sign with the

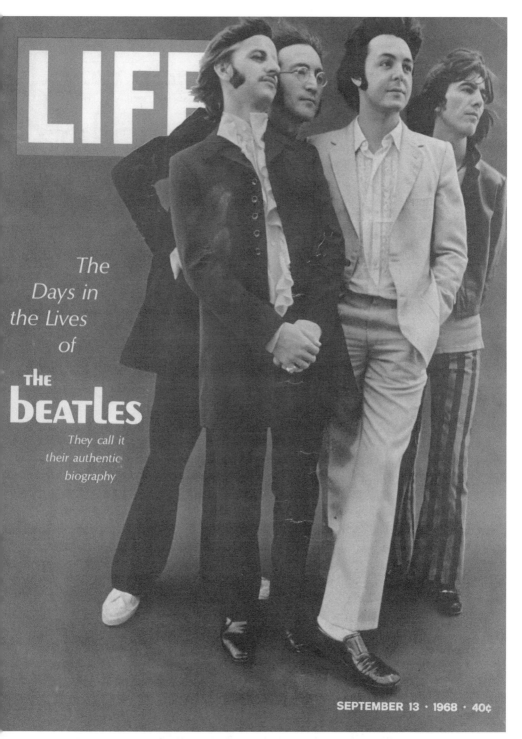

The
Days in
the Lives
of

THE
bEATLES

They call it
their authentic
biography

SEPTEMBER 13 · 1968 · 40¢

Not long after the "Mad Day Out" photo-op, this image from the shoot made the cover of *Life* magazine, in the first of two issues devoted to Hunter Davies's telling of their story.

band's name added was photographed for the back cover. (The seren-dipitous walk-through by an oblivious female passerby irked MacMillan but ended up making the cut.)

The reverberations of the day's work have never ceased. Like *Pepper*, the cover inspired innumerable "tributes." Bowing to public perceptions, the recording facility was eventually renamed "Abbey Road Studios" despite having carried EMI's name since 1931. Meanwhile, life for those who travel daily on the busy street has become an unholy nightmare; hordes of tourists and fans make the pilgrimage, believing that having a photo taken on the crosswalk is their birthright.

As for MacMillan, he continued working with John and Yoko, shooting the *Live Peace in Toronto* cover as well as their "Happy Xmas (War Is Over)" session. Paul brought him back to St. John's Wood to shoot the *Paul Is Live* send-up of *Abbey Road* in 1993. MacMillan died in 2006.

August 22, 1969: The Final Photo Session (Ethan Russell)

With work essentially wrapped up on *Abbey Road*, discussion turned to the promotional needs of the project. Personal appearances were out of the question, but the musicians' contracts with EMI had recently been revamped, and maximizing sales was not far from anyone's mind. Though the band was publicly noncommittal as to their future, tensions between the individual members had never been higher. (It is telling that for the first time in their career, a "promo" film—for George's "Something"—was stitched together with each Beatle shot separately.) Given that the band no longer resembled its last series of promotional photos, a new set was clearly needed, whatever the future held.

John and Yoko's newly purchased home, Tittenhurst Park, provided a locale. The Ascot estate's expansive grounds provided a variety of pictur-esque backdrops, including its Georgian entrance, replete with statuary; a grove of Weeping Blue Atlas Cedars; and a meadow of tall grass. (At one point, a pair of donkeys was invited into the shoot, as depicted in some amateur film footage seen in the *Anthology* documentary). Yoko and a heav-ily pregnant Linda were present; the latter gave birth to daughter Mary six days later.

Manning principal photographic duties was Ethan Russell. Having shot the photos for the book intended to accompany the eventual release of *Let It Be*, Russell was already known to the Beatles. Today he can claim the distinction of being the only photographer to have shot album covers for the Beatles, the Rolling Stones (*Get Your Ya-Yas Out*), and the Who (*Who's Next*).

Russell captured the group in the aforementioned settings, as well as on the lawn, near a retaining wall, and inside, seated at a table. John and George each sport black hats, while Ringo and Paul are each dressed a bit less casually than usual. Photos from the day's shooting would end up being disseminated widely by Apple, but perhaps the most familiar images were those used for an American compilation album, *Hey Jude*, issued in early 1970 (originally titled *The Beatles Again*).

Not since the revamped *Yesterday . . . and Today* sleeve in 1966 had such a somber, seemingly joyless ensemble graced a Beatles album. Coming two days after the foursome had recorded together for the last time (and one week after the Woodstock festival), the images recorded at Tittenhurst document a sad end to a musical force that had defined a decade. Ahead lay a bitter dissolution—happily, largely undocumented in photos—and years of healing.

There Are Places
I Remember

The Beatles' London

There isn't a Beatle fan in the world who would go to London *without* trekking out to St. John's Wood to see the zebra crossing at Abbey Road. (Or leave without annoying drivers by staging photo shoots.)

Hardcore fans will find a wealth of London locales—homes, offices, and film and video locations—with some connection to the Fabs. Depending on the length of one's visit, a tourist can spend an awful lot of time retracing the Beatles' footsteps. Here's a rundown of some of the most worthwhile.

Abbey Road Studios (EMI Studios): 3 Abbey Road, St. John's Wood

First opened in 1931, the EMI recording facility made famous by the Fabs has seen plenty of history, much of it having nothing to do with rock and roll. A complete listing of artists who recorded at the Abbey Road studios would be voluminous; non-rock performers who recorded there include classical composer Edward Elgar ("Pomp and Circumstance"), singer/dancer Fred Astaire (seen on the *Sgt. Pepper* cover), Fats Waller, Judy Garland, and Glenn Miller.

George Martin's work here with the Goons (Peter Sellers, Spike Milligan, and Harry Secombe) helped the producer bond with his future Liverpudlian charges. Employed at EMI studios since 1950, Martin, with his background in classical music (as well as virtually every other recordable idiom), was exactly the right mentor for the talented novices.

Once the Beatles attained stardom, the Abbey Road facility became a mecca for fans. Kept off the grounds by a low wall and a fence, the regulars soon learned that the Fabs could be quite obliging, signing autographs and posing for pictures during their comings and goings.

Though already a draw for fans in the know, the cover and title of the Beatles' penultimate release codified Abbey Road in rock mythology. Never again would signs designating the street be safe; never again would traffic flow unencumbered near the studio. The white wall in front of the property became a repository for ever-changing graffiti from visitors around the world, not all of it complimentary (or printable).

In the 1970s, EMI officially changed the name of the facilities to Abbey Road Studios. During a renovation in 1984, the studio opened its doors to the public for the first time, presenting an acclaimed multimedia show offering tantalizing glimpses into the EMI vaults. The event's success led indirectly to the *Anthology* releases a decade later.

Apple Headquarters: 3 Savile Row, Mayfair

"Savile Row" is linguistic shorthand for exquisite men's tailoring. The meaning came from the preponderance of high-quality clothiers populating this short avenue in the nineteenth century. Also renowned are the district's Georgian townhouses, which by the 1960s were much-sought-after properties. Apple Corps began occupying #3 in the fall of 1968, moving from temporary quarters at 94 Wigmore Street.

The office soon became a hangout for everyone from the young "Apple Scruffs" to a chapter of California Hell's Angels that George inadvertently invited to visit. Employee theft on a grand scale plagued the business, but the atmosphere for all was merry enough—at least until the advent of Allen Klein.

Of primary interest to most fans is the rooftop where the Beatles played their final semipublic gig in January 1969. Visitors may be disappointed to discover that the roof is all but invisible to anyone at street level.

Plans had been made fairly early on to build a recording studio in the building's basement. Despite "Magic" Alex Mardas's total ineptitude at completing the job, Apple Studios did eventually open, though after the Beatles had broken up. George occasionally made use of the facility, as did Mary Hopkin and Badfinger. Non-Apple regulars included Harry Nilsson and Marc Bolan of T.Rex.

Apple lost most of its raison d'être once the four individual Beatles' contracts expired in 1976. Any talent of note had since moved on, as had the ex-Fabs. The studio was soon dismantled and the offices closed. (*Ringo's Rotogravure*, released in 1976 on Atlantic, displayed a photo of Apple's graffitied-beyond-recognition door on its back cover.)

Indica Gallery: 6 Mason's Yard, St. James

"Swinging London" mythology aside, the 1960s saw a thriving underground arts scene in England's capital. Also countering popular perception, it was Paul—not John—who was most plugged into the scene. As the only Beatle living in the city proper, he naturally had greater access, and thus was more attuned to London's happenings.

Peter Asher, of the singing duo Peter and Gordon, was an aficionado of the "experimental" art scene himself. In partnership with John Dunbar, husband of pop chanteuse (and Mick Jagger girlfriend) Marianne Faithfull, and Barry Miles (the future McCartney biographer who preferred being called by his last name), he founded the Indica Gallery in November 1965.

Indica, short for "indications," as in "somewhere to go" (as well as for *Cannabis indica*), opened with McCartney's literal hands-on assistance. An enthusiastic booster, Paul pounded nails, installed shelves, and sawed wood in preparation for the gallery's opening; later, he helped design flyers and Indica's wrapping paper.

Located in the heart of the counterculture community, Indica helped launch many a cutting-edge artist, most famously Yoko Ono but also the Boyle Family (Mark Boyle was responsible for the psychedelic light shows seen at concerts by Jimi Hendrix and the Soft Machine).

Literature was another facet of the gallery. With a bookstore already on the premises, Miles founded the *International Times*, soon to be a well-received underground newspaper. Adding literary credibility were two frequent patrons, legendary Beat writers Allen Ginsberg and William S. Burroughs (who lived nearby). Eventually, the bookstore's success required a move to larger premises at 102 Southampton Row, Camden.

Other renowns making the scene included filmmakers Roman Polanski and Michaelangelo Antonioni. Marc Bolan (née Feld), then a teenager, hung out and ran errands at the gallery.

To Beatle people, Indica's greatest notoriety came as the meeting place in November 1966 of John and Yoko (see chapter 38).

Though quite successful at causing a stir and packing people in, the familiar '60s mindset, which put creativity and business savvy at odds, doomed Indica. The gallery shut its doors in November 1967, a mere two years after its opening, having run up considerable debt.

But nostalgia for the famed place never entirely died; in late 2006, a Soho gallery called Riflemaker (located in a former firearms establishment) re-created Indica, complete with work from the original artists as well as contemporary ones. John Dunbar and Yoko, among others, were on hand to give talks on London's experimental art scene of four decades before.

Apple Boutique: 94 Baker Street, Marylebone

The December 5, 1967, opening of the Apple Boutique promised great things from a group that had been on a roll. With *Sgt. Pepper's* knocking the world for a loop, the "All You Need Is Love" worldwide broadcast, and *Magical Mystery Tour*, their first self-produced film project, completed but unscreened, it seemed as though the Fabs could do no wrong.

Alas, the Beatles' excursion into retail marketing would end ingloriously by the following midsummer. First off, a psychedelic mural covering an entire four-story side of the building (painted without the approval of the city of Westminster) met with universal condemnation by the neighboring

The announced giveaway of all remaining stock at the Apple Boutique on July 30, 1968, caused the final frenzy of Beatle-related activity at 94 Baker Street.

Photo by Cummings Archives/Redferns

merchants. Pressure forced the Fabs to whitewash the mural after just three months.

The shop's overpriced, instantly outdated glad rags were pilfered constantly by staff as well as customers. After losing £200,000 in seven months, the Beatles decided to liquidate via a public giveaway. The experiment ended quickly, but pleasant memories of the shop's brief existence remain strong among Beatles fans to this day.

(A coda to the venture came when, in a burst of inspiration, Paul and girlfriend Francie Schwartz took it upon themselves one night to put the shuttered shop to use as a billboard, painting "Hey Jude" and "Revolution" in the windows. The innocuous plug of the Beatles' newest single shocked their neighbors, especially Holocaust survivors who, with fresh memories of hate messages against the "Juden," feared another *Kristallnacht*.)

The building, today occupied by Reed Employment Agency, remains a tourist draw. The only outward sign of its past life is a commemorative plaque honoring John.

A Hard Day's Night Locale: Boston Place / Marylebone Station, Westminster

Any number of sites around London turned up in videos or as film locales in the first two Beatle films. Most are of only passing interest, but others border on iconic, such as the location of *A Hard Day's Night*'s opening scenes.

As everyone reading this knows, the film begins with a shot of John, George, and Ringo, pursued by fans, running down a sidewalk toward the camera. Underscored by that distinctive opening guitar chord, this electrifying title sequence gave audiences their first glimpse of the boys on the big screen.

After George and Ringo recoup from taking a tumble, three Beatles (save Paul, waiting inside incognito) quickly dash into the Marylebone train station across the street, leaving a scene of mass hysteria in their wake. The two-and-a-half-minute sequence beautifully set up the film as an encapsulation of the Fabs' hyperkinetic existence.

Boston Place is the side street down which the Beatles dash in the opening shot. This otherwise insignificant lane is located on the eastern side of the Marylebone Station. (Eventually, Apple Corps bought some property there to archive their holdings.) Over four decades later, it has retained its 1964 look.

Marylebone Station itself was built in 1899. Cutbacks in service resulted in the station becoming run down and facing threat of closure in the 1980s, but overflow traffic at nearby Paddington station reversed Marylebone's fortunes.

The entrance used by the Beatles is today a Marks and Spencer's sandwich shop, but otherwise appears unchanged. It remains a popular rendezvous point for Beatles walking tours. Alas, the adjoining phone booths inside are long gone, but sharp-eyed visitors can spot where they were.

Trainspotters viewing the film will note that although much of the opening sequence was shot at Marylebone, the Beatles' departure was filmed on a Sunday in 1964, and no trains ran on the Sabbath. The departing train was actually shot at Paddington.

Ringo's Rental Flat: 34 Montague Square, Marylebone

In early 1965, shortly after his wedding to Maureen Cox, Ringo took occupancy of this fashionable townhouse. When firstborn son and future Who drummer Zak was born in September, the family moved to "Sunny Heights," a home near the Lennons in the so-called stockbroker belt of Weybridge.

Ringo maintained the lease on his former residence, however, subletting the first floor and basement to others when the Fabs themselves weren't using it as a convenient trysting space.

Never one to let an opportunity for enriching the musical world pass by, Paul planned to set up a basic recording facility in the flat's basement, intended for use by any fellow musicians and/or poets. These plans fell through, but ex-Animals bassist Chas Chandler did rent the flat, moving in with his protégé, Jimi Hendrix.

After briefly house-sharing with Paul on Cavendish Avenue following the break-up of his marriage, John moved with Yoko into the Montague Square property. The residence became the site of the notorious October 1968 drug bust (as well as the locale for the *Two Virgins* cover shoot). Irked by years of noise complaints and bad publicity in the wake of the arrest, the property managers came down hard on Ringo. Tiring of the whole mess, Starr opted to sell off his interests in early 1969, apparently bearing his bandmate no ill will over the entire affair.

The Asher Residence: 57 Wimpole Street, Marylebone

The Ashers of Wimpole Street were a family of no mean accomplishment. Dr. Richard Asher, a physician, first described Munchausen Syndrome in 1951. His wife, Margaret, had been a professional oboe player in symphony orchestras. After retiring to raise her three children, she continued to give private lessons; her most notable pupil was one George Martin. Siblings Peter and Jane each found fame individually during the 1960s, though both were defined by their relationship with Paul McCartney. Jane was an actress

THE BEATLES

GET BACK

with Don't Let Me Down and 9 other songs

Another London haunt of the Beatles was EMI House in Manchester Square. The site of two album cover shoots (though this one went unused), the building was recently razed.

on stage and screen whose career began at the age of five. Older brother Peter achieved British Invasion success in America as the bespectacled half of pop duo Peter and Gordon.

Paul and Jane began dating in 1963. The story goes that one evening, upon missing his train back to Liverpool, Paul was invited by Mrs. Asher to stay overnight in an attic bedroom. The stopover turned into a couple of years' residence, as Paul continued to live with the Ashers in their posh, well-appointed digs until moving into his own house near EMI studios in early 1966.

In the meantime, the Wimpole Street home became a workplace of sorts, with John and Paul regularly composing songs in the Asher family music room, located in the basement. "I Want to Hold Your Hand," among other tunes, was written on the family piano.

It didn't take fans long to recognize the Ashers' guest of honor, and by early 1965 crowds had begun staking out the residence. With Dr. Asher's help, Paul devised a way to elude them via an adjoining flat and an elevator that opened into Browning Mews, a backstreet to the property. (To thank the owners for their assist, Paul bought them a refrigerator.)

Paul McCartney's House: 7 Cavendish Avenue, St. John's Wood

Never one to rush into things, Paul finally found a home in London that suited his purposes, being somewhat secluded but close to work. The walled residence was purchased in 1965, but renovations kept Paul from moving in until the following March.

Predictably, the property, which functioned as a Beatles hangout around recording dates, was soon overrun by fans and press. The Cavendish house was also the site of frequent parties, with the usual coterie of industry friends and notables in attendance.

Paul was able to return the hospitality extended him by the Ashers when Jane moved in; together, the two set up a household, furnishing the home with artifacts collected on their respective travels.

Paul was generally gracious and accomodating to the gathered admirers, occasionally serenading them from an upstairs window on acoustic guitar. They in turn respected his privacy and helped him out as needed, even walking Martha if asked, and looking after the property during his absences. (Another implied duty was to signal Paul that trouble was approaching, during those all too frequent times when they knew he was inside with a conquest.)

On at least one occasion, a "visitor" went beyond established boundaries. An American girl once boldly scaled the wall, set a ladder against an upper-story window, and entered—into the bathroom, as it happened. This same visitor proceeded to pillage the place, stealing souvenirs including personal photographs and transparencies. Only through the intercession of a trusted "scruff" was Paul able to recover his missing items, just before they were spirited off to America. Turning lemons into lemonade, Paul parlayed the incident into a song on *Abbey Road*.

Paul had a meditation garden and a geodesic dome installed in the back. The latter was the site of one of the last photo shoots done of the Beatles as a group, in July 1968. The home's green wooden gates remain a familiar backdrop for photos taken by fans to the present day.

Brian Epstein's Home: 24 Chapel Street, Belgravia

Manager Brian Epstein bought his first and only London home in December 1964. Located in Belgravia, one of London's most exclusive districts, the residence sat amidst several embassies.

Brian lived for the opportunity to arrange and throw parties, and his new digs were the site of many a fête. As his show-business connections flowered, Brian's Chapel Street home was frequented by some of the biggest stars of the day.

At the May 1967 launch party for *Sgt. Pepper's* at their manager's home, Paul first truly connected with rock photographer/scene-maker Linda Eastman. (The two had first met days earlier at the Bag O'Nails club; at Brian's, the two chatted at length.)

The media event, preceeding huge acclaim for the album, probably represented the pinnacle of Brian's success. Three months later, he died in the house from an accidental drug overdose.

"Mad Day Out" Photo Shoot: St. Pancras Old Church, Euston Road, Camden

Of all the sites listed here, the one carrying the most historical significance beyond the Fabs is this one, a church whose origins date back to the fourth century.

St. Pancras Church, officially designated "old" to distinguish it from its nineteenth-century successor, is among London's most scenic locales. Boasting fountains, the tomb of architect Sir John Soane, an adjoining cemetery, and a magnificent flower garden, the site always draws a stream of visitors, Beatles connections notwithstanding.

Pancras, an orphan, was at age fourteen beheaded in Rome for refusing to renounce his Christianity. The church bearing his name was built some ten years after his martyrdom; though it has been rebuilt many times throughout the centuries, a sixth-century altar remains inside.

July 28, 1968, is commemorated in Beatle lore as the "Mad Day Out," when the Fabs spent the afternoon and early evening posing for promotional photos at a wide variety of settings around London. (See chapter 9 for a detailed itinerary.) The St. Pancras Old Church and its grounds was their last stop before retreating to Paul's home on Cavendish. It is likely that this site was chosen more for its visual aesthetic than for Pancras's standing as patron saint of cramps, headaches, and children.

Dozens of images were recorded around the fountain, in the flower garden, on a bench, and in a Norman doorway. But perhaps the best known is the shot showing the Fabs behind an iron fence, mingling with a crowd of onlookers. A frame from this series graced the inner gatefold to the Beatles' "Red" and "Blue" mid-'70s compilation albums.

I Saw a Film Today

Cinematic Achievements of the Beatles

Just as celebrity females on their way up or trying to avoid the way down must pose for *Playboy*, so it was practically compulsory in the Beatles' day for a rock-and-roll act ascending to stardom to make a film. That the band's body of cinematic work has endured is a pleasant bonus, a tribute to their talent and the high standards of those around them.

Their movie career was bookended by documentaries featuring the Fabs as themselves. In between, they portrayed variations on that theme, establishing, then reinforcing caricatures of their personas.

Though hardly in danger of winning any acting awards, John, Paul, George, and especially Ringo were clearly smitten with the magic of celluloid. Outside the group identity, two Beatles composed soundtracks to films while the other two took on support roles. The solo years would see a continued infatuation, with George even taking on the role of producer.

What's Happening! The Beatles in the U.S.A. (1964); The Beatles: The First U.S. Visit (1994 Reissue)

By the early 1960s, England's Granada Television had built a reputation as *the* source of entertainment and news from Britain's marginalized outer regions (i.e., north of London). As Manchester and Liverpool were their home turf, Granada's bread and butter was documenting the goings-on within those regions.

Granada's ties to the Fabs began in 1962 when a film crew was dispatched to the Cavern to document the hottest thing to hit Liverpool since the Luftwaffe. Two years later, with the Beatles poised to spread hysteria to the New World, Granada contracted Albert and David Maysles to record the events for the viewing audience back home.

The Maysles brothers pioneered a brand of filmmaking called cinema vérité. Using handheld cameras for added intimacy, they acted as flies on the wall, letting the film roll and capturing events without unduly influencing them. The presentation came without narration, allowing viewers to draw their own conclusions *sans* intrusion.

Duly briefed, the Maysles chronicled virtually every move the Beatles made between their raucous February 7 arrival at Kennedy Airport and their debut American concert at the Washington Coliseum four days later, with the *Ed Sullivan Show* appearances as the centerpiece. The resulting documentary, broadcast on English television (minus the D.C. footage) as *Yeah! Yeah! Yeah! The Beatles in New York*, gave home viewers an inside view of a seismic shift in popular culture.

The film depicts the foursome as self-assured, if bemused, and calm amidst the frenzy. It is nothing less than *A Hard Day's Night* minus the plotline. The Fabs are shown inside their limousine, in their hotel, on the train to Washington, at all times surrounded by frantic teens and sycophantic careerists (like DJ Murray the K), anxious to hitch their wagon to the Beatles' star power.

In November 1964, the film was presented on American television, narrated by Carol Burnett. Some years later, Apple acquired the Maysles' raw footage and, with the addition of the Sullivan and Coliseum performances, reedited it as *The First U.S. Visit*.

The resulting release has the benefit of much previously unseen footage (including some of an actual American family watching the Sullivan broadcast), as well as commentary from Albert Maysles. As an encapsulation of 1960s youth culture in transition, it's unbeatable.

A Hard Day's Night, Directed by Richard Lester (1964)

Well before the Beatles broke in America, but after Beatlemania had commenced in Britain, Brian Epstein and United Artists brokered a deal to produce the band's silver screen debut. For Brian, this represented his long-coveted entrée into the world of Hollywood-style glamour; to UA, it meant nothing more or less than an opportunity to take advantage of a passing fancy before it petered out.

As such, the budget was low by cinematic standards, with UA figuring to see a *real* investment return on the soundtrack album. Still, they were willing to indulge the Beatles' desire for a quality writer.

Alun Owen was a curious choice to pen what was expected to be lighthearted fluff. The Liverpool dramatist was best known for his 1959 teledrama, *No Trams to Lime Street*, which all four Beatles had enjoyed. Owen's realistic dialogue and knowing depiction of Liverpudlians won him the Fabs' approval; to close the deal, he spent some time on the road with them to glean insight into their personalities.

He came to the same conclusion as producer Walter Shenson and director Dick Lester: the film *had* to be built around the Beatles' whirlwind existence as prisoners of their own success. (For his efforts, Owen was nominated for an Academy Award.) That the financial limitations precluded expensive locales, sets, or costumes merely enhanced the veracity of the on-screen depiction.

Like Shenson, Lester was an American living in London. Work on the quickie exploitation film *It's Trad, Dad* (starring Beatles tour-mate Helen Shapiro) brought him to Shenson's attention as a talented director who knew how to film music.

But another element helped make Lester the ideal director: his involvement with work that the Beatles appreciated long before they came into professional contact with him. Like George Martin, Lester had previously worked with the Goons, a surrealistic sort of precursor to Monty Python, and on such absurdist offerings as *The Running, Jumping, and Standing Still Film*, a short starring Peter Sellers and future *Help!* costar Leo McKern.

A Hard Day's Night is perhaps the finest film debut of any rock act. Critics unfamiliar with the group's recording output fell all over themselves likening the foursome to a modern-day Marx Brothers. (Groucho himself was dismissive of the comparison, regarding the four Beatles as indistinguishable.)

Lester's intelligent direction played to the Beatles' individual strengths, while his visual innovation sparked almost immediate imitation (most famously by the Monkees). In the words of film critic Roger Ebert, *A Hard Day's Night* stands as "the *Citizen Kane* of jukebox musicals." Its success made it a tough act to follow.

Help!, Directed by Richard Lester (1965)

"It was like putting clams in a movie about frogs," groused John Lennon, perhaps unfairly, about their second big-screen feature. True, the cartoonish plot line, which depicted the Beatles being pursued around the world by Far East thugs and a mad scientist, bore no resemblance to reality, but that was beside the point. Richard Lester was keen to avoid a repetition of their first film together, and on this point, the Fabs concurred.

Instead, they reaped the benefits of a big budget. *A Hard Day's Night*'s success afforded United Artists the wherewithal to send the Fabs anywhere they desired to go; in this instance, the Bahamas and the Swiss Alps. This new freedom extended to the fanciful insertion of songs into the film, giving Lester license to indulge his wildest whims. In addition, *Help!* was filmed in color, making locales that much splashier.

An intuitively gifted filmmaker, Dick Lester got on especially well with John, whom he chose to work with outside of the Beatles.   *Photo by Gunter Zint/Redferns*

His premise was a mixture of James Bond spoof (complete with simulated 007 theme) and action satire, anticipating *Batman*'s over-the-top campiness on television one year later. As such, it tended to diminish the Beatles within their own film.

The original title, *Eight Arms to Hold You*, suggested a decided lack of imagination that the Beatles were challenged to better. As it happened, once again John came to the rescue with an eleventh-hour composition that, on the surface, seemed to capture the flavor of the movie. (That it was a *personal* cry for help escaped virtually everyone at the time.)

Wisely, the filmmakers placed Ringo front and center. Since his stand-out performance in *A Hard Day's Night* a year earlier, the ringed one had impressed all with a presence that translated well to the screen. Though Richard Lester would one day opine that George was the best actor of the lot, Ringo projected personality aplenty, while remaining flexible enough to run with the most unlikely of plot twists.

Though generally at odds with the hurry-up-and-wait nature of filmmaking, the Beatles had by this time found a way to pleasurably pass the time. The incessant smoking of reefer led to uncontrolled giggling on the set and a generally glassy-eyed demeanor. (When visited on the set by an American DJ, John told the incredulous interviewer that they spent their downtime getting "stoned." When the DJ nervously responded with "Of course, you're kidding," the unruffled Beatle replied, "I'm not!")

The Family Way, Directed by Roy Boulting (1966)

With considerable talent, ambition to spare, and a thirst for entering the world of a higher art than the Beatles afforded him, Paul jumped at the chance to compose a film score. *The Family Way* garnered attention as child star Hayley Mills's first "adult" role. Beyond this, it is Paul McCartney's name on the credits that brought notice to this enjoyable but unremarkable Boulting Brothers film.

Twin brothers John and Roy Boulting got their start with the acclaimed drama *Brighton Rock* back in 1947. Alternating the roles of director and producer on each project, the two had been instrumental in building Peter Sellers into a star.

With films like *I'm All Right Jack* (1959) and *Heavens Above!* (1963), the Boultings had carved out a singular niche in classic British satire. *The Family Way* represented a throwback to 1950s-style working-class comedy, in which a pair of newlyweds has difficulty consummating the marriage.

Paul's attraction to *this* film seems rather curious. Given that in 1966 he was immersed neck-deep in London's experimental art scene, such a conventional vehicle for his scoring abilities seemed like underachieving. But for his first try, he acquitted himself well, composing exactly one melody and teasing it out into another dozen variations.

Abetting him on the project was George Martin, who had great experience in film scoring. His orchestra performed on the film's soundtrack; a recording was tailored for radio airplay and issued as a single under the title "Love in the Open Air."

For someone who had just months earlier disdained orchestration as "Mantovani," Paul embraced the experience and, in fact, by early 1967, elected to "conduct" the classical musicians augmenting "A Day in the Life." Decades later, he would branch out into classical work wholeheartedly, composing *Liverpool Oratorio*, *Standing Stone*, and *Ecce Cor Meum*, among other works.

How I Won the War, Directed by Richard Lester (1967)

Just before filming began on *Help!* in February 1965, it was announced that the third film of the Beatles' UA contract would be an adaptation of Richard Condon's 1961 novel *A Talent for Loving*. A Western, it almost certainly would have afforded Ringo a plum role, but the rather adult plot likely made it a nonstarter.

Instead, it would be John alone who worked with Richard Lester in 1966. Impressed with Lester's antiwar take on Patrick Ryan's absurdist novel, and at a loss for what to do with himself after the end of touring, John's respect for Lester made it hard to say no to his film offer.

Set in World War II, the film featured Lennon as Gripweed, an infantry-man under the command of Goodbody (played by Michael Crawford of *Phantom of the Opera* fame). Given the deadly unfunny nature of real war, the film is presented as a black comedy, though viewers accustomed to the snappy pace of *Help!* and *A Hard Day's Night* may find the film slow going. Additionally, though John's presence in the film was heavily trumpeted, in fact his on-screen presence amounts to little more than an extended cameo.

The experience did, however, cure John once and for all of any solo silver screen aspirations he may still have harbored. Easily bored by a film-making process that taxed his patience—especially given the instant gratification he'd come to expect from a concert-going audience or the recording studio—Lennon henceforth limited his cinematic endeavors to work with the Beatles or Yoko Ono.

Magical Mystery Tour, Directed by the Beatles (1967)

Sustaining the trend had that started with *Sgt. Pepper's* and would continue throughout the remainder of the Beatles' career, *Magical Mystery Tour* was Paul's baby. With no further projects on the horizon in a year as eventful as any during their touring career, the time seemed right to produce a film that was wholly their own: no Dick Lester, no United Artists, not even a script.

Inspired by the acid-soaked misadventures of Ken Kesey and his Merry Pranksters (as depicted in Tom Wolfe's *The Electric Kool-Aid Acid Test*), Paul similarly conceived of loading up a coach with friends, family, and a few professional zanies. Then, touring the English countryside with a film crew in tow, everyone could just sit back and wait for the "magic" to begin.

"Mystery tours" (or charabancs)—weekend excursions to an untold destination at a nominal cost—were quite popular in Britain at the time. Fusing that template to Kesey's freewheeling hippie mindset might have been an interesting concept to explore in more capable hands, but an unfortunate hubris permeated the proceedings.

Already a bit of an amateur filmmaker, Paul apparently felt that the Beatles' magic touch and accrued film experience were enough to guarantee the project's success. But by the time film began rolling, Brian Epstein had been dead two weeks; without his zeal for organization and planning, the production was crippled from the start.

Though Ringo, once again anchoring a Beatle film, was game for whatever unfolded, George and John were, literally as well as figuratively, along for the ride. Initially inclined to limit his input to music ("I Am the Walrus") and some on-screen time, John was cajoled by Paul into sketching out a dream he'd had into a "scene" wherein a deranged waiter (played by John, with pencil-thin mustache) heaps mountains of spaghetti onto "Aunt Jessie's" plate.

Whatever creativity and innovation the film might have offered was lost through lack of discipline, focus, and an authority figure to rein in their excesses. Many saw *Magical Mystery Tour* as a self-indulgent cinematic mess, with its disjointed continuity and stoned ambience. (The following year, the Monkees, taking a lesson or two, applied considerable professionalism to their motion picture opus, *Head*, a film equally of its time but produced with better results.)

The film's debut on BBC television on Boxing Day 1967, inexplicably in black and white, gave critics a chance to unload on the Beatles like never before. Terms like "blatant rubbish" were tossed around with such intensity that Paul felt moved to offer a public mea culpa, while ABC canceled plans to broadcast the film in America.

While not up to usual Beatle standards, *Magical Mystery Tour* is not a complete disaster. Though much of the humor may escape contemporary American audiences, supporters liken the film to the inspired lunacy that the Monty Python gang would produce not long after. Besides, noted Paul, it's the only place where you can see the Beatles perform "I Am the Walrus."

Wonderwall, Directed by Joe Massot (1968)

Not to be outdone by his fellows, each of whom had tried his hand at film work outside the group by this time, George Harrison agreed to take on composing responsibilities for this visually engaging piece of "East meets West" psychedelia. Compared to Paul's experience with *The Family Way*, George's duties—composing, arranging, and recording all the film cues—were highly demanding.

Joe Massot had directed a cinematic short in 1966 called *Reflections on Love*. Casting model Jenny Boyd (sister of Pattie) in the lead role brought Massot into the Beatles' orbit. When asking George to compose the soundtrack to *Wonderwall*, his brief was simple: "Anything you do, I will have in the film."

Recognizing the opportunity to offer Western listeners exposure to Indian music as well as a fusion of other styles, George jumped at the chance. Flying to India in January 1968, he gathered a group of musicians at EMI's Bombay studios, getting his compositions recorded fairly quickly (and making sure to take a break at 5:30 each day, when the building's other occupants went home, disrupting the less than fully soundproofed facilities.)

Back in London, more conventional rock tracks were laid down with the help of the Remo Four, Eric Clapton, Ringo, and, on banjo, Monkee Peter Tork (who, according to George, played the instrument as though he had invented it).

As for the film itself, which starred ingénue Jane Birkin, *Wonderwall* was very much of its time. The thinnest of plots framed what might best be described as a period art film. It concerns a decidedly repressed professor's discovery of an opening in his flat's wall that projects Miss Birkin's world into his. Much fantasizing follows.

Massot would go on to direct the equally woolly-minded *Song Remains the Same* for Led Zeppelin (he was fired before its completion). But the soundtrack is *Wonderwall*'s enduring legacy: a world-music sampler before the term had been invented.

Yellow Submarine, Directed by George Dunning (1968)

Producer Al Brodax found success in television with a latter-day version of *Popeye*. Produced on the cheap, the Brodax edition of this venerable character was disdained by critics, loved by networks for its cost efficiency, and accepted by children who possessed no frame of reference.

Brodax was astute enough to recognize the Beatles' universal appeal well before the band had even set foot on American soil. Moving quickly, he struck a deal with Brian Epstein to produce a Saturday morning animated series for television. With backing from ABC, King Features resorted to their tested formula, relying on a platoon of overseas animators to do the actual work while hiring the vocal talent that had supplied voices to *Dudley Do-Right*'s Inspector Fenwick and *Krazy Kat*'s Ignatz Mouse.

The resulting low-rent animation was abhorred by many, particularly Brian Epstein, who refused to allow it to air in Britain. But from a financial

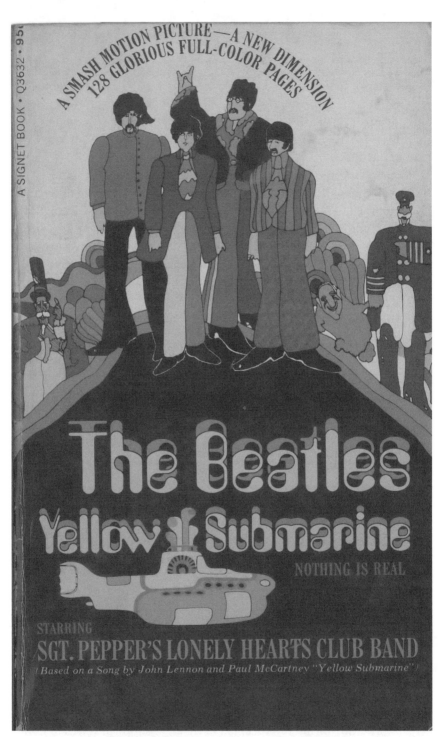

A SMASH MOTION PICTURE—A NEW DIMENSION
128 GLORIOUS FULL-COLOR PAGES

The Beatles
Yellow Submarine

NOTHING IS REAL

STARRING
SGT. PEPPER'S LONELY HEARTS CLUB BAND
(Based on a Song by John Lennon and Paul McCartney "Yellow Submarine")

Yellow Submarine's screenplay was the product of several hands. Oddly, the film's "Hey Bulldog" sequence was deleted from all American film prints and not restored until 1999's home video reissue.

perspective, it was a success, which was enough to give Brodax the qualifications to bring an animated version of the Beatles to the big screen.

George Dunning was chosen to direct, largely on the basis of his experience in commercial work, as well as a series of surrealistic film shorts. Many hands were responsible for the film's script, including Erich Segal, who not long after gained worldwide renown for penning the novel *Love Story*.

Poet Roger McGough played an uncredited but essential role in supplying the film's Liverpudlian dialogue, rich in puns and wordplay. Today he's better known for having been one third of the Scaffold, the musical/poetry outfit that included Paul McCartney's brother Michael.

Much of the film's enduring appeal comes from its stunning visuals, reminiscent of the work of '60s artist Peter Max. Expectations had been for something along the lines of Disney's traditional fare, but Dunning was keen on creating something groundbreaking. Together with the film's art director, Heinz Edelmann, and special effects editor Charles Jenkins, Dunning created a film that appealed to kids who'd grown up on the television series, as well as the college crowd and beyond.

Only the Beatles themselves were unimpressed, at least initially. Not exactly thrilled with Brian Epstein's having pledged them to the project, they distanced themselves, unwilling to commit either themselves or any worthy tunes. (It became a running inside joke that material considered sub-par was instantly consigned to the film's soundtrack.)

But viewing a rough cut changed their minds. Immediately they were blown away by the film's innovation and good-versus-evil theme. Won over, they agreed to appear as themselves at the end of the film, essentially giving their blessing. George Martin seconded their approval, providing a memorable film score.

Yellow Submarine became a hit and has lived on to find a following among successive generations. Although the physical characterizations depict the Beatles appearing collectively in a way they never did simultaneously in real life (the animators modeled them after their "Strawberry Fields Forever" video appearance, but then removed Paul's mustache), enough remained for children born decades later to pick up on. Both Sean Lennon and Dhani Harrison divined their parentage from early viewings of the movie!

The Magic Christian, Directed by Joseph McGrath (1969)

Clearly the critics' favorite among the four Beatles as a screen presence, Ringo inevitably headed toward a film career as his band's downtime increased. First up was his unfathomable casting (as a *Mexican gardener?*) in the decadent-beyond-words *Candy*, Terry Southern's adaptation of Voltaire's *Candide*.

While successfully shattering the lovable mop-top image cultivated in Ringo's first two films, artistically *Candy* has been described as one of the most shocking squanderings of talent ever captured on celluloid. (The cast included Richard Burton, Walter Matthau, Marlon Brando, John Huston, and James Coburn, among others; Buck Henry cowrote the script.)

Nonetheless, the formula was repeated, with better results, a year later with *The Magic Christian*. Based on Southern's 1959 novel, *TMC* concerned the efforts of the cruel, über-rich Sir Guy Grand (played by Peter Sellers) to demonstrate and exploit humankind's innate greed by getting people to do the unthinkable, for a price.

Like *Candy*, *The Magic Christian* is loaded with big names, including Richard Attenborough, Laurence Harvey, Raquel Welch, Christopher Lee, and Yul Brynner. Director Joseph McGrath's biggest credit to date had been the equally star-studded *Casino Royale*, a film not terribly well regarded by James Bond fans.

This blackest of comedies is an acquired taste for most. It's interesting to note that Ringo came straight from the *Let It Be* project to the set of *The Magic Christian*. Notwithstanding the immeasurable cynicism of the film, it must have seemed like a breath of fresh air.

But *The Magic Christian* had plenty of Beatle connections. Apple artist Badfinger recorded the theme for the film, McCartney's "Come and Get It," while a pair of John Lennon and Yoko Ono look-alikes are seen among various celebrities boarding the title cruise ship.

In addition, future Monty Pythons Graham Chapman and John Cleese worked on the script, and both appeared in the film as well. To make things even more Beatley, two other actors from earlier Beatles movies were also in *Magic Christian*: Patrick Cargill, who played the superintendent in *Help!*, and Jeremy Lloyd, who had appeared in both *Help!* and *A Hard Day's Night*.

Let It Be, Directed by Michael Lindsay-Hogg (1970)

The son of actress Geraldine Fitzgerald, Michael Lindsay-Hogg can be regarded with some justification as the father of music video. Cutting his professional teeth on Rediffusion's *Ready Steady Go* musical series in England, he segued very easily into what were called "promo films" back in the day.

As a way to sidestep the demand for more live television appearances than would have been humanly possible, the Beatles began taping lip-synched performances of their new releases for distribution far and wide. As the group tired of miming in stage mode, the filmed presentations soon grew increasingly distant from any pretense of an in-person visit. (An early "video" filmed, but not used, depicted the Fabs consuming fish and chips as "I Feel Fine" blared. Brian Epstein was not amused.)

First among the more thought-out promos were the pair filmed for the "Paperback Writer" / "Rain" release in 1966. Lindsay-Hogg was at the directorial helm for both, which were shot outdoors and in color at the gardens of Chiswick House in London. Work on these clips was followed by promos for the Who ("Happy Jack") and the Rolling Stones ("Jumping Jack Flash"), among others.

In 1968, Lindsay-Hogg was called in to work on the "Hey Jude" / "Revolution" promos. Both were produced to give the illusion of an in-studio appearance, airing on David Frost's *Frost on Sunday* in England and *The Smothers Brothers Comedy Hour* in the States.

Following his work on the Rolling Stones' *Rock and Roll Circus* special in December 1968, the Beatles tapped Lindsay-Hogg to handle directorial chores on their latest effort to engage the public at arm's length. What became the *Let It Be* film (originally titled *The Beatles Get Back*) began as television documentary, depicting the band rehearsing new material for a one-off concert at a visually striking location.

Instead, Lindsay-Hogg documented a band in the throes of dysfunction. The project's logistical setup only exacerbated underlying tensions among the four. Early hours of filming outside their EMI comfort zone virtually guaranteed that the Beatles would be under undue strain, undermining the presumably harmonious working relationship they'd heretofore enjoyed.

With a mountain of footage shot, the finished project could have been steered in any number of editorial directions. But by the time the editing was underway, a sea change mandated something far from the original plan.

To begin with, manager Allen Klein made the decision to have the film released theatrically to fulfill the band's United Artists contract (after *Yellow Submarine* had been rejected as something less than a Beatles film) rather than on television as intended. This meant that film shot on sixteen-millimeter stock had to be blown up for the wide screen, resulting in a grainy, somewhat unfocused presentation.

Next, with disintegration in the air, the movie took on the air of an elegy. As if to enhance the lift given at the film's end during the famous rooftop session, the remainder of the film is largely somber, with lighter moments coming somewhat fleetingly. True, it was undoubtedly less than a picnic for all concerned, especially George, who quit during the proceedings.

But, as hours upon hours of bootlegged recordings reveal, the sessions also produced moments of great camaraderie, not to mention all-out hilarity—something at which the film scarcely hints. An entirely different film could be cut from existing footage, depicting a virtual parallel universe of upbeat Beatles.

Instead, the film seems to follow a curious middle ground between the extremes: hinting at the discord without revealing all the *real* nitty-gritty that went down. (George's walkout is completely ignored.) Also, episodes that may have been a bit sensitive at the time got the axe (e.g., a frank discussion of drug use with a visiting Peter Sellers and a freeform jam featuring three Beatles and Yoko).

John, in fact, complained long and loud that the finished cut had been set up *by* Paul, *for* Paul, showing him in a favorable light at the others' expense. But given John's heroin habit, George's unrest, and Ringo's work-manlike approach to a day job, it's hardly surprising that Paul stands out as the go-getter, if at times an insufferably hammy one.

With the current state of marketing, the available raw material, and the insatiable demand for anything Beatles—particularly *unseen* Beatles—a strong case could be made that Apple should commit to repackaging the *Let It Be* project in a way that puts a more buoyant spin on the proceedings. Perhaps a multiple-disc DVD issue, remastered and presented in 5.1 sound, with director commentary from Michael Lindsay-Hogg and the two surviving Beatles, could fill the gap.

You're Telling All Those Lies

Commonly Believed Myths

Many widely held beliefs regarding the Fabs that have taken root in the public imagination are, on closer inspection, found to be untrue. Some are propagated by hack writers who can't be troubled to fact-check, others come from radio DJs in the habit of imparting some little nugget of knowledge that has no factual basis, and still others emanate from those with axes to grind and scores to settle.

To be sure, some stories originated with the Beatles themselves. (John, while displaying unusual candor for a celebrity, nonetheless seems to have had a particular interest in mythmaking. Certainly, the majority of Beatle tall tales seem to center on *him*.) Many of these fables appear to have a kernel of truth, while others appear to be entirely manufactured.

In the interest of setting the record straight, we examine and correct ten such legends.

John Lennon Was Born in the Middle of a Bombing Raid

John begins his Carrollesque collection of poems and stories, *In His Own Write*, by telling readers his life story in his own inimitable way. His description of being "bored on the 9th of Octover 1940 when, I believe, the Nasties were still booming us led by Madalf Heatlump (Who had only one)," suggests that he was born during an air raid.

It would appear that many subsequent biographers took this fanciful scenario at face value, embellishing the tale of a heated Luftwaffe attack on Liverpool at the very moment John emerged from Julia's loins.

But it isn't difficult to verify specific events during the well-documented Second World War. As it happens, John arrived at 6:30 P.M., during a rare lull in the attacks, which had ended the night before and would resume in another twenty-four hours. Vivid depictions in the works of Hunter Davies and Phillip Norman notwithstanding, it simply didn't happen that way.

John Lennon Named the Beatles

Another Lennon-ism reinforced the much-believed story that the band's name originated with John. In describing the group's early days, even decades later, Lennon seemed particularly adamant about asserting his domination of the group in their formative years. In any number of interviews given by the group during the 1963–64 era, this position was subtly amplified, all of the Beatles laying credit for their name at his feet.

In actuality, according to those around at the time, the name came from Stuart Sutcliffe. Feeling they'd outgrown the Quarry Men moniker, the group (reduced to John, Paul, and George by the end of 1959) tried out for a televised talent show billed as Johnny and the Moondogs. But the experience, as well as the name, left a bad taste with the three, who quickly retired the Moondog label.

In January 1960, Stuart joined the band and soon after suggested "Beatals," as a sonic play on Buddy Holly's Crickets, with the spelling evoking "Beat" music. (The notion that the name was inspired by Lee Marvin's motorcycle gang in the 1953 motion picture *The Wild One* doesn't hold up, as the film was banned in Britain until 1968.)

Here's where it gets confusing. The "Beatals" name appears to have been used very briefly, as the group went through a fallow period, with George moonlighting in another band and John and Paul duetting as the "Nerk Twins" ("Nurk," according to some sources).

But as the group began performing more regularly, their moniker alternated between variations on "beat": The Silver Beats, the Silver Beetles, and—just once—Long John and the Silver Beatles. By the time they headed to Hamburg in August 1960, their lasting name choice had stuck.

John's contribution appears to have been the final spelling, for which he gave a variety of explanations through the years. Cynthia Lennon asserts that John believed reversing the syllables (Les Beat) gave it an appealing French twist, while adding an extra 's' (Beat less) produced an accurate description of the outfit, given their chronic trouble securing a drummer.

John's comic history of the band solidified the notion that "Beatles" was a Lennon concoction. In an article commissioned for Bill Harry's *Mersey Beat* in 1961, he offered up a faux-Biblical explanation of the group's name:

It came in a vision—a man appeared on a Flaming Pie and said unto them, "From this day on you are Beatles with an A." "Thank you, Mister Man," they said, thanking him. . . .

It was this telling that caught the imagination of fans for years to come, leading all to extrapolate that "Beatles" was John's own invention.

John Lennon and Stuart Sutcliffe

It is far more a reflection of our times than of historical truth when a well-known public figure, usually dead, is "revealed" to have been homosexual or to have engaged in homosexual encounters. Such salacious speculation typically arises in books centering on those about whom there is little, or nothing, new left to say, as was recently the case with a biography on Abraham Lincoln ("Log Cabin Republican," indeed!).

John and Stuart shared a deep friendship, based on mutual admiration and shared interests. Though sensitive souls both (despite Lennon's outward

Though any musical influence on his one-time bandmates was out of the question, Stuart Sutcliffe's aesthetic sense certainly left its mark, as John was wont to point out.   *Photo by Jurgen Vollmer/Redferns*

appearance), no one who knew them ever offered a hint of suggestion during Stuart or John's lifetime that their interactions had extended into the physical.

Enter Pauline Sutcliffe. A family therapist by trade, Stuart's younger sister has made it her life's work to keep his memory alive and get him his due as a talented painter outside of the Beatles.

Her first publishing endeavor, a collaboration with Beatle biographer Alan Clayson, led to the 1994 film *Backbeat*, which centered on Stu's relationship with Astrid Kircherr. Pauline then followed with a lavish limited-edition volume for Genesis Publications, *Stuart: The Life and Art of Stuart Sutcliffe*, which offered a reproduction of his sketchbook.

To this point, Pauline's reminiscences of her departed brother treated the Beatles and Lennon with love and respect. So far, so good.

This all changed with the 2001 publication of *The Beatles' Shadow: Stuart Sutcliffe and His Lonely Hearts Club*. Cowritten with Douglas Thomas, the volume was replete with sensational allegations, purportedly based on Stuart's confidences to Pauline. Playing the gay card, the authors contend that Stuart and John's personal "intimacy," as evidenced by letters and flat-sharing, proved that the two were secret lovers, all outward evidence of heterosexuality to the contrary.

Pauline went on to posit that Stu's attempt to end the affair after falling in love with Astrid led to a confrontation with Lennon, who assaulted him so badly that it led to his death of a cerebral hemorrhage months latter. (Pauline attempts to link a supposed indentation in her brother's skull with John Lennon's footwear.)

Others had previously alleged that a dust-up with John led to Stu's premature death, as in Albert Goldman's posthumous hatchet job, *The Lives of John Lennon*. But to everyone within their circle, notably Astrid Kircherr, who was closer to Stu than anyone, the allegation was nonsense. (The examining coroner concurred.) That Astrid continued her friendship with John and the Beatles, and never had an unkind word to say about them, speaks volumes about Pauline Sutcliffe's lurid charges.

John Lennon and Brian Epstein

Though nobody ever suggested that John Lennon likewise offed the group's manager, the allegation has lingered that John enjoyed a romantic interlude with Brian. Besides being a staple of every sensationalistic book in the Beatles' literary canon, the notion was the subject of a heavily fictionalized telling in the 1991 film *The Hours and Times*.

Speculation stemmed from the two-week vacation Brian and John took to Spain in spring 1963—alone. Coming less than three weeks after Cynthia gave birth to his son Julian, the trip soon had tongues wagging among their Liverpool acquaintances—though John vehemently denied that anything untoward had happened.

Fueling the widespread belief of an affair was knowledge of Brian Epstein's physical attraction to John. His own urbane persona notwithstanding, Brian's tastes in men, well known to his closest associates, ran more than a little toward the "rough" side. John, while talented and intelligent, was also verbally cruel, aggressive, and somewhat intimidating (though physical violence was more implied than actual).

On the surface, at least, the trip does indeed raise all sorts of red flags. It does seem to be an odd detour just as the Beatles were starting to take off (not to mention Lennon's splitting so quickly after Julian's birth, but such were the times). Years later, Pete Best would reveal having rejected a one-time proposition from Brian; had anyone been aware of this in 1963, no amount of denials would have erased the taint, and the Beatles' career might have ended there.

One Liverpool cohort foolish enough to crack wise about the story, to an inebriated John Lennon's face, was Cavern Club DJ Bob Wooler. In June 1963, at Paul's twenty-first birthday celebration, Wooler's ill-advised joking resulted in a beating from an enraged John that put the DJ in the hospital. While nursing broken ribs, Wooler received a telegram of apology from Lennon, who was otherwise unrepentant about defending himself after being called "a bloody queer."

The account of the Spanish sabbatical that rings truest came from former Quarry Man and close friend Pete Shotton. Years later he would recount discussing the trip with John, who told of being torn between pity for Epstein and the compulsion to torment him. According to Shotton, John went no further than allowing Brian a one-off toss-off. As Shotton observed, "What's a wank between friends?"

Bernard Purdie Was Hired to Replace Ringo's Drumming; Paul Routinely Replaced Ringo's Drumming with His Own

Maryland-born session drummer Bernard "Pretty" Purdie made a name for himself playing with a plethora of jazz and rock greats throughout the '60s and '70s. With work on tracks by Miles Davis, King Curtis, Aretha Franklin, Cat Stevens, and Joe Cocker to his credit, it hardly seems necessary for the man to embellish his résumé.

And yet, in the early 1970s, Purdie began adding the Beatles to his list of clients. Inferring that the band's management felt Ringo's performances were lacking, Purdie told interviewers that he had been hired by Brian Epstein to overdub drumming onto twenty-one Beatles tracks, all of which appeared on their first three Capitol albums.

For his labors, Purdie stated, he'd been paid double his usual rate of $65 an hour, plus a bonus check in five figures as an incentive to keep his mouth shut (a clause he apparently didn't feel bound to respect after ten years).

With so much evidence to the contrary, it's impossible to know where to begin refuting Purdie's nonsense. Ample evidence of Ringo's drumming prowess exists; furthermore, for Purdie's story to hold, there would need to be substantial audible differences between the drums on the U.K. and American issues of the material, and there aren't any.

What is true is that Purdie *was* hired to overdub over *Pete Best's* rather primitive drumming on four of the Tony Sheridan recordings before their 1964 re-issue. Somewhere along the line, the human mythmaking gene allowed Purdie to inflate his actual role into something far more fantastic.

Rather than come to his senses, Purdie repeated the story endlessly. It's perplexing why someone of his stature would seek to tarnish his legacy so needlessly. (As for Ringo, his curt response was simply "You don't bother fighting that shit.")

Part and parcel of the dissing of Ringo's skills is the tale that Paul habitually wiped out drum parts that he was displeased with and replaced them with his own once Starr had left the studio. (This belief is often illustrated with the following undocumented anecdote: when asked if he thought Ringo was the best drummer in rock, John is said to have quipped: "He's not even the best drummer in the Beatles!")

Those who suggest this are a little unclear on how Paul could have pulled off this secret switcheroo without anyone being the wiser, including George Martin, the Beatles' recording engineers, or the other Beatles. They are also hard put to explain why each of Ringo's fellow Beatles tapped his talents for work on their solo albums.

The Beatles and Marijuana

That the Beatles were turned on to smoking pot by Bob Dylan is firmly established in rock lore. (As the story goes, Dylan believed they already indulged, based upon his mis-hearing of "I can't hide" in "I Want to Hold Your Hand" as "I get high," and was amazed to find they did not.)

While it is probably true that Dylan and his retinue turned on Paul, George, and Ringo (along with Brian Epstein) for the first time in the summer of '64, longtime Fab friend Tony Bramwell asserts that Lennon puffed the magic dragon for the first time earlier that year at a party.

Equally popular are two other tales concerning marijuana: one that the boys bolstered themselves before their MBE investiture at Buckingham Palace in 1965 by indulging in a quick spliff in the Queen's loo; the other that they cheekily included cannabis plants in the floral arrangement gracing the *Sgt. Pepper* sleeve. Neither assertion is true. George Harrison later noted that they had simply shared a legal cigarette at the Buckingham Palace, and Paul wrote that the *Sgt. Pepper* sleeve showed "pot plants . . . not *pot* plants, but pot[ted] plants."

The "Butcher Cover" Was a Commentary on Capitol

This oft-repeated legend holds that the Beatles took revenge on Capitol's routine "butchering" of their albums by posing as the meat-cutters from hell on the original cover art to the *Yesterday . . . and Today* release in 1966.

As delightful a payback as this would have been, as it cost Capitol a great deal of time and money to undo the damage, such was not the case. For a detailed explanation of the cover, see the entry in chapter 9 of this book.

"Lucy in the Sky with Diamonds" Stands for "LSD"

Another specious bit of folklore that is likely to endure is that John deliberately encoded this proto-psychedelic track from *Sgt. Pepper's* with a none-too-subtle endorsement of hallucinogenics. On the surface, the bizarre imagery evoked by the lyrics could, to the uninitiated, seem to describe an acid trip.

In fact, it was more a deliberate cop of Lewis Carroll's *Through the Looking Glass* (just as *Alice in Wonderland* similarly inspired Jefferson Airplane's "White Rabbit" that same year). But the title itself, as Lennon's oft-told explanation reveals, came directly from his son.

Four-year-old Julian Lennon had come home from school with an ornate pastel picture he had drawn and was eager, as four-year-olds are, to show his father. When asked by John what it was, Julian explained that it was "Lucy, in the sky, with diamonds." The girl in question was Lucy O'Donnell, whom Julian years later surmised that he might have had a crush on. Struck by the poetry of the description, John immediately set about to using it.

Others witnessed the scene, and amazingly enough, the drawing itself still exists. But within weeks of the song's release, people all over the world noticed the same distinct pattern and did the math. When it was pointed

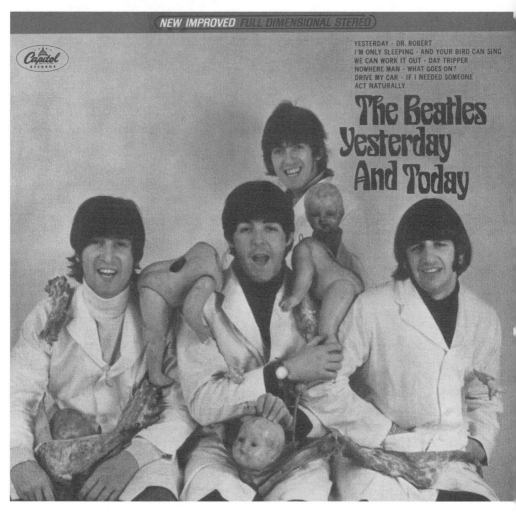

The "Butcher cover" remains one of the most coveted of Beatle collectibles. Pristine copies from a stash found in 1986 in Capitol President Alan Livingston's closet have fetched prices in five figures.

out to him, a flummoxed John then began examining the titles to *all* of his recorded output to see what they spelled out. (Nothing, as it happened.)

What added weight to the notion in the public's mind, John's protests to the contrary, was the admission by Paul (a couple of weeks after *Sgt. Pepper's* release) that the Beatles had, in fact, tried acid. The resulting uproar, ironically unleashed by the Beatle *least* enthused about taking that first trip, set the table for the more conservative members of the public to believe the Beatles capable of *any* abomination.

John would admit to taking hundreds of acid trips (including an accidental one at EMI studios), so the story of his inspiration for "Lucy" makes little sense as an invention. Later that year, he would likewise be pilloried for supposedly having the choir on "I Am the Walrus" sing "smoke pot, smoke pot, everybody smoke pot." As he told an interviewer in his own defense, he would never be so "gross." The lyrics? "Everybody's got one."

George's "Something" Was Written about Pattie

Patricia Anne Boyd Harrison Clapton is often called rock's greatest muse, inspiring some of the greatest classics of the genre. Certainly, most everyone is aware of the romantic torment that Eric Clapton suffered after falling in love with his best friend's wife; he profitably parlayed that obsession into "Layla"—twice. Slowhand's subsequent prom staple "Wonderful Tonight" was written after the two officially coupled up.

Equally believed to have been inspired by the toothy beauty was George's "Something," widely regarded as his compositional high-water mark as a Beatle. Certainly, the song's accompanying video plays up the romantic love angle, featuring footage of all the Beatles and their partners, with particular emphasis on George and Pattie.

Given the sheer romanticism associated with the song, it certainly makes for a sweet story to infer that George had his bride in mind when he began writing it during the "White Album" sessions, except that he didn't. He begrudgingly allowed people to believe that the way Pattie moved attracted him like no other lover, but when pressed, he took great pains to explain that his primary source of inspiration for "Something" was neither her nor any other woman, nor even God, the standard Harrison wellspring.

It was Ray Charles. The American soul legend was foremost in George's mind as he wrote the song on piano, envisioning Charles's gravelly vocals adding a bluesy gravitas that he could only dream of providing. Eventually, Brother Ray would fulfill George's expectations on 1971's intriguingly titled *Volcanic Action of My Soul* release. But prior to that version, Sheffield shouter Joe Cocker did the honors.

The tune itself took some time to finish after the initial inspiration struck. Having cribbed the song's opening line from McCartney protégé James Taylor, George was stuck lyrically for months, substituting "attracts me like a pomegranate" until finally realizing the finished line. Apparently no one else on the Apple roster had any lyrics worth borrowing.

Interestingly, the Beatles' original take featured a four-minute piano-based coda not unlike the one "Layla" would showcase a year later. After the piano part was summarily lopped off in editing, John would revisit the chord sequence, turning it into "Remember" on his 1970 solo outing, *Plastic Ono Band.*

Yoko Ono Broke up the Beatles

Clearly the pairing of an unconventional New York artist with the least conventional Beatle stirred up a torrent of hostility from the public, most of it undeserved. With the group falling apart before the eyes of the world, Yoko became the lightning rod for all the frustration and resentment that the fans had heretofore kept in check.

It didn't help that Ms. Ono's arrival on the scene coincided with a period of transformation that the most devoted of fans would have found challenging to keep up with. By the time she and John went public with their romance, the Beatles had undergone more changes in two years than they had in the several that preceded them.

The end of touring, studio innovations, the trappings of psychedelia (in fashion as well as music) and the musicians' changing looks, with facial hair coming and going at random, combined for a disquieting unpredictability. Though the music, diverse as it was, continued to set rock's standards, the public was losing its sense of who the boys were these days. (Or, as Bob Dylan remarked to Paul after hearing *Sgt. Pepper's* for the first time, "Oh, I get it—you don't want to be cute anymore.")

Their zenith of cuteness behind them, the Beatles' internal turmoil was on the upswing. Caught between the resentment of her boyfriend's partners and hostility from fans in no mood to accept the change foisted on them, Yoko found herself in the center of an extremely volatile situation.

In fairness, it can be said that she did not go out of her way to make herself easy to like. But only the weak-minded could believe that the most successful band in the world could be knocked over so easily. It would be far more accurate to say that Yoko was scapegoated by fans who found it difficult to accept a disintegration set into motion even *before* the passing of Brian Epstein.

Any number of strains contributed to the decay of the Beatles: the financial mess they brought upon themselves with Apple; the infighting over the choice of a new manager; and the need for each band member to assert his individuality and demand a bigger slice of the group pie. But in the end, all four Beatles had grown up, and found that they no longer needed a boys' club from which to draw strength to face the world.

To assert with a straight face that Yoko Ono broke up the Beatles is to demonstrate the need by some for simple (if inaccurate) answers to explain away their hurt. For many, the end of the Beatles and the music they collectively made represents an end to the exuberance of their *own* youth; it is this that they truly mourn.

Will You Read My Book?

The Essential Beatle Bookshelf

Stores all over the world stock literally hundreds of books written about the Fabs. Among the recipe books, trivia tomes, cheap cash-ins, reminiscences of aging B-list acquaintances, paranoid ravings, sloppily researched histories, and airings of dirty laundry, there exists an armful of absolutely necessary books for serious Beatles fans.

Delving into the books mentioned below should give readers a great understanding of the Beatles' history, ranging from their childhoods in Liverpool through their adolescent adventures in Germany, fame in England and around the world, their halcyon days, breakup, and destinies. Here's the best information on their music, their films, their lives, and—yes—their dirty laundry.

And in the great Beatles tradition of fourteen-song albums, giving value for the pound, this list reaches a baker's dozen.

The Beatles: An Authorized Biography, by Hunter Davies (1968)

Davies wrote the "Swinging London" novel *Here We Go Round the Mulberry Bush* as well as its subsequent 1967 screenplay. Around that time, the thirty-year-old Brit approached Brian Epstein about penning an official Beatles bio.

The group, tired of endless interviews, liked the idea of putting all of their frequently asked questions into book form so that they wouldn't have to keep answering the same old queries. Davies received unprecedented journalistic access to the band; he attended the recording session for "Getting Better," witnessed a songwriting session at Paul's house in Cavendish, and visited each of the Fabs' homes, interviewing them, their spouses, and old friends and business acquaintances.

The information on the group's pre-fame history is nearly unmatched, even these many years later, and the portraits Davies paints of the various

Beatle marriages and homes are both sentimental and heartbreaking. *The Beatles*, unstinting in its talk of sex, drugs, religion, fame, and, most of all, music, is the first serious biography of a rock-and-roll act, and as such set the standard for all such books.

In later years, Davies has produced columns for several British newspapers and magazines, written children's fiction, and chronicled his passion for soccer.

Lennon Remembers, by Jann Wenner (1972)

Getting John Lennon to sit down and focus long enough to get facts straight was a fool's errand. Details were just not his thing.

But if you want the intensity, the drive, and the balls-out, "Who cares how the victim feels?" and "I may not even feel this way tomorrow" sting of John's barbed wit, along with insights into the mind of a brilliant and difficult artist/activist/pop idol, this transcription of a harrowing, intense 1970 *Rolling Stone* interview is *the* book (although it must be said that Lennon never intended for his spew to be codified in book form, and was mortified and angry when *Rolling Stone* did exactly that).

In what was, at the time, a truly revolutionary interview, Lennon tore into the Beatle myth ("we were just a band who made it very, very big—that's all"), dissed George Martin for the quality of the band's recordings, ripped Paul and George for their dislike of Yoko Ono, and laid waste to the '60s dream. But amid the vitriol, John also lets slip a few moments of fondness and tenderness for his former mates and shows a passion for his peace work.

Eight years following the book's publication, a happier Lennon also sat for another huge interview, this one with *Playboy's* David Sheff, on the release of 1980's *Double Fantasy*. Mere days after Lennon, Ono, and Sheff concluded the multiday session, Lennon was assassinated.

The book that followed, first published as *The Playboy Interviews* and most recently as *All We Are Saying*, is also a tremendous achievement. Lennon talks about nearly every Beatles song, and Sheff gets the former Fab (and, at times, Yoko) to discuss his musical peers, his personal history, his marriages, and his own demons.

The Longest Cocktail Party, by Richard DiLello (1972)

Of the several books written about the Beatles' disastrous Apple Corps project, this is the most interesting, partly because its stream-of-consciousness approach mirrors the stoned reverie of the company's early days.

As the fledgling company's "house hippie," American-in-London DiLello, hired literally after walking in off the street, first did all sorts of busywork—delivering packages to Buckingham Palace, rolling joints for the office, and listening to demo tapes from groups hoping to be signed to Apple—before eventually graduating into PR man Derek Taylor's assistant.

DiLello's funny and chilling tales of Apple's ambitious plans, endless parties, and spectacular flameout are engrossing as well as cautionary. Taylor reads as a lovable but flawed figure, with the Beatles themselves variously given to micromanagement and utter lack of concern. The glimpses of Apple artists like Badfinger and Mary Hopkin are unparalleled. Allen Klein, who, brought into the save the company, instead destroyed it, comes off the worst.

Two other books written about Apple also have much to recommend them. Peter McCabe's *Apple to the Core*, from 1976, is more thorough in its dissection of why Apple failed, and how the Beatles themselves helped to subvert the project, with their own hippie idealism and through their behind-the-scenes plotting. It's not as much fun to read, though, as DiLello's account.

A third examination of Apple, *Those Were the Days*, by Stefan Granados, is less well known, but also excellent. What Granados adds to the discussion is a review of Apple's history through the 1980s, 1990s, and early 2000s, when, under the auspices of Neil Aspinall, the label reemerged as the chief steward of the band's recorded work.

On the subject of books written by Beatles "insiders," most of them aren't worth much, but a few stand out. Tony Bramwell, a longtime Fab friend who plugged their records for years, wrote *Magical Mystery Tours* (2005), which offers new information and plenty of background on Swinging London. The Beatles' 1968 India sojourn with Maharishi Mahesh Yogi is lovingly and beautifully related in Paul Saltzman's 1999 work *The Beatles in Rishikesh*.

The Beatles: An Illustrated Record, by Roy Carr and Tony Tyler (1975)

This beautifully laid-out package, shaped like a record album at twelve by twelve inches, discusses each Beatles British 45 and LP release, as well as all of their solo material. Chock full of pictures rare even in the '70s, *An Illustrated Record* also features a timeline and a discography.

Carr, a musician in the '60s who played shows on bills with the Fabs, interviewed John and Yoko in 1972, and has remained a champion of new music. Both he and Tyler worked for *New Musical Express* and brought years of observation of the contemporary British rock scene to this work.

While Carr and Tyler made a few mistakes, and are occasionally too cute for their own good (especially discussing some of the Fabs' not-so-listenable solo releases), this still ranks as one of the best Beatles books ever.

An Illustrated Record, updated in both 1978 and 1981, served as a critical text for many a fanatical '70s and early '80s Beatles fan. A further update, twenty-five years on, could be fascinating.

In the last twenty years, several more authors have taken on thorough analyses of the Fabs' music. Among these attempts are Ian McDonald's 1994

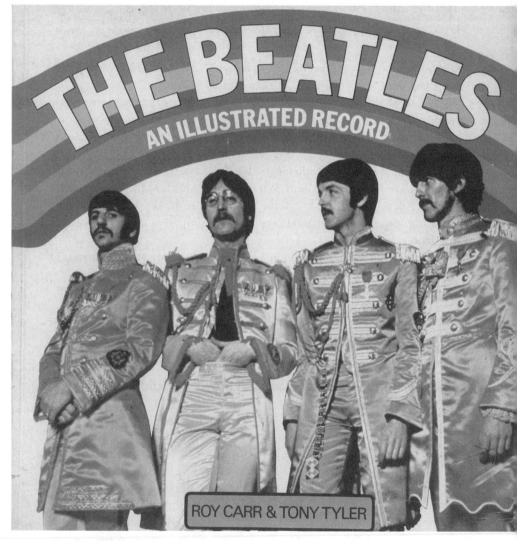

For Beatle fans of a certain age, this snarky but loving assessment of the Beatles' recordings made an indelible impression.

A Revolution in the Head (although it's not really for fans who prefer the group's final three LPs), *Tell Me Why*, by Tim Riley, and, for those obsessed by the seemingly endless early 1969 "Get Back" sessions, Doug Sulpy's *Get Back: The Unauthorized Chronicle of the Beatles' 'Let It Be' Disaster* (originally titled *Drugs, Divorce, and a Slipping Image*).

The Man Who Gave the Beatles Away, by Allan Williams and William Marshall (1975)

Until this book came along, most accounts of the Fabs' early days were founded upon myth, touching on a few salient points before jumping to "Love Me Do." But this book, the would-be memoirs of the band's first serious mentor, tells the story of their origins as musically crude teenage louts, all the way through their joining forces with Brian Epstein as musically focused, slightly older louts.

This volume is unique in all of Beatles literature, from its tone, which swerves wildly between tragicomedy and self-pity, to its insight into the personalities that developed into the most famous foursome in rock. (Ringo, though not a part of the band during their professional association with Williams, figures throughout as a kindred soul within their orbit.) No less an authority than John Lennon endorsed the book in its depiction of the pre-fame Beatles in all their scatological glory.

Though the tales are clearly rooted in Williams's real-life experience, the quotes from conversations that occurred decades before must lead the reader to question their veracity. But this is part of the book's charm; Williams and Marshall's work comes off like nothing so much as the ramblings of a drinking buddy, looking back with pride and regret on a past that earned him the book's title distinction.

The Beatles Forever, by Nicholas Schaffner (1977)

This history of the Beatles, ranging from their early years through 1976, emerges here from the pen of an original 1964-vintage fan who grew up in New York City.

Schaffner's work is almost a Beatles 101, written informatively but in a breezy and witty style. He ties the group's work both to his own growth—though not in the style of Ron Schaumburg's embarrassing *Growing Up with the Beatles*—and that of the entire contemporary culture.

This book, along with Carr and Tyler's *Illustrated Record*, filled a serious void at the time in Beatles history. Schaffner's work is one of the best books about the group ever written, and an entire generation of Beatles fans still swears by it, thanks to Schaffner's excellent prose and organizational skills.

A musician himself and a sometime guest at Beatlefest, Nicholas Schaffner tragically died of AIDS-related complex in 1991. He also wrote two books on Pink Floyd as well as others about the Beatles and the British Invasion, but this is his unquestioned masterpiece.

Paperback Writer, by Mark Shipper (1978)

Shipper's tribute-cum-parody is the funniest book ever written about rock and roll.

Published in the late '70s, at the height of speculation that the Beatles would (and should) somehow reunite, *Paperback Writer* is a remarkably good "alternate" history of the Fab Four—especially considering that it's fictional.

Shipper goes through the group's early releases (their debut album is titled *We're Gonna Change the Face of Music Forever*, while "Shake Your Booty," rather than "Yesterday," is the first rock 45 ever done with a string quartet) and reaches his peak with the *Sgt. Pepper* album, cast as a commentary on the British military. The story doesn't end with their last album, *The Beatles Break Up*, but extends into the dry solo years as well.

Though he's making it all up, Shipper writes about the band's career, aftermath, and eventual letdown of a reunion as only a true Beatles lover could—with humor, knowledge, and empathy.

Shamefully, this great book is currently out of print. But it is available from various online sellers and shouldn't cost you more than $10.

The Unseen Beatles, by Bob Whitaker (1991)

Several photographers have released collections of their Fab photos, including Dezo Hoffman (*With the Beatles*), Harry Benson (*The Beatles: Now and Then*), Ethan Russell (*Dear Mr. Fantasy*), and Robert Freeman (*Yesterday* and *The Beatles: A Private View*). All are good. Whitaker's, however, is on another level entirely.

The Australian photog shared with the Beatles a sense of whimsy and a love for modern, boundary-pushing art. Whitaker also shared manager Brian Epstein's sense of erudition and class, which helped him form a stronger relationship with the band than some other photographers could have done.

This relationship, particularly fruitful in 1965–66, helps explain some of the wilder photos Whitaker took of the band, including the hip, almost

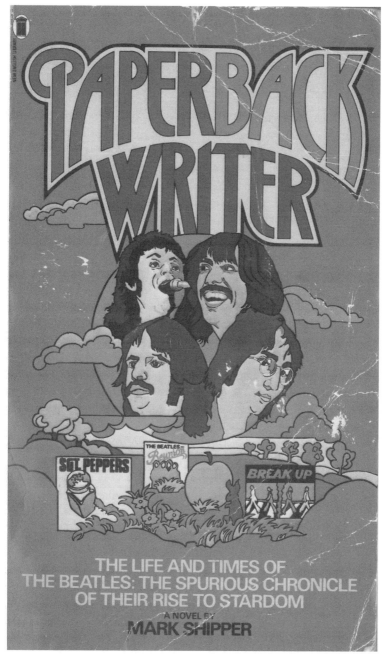

Alongside Eric Idle's Rutles mockumentary, *Paperback Writer* (1977) remains the most spot-on Beatles satire. Today, author Mark Shipper works behind the scenes in radio.

menacing back cover of *Revolver*, the portrait used as the "butcher cover" of *Yesterday . . . and Today*, and various shots of the boys at their homes and on tour in 1966.

The Beatles Recording Sessions, by Mark Lewisohn (1988)

Possibly the most important Beatles book ever published started as an Abbey Road studios project undertaken by terminally ill employee John Barrett. Suffering from a cancer that would kill him in 1984, he stayed busy through his illness by logging the details of every single Beatles master tape (most of which had been recorded at EMI/Abbey Road).

Executives at Abbey Road eventually decided that Barrett's logs would make an excellent book. The hardcover publication of *The Beatles Recording Sessions* was a landmark; never before had the public read so much information about the Fabs in the studio.

For every Beatles song, Lewisohn listed recording dates, studio location, number of takes, original titles, and studio personnel. His accompanying text and interviews covered group arguments and between-songs chatter, inside stories of songwriting, the hiring of outside musicians, Beatle in-studio drug use, and, above all, the evolution of the recording process from the twelve-hour session needed to record the *Please Please Me* LP in 1963 to the more than one hundred takes of the unreleased "Not Guilty."

(In some cases, however, Lewisohn did *not* spill some fairly significant beans, especially considering those songs on which a Beatle for some reason might not have appeared, or a famous, uncredited guest *might* have.)

For those who find the endless details about takes, retakes, and outtakes exhausting, Lewisohn's fascinating *Complete Beatles Chronicle* (1992) is instead recommended. The recording information has been boiled down, and Lewisohn adds in its stead a thorough list of all relevant Beatle doings and news from June 9, 1957 through March 10, 1970. *Chronicle* also features, though in small print, a complete discography, a list of every Beatles live concert, all the songs they ever played onstage, and each BBC radio appearance.

If further recording studio information is what you want, however, George Martin's *All You Need Is Ears* is a fine place to start. And in 2006, Geoff Emerick, Beatles engineer extraordinaire, published his studio memoir, *Here, There, and Everywhere*.

Lewisohn is currently working on what may be the most ballyhooed Beatles book of all, a decade-long project intended as the ultimate Fabs tome. It certainly *won't* be the last word, but given Lewisohn's excellent track record, his Sisyphean task should at least be fascinating—even if, as some claim, there isn't much new to say about his subjects.

Many Years from Now, by Paul McCartney with Barry Miles (1997)

Most official biographies of musicians are long on hyperbole and short on content. But to his credit, McCartney—apparently a control freak par excellence—pretty much let Barry Miles, an old friend and fellow member of the 1960s London underground, do his job.

Since John Lennon's death, McCartney has wrestled with the specter of a Beatle who remained frozen in time and never had to grow older as The Cute One has. McCartney's seemingly endless "But I was hipper than John in the mid-'60s" campaign has embarrassed plenty of fans, but Miles sensibly reins in Paul's tendency toward self-justification (as if such justification were even needed; how many people have a better résumé than *Paul McCartney?*).

While McCartney and Miles didn't do the song-by-song run-through featured in David Sheff's 1981 Lennon book, much of Bassman's career is dissected in impressive detail. Anecdotes about family, friends, Swinging London, songwriting, meeting and "pulling" Linda, and the disintegration of the Beatles abound, although many of Paul's missteps and less stellar moments are papered over or ignored entirely.

John Lennon never commissioned or wrote his own "official" story; Ray Coleman wrote a decent bio (*Lennon*) in 1984, while Albert Goldman's 1988 hatchet job is best suited for a steaming garbage dump.

George Harrison's autobiography, *I Me Mine*, is lighthearted and fun, while those looking for a slightly more linear text are pointed toward Alan Clayson's *The Quiet One* from 1991. Clayson also penned *Straight Man or Joker?* about Ringo Starr in 1998, although both of his books suffer significantly from the scrivener's stultifying surfeit of superfluous syntax.

The Beatles Anthology, by the Beatles (2000)

Five years after the groundbreaking television special and three-volume double-CD issues of the same name, the Beatles finally got around to releasing the long-promised companion book.

Unlike most Beatles books offering historical narratives, this one tells the group's history *entirely* in the words of the Fab Four and, occasionally, trusted friends and colleagues such as George Martin, Derek Taylor, and Neil Aspinall.

The exhaustive collection of interviews (some exclusive for the book), along with some previously unseen photos, makes this a necessary document. It is also one of the most beautiful Beatles books ever published. With Harrison's death in 2001, it is likely to stand as the band's definitive official literary statement.

Beatles Gear, by Andy Babiuk (2001)

Since the early 1980s, Babiuk has been bassist and backing vocalist for the hard-rocking '60s-style garage group the Chesterfield Kings. He also works at Rochester, New York's House of Guitars, one of the country's most celebrated music stores. Babiuk, the store, and the band are *fanatical* about vintage musical equipment, from Rickenbacker guitars to Hofner basses to Vox organs.

Hence Babiuk is on familiar ground for this book, which examines in great detail the equipment the Fabs used on stage and on record. The result of a lot of painstaking research, and some unprecedented access to Beatles equipment, *Beatles Gear* is packed with photos and interviews from unlikely sources. This work answers nearly every question you could ever think up about the drums, axes, and keyboards the Beatles used.

It's one of the few Beatles books that is so good, and so complete, that further exposition on the subject is almost impossible.

The Beatles Are Coming!, by Bruce Spizer (2003)

Spizer, one of the U.S.'s foremost authorities on Beatles history, has written several excellent volumes on the Beatles' various American record labels (Vee-Jay, Capitol, and Apple); all of his books are worth reading.

If you're going to have just one, though—and they're not cheap, at least in hardcover—it might well be this one, the story of how Capitol Records, which had thrice rejected the band's singles, finally got religion and, in late 1963, began their campaign to popularize the Beatles in America.

Spizer interviews Capitol personnel (including label president Alan Livingston), prints original and re-created promotional material and memos, and utilizes a witty, engaging storytelling style to relate how a combination of smart promotion; groundbreaking music; television, radio, and press exposure; and plain old dumb luck converged at the right time to hit America right between the eyes.

He also offers up a very funny "alternate history" examining what might have happened had Capitol chosen to release "She Loves You" in 1963.

Listen to the Music Playing in Your Head

The Recordings

The Beatles on Apple

HEY
JUDE
(Lennon
& McCartney)

THE
BEATLES
Maclen
Music Inc. BMI
7:04
2276
45 X 46414

Produced by George Martin
Recorded in England

Though pressed on labels featuring the distinctive Granny Smith apple from this release forward, records by the Beatles themselves were actually still considered Parlophone and Capitol product, as evidenced by their catalog numbers.

14

It's a Clean Machine

Ten Beatles Instruments

Rockers have long been identified with specific guitars or basses. Chuck Berry had his classic Gibson; the Ventures became spokesmen for Mosrite guitars; the Beach Boys built their sound around the Fender Stratocaster.

The Beatles' instruments have spawned at least one book (Andy Babiuk's essential *Beatles Gear*, from which much of the technical information in this chapter has been gleaned) and articles in countless magazines full of fanatical study about the details of how the Fab Four got *those sounds* on their records.

Several instrument companies, including Rickenbacker, Vox, Gretsch, Ludwig, and Hofner, benefited from their association with the Beatles, who in turn were often allowed to try new equipment and technology before anyone else. Other companies, such as Fender, Guild, and Gibson, tried—usually with little success—to get the band to use their products.

Here are some of the tools that John, Paul, George, and Ringo used to make *those sounds* on *those records*.

Rickenbacker 325 Electric Guitar

Back in the late 1950s, British kids idolized American guitars—any American guitars—because, due to trade issues, U.S.-made axes were unavailable in the U.K. except by long-delayed mail order.

On a 1960 Beatles trip to Hamburg, Lennon found a Rickenbacker 325 guitar in a music shop. Having already seen pictures of Rickenbackers, he liked the guitar, which was smaller than most electric guitars but had an interesting, pointy-ended shape and a natural-wood finish. (Lennon would later have the guitar painted, the black 325 providing one of many iconic images of Beatlemania. The newer 325 he bought in 1964 was also black.)

Lennon loved the Rickenbacker 325, and in fact retained his first "real guitar" until his death. He enjoyed its extremely small fretboard, which made it easy to hold down barre chords and play high up the neck. In addition, these short Rickenbackers have excellent "action" (i.e., the strings are very close to the neck, making playing that much easier).

The 325 has a chunky, trebly tone, as do most Rickenbackers, but due to its solid body does not jangle as much as the hollow-body Ricks that George Harrison later used. You can hear Lennon's 325 tone in the triplet-strumming on "All My Loving," the chugging rhythm of "I Want to Hold Your Hand," and the almost honking sound of "When I Get Home."

Every current Beatles sound-alike band has to have the 325 for its rhythm guitarist, but the most famous recent user of the Lennon-styled guitar is Susanna Hoffs of the Bangles. After years of playing a 325, she asked Rickenbacker to design her a custom 350, a hollow-body guitar close in size, shape, and tone to the 325.

Gretsch Country Gentleman and Gretsch Tennessean Electric Guitars

George had liked the sound of Gretsch guitars ever since he first heard Chet Atkins and Duane Eddy play them in the late 1950s. But buying American guitars in England wasn't easy.

A lucky break got George his first Gretsch, a black solid-body Duo Jet, in July 1961. An American sailor had brought the guitar to the U.K., and Harrison's eyes popped when he saw the "for sale" ad in the Liverpool *Echo*.

Harrison loved his Gretsch Duo Jet but wanted the deeper, richer sound of the hollow-body guitar, which was what Atkins and Eddy were playing. He eventually supplanted the Duo Jet with a hollow-body Country Gentleman model in 1963, which he soon had painted black from its natural dark-wood finish.

The Country Gent is a large but not overly thick or heavy guitar. This was George's axe on many great *With the Beatles* songs, including "Roll Over Beethoven," "It Won't Be Long," and "All My Loving." He also used it on "She Loves You" and "I Want to Hold Your Hand."

In December '63, shortly before the group first came to America, George also acquired a smaller Gretsch, a red Chet Atkins Tennessean, which he used often in 1964–65. This beautiful bright-red instrument emitted a slightly more country-ish sound than the Country Gentleman and helped give a twang to such tracks as "Act Naturally," "Baby's in Black," and "I Don't Want to Spoil the Party."

As is true with the Rickenbacker 325, every Beatles tribute band worth its imported salt has to have a Country Gent in stock for the early numbers. Otherwise, however, these classic Gretsches have fallen from popular use, which is quite a shame—they are majestic guitars with impeccable tone.

Hofner 500/1 Electric Bass

When Stu Sutcliffe's departure from the Beatles necessitated a new bass player, Paul McCartney didn't exactly jump. He wanted to remain on guitar, or maybe move to piano, but given Harrison's stature as lead player and Lennon's stature as lead vocalist, McCartney was—to his regret—a natural choice for bass.

Since Sutcliffe had been using a large, hollow-body Hofner 333 bass, and McCartney a left-handed-strung Hofner Club 40 guitar, making the change to the Hofner "violin"-style bass wasn't a complete leap of faith.

So during 1961, in Hamburg, when he saw a Hofner in a shop for a relatively affordable £30, McCartney, chary of going too deeply into debt and liking the bass's small, symmetrical shape, ordered a left-handed version, which he picked up not long afterward.

The 500/1's distinctive "violin" body made it stand out from its larger, bulkier competitors such as the Fender Precision bass and the Gibson SG. The tone of the Hofner was thumpy but clean, with little distortion, which suited McCartney's innovatively melodic and solid bass playing on the early Beatles records.

McCartney later upgraded to a '63 Hofner bass, which he used on the group's subsequent tours and recordings.

After taking up the Rickenbacker 4001 bass in late 1965, Paul let his Hofners lie unused for a while, but he picked up his original Hofner in early 1969 when the Beatles began the "Get Back" sessions. Perhaps McCartney was hoping to regain some of the feel of the group's rock-and-roll origins. The '61 model was soon stolen, but McCartney played the '63 on most of the *Let It Be* LP.

The most famous bassist in the world has continued to rely on the Hofner during his solo years, for recording, on tour, and in videos such as 1979's "Coming Up," when he donned a collarless jacket and swept his hair into a mop in an imitation of . . . guess who?

Ludwig Drums

Pete Best, longtime Beatles drummer, was a Premier drums man. Although Ringo Starr, who replaced Best in August 1962, later became famous for his Ludwig drums, he started off with the band playing a Premier set. This was a simple kit with 1) a bass drum with an attached tom-tom, 2) a freestanding floor tom-tom, 3) a very shallow snare drum, 4) high-hat cymbals, and 5) a freestanding crash cymbal.

In April 1963, Starr upgraded to a new Ludwig set and stayed with that manufacturer for his entire time with the Beatles. All of Ringo's drums in the early days had what was called an "oyster pearl" silver-and-black finish.

Starr, a rocking drummer who played his cymbals hard and could drive the kick with the best of them, found Ludwig kits a perfect match. By 1964, he was on his second Ludwig, with a larger bass drum and a pair of upgraded cymbals (replacing his Paistes with the less "European"-sounding Zildjians).

That kit, delivered in early 1964, served Ringo well for four years, on tour and on record. During that time, improvements in recording technology made Starr's already inventive drumming sound even better; one would scarcely recognize the superb fills on *Sgt. Pepper's* as coming from the same kit that gave us his groundbreaking performance on "Rain" one year before. The "White Album" sessions saw the 1964 kit's final use, for early in 1969 Ringo upgraded to his fourth Ludwig kit, the "Hollywood," featuring a natural wood-tone finish and dual rack-mounted toms.

For Ringo, the real breakthrough came when he replaced his standard plastic drum heads with the more unusual calfskin ones. His tom-toms now had a richer, warmer tone that tea-towel muting couldn't equal. With this new inspiration, his fills became ubiquitous, culminating with the understated but rock-solid solo on *Abbey Road's* "The End" (which the ever self-effacing Ringo had to be *convinced* to record).

Gibson J-160e Acoustic Guitar

After being signed to Parlophone in 1962, the Beatles had to think about how to adapt their sound to records. This process entailed the use of acoustic guitar as a background "space filler." Had the group simply gone into recording sessions with its two-electric lineup, the guitars would have been a bit thinner, and the material possibly not as distinctive.

Both George and John's acoustic guitar of choice in those days was the Gibson J-160, which provided a rich and full sound with a built-in electric pickup. The Gibson wasn't an inexpensive guitar, and Lennon was crushed when his was swiped, probably from a dressing room, around the time of the band's Christmas shows in London in December 1963.

By now, however, Lennon could afford another J-160, and got it shortly afterward. He played it on many of the group's songs in 1964, including "Can't Buy Me Love," "Things We Said Today," "I'll Be Back," and "And I Love Her," among others.

While the group fiddled around with all sorts of acoustics during the 1960s, including models by Framus (their twelve-string was a favorite of

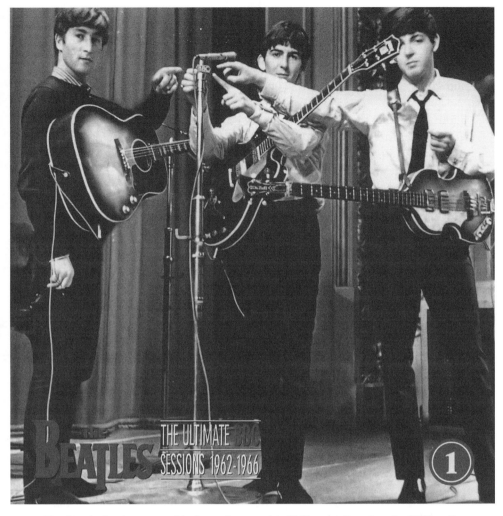

The Beatles' guitar arsenal is shown here at this 1963 recording date for BBC radio. They are (from left to right) John's Gibson J-160E, George's Gretsch Country Gentleman, and Paul's distinctive violin-shaped Hofner 500/1 bass.

George's) and Martin (Paul and John played them on much of *The Beatles*), the J-160 was nearly always Lennon's go-to acoustic.

After a couple of different paint jobs, including one in a psychedelic blue-and-lavender pattern, Lennon stripped the color from the Gibson in 1968 and continued using it on tracks such as "Hey Jude" and "Give Peace a Chance," which was recorded live in a Montreal hotel room in 1969.

Rickenbacker 330-12 and 360-12 Twelve-String Electric Guitars

When Harrison went to visit his sister Louise in the United States in 1963, he bought a solid-bodied Rickenbacker 425 guitar. This first Rick served him only briefly, including once on a telecast of *Ready Steady Go!*, a British pop show. Harrison soon gave it to a guitarist playing with fellow Liverpudlians the Fourmost.

In early 1964, Rickenbacker aggressively courted the Fab Four in New York, presenting a sick-in-bed George with a recent company innovation—a 330 model with twelve strings—on February 8. Perhaps the company had seen the recent "folk music" boom, and its use of twelve-string acoustic guitars, as an inspiration.

The ringing quality of the hollow-body guitar entranced Harrison, who immediately began using it on Beatles recordings. The first appearance of the 330-12 came as a rhythm guitar on "Can't Buy Me Love," recorded in Paris on January 29, 1964. George continued to work with the guitar and used it for several iconic Beatles lead parts, including those on "A Hard Day's Night," "I Should Have Known Better," and "Ticket to Ride."

John Lennon, impressed with the expanded sound of the 330-12, asked Rickenbacker to custom-make a 325 with twelve strings, but the small, solid body of the guitar did not allow the strings to "ring" properly. (Lennon also played, briefly in 1964, a 1995 model; this hollow Rickenbacker was similar to but larger than his 325.)

Starting in summer 1965, Harrison began to use another Rickenbacker twelve-string, a 360, which is physically differentiated from the 330 by the rounded, rather than pointed, borders to its curvier body. Sonically, it's a bit creamier and richer than the 330.

Harrison used the 360 twelve-string for performances of "If I Needed Someone" on the 1966 world tour and *Rubber Soul*. The electric twelve-string was last used on a Beatles session in early 1966 in an early, rejected take of "And Your Bird Can Sing."

Of all Beatle instruments, the twelve-string electric guitar had the biggest impact on other rock musicians. Upon seeing Harrison play the twelve-string in *A Hard Day's Night*, Jim McGuinn bought one, helping give the Byrds their signature sound. All sorts of singers and bands from the mid-'60s onward—including the Who, Steppenwolf, Tom Petty, the Jam, the Romantics, XTC, and R.E.M.—have relied on the magical, jangly, and surprisingly muscular tones of Rickenbacker guitars.

Sitar

In his capacity as lead guitarist, George Harrison took it upon himself to search for new sounds to color Beatles records. He used tremolo on 1963's "Don't Bother Me," explored the twelve-string sound in 1964, and utilized the volume/tone pedal on "Yes It Is" from early 1965.

Around the same time, while on the set of the group's second film, *Help!*, George became intrigued with the exotic (at least to an English twenty-two-year-old) sound of the sitar, a multi-stringed Indian instrument.

Harrison's curiosity led to him purchase an inexpensive sitar and pick up a few elementary licks. (The Byrds' David Crosby, a Beatle-hangout friend in America, credits himself with pointing George toward some Ravi

Prevailing upon the world's foremost sitar maestro for private lessons is a little like asking Yo-Yo Ma to teach you to play the cello. Despite his hubris, George and Ravi became lifelong friends.   *Photo by David Redfern/Redferns*

Shankar records). Eventually George felt comfortable enough to use a sitar as a central instrument on *Rubber Soul's* "Norwegian Wood (This Bird Has Flown)" although his playing sounded worse than amateurish to any experienced sitar player.

The sitar operates on a different musical scale than the guitar, piano, or any Western instrument. While one can pick out rudimentary notes on the sitar by playing it in a guitar-like fashion, truly learning the instrument, Indian music theory, and its entire system of tuning requires years of study.

After being introduced to Ravi Shankar in 1965 through the offices of London's Asian Music Circle, George took some lessons from the master, who himself was no stranger to the idea of bridging Eastern and Western music, having recorded an often thrilling album of jazz/Indian fusion with session men extraordinaire Bud Shank and Dennis Budimir in Los Angeles in 1961. George became reasonably proficient at the instrument and, in 1966, following the end of the group's final tour, he and his wife, Pattie, even traveled to India for several weeks.

Harrison composed "Love You To" and "Within You Without You" in the Indian style, creating entrancing East/West soundscapes that sounded like no pop music that had come before. He also added drones and Eastern patterns to many of his other mid-to-late-'60s compositions, such as "Blue Jay Way," "The Inner Light," and "Long Long Long." Late in 1968, George decided to give up his intense sitar lessons, but he continued to champion Ravi Shankar and his music, taking him on tour in 1974 and producing Shankar's *Chants of India* CD in 1997.

While Harrison lacked the time and the discipline to truly master the sitar, he did wonders for the popularity of the instrument, and, more important, he learned to integrate Eastern philosophy into his life. As much as George Harrison did to introduce Westerners to Eastern instruments, he did more for himself by embracing a spiritual path, crediting meditation and prayer with getting him through rocky times and allowing him to live more peacefully.

Epiphone Casino Es-230 Electric Guitar

Every electric guitar maker in the world spent the mid-'60s trying to get its newest instrument into the hands of a Beatle. Even one photo of a Beatle with a particular guitar was advertising heaven for the lucky instrument maker.

Representatives of Fender, Martin, Guild, Vox, Coral, Burns, Gibson, and others did their best to get guitars, electric sitars, and basses to the

Fab Four. The group did use Fender Stratocasters on "Nowhere Man," but mostly stuck to Gretsch, Hofner, and Rickenbacker through 1965. (George would later drench his Strat in psychedelic colors, as seen in *Magical Mystery Tour*. Later, after the instrument had been set up for slide playing, it made an appearance—along with George, though not together—in the video of Tom Petty's "I Won't Back Down.")

Late in 1965, however, Paul purchased an Epiphone Casino ES-230, and both John and George, impressed with the guitar's sound, bought identical models early in 1966. The Casino, a hollow-body guitar that produces chunky, raw leads with bluesy overtones, remains to this day Paul's favorite electric guitar. It's a relatively thin hollow-body that works well with effects pedals and has a bridge strong enough to benefit from a whammy bar.

Both George and John used their Casinos for the recording of *Revolver* and on the Beatles' 1966 world tour. In addition, the Casino was the dominant electric guitar played on the *Sgt. Pepper* LP.

As the Beatles continued to search for new sounds, they also played new and different electrics. George played a Gibson ES-345 on a 1965 British tour, then picked up on Fender Stratocasters and Telecasters, the Gibson Les Paul, and the Gibson SG (which he would give to Badfinger's Pete Ham).

John played Gretsches and Fenders on occasion, although, being less of a guitar hound than George, he mostly stuck to his Casino. His Epiphone, scraped clean of its original finish, made appearances beginning in 1968, most notably on the hard-rocking "Revolution," on through the *Let It Be* and *Abbey Road* sessions, and well into his solo years.

Paul still uses the Casino for recording and touring purposes. Oddly enough, however, the Epiphone, like most other hollow-body guitars, has fallen out of favor with many modern guitarists, who seem far more interested in guitars that deliver flash, volume, and distortion.

Rickenbacker 4001 Bass

Paul McCartney was, bar none, the most innovative bass player in rock music during the mid-1960s, fusing elements of pop and Motown (in particular, James Jamerson) into a style that mixed rock-solid rhythm with melodic flights of fancy completely unprecedented for a pop music bassist. Others had more technical flash than Macca, but none outshone him as a melodist or colorist of songs.

Shortly after George and John completely stopped using Rickenbacker guitars on their recordings and tours, Paul began a relationship with the instrument manufacturer's new 4001 bass. The Rickenbacker people had been trying since 1964 to get Paul to accept a custom-made left-handed prototype, and he finally played it while in Los Angeles in August 1965.

McCartney began using the 4001 almost immediately; it had a very long neck, which allowed the bassist to play very high notes with greater ease, and an innovative design that looked like no other bass guitar; the body was large and asymmetrical, far stranger looking even than the Fender design.

While it's a very heavy instrument to hold, the classic Rickenbacker bass produces impeccable sound, providing chunky treble and deep bass as well as allowing access to the high end of the neck. Most of *Rubber Soul* boasts the 4001 sound, and McCartney used the bass on all or nearly all of the Beatles' output until 1969.

The increased bass presence on Beatles recordings from "Paperback Writer" onward must be credited not only to improved recording techniques and McCartney's forceful presence, but also to the sheer power and advanced sonic capability of the Rickenbacker bass.

Fender Rhodes Electric Piano / Blüthner Grand Piano

While remaining a two-guitars-bass-and-drums quartet, the Beatles still chose to use a variety of keyboards on their recordings, including a Vox organ ("I'm Down"), a Hohner Pianet ("The Night Before"), a Clavioline ("Baby, You're a Rich Man"), and a harmonium ("We Can Work It Out") as well as various organ, piano, and "tack" piano sounds. Lennon would play the Vox Continental organ during the group's 1965 American tour, and McCartney occasionally accompanied himself on that keyboard on "Yesterday."

The essential sonic palette of "Strawberry Fields Forever" comes from the Mellotron, a keyboard instrument whose keys activate the playing of "tapes" of other instruments. A harpsichord is featured prominently on "Fixing a Hole" and "Piggies," while a George Martin–owned clavichord gives "For No One" a chamber-music feel. But only around the time of the "Get Back" / *Let It Be* film and album sessions in early 1969 did the Beatles begin to *emphasize* keyboards.

First, they asked American soul/R&B/gospel singer and keyboardist Billy Preston, whom George had spotted in London at a Ray Charles concert, to sit in with the band. Preston, who had played shows as a sideman for Little Richard on bills with the Beatles in 1962, used a Fender Rhodes seventy-three-key electric piano to give the group a richer sound in their rooftop concert on January 30, 1969, banging out solos on "Get Back" and "Don't Let Me Down." He also used the Rhodes, as well as other keyboard instruments, on the myriad of rock oldies the now Fab Five played at Twickenham Studios during the filming of *Let It Be*.

In addition, Paul was doing much of his composing on piano, including his stately ballads "Let It Be" and "The Long and Winding Road." Only a grand piano would satisfy the needs of such grand compositions, so the Beatles had a Blüthner concert grand brought into Twickenham (as shown in *Let It Be*'s opening sequence).

Blüthner's musical history extends back to 1853, originating in Leipzig, Germany. Featured onboard the doomed airship *Hindenburg* in 1936, the Blüthner was the first piano ever used for a recital broadcast from midair. Of course, the May 1937 *Hindenburg* explosion was a far more serious disaster even than *Let It Be*.

15

Every Sound There Is

What *Was* That, Anyway?

Much of the beauty of the Beatles' recordings comes from their penchant for thinking outside the established box. Found objects, serendipitous noises, and unfamiliar instruments were all fair game for inclusion into the final mix. For those who enjoy the finished product through headphones, here are a few things to listen for.

"Words of Love" from *Beatles for Sale*; Recorded October 18, 1964

As crazy for Buddy Holly as the Beatles were, they showed great taste and restraint in approaching their hero's material. Having tackled "That'll Be the Day" on record as the Quarry Men (not officially released until 1995!), they demonstrated excellent judgment years later in choosing this understated number, the original of which featured Holly harmonizing with himself and stifling his idiosyncratic "hiccups."

As such, "Words of Love" thoroughly lends itself to typically pleasing vocals from John and Paul. (It also would have made sense as a title for Capitol's 1977 *Love Songs* ballads compilation, in keeping with the previous double record set—named, after a cover version whose title succinctly described its contents, "Rock 'n' Roll Music.")

The Beatles' version of this track includes Ringo tapping what has been described as a "packing case." Perhaps the Beatles were drawing further inspiration from Buddy, who recorded "Not Fade Away" with drummer Jerry Allison applying his sticks to a cardboard box, or, more subtly, "Everyday," on which Allison beat out the song's rhythm by slapping his thighs.

In any event, this recording brought an end to a productive day, which saw the band nailing a slew of tunes: "Kansas City" / "Hey Hey Hey Hey," "Mr. Moonlight," "I Feel Fine," "I'll Follow the Sun," "Everybody's Trying to Be My Baby," and "Rock and Roll Music."

"You Won't See Me" from *Rubber Soul*; Recorded November 11, 1965

Often described as the Beatles' first artistically "mature" album, *Rubber Soul* was recorded near the end of the group's second straight year of nonstop international jet-setting activity. In 1965 the Beatles undertook a second world tour, cinematic obligations, and television and radio appearances, and—oh, yes—received honors from their queen.

Despite the exhaustion they must have felt, the Fabs turned in their second album comprised entirely of self-penned songs. Stylistically, *Rubber Soul* ran the gamut from acoustic introspection ("Norwegian Wood," "Girl") to roots ("Run for Your Life," "What Goes On"—the latter a co-composition with Ringo) to Euro-pop ("Michelle"). Additionally, the record boasts two tunes from George, "Think for Yourself" and "If I Needed Someone," that document his growing prowess as a writer.

Added to the mix of original songs were the Beatles' continuing adventures in sonic color. The album offered a first taste of Indian instrumentation on "Norwegian Wood," kicking off a growing sitar obsession for pop groups during the next couple of years. Ringo would make his keyboard debut (!) on "I'm Looking Through You," a complete recasting of a song heard embryonically on *Anthology 2*. On the *Rubber Soul* version, Mr. Starkey, in addition to his usual drumming, provides the "one-two" organ fills between each verse.

In addition, the rush-recorded "You Won't See Me" introduced another unlikely sideman: one Mal "Organ" Evans. The group's beloved gofer apparently provided an extra hand—or, in this case, finger—because George Martin was busy playing piano on the track. Evans's contribution, even less complicated than Ringo's, consisted of a single, hornlike note held down beginning at 2:29 and continuing for another half-minute.

Another point of interest is the song's decreasing tempo throughout; "You Won't See Me" begins at 119 beats per minute and ends *dragging* at 113. Were they just getting tired?

"Tomorrow Never Knows" from *Revolver*; Basic Track Recorded April 6, 1966

For a rock band in its prime to begin working on a release that its members have no intention of promoting on their upcoming concert tour is, to say the least, a curious career move. But in spring 1966, the Beatles set about laying down tracks for their boldest, most experimental album yet, most of which would have been difficult, if not impossible, to reproduce onstage with their standard lineup of two guitars, bass, and drums.

Whether or not they had already made the decision to quit touring, it's evident that the Beatles saw themselves wearing two musical hats: one as a performing band of entertainers, the other as studio craftsmen seeking to move their artistic and technological goalposts.

The most adventurous track intended for release was the first committed to tape. Beginning life as "Mark I," but soon rerecorded and graced with a new title thanks to a Ringoism, John's composition was built entirely on a C-major chord with no changes, although an occasional B-flat was eventually grafted on.

Naturally, such a monochromatic opus on a pop record could be expected to need some sort of embellishment. Enter Paul McCartney and his collection of tape loops. These short bits of recorded found objects, captured at his home on a Brenell tape machine, could be electronically manipulated to create new sounds out of nothing. When fed into the recording console, these sundry noises added texture to the track when brought forward randomly in the mix.

To that end, the other three Beatles, all of whom owned Brenells, brought in various home recordings they'd made. With engineers assisting, an assortment of sounds were chosen and spooled onto a platoon of machines with pencils. (The song's signature "seagull" sound has been reported variously as a "distorted guitar" and sped-up McCartney laughter.)

An Indian-style drone permeates the recording, while assorted loops of stringed instruments, backwards guitar, and even the rubbing of the rim of a wine glass enter and exit the unfolding sonic sojourn, atop Ringo's bedrock drumming. With far too much precision to have come by accident, a "beep" tone sounds at 1:28, the song's exact halfway mark.

All in all, "Tomorrow Never Knows" made an audacious beginning to the next phase of the Beatles' career.

"Yellow Submarine" from *Revolver*; Basic Track Recorded May 26, 1966

For Ringo's star turn, Paul conceived a whimsical children's sing-along. Musically, it's simple and direct, featuring lyrical contributions from Donovan. But for recording purposes, the band evidently felt that some special effort was in order to underscore the nautical theme.

To that end, the effects closet at EMI studios was raided, presenting a wealth of possibilities that the resourceful boys quickly put to use. A metal bathtub was filled with water, and waves were effectively simulated by churning chains inside of it. Blowing water through a straw provided the requisite bubbles.

Furthering the ambience of underwater life, John commandeered the studio echo chamber and began barking out maritime gibberish. (Some deep listeners swear that the hard-to-decipher verbiage spoken during the instrumental break is, variously, Swedish, Czech, or Danish. When pressed for an explanation as to how Lennon would have spoken in those languages, the fallback answer is, "Well, obviously, an engineer from that country was around!")

The resulting sound collage helped bring "underground" recording techniques and a bit of the avant-garde into the mainstream. "Yellow Submarine" wouldn't be the Beatles' last foray into the idiom, but it was unquestionably their most popular, reaching #1 around the world.

"Strawberry Fields Forever" Single; Recording Began November 28, 1966

The first product of the band's newfound freedom from the road was a tune John composed in Spain during the filming of Richard Lester's *How I Won the War*. Bereft of his usual companions and removed from familiar surroundings (possibly for the first time in his adult life), John was forced to tap his inner resources to come to terms with an uncharted future. Typically, he reached back into childhood to find a prism through which to assess his situation.

The version he played for George Martin upon his return to England featured only his voice and acoustic guitar, a treatment John never bettered, in Martin's estimate. But both Lennon and his bandmates were keen on extending the sonic ideas they'd begun exploring in their recordings earlier that year.

A version featuring slide guitar was cut first (see *Anthology 2*), which, despite being satisfactory to everyone but the song's creator, yielded to an orchestration-laden remake. This too falling short, both versions were famously spliced together, taxing George Martin's creativity to the hilt as he sped up one version and slowed down another to get them, improbably, into the same key and tempo.

Among the heretofore unknown-to-pop-music sounds embellishing the finished release is a harp-like Indian instrument (spelled variously as "swarmandel" or "swordmandel"). Not unlike a Western zither, it first pops up at 1:18, after the second chorus, and again at 2:04. It's an intriguing sound, somewhere between guitar and sitar, and as such, perfect for establishing mood.

Oddly, one of the song's most memorable moments was produced not by George Martin, but by technical engineer Dave Harries. With Martin and engineer extraordinaire Geoff Emerick absent (attending, of all things, a Cliff Richard film première), Harries was drafted to oversee the recording of the track's drum-heavy coda.

With Paul and George pounding away on timpani and an out-of-control Ringo flogging his kit, the top- and bottom-heavy cacophony prompted one of John's more memorable non sequiturs: "Cranberry sauce." (Lennon then admonished his bandmate, "Calm down, Ringo!")

"A Day in the Life" from *Sgt. Pepper's Lonely Hearts Club Band*; Basic Track Recorded January 19, 1967

Though its landmark status among the group's albums is regarded as somewhat overblown today, *Sgt. Pepper's* impact "way back when" was not. Though most fans today hold *Abbey Road* and *Revolver* in slightly higher regard, most anyone listening to pop music at the dawn of the Summer of Love can, without fail, describe his or her first impression of *Sgt. Pepper*. That the release would spawn legions of imitations is also demonstrable, for better or worse. One thing is certain: the artistic approach to crafting a rock album changed forever in *Pepper's* wake.

The album's stunning closer began its life, like "Strawberry Fields Forever," as a simple acoustic piece. But instead of emulating that recording's fractured creation, this song was assembled in a workmanlike manner.

For example, when the four Beatles laid down the initial instrumental bedding of the song, in which John had left a vacancy right in the middle, someone had the canny idea of marking off the "empty" bars of music, pending a better idea. Everyone knew that *something* amazing had to bridge the song's sections, but no one knew what yet, so Mal Evans was tabbed to count aloud the twenty-four measures that needed filling. Some of the counting can be heard on the original release, while *Anthology 2*'s outtake reveals all the hidden details. And, lest anyone miss the point of return, Mal set off an alarm clock.

Eventually, an orphaned song fragment by Paul ("Woke up . . .") was plugged in. The fact that his opening lines were exquisitely appropriate following the alarm clock's bell made it unthinkable to remove the serendipitous sound.

Once the adrenaline-like orchestral rush, a revolution in itself, had been folded into the recording, the problem of a fitting ending to the build-up arose. After nixing the original idea—eight beats of group humming—

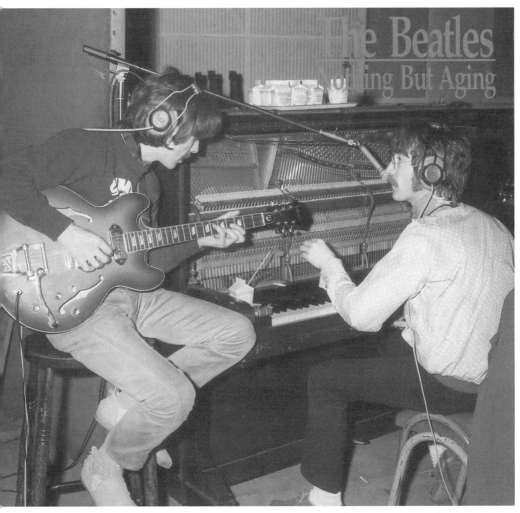

The *Sgt. Pepper's* sessions were marked by a high degree of musical interaction and experimentation, in direct contrast to *The Beatles* recordings a year later.

the apocalyptic E-major chord was chosen, with John, Paul, Ringo, and Mal hitting three pianos at once.

Some claim that the high level of attenuation made it possible to hear studio air conditioners as the note decays. But since this part of the song was recorded on February 22, 1967, it is unlikely that any AC was in use. You *can*, however, hear three separate bench squeaks.

"I Am the Walrus" from *Magical Mystery Tour*; Basic Track Recorded September 5, 1967

John's last real foray into psychedelic music is a talking blues piss-take directed at dissectors of his songwriting, and simultaneously a send-up of the work of others, specifically Dylan (who he believed got away with murder in his nonsensical lyrics). Part LSD-induced inspiration, part schoolboy doggerel, "Walrus" actually aligns itself with the character John later came to believe was the *bad* guy in Lewis Carroll's poem "The Walrus and the Carpenter."

"I Am the Walrus" is one of the busiest Beatles recordings, with layers of orchestration and voices (the Mike Sammes Singers, to be exact) stacked precipitously atop the band's basic track. But, as often happened in Beatledom, pure happenstance provided textural depth to the track along with fodder for conspiracy-minded critics.

Three weeks after recording commenced, John made a rare appearance at the song's mixing session. His presence suggests that the incorporation of a live radio feed into the track was planned, and not simply some spur-of-the-moment epiphany. What *was* spontaneous was the particular broadcast that ended up on the record: a BBC production of Shakespeare's tragedy *King Lear*.

Sharp-eared listeners could hear the broadcast enter the "Walrus" recording at 2:26, with Act IV, Scene VI in progress. Those unfamiliar with the unfolding drama, which in this vignette depicted the killing of Oswald by Edgar, may have been astonished to hear such dialogue as "Bury my body" and "O, untimely death!" emanating from their speakers. It wouldn't be long before the "Paul is dead" crowd read sinister meaning into the inclusion of this verbiage.

"I Will" from *The Beatles*; Basic Track Recorded September 16, 1968

Not since their EMI debut had a Beatles album been so thoroughly mapped out in advance as *The Beatles*, better known as the "White Album." With so many songs written during the Rishikesh sojourn, an organizing principle was needed to sort them out. In May, the group gathered at Kinfauns, George's residence at Esher, to demo twenty-three compositions for possible inclusion.

Unknown to George Martin at the time were the details of a new EMI contract, calling for the Beatles to continue delivering albums through 1976. In order to fulfill their end of the deal ahead of schedule, the Beatles insisted on making the new album a two-record set. Martin would go on record as urging the group, to no avail, to pare down the thirty tracks in order to produce "a really fine single album."

The sessions marked the beginning of tensions between band members that spilled over into the studio. At one point, the atmosphere became so toxic that Ringo walked out, various engineers threatened to quit (and one did), and even the unflappable Martin absented himself from the proceedings to go on holiday, leaving Chris Thomas, a future ace producer but then just a callow twenty-one-year-old, in charge.

In slogging through so much material, the band sometimes worked on separate recordings concurrently. John would later recall feeling slighted whenever Paul went off on his own to work alone. Conversely, John's insistence on having Yoko around every waking moment couldn't help but

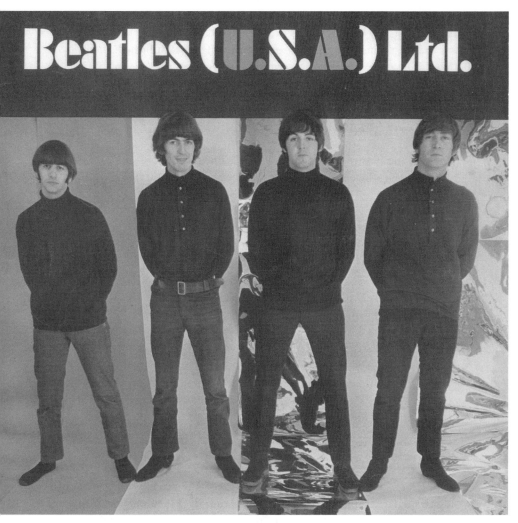

Perhaps knowing the outcome ahead of the others, only George seems enthused on the cover of their 1966 tour book. Strikingly, they were in the midst of recording an album that they would never perform live.

alienate his bandmates. All in all, the inexorable slide toward disintegration had begun.

George was not present on September 16, when the other three Beatles captured a solid take of Paul's gentle ballad. (Also taped was Paul's intriguing "Can you take me back where I came from" fragment that would be grafted onto the end of John's "Cry Baby Cry.")

With the song's author playing guitar, Ringo handling maracas and cymbals, and John tapping on a wood block, the track lacked a bass foundation. Normally, Paul would add a bass guitar later, but after cutting a backing vocal the next day, he opted instead to *sing* his bass part. Listen carefully; without camping it up, he does a creditable job. Five years later, Paul extended his oral instrumental repertoire by vocalizing a saxophone solo in Ringo's "You're Sixteen." Contrary to common belief, it is not a kazoo.

"Long Long Long" from *The Beatles*; Basic Track Recorded October 7, 1968

The backing to what is arguably George's finest contribution to their double album was produced in a marathon sixteen-hour session. Following his habit of coming in late (or not at all) when George's tunes were recorded, John was absent.

Even when Lennon did deign to show up during Harrison's sessions, his input, unless integral, such as the slide guitar on "For You Blue," was wiped (the rhythm guitar on "Old Brown Shoe") or minimized in the mix (his piano on "Something"). This interesting dynamic would come to a head in January 1969, with George quitting the group after a row with John (not Paul, as is commonly supposed).

"Long Long Long" is an intriguing mixture of styles: part folk ballad, part jazz waltz (with a preponderance of ninth chords), and more than a hint of Eastern-style psychedelia. For all that, it hangs together wonderfully, if softly, punctuated by Ringo's thundering drum fills. Lyrically, it typifies a long-running theme of George's—songs that could as easily be about a lover as about God.

Three Beatles set to work on the track, with Paul on organ. Despite the length of the session and some sixty-plus takes (!), the atmosphere was light-hearted, with rare Indian incense burning at all times. At the climactic end of one take, a bottle of wine (Blue Nun, according to Chris Thomas) atop a Leslie speaker cabinet began to vibrate when Paul hit a particular note. The resulting sound met with the approval of all, compelling engineers to mike the bottle and re-create the accident for inclusion in the finished master.

"The Continuing Story of Bungalow Bill" from *The Beatles*; Basic Track Recorded October 8, 1968

Those following the Beatles' career closely must have been baffled by this song's flamenco guitar opening. Who played *that*? Clearly, no one in the band had the chops for that kind of intricate playing . . . or did they? George had two years of sitar lessons behind him, and all the Beatles save Ringo had been tutored in fingerpicking earlier that year in Rishikesh by Donovan. Then there was the issue of guitar-slinger extraordinaire Eric Clapton attending the sessions; might he or someone of equal caliber have been brought in for an assist?

The truth is far simpler. What listeners hear is the "Spanish guitar" voice from the Beatles' Mellotron. The elegant, evocative intro for John's cautionary tale is actually a pre-recorded tape. Which goes to show that, as in so much else, the group was ahead of the curve in sampling. For those keeping score, the last "instrument" heard on "Bill," underneath the clapping during the song's outro, is also the Mellotron—played by Chris Thomas—with voice set for "trombone."

No One (I Think) Is in My Tree

Recording Innovations

The Beatles didn't invent most of the recording tricks they used to expand their sonic palette, but one could certainly make the case that they used them the most artfully. A part of what made the Fabs sound so fresh was their tendency to pull back from beating a sound to death, opting to stay fresh and not repeat themselves.

Here are ten elements that George Martin, engineers like Norman Smith and Geoff Emerick, and the Beatles themselves used to great effect in their musical collaborations. When it came to producing every sound there is, the Fabs led the way in the 1960s.

Double Tracking

This standard studio tool is used to beef up thin singing voices and lead guitar lines. In a nutshell, the artist records a second take of a given part on a separate track, attempting to follow the original as closely as possible. Ideally, the two parts will mesh, giving the part a fuller, richer sound. (This is why the lousiest live singers can still sound great on record.)

The Beatles used this trick extensively, beginning with 1963's *With the Beatles*. Close listening to several tracks reveals slight differences between the two takes. (As an example, listen to the sound of the word "will" at 0:33 in "All My Loving.") In less skilled hands, the delay effect can be comically exaggerated; see Ringo's vocal on "Matchbox," especially at 1:32 on "Well . . . ." Hilarity ensues.

Lead guitar was also sometimes double-tracked, as on the solo in "Can't Buy Me Love." The more obvious deviations throughout actually enhanced the guitar's sound.

Over time, the Beatles—John in particular—began to view double-tracking vocals as a bothersome chore and entreated EMI engineers to find a way around it. This request led directly to the invention of ADT (see below), but even afterward, double-tracking remained a tool in the Beatles' arsenal. Eventually, they became more judicious in its application, using it for effect intermittently within a song. "Revolution" would be one example, "Julia" another.

Feedback

Lacking security in their own gifts, at least during the early years of recording, the Beatles simultaneously embraced and were wary of gimmicks to create an ear-catching, radio-friendly sound. Their first three singles and many album cuts used harmonica as an identifying voice; this was dropped after Lennon reported that it was becoming "embarrassing."

Still, they stayed on the lookout for any distinctive device they could use to engage listeners. During the *Beatles for Sale* sessions in late 1964, John, already experimenting with the riff to Bobby Parker's "Watch Your Step," had the notion of kicking off the song "I Feel Fine" with a sound heretofore avoided in the recording studio: feedback.

This term refers to the sound of an electronic signal re-amplifying itself. If a microphone or a plugged-in guitar is left too close to the speaker amplifying its sound, the microphone or guitar pickup will receive the sound emanating from the speaker and re-amplify it (picture a dog chasing its tail), creating a circle of noise that, unchecked, will rise in intensity.

Well before guitarists like Jeff Beck, Pete Townshend, and Jimi Hendrix made a career out of this effect, John purposely recorded it for the start of "I Feel Fine," a fact that he was inordinately proud of: "I defy anybody to find a record . . . unless it is some old blues record from 1922 . . . that uses feedback that way."

Less contrived feedback would pop up in other Beatles records, notably *Rubber Soul*'s "I'm Looking Through You," where its presence seems far from deliberate. It also crops up near the beginning of the "Revolution" promotional film, adding to the overall illusion of a live performance.

ADT

In response to Lennon's demand for an end to the tedium of nailing the perfect vocal twice, EMI engineer Ken Townsend developed an electronic gadget that he called Automatic Double Tracking. The device took the incoming signal (in this case, the vocal) from the tape machine's recording head, sent it off to a second recorder running at an ever-so-slightly different speed, then fed it back into the first recorder so that the receiving tape at the end of the line would receive the composite vocal.

The Beatles were thrilled with the device and began using it extensively, beginning with *Revolver*'s "Tomorrow Never Knows," to fatten up vocals as well as other components of their work.

Lennon, as was his habit, had arrived with a new composition, bearing technical demands that he expected George Martin and crew to fulfill. To execute his vision, he told Martin that he needed his voice to approximate the sound of the Dalai Lama singing from the highest mountaintop in the Himalayas.

No problem, Martin assured him. He treated John's voice to ADT for the first half of "Tomorrow Never Knows"; after the backward guitar break, he ran the vocal through a Leslie speaker. This rotating device was built for use with electric keyboards, but the Beatles soon discovered that it produced a pleasing, oscillating effect when other sounds were fed into it. (George would use it heavily for recording guitar in later years; it can be heard on "Something" and on his guitar solo on the single version of "Let It Be." He also made a point of running friend Eric Clapton's "While My Guitar Gently Weeps" solo through it, feeling that, as recorded, it wasn't "Beatley" enough.)

Though the ADT was widely used for many years, the advent of digital technology in later years rendered it and other analog tape-dependent gear obsolete. Today, it is used, if at all, by old-school aficionados.

Volume Pedal

Beginning in 1963, Vox musical equipment was officially linked with the Beatles. In a deal brokered by Brian Epstein, the Fabs, in exchange for a lifetime's worth of free gear, agreed to use the brand's amps and guitar accessories exclusively; Vox, in return, received unlimited use of the Beatles' image for advertising.

In early 1965, George began using a Vox V-850 volume pedal. This device gave him the ability to "swell" the volume of his guitar as he played, lending his leads and fills a stylish, almost vocal effect.

He first tried out his volume pedal on "I Need You," from *Help!*, working it into the song's guitar riff. This marked a decided improvement from the last time he'd attempted that sound; during the *Beatles for Sale* sessions six months earlier, he'd needed John to twiddle his knob during "Baby's in Black" to achieve the same result.

Recorded the same day as "I Need You," "Yes It Is" proved an even better showcase for the Vox pedal. George's lilting lead is characteristically weepy, perfectly suited to the song's theme. Indeed, it directly forecast the slide playing that would become George's signature sound during the solo years.

George would trot out the pedal again later that year on "Wait," cut for *Help!* but released on *Rubber Soul.*

Fuzz

Vox wasn't the only manufacturer whose gear the Beatles would play around with. Sound engineer Gary Hurst introduced the Tone Bender in 1965, intended as an improvement upon Gibson's Maestro Fuzz Tone. (The latter effect was nearly used by John on George's "Don't Bother Me" in 1963 before George Martin and the other Beatles vetoed the idea.)

What *is* fuzz tone? A fuzz box is a distortion device intended to dirty up a guitar's sound, sparing the guitarist from shredding his speaker cones to achieve the same result. Millions of music fans were first exposed to fuzz in 1965 via the Rolling Stones' smash "(I Can't Get No) Satisfaction."

It would be unthinkable for the Beatles to ape a sound effect on a Rolling Stones record, and a well-known one at that. So for *Rubber Soul's* "Think for Yourself," the Tone Bender was applied to Paul's *bass,* in a departure from all precedent (as was having two bass lines on the track: regular and fuzz).

Given the distorted guitar heard on many subsequent Beatle recordings, it can be taken on faith that the Tone Bender saw further use, perhaps on "Happiness Is a Warm Gun." Many people assume that the ultra-distorted guitar heard on "Revolution" three years later was generated by some sort of fuzz effect, but it wasn't. The speaker-punishing tone (best heard on the mono single mix) was created by plugging the guitar directly into the recording console, increasing the volume and intensity of the sound while "pegging" the tape machine's volume needles. EMI supervisors frowned upon this maltreatment of property, to say the least, but the studio was in no position to kill the golden goose.

Tape Echo

EMI's Abbey Road facility had three separate echo chambers operating in the 1960s. These were implemented to achieve natural-sounding reverb on the Beatles' recordings, not unlike that found on Elvis Presley's echoey Sun Records output, which all the Fabs were thoroughly enamored of.

To enable greater control over the echo's application, Martin and company utilized a gadget called STEED (single tape echo and echo delay). This device was basically a self-contained tape-recording unit. A signal fed into it

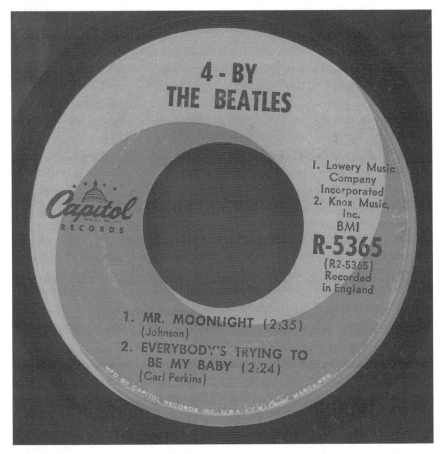

The reverb-drenched *Beatles '65* track "Everybody's Trying to Be My Baby" found issue from Capitol on their second EP, a format they would abandon after this release.

was recorded onto a tape loop, which would then repeat the signal according to a pre-set speed and duration.

Despite John Lennon's chronic dissatisfaction with the sound of his own voice (which he fixed during the solo years by smothering it with delay), George Martin generally took great care to apply echo sparingly. Over in America, however, where excess reigned, no such qualms were felt. Believing record buyers in this country were oblivious to subtlety, Capitol's mastering engineers routinely slathered the Beatles' recordings with extra echo and reverberation before release, at times making the recordings sound as if they had emanated from the bottom of Death Valley.

On at least one occasion, however, Martin inexplicably beat Capitol at its own game. STEED made an appearance bordering on overkill for George's vocal on "Everybody's Trying to Be My Baby," recorded during the cover-happy *Beatles for Sale* sessions. It is indicative of how little care was taken with compositions not of their own making that this echo-drenched track was ever issued (that, and the presence of "Mr. Moonlight" on the same release while "Leave My Kitten Alone" sat unused in the can).

Far better results were achieved over a year later on "Paperback Writer." There, the tape-delay echo was used on alternating verse endings, nicely enhancing the track without bludgeoning the listener.

Vari-Speed

By 1966, when their infatuation with recording experimentation was in full bloom, the Beatles had been clued in to the effects of vari-speed (or pitch control). This was the practice of tweaking the tape speed on a given record-ing to alter the normal sound of the instruments and/or voices.

Sometimes this was done to suit the nature of the song. For example, Paul wanted to sound youthful on "When I'm Sixty-Four," he recorded the vocals with the backing track slowed down, which had the effect of *speeding up* the vocals when the finished product was played at normal speed. "I'm Only Sleeping" is another example of the use of this effect.

Conversely, recording the song at a faster tempo than preferred facili-tated slowing the entire track down afterward to the desired tempo while also affecting the vocal and instrumental texture. On "Rain," slowing the backing track created the requisite leaden, detached mood.

Perhaps the best example of vari-speeding done *without* intending to change the pitch of either the backing or the vocals is found on "In My Life." The track was all but finished, save for an empty space where the instrumental break would go. George Martin was given leave to fill the void with a keyboard obbligato of his own composition, but discovered to his chagrin that his hands weren't quick enough to play what he had written.

The problem was solved when he slowed down the entire track and then laid down his piano solo at a tempo unhurried enough for him to perform it. When the entire track was played back, he discovered that the piano had assumed a sound approaching that of a harpsichord or clavichord. The resulting Baroque-sounding interlude perfectly complemented Lennon's wistful, timeless composition.

Flanging / Phasing

Though Lennon used the term "flanging" to refer to ADT, the actual record-ing effect by that name was invented well before the advent of the Beatles.

The 1959 chart hit by Miss Toni Fisher, "The Big Hurt," made extensive use of flanging, an effect that provides a "whoosh" effect when used on a particular sound.

To explain how flanging is produced would require a technologically heavier discussion than anyone should be obliged to sit through. (The distinction between flanging and phasing, for instance, is very subtle. Briefly, the delay cycle for phasing is ten to twelve milliseconds; for flanging, twelve to forty or fifty milliseconds. For further explanation, see your nearest sound engineer.)

Therefore, to give a familiar example of what flanging sounds like, listen no further than "Itchycoo Park" by the Small Faces: the drum breaks occurring after the lyrics "be nice and have fun in the sun" are "flanged."

Flanging was used liberally during the psychedelic era, as it evoked a hazy, trippy sort of reverie. Hendrix included it on "Bold as Love"; in a less weighty context, it featured in Status Quo's "Pictures of Matchstick Men."

The Beatles were usually not given to jumping on the effects bandwagon, preferring to set trends rather than follow them. Their use of flanging was spare, coming most notably on "Blue Jay Way" and briefly on "Lucy in the Sky with Diamonds."

Tape Loops / Backwards Taping

By definition, a tape loop is literally a loop of recording tape; that is, a bit of recorded sound spliced to itself, creating literally an endless piece of sound that repeats ad infinitum until mixed out. In the Beatles' recorded output, perhaps the best known example of this is the incessant "Number 9, Number 9 . . ." heard on "Revolution 9." Without tape loops, the aural soundscape thus created wouldn't even exist.

A phalanx of tape loops on "Tomorrow Never Knows" added atmosphere to the song. Each Beatle brought in home recordings of various sounds, which were then looped and fed into the mix. They conducted a similar experiment in affixing a loop of gibberish to the inner groove of side two of *Sgt. Pepper's*, inadvertently providing a "clue" to Paul McCartney's demise, at least for the weak-minded.

Backwards tapes were something entirely new, or so John claimed in 1980 to David Sheff: "That's me again, with the first backwards tape on any record anywhere. Before Hendrix, before the Who, before ANY fucker."

While this claim is debatable, we *can* say, with no doubt, that the first backwards recording on a *Beatles* record can be found in the coda to "Rain," where the vocal line ("When the rain comes . . .") was inserted in reverse, creating an odd-sounding intonation that was subject to a wide range of inter-pretation. (One such "clue" says, "Bed her down and worry later. . . .")

The Fabs soon found that guitar lines sounded great when recorded backwards. Sketching out in his head what he wanted a finished guitar part to sound like, George Harrison picked out the notes he needed to play "forward" in order to achieve the desired results in reverse. As with so many other effects, "Tomorrow Never Knows" pioneered this technique.

"I'm Only Sleeping" also benefited from the use of backwards guitar, and the fact that the song was released in nearly half a dozen variations gave Beatle audiologists plenty of material to dissect.

So identified with the Fabs was this trick that in 1967, Peter, Paul, and Mary's "I Dig Rock and Roll Music" lampooned the Beatles' sound with a sampling of backwards guitar, betraying considerable bile in a sardonic commentary on their peers.

Moog Synthesizer

Though technically an instrument, and not an effect per se, the Moog (pronounced to rhyme with "rogue") was an important, if eleventh-hour, innovation in the Beatles' sound, typifying their use of cutting-edge technol-ogy well before many of their peers. (Others attracted to the new contrap-tion included California rock band the Turtles and the Monkees' Micky Dolenz.)

Thanks to the invention of the microchip, long after the Beatles had passed from the scene, synthesizers are now available in ever-smaller sizes, but in 1967–69, they were monstrous affairs, including a keyboard *and* a finger-activated "ribbon" to control the pitch of the notes; a thicket of patch cables; and very little documentation for the consumer on how to use the whole package.

But George Harrison was never daunted by a musical challenge. He bought a Moog IIIp in Los Angeles in late 1968, and, after consulting first with Bernie Krause of the electronic music duo Beaver and Krause, and later with Mike Vickers of Manfred Mann, he was able to get a handle on the Frankensteinian machine.

George had the synthesizer delivered to the facilities at Abbey Road, where its sheer bulk required a separate room for setup and a cable to con-nect it to the recording console. The other Beatles and EMI staff hovered over the novel device, oohing and ahhing at this latest toy.

It is to their credit that the Beatles had the restraint to use the Moog tastefully. *Abbey Road's* synthesizer embellishments are nearly all subdued, adding finishing touches to songs without drawing undue attention.

George made first use of the Moog on John's "Because." With George Martin on electric harpsichord, George entered the track at 2:12, contributing an adornment as timeless as it is effective. It's striking how incredibly dated the instrument soon sounded in lesser hands; not so the Beatles'.

Paul commandeered the synth for "Maxwell's Silver Hammer," adding fills between the verses. According to engineer Alan Parsons, of later "Project" fame, Paul mastered the parts very quickly, playing the notes by sliding his finger up and down the ribbon (not unlike playing a violin).

For someone with no use for purely experimental sounds ("avant garde a clue" he'd call it), George startled many with this, his second solo (and only Zapple) release in 1969.

Perhaps lacking the patience even to simply come to terms with the intimidating electronic behemoth, John limited his use of the Moog to adding "white noise" to "I Want You (She's So Heavy)."

George concluded his Moog work on *Abbey Road* by applying some light touches to "Here Comes the Sun," adding an extra dash of sparkle to his luminous composition. Interestingly, he would never implement the synthesizer in his solo work as he had with the Fabs. Only Paul, among the four Beatles, seemed eager to realize the instrument's capabilities, with "Jet" a prime example.

17

If I Knew What I Was Missing

Some Recording Variations

O dd as it may seem today, the Beatles' records were issued around the world with astonishingly little uniformity. The wake of their international success saw mixes vary from market to market, most notably in America, where rebalancing and applying echo—apparently with a spatula—was the order of the day. (This practice reached the peak of its excess in late 1964, when Capitol released the "I Feel Fine" / "She's a Woman" single, which sounded as though the Beatles were playing in a *real* Cavern.)

Similar variations arose with distinct mono and stereo releases. The Beatles, George Martin, and most recording artists of the day felt that stereo was a novelty enjoyed by all too few, mostly hi-fi buffs who were likely listening to jazz or classical anyway. Stereo mixes were tossed off fairly quickly, and occasionally even faked, but mono mixes were labored over. (To contemporary ears, that mid-'60s stereo formula of placing the backing track on one channel and the vocals on the other is especially maddening.)

The release of their music in compact disc form, using the original U.K. mixes, confronted the band's longtime American fans with a quandary: on the one hand, they could at last replace their worn-out vinyl and cassettes with something approaching sonic perfection; but on the other hand, listeners were now hearing the music in "altered" form.

Having grown up on the Capitol versions, or on the stereo issues released subsequent to the '60s, American listeners were being hit for the first time with a different sound: the Beatles as originally intended. For many, it would take an emotional adjustment to accept the music that had become embedded in their DNA in an alien form.

While a full accounting of every single Beatles mix variance would be (and, in fact, *is*) a book unto itself, here are ten notable examples of releases that varied in some way from one audience to another.

"From Me to You" B/W "Thank You Girl"

Both sides of this, the Beatles' third single, differ substantively from mono to stereo in the same way: the harmonica riff. In the case of the A-side, the stereo version omits the harmonica heard in the mono version's opening. For the B-side, a harmonica completely absent in the mono release is *over-dubbed* into the song's intro and outro for the stereo release.

What all this means is that fans accustomed to the original mono single enjoyed a very different listening experience than did those first exposed to these songs via the stereo album issues, *The Beatles' Second Album* (in America) and 1973's *1962–1966* ("The Red Album").

CD buyers wishing to recapture the stereo buzz of "From Me to You" are, sadly, doomed to frustration. All authorized compact disc issues of that song (*1962–1966*, *Past Masters Volume One*, and *Beatles 1*) opted to use the mono take. But "Thank You Girl" can be heard in all its stereo splendor, courtesy of the controversial *Capitol Albums Volume One* box.

"All My Loving"

Evidence of the liberties taken around the world with the Beatles' masters is demonstrated by the German and Dutch issues of this song, both as a single and on the compilation *The Beatles Greatest*.

Heard nowhere else in the world is a five-tap hi-hat cymbal count-off from Ringo, followed by McCartney's intake of breath just before the singing begins. Lopped off every other official release, it's a neat little variation.

If one needs further incentive to seek out these releases, note that as a general rule, Germany's EMI took great care to only issue recordings with true stereo first-generation masters. The fidelity of the Germany EMI catalog is equaled only by Japan's Toshiba-EMI.

"Money (That's What I Want)"

The original British mono mixes of this song, included on the *With the Beatles* album, the *All My Loving* EP, and now the *With the Beatles* CD, contain a radically different introduction than do all the stereo and subsequent mono mixes. It features George Martin's piano, mixed dry and sparse, with some tapping.

The version heard by most people before the advent of CDs contains a double layer of piano, slathered with echo, and no tapping. (Even the U.S. mono mixes of *The Beatles' Second Album* release were derived from this

Fans in the know would make a point of seeking out the vastly superior German pressings, both for the mastering quality and higher grade of vinyl.

alternate intro.) Some latter-day George Martin refining of this mix was included on the 1976 *Rock 'n' Roll Music* compilation.

"I Should Have Known Better"

One can readily discern the difference between the mono and stereo versions of this popular tune from *A Hard Day's Night* by listening to the distinct variations in the opening harmonica riff.

As seen in the film and heard on all mono issues (including the U.S. B-side of the "A Hard Day's Night" 45), John plays the same phrase four times before the vocal begins.

In the stereo version (unreleased in America until 1970, when it appeared on the *Hey Jude* album), he stumbles on one of the phrases as if to take a breath, picking it up in time for a bad note before the singing starts. (It's likely that the "corrected" mono versions were created by simply repeating the flawless phrases of this very take.)

One might ask: what about the stereo 1964 United Artists issue of the film's soundtrack? Bizarrely, the only true stereo contained on that release is on the George Martin instrumental tracks. All seven Beatles songs are sourced from the mono masters, crudely tweaked into a simulation of duo-phonic stereo by adding a slight delay.

"I'll Cry Instead"

Clocking in at a brisk 1:44 in most places, the U.S. 45 and mono album release (from *Something New*) run 2:06. Why? Because of some unique splicing.

Mark Lewisohn informs us that the finished master was created by editing two separate performances together. What he doesn't say is that every version *except* the U.S. mono LP and 45 release is shorter, due to the deletion of a repeat of the opening verse midway through the song. (It is a *performed* repeat, and not one created purely through editing; slight vocal variations confirm this.)

A likely reason for the alteration is this: "I'll Cry Instead" was originally intended for big-screen use in *A Hard Day's Night*, to be played during the sequence where the three Beatles retrieve Ringo from the arms of the law. An extended take of the song fits the action nicely, more closely matching the running time of what was eventually used: a repeat of "Can't Buy Me Love." (According to John Lennon, director Richard Lester just never cared for the song. As an added insult, United Artists' pressings of the film's soundtrack mistakenly retitle the track "I Cry Instead" on the sleeve and label.)

The song finally made it into the film in 1982, when producer Walter Shenson used the song to accompany a newly contrived opening montage of stills for the cinematic rerelease.

"I'm Only Sleeping"

The unorthodox release history of this track, recorded by the band for release on *Revolver*, sparked a myriad of mixes. With Capitol loath to let a full half-year go by without new long-playing product, *Yesterday . . . and Today* was conceived, gathering leftover *Help* and *Rubber Soul* tracks along with the recent two-sided hit single "Day Tripper" / "We Can Work It Out."

For all that, eight songs were hardly enough to fill an album, even by Capitol's low-rent standards. They'd managed to skate by with *seven* Beatles songs on *Help!* the year before by filling the grooves with superfluous incidental music. (Why they didn't pad the release by adding the perfectly fitting B-side to the "Help!" single, the popular live-show set-closer "I'm Down," is a mystery.) Had they opted to throw in some dialogue from the movie (as the Monkees would do with *Head* three years hence), it might have been worth it.

Given the demands of the American market, Brian Epstein was forced to request some tracks from the group's work in progress, slated for release two months later. Three of John's tunes were selected: "Dr. Robert," "And Your Bird Can Sing," and this one, perhaps simply because they were already finished.

Therefore, while the U.K. *Revolver* was issued in its full fourteen-track glory, its American cousin was a truncated affair, tipping the compositional balance heavily toward Paul.

The album would prove a watershed for George, for, in addition to contributing an unheard-of *three* compositions (thereby exceeding John in America), he offered the first well-documented instance of "backwards guitar." This effect, a sonic embellishment of the first order, is created by playing guitar on tape and then reversing the tape. Harrison labored over his parts, composing the patterns "forward," then learning to play them from listening to the tape played backward.

Ultimately, no less than four and possibly five variations of the track were released, each offering a different composition of the backwards guitar throughout the recording. The mono U.S. version is the most barren, with the effect not beginning until the solo. Its U.K. mono counterpart, conversely, contains the *most* separate fills—all those featured on the stereo release, plus one more during the line "lying there and staring at the ceiling."

A French EP release is alleged to contain a unique mix, but all American tape releases and Apple pressings released in the mid-'70s contain a true stereo version heard nowhere else.

"Got to Get You into My Life"

It is an exasperating fact of life that the most satisfying (to the authors' ears) mix of Paul's soul pastiche is also the most elusive. But first, to address the more accessible mono/stereo differences:

Virtually every track on *Revolver* has distinctions between the two formats, largely length issues (one version of each song seems to run a few seconds longer). More complex recordings feature more significant differences. "Tomorrow Never Knows," a mixing engineer's wet dream, includes a wide array of differences in sound effects between the two issues.

"Got to Get You into My Life" also contains a disparity, noticeable mainly in the fade-out. The mono version runs a few seconds longer and contains different ad-libbed vocals, probably from a vocal cut for double tracking purposes.

The song's more lamentable distinction is that the stereo mix on every commonly available version (the U.K. and Capitol albums, the *Rock 'n' Roll Music* compilation, and its accompanying 1976 single release, and even the *Revolver* CD) is far inferior to Apple's mid-'70s mix.

At some point in the decade, albums originally released on Capitol were reissued on the Apple label. Coinciding with this cosmetic move was a more substantive one: stereo mixes were tweaked to rein in the awful wide-panning done the previous decade, bringing the instrumentation closer to the center.

This updating provided a fringe benefit to this track in particular. Ringo's drum fills, coming at the end of each verse and heretofore somewhat buried, suddenly leapt from the speakers, giving the song some percussive pop to match the brass. The difference on the Apple release of *Revolver* is truly striking, making all other releases sound anemic by comparison.

"I Am the Walrus"

The release of this song in EP, single, and album form showcased significant mono/stereo differences. With mono the preferred format at the time, the Beatles showed distinct preferences in how they presented their music.

To begin with, the song's very opening—the six-repeat, two-note Mellotron imitation of an English police siren—is two repeats shorter on the mono issues than on the English stereo release. (All American pressings, mono and stereo, are also four repeats, with an exception cited below.)

As the song proceeds, the mono mix removes a drum fill that comes after the first "I'm crying," as well as a cymbal crash that follows the first "goo goo g'joob." More striking are the extra four beats of music falling between the next "I'm crying" and "yellow matter custard" (coinciding with a premature vocal entrance by John, as shown on *Anthology 2*). It adds a more leisurely pacing to the track; its removal in all stereo issues merely hastens things along. While the single release, being mono, kept this extra bit intact (making the single version longer than the album track), the monaural albums removed it, thereby maintaining some uniformity between LPs.

Eventually, the stereo versions superseded the outmoded mono ones, codified with the *1967–1970* ("Blue Album") compilation in 1973 and the 1976 *Magical Mystery Tour* U.K. album release. Hence the version apparently favored by the Beatles is simply not available on CD.

In 1980, Capitol served up a compilation aimed strictly at collectors and Beatle geeks that thrive on these small mix variations. The *Rarities* album sought to placate listeners who wished to own all the idiosyncrasies in LP form. Their issue of "I Am the Walrus," however, merely generated yet another variation by restoring the edited music, the longer intro, deleting the drum fill, and presenting the whole shebang in stereo.

"Across the Universe"

On February 4, 1968, the Beatles committed John's inspired composition to tape. It may surprise some listeners to know that they never tackled it again; the three commercially available versions are variations of the very same recording. (*Anthology 2*'s version is an *earlier* take.)

Dissatisfied with what everyone else believed to be a fine master, John shelved the track. George's "The Inner Light" was instead chosen to back Paul's "Lady Madonna" single, while "Universe" was consigned to oblivion. (Talk of adding the song to the proposed *Yellow Submarine* soundtrack EP as filler went nowhere.)

Then, in 1969, Brit comedian Spike Milligan, a Beatle acquaintance, learned of the song's existence and finagled the band into contributing it to a charity album project he spearheaded for the benefit of the World Wildlife Fund (the LP also included contributions from the Bee Gees and the Hollies, among others). The addition of Beatle prestige compelled organizers to title the release, in honor of this rarity, *No One's Gonna Change Our World*.

Keeping to the nature theme, George Martin added bird sounds and flapping wings to the beginning and ending of the song. This version flew beneath the radar of most fans until being rediscovered in the late '70s and included on both the U.K. and American *Rarities* compilations.

But before that, the *Let It Be* project presented a dilemma. The final cut of the film depicted an apathetic band going through the motions of performing the song in January 1969, thereby necessitating its inclusion in the soundtrack. The rehearsal takes being rubbish (and securing all four Beatles to recut the track being out of the question), Phil Spector opted instead to revisit the previous master.

For better or worse, he stripped the track of its amateurish backing vocals (which included two lucky fans recruited from the steps of the studio), slowed it down a halftone, and added tasteful orchestration, providing a heretofore absent majesty. This was how the world came to know and love the song throughout most of its existence.

But *Let It Be* remained something of a canker sore for Paul, who in 2003, with two band members forever beyond reach, commissioned a reworking of the album. *Let It Be . . . Naked* offered a *third* version of the same recording. This time, rather than err on the side of excess, the take was deconstructed down to little more than a solo John performance. Adding the lovely outtake on *Anthology 2*, "Across the Universe" stands alone within the Beatles catalog as a song available in arrangements to suit everyone's tastes.

The Beatles on Reel-to-reel

Tape issues of the Beatles albums began appearing in the mid-1960s as manufacturers tried one format, then another, in hopes of catching on

"Open reel" tape issues were an audiophile's dream, featuring a click and pop-less listening experience. These rare releases trade for high figures today.

Courtesy of Frank Daniels

with the public. Four-tracks, eight-tracks, cassettes, and something called a "Playtape" were manufactured throughout the '60s and '70s.

But for our purposes, the "open reel" (or "reel-to-reel") releases warrant special interest. Manufactured by Ampex, these were an audiophile's dream, offering superb reproduction, free of pops and ticks, generated from true stereo masters. Typically, they ran at 7½ ips, making for optimum fidelity. (Longer releases, like George's *All Things Must Pass*, ran at 3¾ ips in order to fit three records onto a single reel.)

Such care in presentation makes the severe editing of this format's "White Album" release baffling—and highly collectible. Split over two reels dubbed *Volume One* and *Volume Two*, the cuts are clean, if arbitrary. *Entire verses* were removed from "Glass Onion," "Don't Pass Me By," and "Yer Blues." Minor cuts were made on "Dear Prudence" and "Why Don't We Do It in the Road," while "Cry Baby Cry" saw Paul's "Can you take me back . . ." coda removed entirely.

18

Half of What's Wrong

Ten Mistakes That Slipped onto the Vinyl

A s they accumulated years of stage experience, the Beatles developed truly impressive musical chops and an exceptional capacity for instinctively reading one another. (Their tightness probably reached its peak by the fall of 1963; Beatlemania's accompanying hysteria and shortened sets soon hastened the band's onstage musical decay.)

That said, recording is an entirely different discipline, requiring extra focus to incorporate changes in a song while going through numerous takes. In the Beatles' day, recording was often rushed. Out of necessity, songs were developed as tape rolled, with vocals and other cueing points absent. The pressure to come up with high-quality material on demand made perfectionism a luxury that could not always be afforded.

Despite having the best quality control in the world in the form of George Martin, the Beatles' vinyl catalog is riddled with little flubs and playing errors that all point to one conclusion: these guys were *human*. (Lennon would later claim that the band *purposely* left in little mistakes just to see if anyone noticed.) Subsequent CD releases have frequently "fixed" the errors, so it is largely through the original vinyl issues that these slips can be heard.

"Please Please Me," Recorded November 26, 1962

For their follow-up to "Love Me Do," the Beatles on this evening nailed the newly revamped "Please Please Me," prompting George Martin to accurately forecast its chart-topping future. After eighteen takes (not all complete), one was deemed best and mixed for mono release. Not until the following February did the song's hit status necessitate a stereo mix. With the master take's multitrack tape long since erased, Parlophone was forced to revisit the session tapes, choosing an alternate for stereo mixing.

Unfortunately, the pickings were slim, and a near-identical take spoiled by John and Paul singing two different lines simultaneously in the last verse made the cut:

John: "Why do I . . ."

Paul: "You know you . . ."

John's chuckle at the error is evident in the subsequent "Come on!"

Of course, many mistakes of this kind occurred during recording sessions and shows. (As Daffy Duck would say, "Pronoun trouble!") "I Feel Fine," "Baby's in Black," and many other songs would suffer from similar uncorrected gaffes in the studio—to say nothing of live performances.

Throughout the 1960s, mono was the common currency, as pop records were broadcast in monaural on AM radio and most kids couldn't afford the more expensive stereo records or the equipment to play them on. So Parlophone was pretty safe in issuing a "mistake" that few would ever hear.

BEATLES VI

(See label for correct playing order)

SELECTION	SUNG BY
EIGHT DAYS A WEEK	John, Paul & George
KANSAS CITY	Paul
WORDS OF LOVE	John & Paul
YES IT IS	John, Paul & George (solo by John)
I DON'T WANT TO SPOIL THE PARTY	John & Paul
EVERY LITTLE THING	John & Paul
WHAT YOU'RE DOING	Paul
YOU LIKE ME TOO MUCH	George
TELL ME WHAT YOU SEE	John & Paul
BAD BOY	John
DIZZY MISS LIZZIE	John

Produced by GEORGE MARTIN

Cover photo:
Fabulous Magazine—Fleetway Publications Ltd.

Other errors came from rushing releases to market, particularly from Capitol. First pressings of *Beatles VI* jackets, for example, appeared with the songs listed randomly.

But the following decades saw a mono/stereo paradigm shift. Through stereo re-releases, compilations, and FM oldies radio, the stereo "mistake" version of "Please Please Me" became widely heard, a situation not redressed until CD issues, in mono, of the first four albums arrived in the 1980s.

"Do You Want to Know a Secret," Recorded February 11, 1963

On this historic day, which saw completion of the ten tracks that supported two hit singles (and their B-sides) in comprising the *Please Please Me* LP, precious little room for error existed. It's easy to surmise that George Martin accepted as a successful take this otherwise smooth cut in which lead singer George inadvertently switches two words.

This occurred during the song's bridge. "I've known a secret for the week or two," sings George, a lyric that makes little sense until you transpose "a" and "the." But with the group tearing through so much material that day, they probably lacked the time to fix such a relatively minor error.

"If I Fell," Recorded February 27, 1964

Most of the charm of this exquisite *Hard Day's Night* ballad lies in the close harmonies between John and Paul, who were recorded standing at a single microphone. But Paul's performance adds pathos simply through the quality of his voice.

Since the notes of his part are at the upper end of his range, Paul's voice gets somewhat quavery as the track progresses, until finally, at 1:45, it cracks completely on the word "vain." This error was corrected with a simple splice for the mono mix, but survives, as is, in stereo.

"She's a Woman," Recorded October 8, 1964

The *Anthology 1* run-through (as well as various bootleg recordings) of this McCartney rocker shows John and George struggling to get a handle on this deceptively simple song's rhythm. This challenge evidently carried on into the released take, for at 1:25, an expected upstroke is simply gone. *Someone* completely missed the strings; the probable culprit is John.

"You're Gonna Lose That Girl," Recorded February 19, 1965

George Martin would one day pen a tell-all titled *All You Need Is Ears*. With hindsight, he may have had this day in mind as an occasion when he should have heeded his own advice.

As was typical from mid-1963 onward, the group was under severe time constraints, obliged to generate product while attending to a plethora of other activities. With filming soon to begin on their follow-up feature film, *Help!*, songs for the soundtrack needed to be cut—and fast. This may in some way explain how this track ever made it into production as is.

The backing track was laid down in one complete go. Such pros were the band by this time that even a new song with a rather intricate vocal arrangement was nailed quickly. The trouble came with the additions of bongos and piano.

The keyboard is horribly out of tune with the rest of the instruments, making the guitar sound flat. It doesn't help that the third chord Paul hits in the song's opening seconds is either a misfire or purposely dissonant. In any event, the results may help to explain why Richard Lester chose *this* song to mask with an electric saw in the film. ("It *was* you buzzing! You naughty boy!")

"Dizzy Miss Lizzie," Recorded May 10, 1965

In this recording the listener can hear evidence of the pressure on the lads to quickly fill out an album. Given the opportunity to record a tune they'd played innumerable times on stage, the Fabs produced and released a track riddled with mistakes. After two takes, they evidently believed they'd nailed it, but later returned to it for another five passes, following a successful stab at "Bad Boy," another Larry Williams original.

Most of the errors involve the lead guitar, which misses notes throughout, but loses the plot completely at 1:31. Unsure of his place, George—using, oddly enough for a straight rock number, a twelve-string guitar—is suddenly tentative, playing somewhat mutedly until regaining his confidence.

All of which is emblematic of the lackadaisical attitude the Fabs had by then toward recording any song not of their own creation. The *Help!* LP would be their last album containing old rock-and-roll chestnuts; artistic growth and a shift in attention to studio craftsmanship made future detours down memory lane unnecessary, at least until 1969.

"I'm Looking Through You," Recorded November 10, 1965

The unbelievable sloppiness of this track has given rise to conspiracy theories (more on that below).

Out-of-tune guitar notes abound; feedback pops up twice; even the rock-steady Ringo, at 1:58, misses the snare completely! American fans were even treated to two false starts on the stereo mix. So what was going on with a track that sounds like it was recorded with nowhere near the precision of the rest of the album?

History shows that the recording was a complete remake of an earlier take (released on *Anthology 2*) with the addition of a newly composed bridge. We also know that "I'm Looking Through You" was recorded a day before the finish of the *Rubber Soul* recording sessions, squeezed in before an all-night marathon that saw the completion of "You Won't See Me" and "Girl."

Rubber Soul was mixed shortly thereafter, when "Wait," a *Help!* leftover, was dusted off, polished up, and added to the album to make up the fourteen requisite tracks. With a deadline looming, was a proper remake of "I'm Looking Through You" simply too taxing for the band to produce?

Rumor-mongering Internet Beatleologists note that the recording bears all the earmarks of a McCartney one-man band project (or two, with Ringo on organ). The guitar stylings, the amateurish percussion (at 1:20, a dropped tambourine can be heard), and the apparent absence of Lennon and Harrison's instrumental presence points to this provocative conclusion. One thing is certain: no one has ever stepped forward to account for this track's deficiencies, one way or another.

"Ob-la-di, Ob-la-da," Recorded July 9, 1968

A certain amount of tension permeating the "White Album" sessions is traceable to the band's songwriters asserting individual control over their compositions rather than submit to group collaboration. While Ringo and George had generally been subjected to "direction" by the band's chief songwriters and George Martin, a more overt need now emerged, especially in Paul, to reduce them to supporting roles.

The upshot of this new dynamic was that either the song's author would perform the critical parts himself (usually Paul), or he would run the band ragged attempting to capture a "perfect" performance (also usually Paul). Nowhere during the sessions was the latter approach more evident than in the recording of this number.

It couldn't have helped that the song was the very encapsulation of the McCartney tendencies that most irritated John and George: "made-up" characters in silly, unlikely situations, glibly characterized and scored with a bouncy melody certain to engage a lowbrow audience. With the song's composer certain that, despite take after take, the band's performance was lacking *something*, the track's status among the three other members as their least favorite of thirty was assured.

Work on this tune alone consumed five straight days, encompassing three separate versions, of which version two would be the keeper. The finished master came about when John, already heartily sick of the song, sat down at the piano and agitatedly pounded out the opening, the rest of the band falling in (although Ringo's participation in the released track has been questioned). Through sheer force of will, the pieces fell into place; the resulting spontaneity is not quite belied by the aggravation that ultimately produced it.

With interjections from George and John (the two chime in with "arm" and "leg" following the line "children lend a hand") and laughter throughout, Paul's mix-up in the last verse ("Desmond stays at home and does his pretty face") seems scripted. It wasn't. Despite the take's evident quality, Paul attempted a *second* remake the following day before finally conceding that there could no bettering of what they already had.

"Hey Jude," Recorded August 1, 1968

The Beatles' last truly great song recorded expressly as a single drew as much attention for its uplifting theme as for its groundbreaking, sprawling length. Clocking in at 7:11, it also marks the band's last thoroughly innovative attempt to disrupt the pop world's natural order.

Another broken barrier might have caused even more ripples, if anyone had picked up on it at the time. During the last verse (beginning at 2:52), John suffers a playing mishap that leads him to burst out, beneath the line "let her under your skin," "Got the wrong chord—fucking hell!" Coming within a song possessing so many other elements drawing attention, it is not surprising that John's expletive has gone largely unnoticed.

"The Long and Winding Road," Recorded January 26, 1969

The "Get Back" project's free-form, unscripted path sometimes meant that tracks were selected for release that would not have been let out in other circumstances. Passing through the hands of Glyn Johns—who displayed appallingly bad judgment in choosing takes—before reaching Phil Spector, the selections that eventually comprised the *Let It Be* album were cobbled together from hours upon hours of tape that the biggest Beatles fan in the world would have had a hard time suffering through.

Nowhere is this clearer than in the decision to pass up a superior January 31, 1969, remake of "The Long and Winding Road" in favor of this version. John once likened playing bass to being asked to stay after school; it was a punishment that he'd just as soon pass on. His disdain is rendered crystal clear with the embarrassingly bad performance he turned in here (McCartney was busy singing and playing piano). Fluffed or entirely

Another domestic "oops" occurred when initi al *Hey Jude* pressings featured a provisional title that was later changed. (The title song was shortened by five seconds on this LP release.)

missed notes abound, leading at least one critic to accuse Lennon of willful sabotage.

This song inspired considerable bile during the band's split, chiefly in response to Spector's perceived overproduction. For his part, Spector claimed that he *had* to lay the strings on with a trowel in order to spare listeners from the song's awful underpinnings. Not explained is why he simply didn't just ask Paul, or someone, to recut Lennon's bass track.

19

There's Nobody There

Solo Performances Within a Group Context

A s the Beatles grew in confidence, artistry, and studio mastery, it became obvious that not every tune slated for recording was suitable for a beat group arrangement. (Even the sparer songs recorded early in their career found musical roles for everyone, if only in a percussive capacity.) "Yesterday" set the precedent when George Martin informed the group that three of them need not trouble themselves to show up for the session. This opened the door to releasing recordings under the Beatle moniker that used less than the full group. The notion that a Beatles record needn't include all four musicians reached its peak during the "White Album" sessions.

The most casual of readers will notice a pattern throughout this roll call of tunes recorded mostly unassisted: if only one Beatle was on a track, it probably was Paul. It is ironic that the member who worked the hardest at keeping the act going was unquestionably the most well-rounded musician (and wasn't shy about proving it, much to the consternation of his fellows), and therefore least needed the others around. It is no coincidence that the frequency of solo recording increased as tension between the musicians grew.

"Yesterday," Recorded June 14, 1965

When presenting what became his magnum opus to George Martin, Paul wasn't thinking in the slightest of the song's eventual recorded arrangement. Instead, he looked for input on a tune he simply did not know what to do with. Paul would speak often and at length through the years on the song's origin as a thunderbolt of inspiration that hit him upon waking one morning in early 1964. (The finished product's heartfelt sentimentality is belied by its working title of "Scrambled Eggs.")

That the band sat on what became a signature song for nearly a year and half before approaching it (as a near throwaway to fill space on the *Help!* LP)

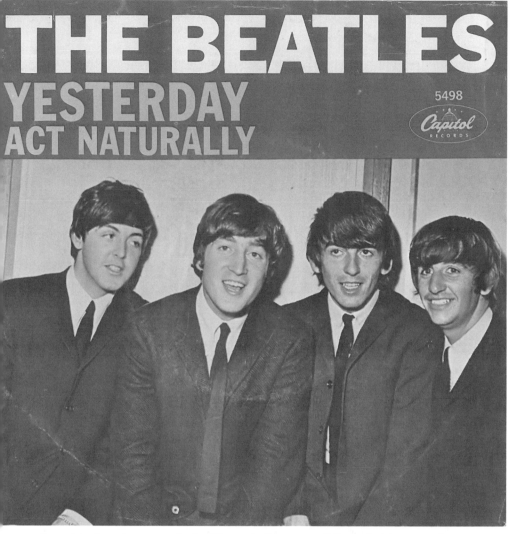

THE BEATLES
YESTERDAY
ACT NATURALLY

5498

Capitol RECORDS

Issued in American as a single, "Yesterday" presented Capitol with a quandary. Though clearly a solo recording in every sense, it was released as "Beatles" product. A year later, Capitol released "Caroline, No" from the Beach Boys' *Pet Sounds* under Brian Wilson's name only.

speaks volumes about their indecisiveness and/or self-consciousness about a composition that was a decided departure from their sound.

Still, Paul gamely submitted it for group consideration, with initial thought being given to putting John on organ for the recording. (Session tapes reveal George and Paul discussing the key it is to be laid down in.)

But George Martin had other notions. Impressed with Paul's solo performance on acoustic guitar when demonstrating the composition, he immediately "heard" an arrangement for string quartet, an idea he had to sell to the song's composer, who was alarmed at the prospect of entering "Mantovani" territory.

With Martin's explicit encouragement, Paul warmed to the idea, eventually contributing input to the producer's score. The others didn't seem in the least put out by their redundancy, praising the song privately while mocking it publicly, such as during televised performances on *The Ed Sullivan Show* and *Blackpool Night Out* in Britain, and on their 1965 year-end "Christmas Message."

This singular track, a Beatle recording in name only, was released as a single by Capitol in late summer of 1965. (U.K. fans would have to wait until *1976* to buy it as a 45.) The following year saw the Fabs perform it, as an ensemble, on their final tour.

"Love You To," Recorded April 13, 1966

George's first full-blown excursion into the exotic East began its recorded life as "Granny Smith" before giving way to a more familiar if equally inexplicable title. By the recording date, George had been dabbling with the sitar for at least six months; not until the end of touring later that year did he take up lessons in earnest at the foot of the maestro, Ravi Shankar.

Obviously, it would be unrealistic to expect proficiency from George when mastering even the rudiments of sitar playing requires years of study. For that reason, a platoon of Indian musicians from the North London Asian Music Circle did the heavy lifting on this track, with George tackling lead vocals. (Some sources credit him with playing acoustic or electric guitar on the recording.)

A harmony vocal from Paul did not make the final mix, although Ringo's shaking of a tambourine qualifies this as a two-Beatle track.

"Eleanor Rigby," Recorded April 28–29, 1966

The sharp focus of the finished product belies this song's rather haphazard gestation. Originally inspired by an opening line that popped into Paul's head to accompany a piano lick (with "Miss Daisy Hawkins" in place of "Eleanor Rigby" at that point), the song's storyline went through a variety of zigs and zags before arriving at its final destination.

Original Quarry Men member Pete Shotton was around for much of the song's creation. He recalled advising Paul to rethink naming the priest "Father McCartney," lest he give listeners the wrong idea. (Shotton's further suggestion that the song end with the clergyman officiating over Eleanor's funeral was met with snorts of derision from John.) Ringo offered the "darning his socks" scenario, while George is credited with helping to craft the "Ahh, look at all the lonely people" refrain.

John's claims of substantial lyrical contributions are contradicted by virtually everyone else who was present. What is clear is that on this particular number, Paul's penchant for soliciting input from anyone around was regarded as highly insulting by his songwriting partner.

Building upon the precedent of "Yesterday," George Martin again saw no need for any instrumental input from the group, selling Paul instead on the idea of a string *octet*. The latter gave some general direction for the orchestration, which Martin then proceeded to write drawing inspiration from Bernard Herrmann's *Fahrenheit 451* score. Paul recorded layers of vocals himself, with minimal assistance from George and John.

"Within You, Without You," Recorded March 15, 1967

Landmark status notwithstanding, *Sgt. Pepper's Lonely Hearts Club Band* was far less of a group effort than is commonly supposed. John contributed tunes somewhat begrudgingly for this conception of Paul's, as Ringo battled ennui through hours of standby duty while the two chief composers caucused with George Martin. For his part, George eschewed his rock guitarist role to pursue serious study of the sitar, all but abdicating his lead guitar duties to Paul.

Despite clear indications that this album was destined for greatness, George's initial contribution to the project ended up, eighteen months later, as an effects-laden piss-take. "Only a Northern Song," a dig at their publishing arrangement, was met with a decidedly tepid response from his fellows. Pressed to dig a little deeper, George fused his India/meditation fixation to a more musically serious attempt at a statement. The resulting opus, composed on a harmonium at Klaus Voormann's house, wedded Eastern and Western elements to a sing-songy sermon.

Initially skeptical, George's bandmates and producer were eventually won over by his exceptional efforts at getting the track *just so*. George Martin had the daunting task of melding the Western strings to Indian scales before succeeding in creating a seamless musical tapestry. George's trancelike vocal atop a lush instrumental bedding proved a perfect fit to the track destined to become *Pepper's* spiritual centerpiece. (The composer himself would insist on relieving the weightiness of his preaching with a burst of laughter at the track's end.)

Though it was not everyone's cup of chai, no less an authority than John Lennon himself would declare the song a favorite, a lucid encapsulation of George's singular mindset.

"Blackbird," Recorded July 11, 1968

This charming acoustic composition, commonly regarded as a metaphor for the 1960s Black Power movement, got its start as an attempt to play Bach's Bourrée in E minor from memory. It is perhaps for that reason that guitarists adept at fingerpicking find it irresistible.

Paul recorded it at the same time John was working on "Revolution 9" in another studio at EMI. (The contrasts in their work could not be more striking.) He recorded in solitude, accompanied only by his guitar and a metronome. (Some insist that it is his tapping foot, but the precision is too spot-on to be human.) Engineer Geoff Emerick claims an effort was made to record natural ambient sounds outdoors (using a very long microphone cable), but ultimately he turned to EMI's ever-reliable sound effects library.

Never afraid to echo his past, Paul would later record "Bluebird" for 1973's *Band on the Run* album, and later still, "Jenny Wren" for 2005's *Chaos and Creation in the Backyard*, creating an avian trilogy of sorts.

"Good Night," Recorded July 22, 1968

As most of the world knows, Julian Lennon sparked Paul's initial burst of inspiration for Paul's "Hey Jude." Less remembered is that John himself wrote "Good Night" with his son in mind. This song is usually brought up as Exhibit A to refute the charge that Lennon was incapable of writing a tender, melodic ballad. (Though it must be said that handing the song off to Ringo suggested some insecurity on John's part about performing something so saccharine himself. According to Geoff Emerick, the vocal John recorded as a guide was never bettered.)

In a rare occasion of full group support, all three non-featured Beatles assisted in the recording of this, the obligatory Ringo showcase on the album in progress. (Though "Don't Pass Me By" was already in the can, one vocal among thirty tracks wasn't going to cut it.) A spoken-word intro was planned, to set the mood of sending one's child off to slumber, but was later abandoned. Left in was Ringo's whispered parting to the world at the song's end.

John requested that George Martin orchestrate the ballad with a real "Hollywood" feel; years later, he assessed the finished product as "possibly overlush." But the song provided a sympathetic setting for Ringo's limited vocal prowess, with ample support from the Mike Sammes Singers (the same outfit heard on "I Am the Walrus" less than a year before).

"Mother Nature's Son," Recorded August 9, 1968

While in India studying meditation with the Maharishi, the Beatles attended a lecture addressing the relationship between mankind and the natural world. Whatever else they may have gotten out of the lesson, John and Paul walked away inspired, channeling their respective reactions into music.

For John, this took the form of a gentle, vaguely spiritual commentary. "I'm just a child of nature," he would sing. "I'm one of nature's children." Maybe it was the uncharacteristically hippy-dippy lyric; perhaps it was the association with the Master, whom later he would loudly denounce as a charlatan. But for whatever reason, John all but abandoned the tune, revisiting it three years and a sea change later. Retooled as the first of an ongoing series of mea culpas to his missus, the world would know the song as "Jealous Guy."

Paul, on the other hand, rarely evidenced a need to rethink his position on anything. His response to the lecture was, typically, to conjure up a persona that could not be mistaken for himself, all future pastoral leanings aside.

In typical McCartney fashion, his reading reeks of sincerity from the opening line. All in all, "Mother Nature's Son" is a fine, understated performance, punctuated with tasteful brass (suggested by Lennon, of all people).

Despite his input on the song, the presence of John—or any other Beatle—was decidedly unwelcome. Some eleven days after recording the basic track alone, Paul revisited the song to supervise the brass overdubbing and lay down some percussion. Engineer Ken Scott would recall the lighthearted vibes that evening, disrupted only by the unexpected intrusion of John and Ringo into the proceedings. Then, Scott reported, you could cut the tension with a knife. The hostility only dissipated with their departure.

"Wild Honey Pie," Recorded August 20, 1968

That same evening, still in one-man-band mode, Paul laid down the tracks to this piece of musical ephemera. Bearing no resemblance whatsoever to the similarly titled music hall pastiche tucked away on side four, the song's apparently off-the-cuff flavor is belied by the fact that it had been bandied around in Rishikesh months earlier as an instrumental. Pattie Harrison was particularly fond of the tune, which was probably enough reason for Paul to spend studio time capturing it.

It also may have served as a transient distraction from heavy doings afoot. Three days earlier, with no warning, George had taken off for a brief vacation in Greece. It may have been simply a way of blowing off steam, given the increasingly heated tone of the sessions. Two days after this session, Ringo would walk out, with no intention of returning.

Engineer Geoff Emerick had quit mid-session a month earlier, while George Martin would himself go on an unannounced holiday in early September. The sense of purpose and exploration that had been the hallmark of the band's previous collaborations had disappeared, and evenings like this one were certainly emblematic of the ongoing turmoil.

"Julia," Recorded October 13, 1968

This most personal of tunes offered listeners a look into the composer's unvarnished psyche. While he was certainly not averse to revealing his innermost thoughts publicly, this was the first time John had addressed an actual person by name in a song. Evocations of his long-departed mother served as a starting point, but the tune is as much an embracing of his present as wistful look back at his past. In "Julia," John melded the first significant female in his life with the newest.

To mark the advent of an increasing directness in his writing—a hallmark of his solo career—John, for the first and only time, recorded this Beatle tune by himself. He utilized the fingerpicking technique picked up from Donovan in India (a style he would employ extensively in his next several compositions, including "Sun King" and "Everybody Had a Hard Year," eventually grafted onto "I've Got a Feeling.")

This would be the last tune recorded for the sprawling double LP, providing closure to the most tumultuous chapter in the Beatles' career. It ended on a gentle note; as an extra set of ears, Paul offered encouragement, with John nailing the song in a couple of passes.

"Her Majesty," Recorded July 2, 1969

Paul arrived at EMI studios ahead of the others this day—one day before Brian Jones of the Rolling Stones was found dead in his pool—and laid down this slight concoction for inclusion in what everyone perceived to be the band's farewell recording. An era was rapidly closing; tuneful melodic pop as epitomized by the Beatles was giving way to heavier, less song-oriented sounds. In a few days, the Atlanta International Pop Festival would showcase artists whose ascendancy would dominate the coming years: Led Zeppelin, Chicago, and Grand Funk Railroad.

It's hard to imagine how the Beatles would have competed alongside these acts. Their artistic and sales domination of the decade would have been challenged by newcomers with more energy and something to prove, just as the Fabs had grown weary of the game and each other. Having enjoyed rock-and-roll supremacy for so long, would they have been compelled to reach farther to stay ahead of their peers, or would they simply have abdicated their position, assuming the role of elder statesmen?

We'll never know, for by this time each was off pursuing an individual path, a practice already increasingly manifest. Paul used this day to record

The "White Album" individual portraits are shown on the cover of this Spanish compilation. The 1968 sessions marked a distinctive lack of unity and group spirit, in direct contrast to previous projects.

"Her Majesty" without interference from George and Ringo, who arrived in due course to tackle "Golden Slumbers" / "Carry That Weight." (John was recovering from a car accident in Scotland; his bandmates would use his absence to tackle a raft of tunes before he rejoined them a week later.)

As originally intended, the song served as a link between "Mean Mr. Mustard" and "Polythene Pam," breaking up two John songs in a row. Paul didn't like the result, however, and ordered engineer John Kurlander to remove "Her Majesty" and discard it. Under house rules to never dispose of *anything* recorded by the Fabs, Kurlander simply stuck the song at the end of some leader tape and spliced it onto the end of the *Abbey Road* master, inadvertently creating the world's first "hidden track." (The opening crash is actually the ending to "Mean Mr. Mustard," while the "missing chord" at the end of "Her Majesty" still exists, buried in the opening strums of "Polythene Pam.")

Oh, Rock On, Anybody

Ten Recordings Featuring Musical Role-switching

Eventually, territorial issues were bound to rise within the Beatles, a group blessed with a bass player who had originally been a guitarist, and just happened to be more than competent on a variety of other instruments. As cocomposer, Paul more than occasionally asserted his right to brush George aside on lead guitar duties. (In a pinch, he was fair to good behind the drum kit, as well.) For his part, George tended to stick to his traditional role, while John was good for the occasional surprise guitar solo or bass slot. Here are some shining examples of "Beatle musical chairs" that marked a departure from the established order.

"You Can't Do That," Recorded February 25, 1964: John on Guitar Solo

With George celebrating his twenty-first birthday in the studio on this day, the band laid down tracks for possible inclusion in their upcoming film debut. The first song tackled would eventually see release as the B-side to "Can't Buy Me Love."

Thoroughly enthralled with his newly acquired Rickenbacker twelve-string, George was more than happy to occupy himself with the song's opening riff and rhythm. For the solo, John took over, weighing in with his brand-new Rickenbacker 325. Certainly a departure from George's more fluid lines, Lennon's shining moment is, typically, kinetically rhythmic and perfectly serviceable while more than slightly raucous.

"Ticket to Ride" and "Another Girl," Recorded February 15, 1965: Paul on Lead Guitar

On this day, the group recorded a pair of tracks destined for their second film, *Help!*, both of which featured Paul on lead guitar. Brandishing his new Epiphone Casino electric guitar, Paul played lead fills throughout the first recording while George supplied the chiming central riff on the twelve-string.

It made practical sense to hand off the lead guitar to Paul on this guitar-laden song, with John busy singing lead and supplying his standard rhythm contribution. Onstage, where exact duplication of records was fast becoming unfeasible, George handled the riff and lead parts.

Less explicable is how Paul came to handle the lead fills on "Another Girl," a song devoid of any guitar intricacies. His busy, sloppy doodlings permeate the track while George is reduced to playing simple down strokes. (Whatever his feelings toward the "demotion," George may have exacted his revenge in the film, miming Paul's leads with comically overblown guitar heroics—on John's guitar, no less.)

"Drive My Car," Recorded October 13, 1965: Paul on Lead Guitar

Rubber Soul's opening track is a sprightly little McCartney concoction, powered by a driving bass line copped from Otis Redding's "Respect." Paul set up the rhythm with another newly acquired axe—in this case, a Rickenbacker 4001 bass—and George doubled McCartney's part on guitar.

The song contains some of the group's most dissonant vocals *and* lead guitar fills, which Paul—using a slide to approximate a bluesy sound—managed to shoehorn into the intro, solo, outro, and even beneath the vocals on the last verse. For all that, it's a powerful track, with more bottom end than the Beatles had ever managed on a record before.

"Taxman," Recorded April 21, 1966: Paul on Lead Guitar

For their final album release during the touring years, George reached his high-water mark. *Revolver* saw the inclusion of *three* Harrisongs, a per-disc ratio he would never again match. (Their next two album releases, *Sgt. Pepper's* and *Magical Mystery Tour*, would see him drop back to pre-*Help!* levels, with just one lead vocal per record. For their remaining four LPs, he rose to an average of one track per side.)

Winning this latitude on *Revolver* may have required some finesse. Perhaps it was for this reason that George *asked* Paul to take the lead on the album's opening track (another distinction he would never again enjoy). "Taxman" boasted some truly exceptional lead guitar, praised by the song's author as sounding vaguely Indian. Indeed, the finished track utilized Paul's singular solo break twice; the original "cold" ending was ditched in favor of splicing a repeat of the solo onto the end and fading it out.

"She Said She Said," Recorded June 21, 1966: George on Bass (?)

Recorded at the end of the *Revolver* sessions, this track was famously inspired by a 1965 encounter in L.A. between the song's LSD-addled author and an equally woolly-minded actor Peter Fonda, who insisted on recounting his clinical death to a mortified Lennon.

The song's well-remembered origins are countered by the murky circumstances of its recording. Completed from start to finish in a single session, "She Said She Said" was the very last song taped for the album. The following day, the album's mixes were rushed for completion before the Beatles kicked off their world tour.

Some sources report that a serious row, ending with an infuriated McCartney storming out of the studio, marred the session, and forced the track's completion by a three-piece band. (Mark Lewisohn's otherwise exhaustive books, which should have settled this matter, don't even mention it, while McCartney cops to the argument in his bio *Many Years from Now*.)

Circumstantial evidence supports the possibility of George being pressed into service to tackle Paul's usual role. To begin with, the bass line is not typical of Paul's style. It is measured and thoughtful—a Harrison trademark—rather than powerful and boundary-pushing, as so much of Paul's work was at this time.

More importantly, no traces of Paul's vocals are evident on the track, whereas John's and George's are plainly obvious. Was McCartney's absence the result of an unpleasant confrontation, or something more benign? With memories fading over time and two of the principals beyond asking, the matter may never be settled.

"Back in the U.S.S.R.," Recorded August 23, 1968; "Dear Prudence," Recorded August 28, 1968: Paul on Drums

Far better documented is Ringo's departure from the band during the "White Album" sessions. Feeling fed up and unloved, he departed a day after the August 21 recording of "Sexy Sadie." Unfazed by the unexpected loss, the three remaining Beatles adhered to their recording timetable.

With Paul commandeering Ringo's forsaken kit and John plunking away on a six-string bass, the Threetles laid down "Back in the U.S.S.R." in a workmanlike manner. Even so, apparent deficiencies in the recording neces-

Though a decent enough hand on the skins, Paul's abilities gave Ringo nothing to worry about. Still, Mr. Starkey often lamented the fate that placed him in the company of *three* frustrated drummers.   *Photo by Tom Hanley/Redferns*

sitated numerous overdubs of additional bass, and eventually drums—by Ringo himself—to bring the recording up to snuff. So cluttered were the results that properly assessing Paul's work is somewhat challenging.

Less so is his exemplary, tasteful stickwork on "Dear Prudence." It's hard to see how Ringo might have bettered it. Strangely, Paul seemed to have more difficulty handling rockers, which are fairly basic, than more complex recordings like this one.

"Honey Pie," Recorded October 1–2, 1968: John on Lead Guitar

For all the disdain he and George heaped upon Paul's "songs for Grannies to dig," John lent unexpectedly effective support to this, the latest in Paul's series of vaudeville throwbacks.

In a performance that George would describe as "brilliant," John channeled his inner Django Reinhardt, providing a pitch-perfect imitation of 1930s jazz guitar. Despite any posturing to the contrary, it's evident from this song and others how much the Beatles were steeped in old-time show-business tradition, able to conjure up passable renditions seemingly at will.

Ringo would reveal this with his LP debut of 1930s and '40s standards, *Sentimental Journey*, while George would record tunes by Hoagy Carmichael, Harold Arlen, and Cole Porter during his solo career (and display a fondness for English ukulele player and music hall legend George Formby). Paul's dalliances with old-timey styles are well documented.

"For You Blue," Recorded January 25, 1969: John on Lap Steel Guitar

The troubled "Get Back" project only regained its footing once the band ditched the austere atmosphere of Twickenham film studios for the cozy surroundings of their own Apple studios on Savile Row. This, plus the addition of keyboardist Billy Preston to the proceedings, lightened things considerably for the duration of the project. Minus Billy on this day, the group took the time to record one of George's songs.

Following George's departure and conditional return to the fold, he had withdrawn his compositions from serious consideration for the proposed, but still nebulous, live performance. Stung by his bandmates' complete apathy toward the quality tunes he had brought in (several of which ended up on his solo debut album), Harrison instead presented this cute but slight offering.

Perhaps the track's most interesting feature (aside from being an upbeat blues song) was the "Hawaiian" guitar. With George playing acoustic throughout and Paul on piano, it fell to John to give the tune some color. Displaying a heretofore unsuspected talent, he played his heart out—in effect, justifying the song's existence. In his overdubbed vocal, taped a full year after the band's performance, George would invoke the name of a classic blues guitarist in admiration of John, exclaiming, "Elmore James got nothing on this, baby!"

"Get Back," Recorded January 28, 1969: John on Lead Guitar

Remarking on Paul's dictatorial manner, John, spewing resentment in his famous post-breakup "Lennon Remembers" *Rolling Stone* interview, noted about "Get Back" that "I played the solo on that, yeah. When Paul was feeling kindly he would give me a solo." Reading between the lines, it is not

As shown here in the *Beatles Monthly Magazine*, John too was eager to play around on the kit, though wisely not on any recordings.

inconceivable to suggest that Paul instinctively knew that the best way to engage Lennon's meandering attentions was to give him a task to do.

That said, John certainly ran with the part on "Get Back," playing in a rootsy style that suggests, without aping, rock and roll's early days. Given the song's somewhat primitive dynamics, one could imagine that George's treatment of the same material might have underscored how compositionally thin the track really is; "Get Back" is more a groove than anything else.

It's interesting to watch the rooftop performance of this song in *Let It Be*. The band seems to enjoy playing it, even as John struggles manfully with the lead in the winter wind, blowing on his fingers at one point. (Despite having witnessed the song's origins as a racially tinged satire earlier that month, director Michael Lindsay-Hogg seems to have forgotten who was doing what, cutting to *George*, hacking away on chords, during the first guitar solo.)

"The Ballad of John and Yoko," Recorded April 14, 1969: John on Lead Guitar, Paul on Drums

Never one to let regard for others stand in the way of personal impulse, John wanted a ditty chronicling his recent nuptials and honeymoon with Yoko to be released to a breathless public *immediately*, notwithstanding the presence of "Get Back" on the charts and the unavailability of George and Ringo. With the former out of the country and the latter filming *The Magic Christian*, this left John and Paul to trot out their Nerk Twins act for the last time, meeting up at EMI to tackle the musical duties themselves.

Paul, recently married himself, jumped at the chance to work with his (of late) disinterested and distracted partner. With a thicket of business and personal issues ensnaring the band, it must have seemed refreshing to engage in *any* musical activity, self-serving as the offering was.

Much care went into maintaining the illusion of group unity with this release, with footage of a *group* performance used in the promo film, and a *group* shot of the band—plus the ever-present Yoko—on the American single sleeve. It is hard not to read all of this as Lennon's trading on the public's goodwill toward the Beatles as a way to win approval for his personal union. The fact that he'd all but left the Beatles in his heart by this time makes the entire enterprise somewhat hypocritical.

Session tapes reveal that while John's rhythm and lead guitar duties went smoothly enough, Paul struggled mightily with providing a simple backbeat, repeatedly losing the plot at the end of the middle-eight section ("Think!"). Eventually, he nailed the timing at this hurdle, growing noticeably bolder in his fills as the track concluded.

Perhaps as a sop to George, the band regrouped in toto just two days later, this time to cut his bouncy pop charmer "Old Brown Shoe" as a B-side. (This was only George's second flip, coming one year and three singles after "The Inner Light" had graced "Lady Madonna.") While John contributed rhythm guitar in support of George's and Paul's marvelous unison runs, the song's author had a change of heart two days later, erasing Lennon's superfluous guitar part and adding an organ track. As a single, this release averaged 2.5 Beatles per side.

21

All Right, George!

Following the release of "Love Me Do," the Beatles' Parlophone debut, George recalled hearing it on the radio for the first time. He describes focusing his ear on "the lead guitar work," which begs the question: what was he *listening* to? The only notable instrumental work on *that* record comes from John's harmonica; there's no guitar solo, and only an acoustic rhythm guitar chugs along in the background. Thereafter, George would build a glorious body of work throughout the band's career, but "Love Me Do" isn't included in it.

Here are ten truly shining moments that illustrate the Quiet One's way with an axe. To those who equate fretboard mastery with speed, effects, and volume, his oeuvre seems laughably inadequate. But true aficionados know that greatness goes beyond playing fast blues scales. For all the deriding of his abilities, the following examples prove what the faithful already know: George had a gift for composing melodies within melodies and providing exactly the lift and elegance needed to turn already unforgettable songs into true classics.

"Till There Was You," Recorded July 30, 1963

In 1963, Beatles fans learned of a little-suspected influence on George: classical guitarist Andrés Segovia. Though anyone hearing George's rockabilly stylings at the time might have doubted it, the twenty-year-old named the famous Spaniard as a favorite in a band profile published that year.

The first evidence of this influence came that autumn with the release of *With the Beatles*, which contained "Till There Was You." Though the tune had long been a staple of the group's stage act, the recording process required more suitable instrumentation. At George Martin's suggestion, George ditched his electric guitar to record "Till There Was You" on a nylon-stringed guitar, enhancing the Latin-style arrangement the boys had worked up.

Though he'd composed his solo long before (having played it at the Decca debacle eighteen months earlier), by July 1963 he had honed it to perfection. Within McCartney's otherwise pedestrian cabaret interlude, George's flamenco-style solo shines. Those not aware that they were listening to pop album by a group of rough-and-tumble rockers may have mistaken the recording for that of a "serious" musician. Years of stage experience had also shaped George's *visual* presentation, as showcased by his highly memorable performance on *The Ed Sullivan Show* in early 1964.

"All My Loving," Recorded July 30, 1963

Sullivan's show provided America with its first opportunity to size up the dynamic newcomers visually. First impressions proved lasting, establishing character types amplified months later in *A Hard Day's Night.*

On this night, in their first New World performance, George was afforded a generous platform to show what he did best. The Fabs' first number, "All My Loving," represented the culmination of Harrison's Chet Atkins fixation, which had led to the acquisition of a Gretsch "Country Gentleman" electric guitar.

It's interesting to watch the *Ed Sullivan* performance today, for rarely did George—suffering from the flu, no less—display such a carefree, crowd-pleasing persona.

On the recording, Harrison's jaunty lead, suspended over a bed of spastic strumming from John, is a marvel of economic composition, thoroughly summing up his strengths. (Slight imperfections in the double tracking only enhance the song's appeal.) Melodic and memorable, George's solo builds to a tidy finish before giving way to the harmonized first-verse reprise (while Paul sang both parts on record, George dueted with him in live situations).

"A Hard Day's Night," Recorded April 16, 1964

The band's film debut could scarcely have kicked off with a bigger splash than the one provided by George's newly acquired twelve-string Rickenbacker. The title tune opened with a shimmering chord unheard of in rock—or just about anywhere else, for that matter: a G7 suspended ninth, with an added fourth, for those keeping score. (The Kinks would ape this opening years later on "Do It Again.")

The Beatles' thirst for innovation found expression here, signaling progress from mere bandstand competency toward studio mastery. Though compositionally the song is not one of John's finer moments (rhyming "buy you things" with "everything"?), the performance itself is breathtaking.

Momentum carries the song, perfectly encapsulating the frantic pace of the Fabs' lives depicted in the film.

George's work on the recording, literally from start to finish, is stunning. Dramatic kickoff aside, his guitar break sounds like nothing he'd ever played before. Simultaneously dark and elastic, with bottom-note riffing giving way to some speedy picking, it sounds more difficult to play than it actually is. Adding to the unusual flavor is an underpinning of piano from George Martin doubling Harrison's notes on the solo.

The song's exotic, chiming outro portended the folk and Indian stylings George would bring to the table in 1965–66.

"I Don't Want to Spoil the Party," Recorded September 29, 1964

Though buried among the more obviously commercial tracks on the late 1964 *Beatles for Sale* album, this song represents a tribute to the Beatles' country-and-western influences. Demonstrating a command of the idiom within their own style, "Party" contains interesting touches.

The verses, for instance, feature John harmonizing with *himself*, instead of his usual partner. (As a result, the vocals are somewhat less precise than they would have been, had Paul sung along.) The subject matter is rather downbeat for a Beatles track: the narrator, having been stood up, would rather go off and drink alone than ruin other people's good time with his foul mood.

But all is not bleak, for with the instrumental break George displays the culmination of his rockabilly studies. Typical for him is the great effort put into the solo, which contains some memorable phrasing before reaching a satisfying conclusion. Less common is the marvelous attack he delivers with his fingerpicking, producing a ringing, stinging solo. The effect is to give voice to the singer's bitterness without being heavy-handed. "Party" is proof positive of the vastly underrated sympathetic support that informs George's best work.

"Nowhere Man," Recorded October 22, 1965

The best of the Beatles' radio hits were pitch-perfect creations: accessible without being predictable, and with a richness of detail that always rewarded repeated listenings. Unexpected twists provided added bonuses.

Such was the case with this song, a *Rubber Soul* album track in England but a single in America. The *a cappella* intro in three-part harmony was

THE BEATLES
I DON'T WANT TO SPOIL THE PARTY
EIGHT DAYS A WEEK

5371

George's fine rockabilly picking on "I Don't Want to Spoil the Party" was showcased on the flip side to "Eight Days a Week" in America.

certainly arresting (a trick the band would elaborate on soon after with "Paperback Writer"), but even more so was the structural innovation of inserting of the guitar break after the *first* verse, rather than toward the middle or end of the song.

And what a solo it is: in a reversal of standard procedure, which demands that one start on the low strings and end high, this one starts high and ends *low*, just before a single sparkling harmonic note played *high* on the neck. Anyone doubting George's capacity to construct neat little sub-melodies for insertion into the group's offerings must only listen to "Nowhere Man."

Some of the solo's sheen comes from George's adoption of a Fender Stratocaster on this number. Popularized by Buddy Holly, the instrument

THE BEATLES
NOWHERE MAN
WHAT GOES ON
5587

The obvious commercial appeal of "Nowhere Man" led Capitol to hold back the track from the domestic release of *Rubber Soul*, saving it instead as an ace in the hole for their next cobbled-together album.

hardly ever found its way onto a Beatles record, but on this occasion, its rare use resulted in a gem.

"And Your Bird Can Sing," Recorded April 26, 1966

This powerful track, buried on side two of *Revolver*, stands as evidence of the Beatles' talent for *orchestrating* their individual parts.

Built upon the bedrock of Ringo's solid drumming and John's chiming, four-in-the-bar strum, "Bird" also features Paul's percolating, walking bass line. But it is the magnificent twin-guitar riffing that takes the song to another level. This sinewy melody line sounded like *nothing* heard on a pop record, much less a *Beatles* record, in 1966—which says something, considering Jeff Beck's work in the Yardbirds, Clapton's with Cream, Roger McGuinn's Byrds output, and the flights of young Jimi Hendrix.

For those who revel in guitar glory, it doesn't get any better than this. (As usual, the *Revolver* mono mix is preferable for anyone seeking the full slab of six-string ecstasy.)

Though clearly comprised of two guitar parts played in unison, the riff that forms the song's backbone is a marvel. Never satisfied to diddle away on blues scales, George provided an engaging yet muscular melody that was light years ahead of anything he'd attempted heretofore. As such, it makes a convincing case for the enlightening powers of LSD, though the drug's effects on lesser talents were demonstrably less stunning.

The groundbreaking riffing provided a blueprint for guitarists in years to come, when use of the "twin lead guitar" effect (by groups like Boston and Molly Hatchett) became a rock staple, often with disastrous results.

(An earlier, rejected version of the song, found on *Anthology 2*, featured twelve-string folk-rock picking. Less than a week later, the band redid the song, consigning the Rickenbacker twelve-string to Beatle history and converting the "solo" section into the beefy opening riff that we know today.)

"Hey Bulldog," Recorded February 11, 1968

On the eve of their departure for Rishikesh to study with the Maharishi, the Beatles took care to assure "Lady Madonna" a proper launch as the final single before their sabbatical. The group dutifully filed into EMI studios with a film crew in tow, eager to get the chore of making what was then called a "promo film" out of the way.

Before shooting began, someone had the bright idea of actually recording a song in front of the cameras, rather than just lip-synching a track that they were doubtless already sick of. John brought in a new song called "She Can Talk to Me," and before they were finished recording, Paul's misreading of John's scribble had re-christened the track "Hey Bulldog."

George was never famous for making up his parts on the fly. Typically, he worked out his contributions in advance, composing riffs and melodies that would enhance the finished product. In this case, compelled to solo "on the spot," he rose to the occasion. (Existing footage shows him going over the song with John before tape rolled, no doubt to become familiar with the composition's structure.) What resulted was one of George's shining moments, offered in the service of a song cut as little more than a throwaway.

It is perhaps less the notes played and more the overall sound of George's Gibson SG that elevates this performance to greatness. The snarl in his incisive solo perfectly matches the acerbic tone of John's vocal. Once again, the sympathetic musical understanding between the two was displayed in a collaborative effort that, at the best of times, made for a heightened listening experience.

The pity here is that the resulting track, undervalued by its author, was consigned to *Yellow Submarine* soundtrack oblivion and cut from the film, only to be rediscovered years later for the *Songtrack* release.

"Yer Blues," Recorded August 20, 1968

John Lennon went through a series of transitions in 1968, his creative output ascending as the group's Indian meditation excursion mutated into a songwriting camp. His offerings to the *Sgt. Pepper* follow-up ranged from gentle whimsy ("Cry Baby Cry") to hard-rocking rave-ups ("Everybody's Got Something to Hide Except for Me and My Monkey") to introspective catharsis ("Julia") and bold experimentation ("Revolution #9").

Then there's this track, a send-up of the current blues craze in Britain. John had little use for Clapton/Beck/Page-style *blooz*, yet could not resist taking a stab himself. Wisely, instead of simply mocking the style, he equipped it with lyrics that reveal a dark wit masking an undercurrent of genuine despair.

George might have expected to feel daunted upon finding himself in the blues territory of his best friend, Eric Clapton. But instead of faltering, George reached deep into his own bag of tricks to come up with a solo that takes on the blues-rock gods directly and bests them on their own turf.

The instrumental break in "Yer Blues" begins with John, who had lately become a little more forward in demonstrating his guitar prowess. While making no claim to virtuosity, he does a more than adequate job in establishing a groove.

George then steps in, offering an unearthly sonic assault. His astounding, banshee-like wail rises in intensity, acknowledging existing musical boundaries before transcending them. It is an amazing display, utterly bereft of clichés. Clearly evident is a quality that began appearing in his playing around this time and would define his solo work: the guitar as *voice*. His performance here is less a display of rock star heroics than the sound of a soul in agony.

Just weeks later, Clapton himself, drafted into a band with Lennon, Keith Richards, and Mitch Mitchell, did his own take on "Yer Blues"—competent, but hardly earth-shattering—for the Rolling Stones' *Rock and Roll Circus* film.

Soon Clapton would abandon the musical base on which his deity status was built for the somewhat greener pastures of Blind Faith and Delaney and Bonnie.

"Dig a Pony," Recorded January 30, 1969

As is well documented elsewhere, what became known as the *Let It Be* sessions were not the Beatles' finest hour. Long-simmering tensions that had first surfaced during the creation of the "White Album" were now publicly displayed, though rarely in the form of outright bickering; George would later say that when the four were at odds, they simply stopped communicating, or went at each other passive-aggressively. Ennui, stardom fatigue, heavy drug fallout, and sibling-like rivalry now came into play all too evidently before the cameras.

Yet no amount of collective disinterest in carrying on kept these seasoned professionals from marshalling their forces for one final shining moment of greatness as a performing band.

The famous "rooftop concert" was an eleventh-hour climax to thirty days of recording and rehearsing, which Lennon later called "the most miserable sessions on Earth." Temporarily short on quality material, Lennon provided "Dig a Pony," which hardly measures up to his best. Yet the band's performance in wintry outdoor conditions somehow transforms the track, due in no small part to George's creative guitar work.

Thundering in with a pounding riff (followed by a superfluous refrain that Phil Spector wisely edited out), the song quickly settles into an oddly metered waltz tempo, a frequent Lennon trademark. His plaintive, world-weary vocal receives direct counterpoint from George's rosewood Fender Telecaster. Utilizing an uncommon (for him) formula, George responds to John's free-associative wordplay with a series of near-rockabilly phrases.

The solo, cued by trade-off whooping between John and Paul, is a gem. Bent notes again presage what would become George's signature sound. Though he didn't have a slide on his finger that chilly afternoon, his playing instinctively took steps toward what became his defining "voice" in coming years. Amazing that a bit of six-string magic can lift an otherwise unremarkable tune beyond its origins.

"Let It Be" (Album Version), Solo Recorded January 4, 1970

The day after their public swan song, the Beatles were back indoors, performing three Paul compositions—"Two of Us," "The Long and Winding

Road," and "Let It Be"—for the benefit of the cameras and the recording console.

But the continued tweaking of the title track toward its final release demonstrated the chaos and ambivalence the Beatles felt toward the entire project. This recording passed through the hands of *three* producers (Glyn Johns, George Martin, and Phil Spector) before arriving at a reasonably satisfactory conclusion.

George revisited the January 31, 1969 recording of "Let It Be" three months later in order to dub in a smoother solo. As if to better, but not significantly alter, his film performance, he again ran his guitar through a rotating Leslie organ speaker, giving his sound an oscillating texture. Wholly fitting with the tune's churchy, quasi-spiritual tone, the guitar line is functional without drawing undue attention to itself, and approximates the filmed performance quite nicely.

Months would pass before the band dusted off the track for public release. As mastered by George Martin, the April 30, 1969, guitar solo version of the song was chosen to grace the Beatles' final U.K. single in March 1970.

But back in January 1970, a day after recording "I Me Mine" with Paul and Ringo, George re-approached "Let It Be," this time dropping the Leslie speaker effect and infusing his performance with a previously unheard bite and emotion. Having come back to tidy up some loose ends, he seemed to be taking the opportunity to close the door on one career before venturing into the unknown. As such, this solo must be regarded as his valedictory statement.

The "Let It Be" album cut is a triumph. Despite the continual bad rap Spector is accorded in Beatles lore, his work on this recording is magnificent. George's emotive guitar fills throughout are brought up in the mix; the touch of brass serves, as one writer put it, to "deflate the pomposity" inherent in the song.

For all of Paul's subsequent bellyaching over Spector's methods, the majesty and power of this version is undeniable. Demonstrating one last time his gift of razor-sharp counterpoint, George's work provides a fitting end to a remarkable Beatles career.

22

Way Beyond Compare

The Cute One Can Play, Too!

Paul McCartney made plenty of mistakes during the Beatles years, but also drew more than his fair share of blame. For instance, his "come on, guys" rallying during *Let It Be* may be insufferable, but he was the only Beatle who showed any enthusiasm in the entire process.

From various quarters, Macca's virtuosity, his ability to write popular songs, and even his happy-go-lucky nature have unfairly come in for criticism. To be blunt, John Lennon only looks cooler now than his bandmate because he had the ill fortune to become a martyr in 1980.

McCartney was the best musician in the Beatles, and certainly the best craftsman. Sure, he wasn't as "artistic" as Lennon, as funny as Ringo, or as mysterious as George, but every band in the world would be blessed to have a Paul McCartney on board—not only to create his own classic compositions, but to add color and depth to his bandmates' songs as well.

"I Saw Her Standing There," Recorded February 11, 1963

The first track of the first Beatles album proved one of the most exciting of the band's entire career.

"I Saw Her Standing There," originally titled "Seventeen," featured a thundering drum part from Ringo and clattery guitars from John and George. But aside from providing an enthusiastic lead vocal, McCartney also added the song's jet propulsion in the form of an incredibly aggressive, in-your-face bass line.

Paul could have easily played a much simpler bass part, perhaps using only half the notes, which would have given the song a more "swinging" tempo. But instead, he attacked the song, jamming it home Hamburg-style with a relentless, throbbing run on his Hofner that made "I Saw Her Standing There" sound like no previous rock song. And few other songs have followed its tracks.

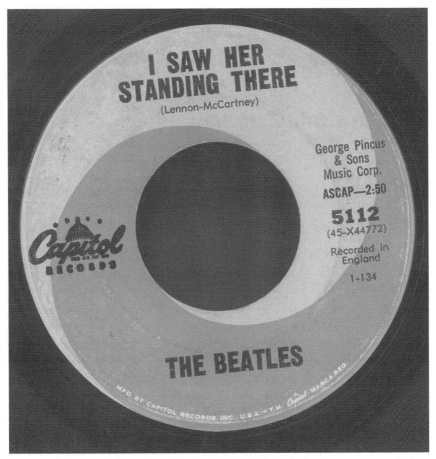

The Beatles' own choice of a b-side for their initial Capitol release was overridden.
The ballad "This Boy" was swapped for the rocker "I Saw Her Standing There" (from
their LP debut), creating an instant classic.

"Rain," Recorded April 14 and 16, 1966

During the early Beatles years, Paul McCartney's bass playing was more
than functional, keeping the beat and perfectly complementing Ringo's
drumming. His inventive runs during songs like "The Night Before," "Day
Tripper," and "Drive My Car" showed that by 1965, he was already ahead
of the pack.

The Beatles' first product of 1966, the "Paperback Writer" / "Rain"
single, was a whole new thing. Aside from the deeper lyrics and more caustic
guitars on both songs, the bass frequencies on this 45 were much more

interesting than those on any previous Beatles record, thanks to Paul's new Rickenbacker 4001 bass, his relentless pushing of the envelope, and the willingness and ability of Abbey Road engineers to break the studio's "rules" in order to improve the band's bass presence.

Paul's work on both sides was stunning, but his sound on "Rain" was particularly special. He worked against Ringo's unconventional but thrilling drums with a gobbling bass line that provided its own melody.

The song, recorded at one speed and then slowed down before Lennon added his vocals, sounded as a result heavier than any previous Beatles record, almost ponderous in its crunching but graceful pace.

"Taxman," Recorded April 20–22, 1966

McCartney's distinctive "Taxman" bass line has provided a foundation for countless other rock songs in the last forty years . . . which by itself would be nearly enough to put it in the pantheon. But his sizzling guitar solo added even more to Harrison's turbo-charged song, eventually the leadoff track to *Revolver*.

During the *Help!* sessions, McCartney had for some reason assumed lead guitar duties on "Ticket to Ride" and "Another Girl," deciding to throw his fairly sloppy blues licks over otherwise completed songs. This must have been especially hurtful to George.

But on "Taxman," Paul's lead guitar was utterly distinctive, working in both a blues edge and an Indian scale, which greatly pleased Harrison. The tone of McCartney's newly acquired Epiphone Casino provided an edge lacking on previous Beatles records, and as a left-hander, Paul played a line that no right-hander could have easily devised. This song provided, for the first time, conclusive evidence that Macca could play some guitar.

"For No One," Recorded May 9, 16, and 19, 1966

While the Beatles had fooled around with exotic keyboard sounds in the recent past (George Martin's chamber-type piano on "In My Life," Lennon's harmonium on "We Can Work It Out"), Paul hadn't yet made a truly distinctive contribution to a Beatles record while playing the keys.

In this number, however, McCartney raised the stakes and truly went for Baroque. Using a piano as well as a clavichord—a keyboard that resonates, like a harpsichord, but with more body—Paul added a period drawing-room frisson to an already lovely song.

In addition, Paul's bass playing on "For No One" was typically excellent, providing sonorous, cello-like rhythmic underpinning to the melody. Neither George nor John is present on this record; Ringo provides high-hat cymbal and percussion, while Alan Civil's horn adds yet more period authenticity.

The results here are stunning, certainly. But it is important to note that when McCartney began playing keyboards, guitar, and the like, supplanting the others, he helped, however accidentally, to drive a wedge into the band that culminated in the "you do your song, I'll do mine" dynamics of the "White Album."

"Strawberry Fields Forever," Recorded November 24, 28, and 29, and December 8, 9, 15, and 21, 1966

One of Lennon's simplest, most beautiful songs became a full-blown psychedelic festival of otherworldly sounds when the Beatles took their turn at it.

George Martin's accidental genius in slowing down one version and speeding up another to get the two takes of the song to fit has been well documented. But what is often lost is the critical importance of Paul's contribution on the Mellotron.

McCartney's stylings on the odd keyboard provided the final product with much of its appeal. He set the mood from the opening with a pretty, yet somehow unsettling flute approximation that felt, despite its harmony, just discordant enough to convey a puzzling sense of reverie.

Paul's rock-solid bass part also helped center the song, which featured great guitar from Harrison and extremely innovative drumming from Ringo that didn't always hew directly to the beat.

Lennon argued at length during his late 1980 interview with David Sheff that McCartney would sometimes work to "sabotage" a great song, becoming too interested in fussy arrangements for John's taste. But Lennon's utter lack of interest in technical matters, and his often unclear notions of how his own songs should sound, led to a vacuum that Macca, George Martin, and others would *have* to fill in order to get John's songs done.

"Hey Jude," Recorded July 31 and August 1, 1968

McCartney, despite his kitchen-sink instrumental ability, does not play drums, guitar, recorder, clavichord, harpsichord, tamboura, or organ on this recording.

What Macca does on "Hey Jude" is summon up some of the most soulful piano pounding of his career—or, for that matter, anyone's. Never before had Paul channeled his obsession with various Fat pianists (Waller, Domino) into such a slow, thoughtful gospel-style stroll, eschewing silly fillips and going instead for the dramatic jugular. He knew enough to let the song stand on its own.

Lennon took on the acoustic guitar chores, while Harrison softly stroked an electric guitar. (His suggestions for a guitar line "answering" the lyric had been gently rebuffed by Paul, who wanted a simple, uncluttered arrangement—at least until the explosive group-sing fade-out.)

"Jude" is so perfectly realized, in Paul's playing, its overall pacing, and its rising intensity, that the 7:11 masterpiece seems to have emerged, perfectly formed, from some alternate pop song universe.

And that's not even discussing McCartney's lead and backing vocals on "Hey Jude," which range from subtle, inspirational pleading during the song's verses to wild, raucous shouting on the fade.

"I Want You (She's So Heavy)", Recorded February 22, April 18, and August 8 and 11, 1969

Once again McCartney did some of his best work in the service of a Lennon song chronicling the author's obsessive love for Yoko Ono.

During the first, anguished section of this typically heavy John composition, Paul contributed a bass guitar that alternated between descending runs and up-the-neck flutters. His part, solidly swinging but not nailed down, perfectly underscored the graceful, desperate misery of the lyric.

During the "She's So Heavy" portion, Paul's bass bubbles through at various times, playing quick descending notes when appropriate.

"The Ballad of John and Yoko," Recorded April 14, 1969

This isn't the best Beatles record ever made, or the most virtuosic performance, but the mere fact that John and Paul recorded this themselves (George and Ringo were out of the country at the time) is significant.

For the first time on a Beatles record, McCartney handled the drums (he'd chipped in on "Dear Prudence" and "Back in the U.S.S.R.,") along with playing his typically solid bass. In addition, Paul banged on the piano and shook maracas. Lennon laid down the acoustic and electric guitars.

Even while the Fabs were struggling just to stay together, the partnership of John and Paul still made magic. One can almost see the duo in the studio, obviously having fun with this slight but catchy number that captured John's witty, journalistic approach as well as his growing megalomania.

The breakdown in the Beatles' esprit de corps on this release, essentially a John solo effort with Paul as sideman, would surely have alarmed fans. George and Ringo's non-participation was carefully papered over, as shown on the American single sleeve.

Courtesy of Mitch McGeary

Paul's willing participation in "The Ballad of John and Yoko" also gives the lie to the revisionist notion that he never supported Lennon in the latter's personal affairs or in his romance with Yoko Ono.

"You Never Give Me Your Money," Recorded May 6, July 1, 15, and 31, and August 5, 1969

It's telling that one of McCartney's most honest, emotional songs about the Beatles should come on the last album they recorded. The financial problems plaguing the Apple enterprise, and the fallout such money-oriented squabbles precipitated in the band, were only getting worse.

Paul's virtuosity helped carry the song, although he was ably supported by Harrison's chiming guitars, Lennon's unmistakable harmonies, and Starr's rock-steady drums. McCartney plays both grand and pub piano on this song, with the honky-tonk, player-piano style of the "out of college" section especially impressive.

Add to that his typically agile bass playing and you have yet another terrific performance. The fade-out includes several examples of the bubbling "up-the-neck" fills that he made a trademark on *Abbey Road*.

"Come Together," Recorded July 21–23, 25, 29, and 30, 1969

Originally a product of John's 1969 "back to basics" rock-and-roll obsession, the quick-tempo "Come Together" seemed just a little derivative to Macca's ears. So he suggested John slow it down and make it funkier.

On top of this, Paul then added two critical elements, beginning with his bass playing. George's guitar provides some backbone, but it's Paul's bass that moves the feet and establishes the mood, especially leading up to the chorus.

Second, the solo section features an electric piano, an instrument not often used by the Beatles. McCartney's nimble-fingered mastery of the Fender Rhodes took "Come Together" even farther into funky territory, and his undulating keyboard tones were swampy and soupy enough for Lennon to voice his approval. Which pleased Paul no end.

I Got Blisters on My Fingers

The New Guy Shows George Martin What For!

The last to join the group and the first to be dissed in the studio, the former Richard Starkey may be the Rodney Dangerfield of rock and roll. Characterized early on as (in John's words) "dumb and cute," Ringo had an everyman persona that encouraged the public to regard him as either the Beatles' Fool or the luckiest guy in the world, plucked from obscurity to hitch a ride on rock's greatest bandwagon.

Some have even said that somehow his skills were sub-par, and that as far as rock drummers go, he wasn't in the same league as his peers. This issue was first raised while the Beatles existed, and no amount of commendation to the contrary has eradicated it.

The truth is that Starr's self-effacing manner probably contributed to his image as a percussively inept dupe. Ringo's genius, as asserted by every qualified observer, is his ability to play *the song* rather than simply play the drums. He never contributed anything gratuitously; every fill was spot on, fitting the mood and flavor of the composition.

While certainly lacking the technique of, say, Keith Moon, or even Kenney Jones, Ringo became possibly the most imitated drummer in rock for a reason. (Many a session drummer has spoken of being ordered to "play like Ringo.") Even George Martin, not entirely sold on him at first, gave him his due as a creative, intuitive drummer, and a perfect timekeeper to boot.

With such a rich body of work to choose from, it's hard to pick his absolute finest moments. But here are ten examples that should silence the doubters once and for all, and show that the man earned his keep as an essential component of the greatest rock band in history.

"Roll Over Beethoven," Recorded Live in Sweden, October 24, 1963

Despite being thrown off balance by George Martin's efforts to displace him on their debut Parlophone single, Ringo recouped sufficiently to provide superlative percussion on "Please Please Me" two and a half months later. In between, a steady stream of live shows solidified the foursome as a tight, versatile powerhouse.

Not counting the Hamburg club stints, the Beatles embarked on their first foreign tour in the fall of 1963. Their electrifying reception seemed to spark something within them, as documentation of their trip showed the four consistently outdoing themselves in terms of excitement and musical muscle.

During their Swedish stay, the Beatles performed before an audience at Karlaplansstudio for a radio broadcast. Unmarred by the hysteria soon to come, this well-engineered recording showcased the band at perhaps their live peak, before the inability to hear themselves turned concerts into "events."

The Fabs played seven songs, five of which turned up years later on *Anthology 1*. For sheer audacity, this umpteenth performance of "Roll Over Beethoven" is a marvel. Differing from the approach they took in other recorded versions (e.g., *Live! at the Star Club*, *With the Beatles* LP, *Live at the Hollywood Bowl*), this one *swings!*

Ringo played like a man possessed by the spirit of Max Roach, displaying remarkable finesse and a light touch while throwing in stylish rolls at every turn. His fills were crisp and measured, never superfluous, as he kept perfect time and resisted the temptation to speed things up.

Though Ringo was never particularly known as a jazz aficionado (unlike Rolling Stones stickman Charlie Watts), his performance on this recording rivals anything found in London's myriad Trad clubs. His swing treatment on this occasion would not be repeated, but for Swedish fans, the approach was an unexpected bonus.

"I Saw Her Standing There," Recorded Live in Washington, D.C., February 11, 1964

Once again, the effect of pure adrenaline on the Beatles' live skills was manifest. Nowhere was the contrast between studio and concert performance more vividly delineated than in this floor-pounding version.

As Ringo later recalled, the Fabs' debut American concert was a dynamic experience for both the performers and the audience. The energy projected by the fans was met and returned by the musicians, no one more than Ringo on this song.

At his best on rockers like this one, Ringo unleashes a punishing attack on his cymbals while hammering out a bone-jarring beat on the kick. Applying the odd crash cymbal accent for emphasis, he plays like nothing so much as wind-up monkey keeping perfect rhythm with mechanized arms while appearing to remain oblivious to his surroundings.

This showstopper from their Washington Coliseum concert can be seen in *The Beatles: The First U.S. Visit*, on DVD. Exactly one year to the day after recording their debut album, the Beatles had truly conquered the world.

"Long Tall Sally," Recorded March 1, 1964

The recording of the throat-rending "Twist and Shout" in one take has become the stuff of rock-and-roll lore, coming at the end of the Beatles' day-long debut album recording session. No less remarkable is the equally ferocious recording of this song, similarly a staple of their live show, nailed in one take.

While Paul codified his renowned Little Richard impression in this session, Ringo's drumming is not to be overlooked. Beginning with his sharp-edged stop-and-start percussion on the verses, Ringo quickly kicked the song into gear, adding a swing feel to his bedrock foundation for George Martin's rock-and-roll piano and Paul's soaring vocal.

The recording displays Ringo's command of backbeat between the snare and bass drum, while his ride cymbal rhythm provides the perfect ambient wash beneath George's ascending lead guitar solo. For the home stretch, Ringo reverted to a four-four beat on the hi-hats before throwing in a stunning flourish of cymbal and toms on the last refrain.

Often overlooked in the Beatles' canon, "Long Tall Sally" may be the best studio encapsulation of their live act ever captured. Only the sound of adoring fans is absent from this remarkable recording.

"Boys," Recorded Live in Los Angeles, August 23, 1964

Though possessing the means to provide themselves with the best sound reinforcement gear in the world, the Beatles had changed their approach to playing live not one iota since their club days. Consequentially, when Ringo's turn came to sing, he simply moved his one drum mic from overhead to somewhere near his mouth.

As this was usually a hit-or-miss proposition, more often than not Ringo's vocals were simply inaudible. As this first appearance at the Hollywood Bowl

THE BEATLES
LONG TALL SALLY

Recorded quickly in the wake of *A Hard Day's Night*, the *Long Tall Sally* EP offered three of their nightclub favorites, along with an early Lennon composition, "I Call Your Name."

was being captured for posterity, however, care was taken to make sure his lead was heard. (The bootleg recording of the show comically documents Paul stalling for time as Ringo's mic is adjusted and tested.)

As always, Ringo fed off of the audience's concentrated adoration; he was by this time a firm fan favorite. The announcement of his pending Starr turn provoked a frenzied reaction.

Ringo plunged straight into the tune, rushing the tempo slightly as he went. Rhythmically, his assured if unsubtle vocal fell in somewhere between his punchy bass drum on the bottom and flogged cymbals on top. In an unmistakable triumph of spirit over finesse, his performance would, on another composition, qualify as "punk."

Despite his apparent rush to finish it, the song just makes it past the two-minute mark, a "thank you" issuing from Ringo's mouth before the last note from George's twelve-string has decayed. The sonic boom–inducing performance ended as suddenly as it had begun, with John chuckling in its wake.

"Ticket to Ride," Recorded February 15, 1965

By way of diminishing his talent, some critics point out that Ringo, like George, was on occasion given direction on his parts from the chief composers or producer. But why should the composers' desire to bring a song to life as they first heard it in their heads be counted against their fellow musicians? That the band's drummer and lead guitarist unfailingly stepped up to help fulfill John and Paul's vision should win them praise, not derision.

The drum pattern on "Ticket to Ride" was as groundbreaking as was the song's overall construction. Purportedly at Paul's request, Ringo departed from the norm by laying off the cymbals completely throughout the verses, playing instead a rhythmic pattern on the snare and toms.

With each verse, the pattern varied slightly, until on the second-verse reprise it became something approaching (but not embracing) convention. Not until the bridge segments ("I don't know why . . .") did Ringo revert to a "normal" backbeat. As an added variation, he placed a different fill in every refrain (right after "she's got a ticket to ri-i-ide"), adding to the song's unpredictability.

"Ticket to Ride" was a highlight of the Beatles' 1965 tour, with the band performing the coda in double time. The song represents an early attempt by the Fabs to vary their format, coupling a somewhat conventional lyric with a most unconventional arrangement. Whether conceived by him or not, Ringo's execution of the off-kilter groove laid the foundation for the song's overall departure. As the group embraced experimentation, musical and otherwise, their drummer became increasingly vital to breaking new ground.

"Tomorrow Never Knows," Recorded April 6, 7, 22, 1966

The first song taped for *Revolver* represented a quantum leap forward from everything the Beatles had done previously. Laid down just as they were about to embark on their final round of live dates, this remarkable amalgam of sounds shouldn't hang together but does, unified around a central element: Ringo's drums.

The addition of engineer Geoff Emerick to the production team proved fortuitous. Just as the Fabs were becoming more demanding in altering sounds produced in the studio, they found the perfect partner in Emerick, whose resourcefulness, artistic vision, and talent for sonic innovation proved equal to the task.

Dissatisfied with the way the drums sounded on the band's previous records, Emerick willfully broke an EMI taboo by removing the front drumhead on Ringo's kit and (shudders!) placing the microphone as close to the rear head as possible. Further, he dampened the kick with a blanket—now common practice, but not so then—thereby producing a powerful cannon-shot "boom."

For this recording, the drums were heavily "compressed"—an electronic alteration that in lay terms brought every sound, soft and loud, up to the same volume level. Thus the persistent wash of the ride cymbal, the snare, and the tom-toms provided a solid backbone for the song as it drifted along in its near-constant C major drone.

Ringo's hypnotic drum pattern on this track has proved irresistible to many a musician through the years. The oft-imitated lick pops up in Beck's "The New Pollution" as well as in "Setting Sun" by the Chemical Brothers.

In 2006, the Beatles in effect sampled themselves when the drum track from "Tomorrow Never Knows" was grafted onto "Within You Without You" for a so-called mash-up mix on *Love*, crafted by George Martin and son Giles.

"Rain," Recorded April 14, 1966

Beginning with a resolute "tat-tat tat-tat-tat," Ringo's drumming on this psychedelic number ranks as his own personal favorite performance. It isn't hard to see why: on "Rain," Ringo plays a pattern of measure-defying fills, punctuating the vocal but not waiting for a line to finish before entering the sonic landscape.

As Paul's bass became increasingly prominent in the Beatles' recordings, Ringo's percussive role was similarly accentuated. Their musical lockstep became ever more evident, nowhere more so than on "Rain."

Paul's sinewy lines percolated throughout the verses, met by a rhythmic response from Ringo. The parallel performances coalesced at the song's conclusion; just before the backward-vocal coda begins, bass and drums contribute a distinctive fill, as one.

In the first instance of many such sonic experiments, the drums were laid down at one speed and then slowed down on the finished track, adding to the somnambulant feel of John's detached lyrical observations. From 1966 onward, the effects of the Beatles' chemical experiments became increasingly manifest in their recordings.

"Strawberry Fields Forever," Recorded November 24, 28, and 29, and December 8, 9, 15, and 21, 1966

Though emanating from the same throne on the same Ludwig kit in the same recording studio as it had since 1963, Ringo's drum sound had in the past few months changed immeasurably for the better.

Geoff Emerick's input, coupled with advancements in recording and miking technology, added a discernable punch, giving the drums greater color and thump. This sonic leap forward in turn inspired greater creativity from the now studio-bound drummer.

This tom-tom-heavy production constituted a foray into uncharted waters. To add color to a composition far removed from anything else in rock at that time, Ringo was forced to dig deep to come up with appropriate percussive backing.

He achieved this by making his every entrance an event. On the choruses, Ringo's drums came in halfway through the opening line; on the verses, just after the first line. The effect added drama to John's lyrics, with cascading tom-tom fills providing gravitas to what otherwise might have remained a series of fanciful observations.

"Strawberry Fields Forever" broke new ground on several levels, as Mellotron, Indian instrumentation, and orchestration wove a unique tapestry. The song's coda saved the best for last, as Ringo steered the percussion into the closest he would ever come to "jamming" on a Beatles record.

His signature tom-tom fills gave way to a ride cymbal sheen, as George and Paul added bottom end by pounding on a pair of timpani. So freewheeling was the ensuing percussive cacophony that Ringo lost his place in counting out the measures; it was at this point that the record faded down before returning.

Fading back in, the performance continued on just a little longer, with John throwing in his "cranberry sauce" ad lib, before the whole ensemble collapsed with the admonition, "Calm down, Ringo!" The exercise proved to be a taste of things to come, with Ringo building upon his toms-as-lyrical-punctuation theme on the even more complex "A Day in the Life" two months later.

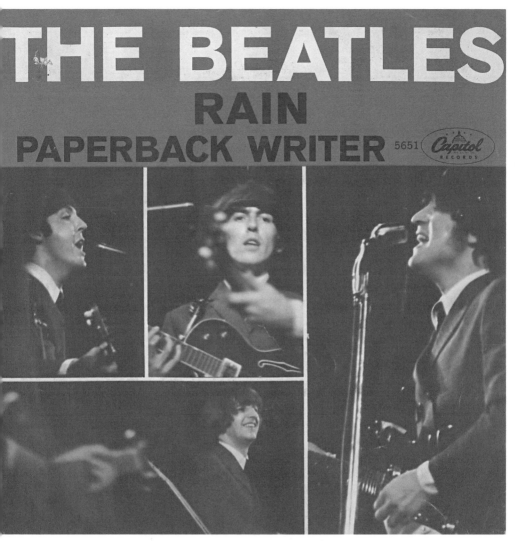

The Beatles
RAIN
PAPERBACK WRITER
5651
Capitol RECORDS

Though released as the flip to the more obviously commercial "Paperback Writer," John's "Rain" was a landmark in many ways: from Ringo's drumming to Paul's bass line and the first use of backwards vocals at the end.

"Long Long Long," Recorded October 7, 8, and 9, 1968

This otherwise pastoral, airy ballad by George gained a dollop of dynamic punch from Ringo's measured tom-tom fills. Arranged so gently as to be all but inaudible after the sonic assault of "Helter Skelter," "Long Long Long" featured acoustic guitar figures over a bed of soft organ chords, lulling the listener into a meditative mode.

But the milieu was shattered when Ringo's authoritative toms and cymbals came crashing in at 0:27. Rather than crude intrusion, his input came as punctuation, accenting and underscoring George's subtle vocals. The contrast is truly sublime, showing once again that what *shouldn't* work often *does.*

The track embodies Ringo's "less is more" talent. Resisting the temptation to overplay, again and again he pops in, then sits back. Nowhere in the Beatles' canon is there more compelling proof of the band's ability to create tension and release.

Shifting seamlessly between brushes on the verses and powerful fills in between, Ringo was seldom called upon to use so much range within one song. One of the most underrated tunes in the Fabs' entire catalog, this song's timelessness gives hope for an eventual rediscovery.

"The End," Recorded July 23 and August 5, 7, 8, 15, and 18, 1969

Musical excess was anathema to the Beatles. Ringo hated soloing, regarding it as discordant bloviating, the domain of those seeking to show up their bandmates. The ringed one preferred to reserve any musical statements for integration within the whole, as a contribution rather than a distraction.

Nonetheless, on this, the penultimate track on their final group recording, the others ganged up on the hapless skinsman, managing to cajole a reluctant Ringo into taking the spotlight. As an eight-bar lead up to Paul, George, and John (in that order) trading off on lead guitar, Ringo dutifully laid down a drum break that was solid, distinctive, and, most challenging of all for a drum solo, not boring.

While Ringo later copped to drawing inspiration from the *long* version of "In-A-Gadda-Da-Vida" from Iron Butterfly's 1968 album of the same name, the drum sound itself distinguished the solo from anything else and made the piece scream "Ringo."

In early 1969, Ringo took delivery of a new Ludwig kit, the "Hollywood" model, which came tricked out with calfskin drumheads. These heads are rather high-maintenance, being extremely sensitive to temperature and humidity, but the resulting sound makes them worth the bother. (Hauling the kit up to Apple's rooftop in London's January weather must have given Ringo pause, but only for a moment.)

In George Martin's estimate, Ringo took great care in getting exactly the sound he sought from his drums. Through the Beatle years, Ringo would alternate snare drums (listen to the difference between the sound on "Drive My Car" and "I Am the Walrus," for example), and adjust his kit with sheets and tea towels for dampening.

But the "organic" sound achieved by dispensing with plastic heads brought his toms into a new realm. Under Ringo's capable sticks, his idiosyncratic tom-tom fills, now spread out on vinyl over two tracks, took on a warmer hue. "The End" represents the culmination of his exploring sonic boundaries while remaining unmistakably "Ringo": no easy feat.

It's a pity that Ringo spent so many of his solo years running from his own greatness. Instead of wisely building a band around his own distinctive sound, he largely chose to abdicate the heavy percussive lifting on his projects by sharing drumming chores with session great Jim Keltner, thereby diluting his talents. Not until hooking up with producer Mark Hudson was Ringo consistently challenged to rediscover his gifts, returning to what he did best with a vengeance.

Oh, Look Out!

The Witty One, When He Still Believed

John Lennon was the leader of the Beatles. Even in this most democratic of bands—and just ask anyone who's ever been in a band how difficult democracy is—when Paul, George, or Ringo was singing lead, Lennon was the focus, because he was the one constantly pushing the envelope.

Lester Bangs wrote, after Lennon's death in 1980, that it made perfect sense that John would be the first Beatle to die, since he was the one farthest out, the one on the edge. And that quality of adventurousness, which led to his willingness to give body, mind, consciousness, and soul for his art—and at times to make others suffer for it, too—lent his Beatles work an inimitable stamp.

While Lennon was never the group's best instrumentalist, some fans and critics have underrated his skills. As only a true original can, John blended his influences into a heady concoction that could never have cohered in the hands of someone less artistic and less creative.

What John had in common with the other greats was a desire—a need—to keep progressing, keep moving, keep going higher and higher. That can make for a tough life, but at least Lennon left us with dozens of classic songs, performances, and works of art. Here we focus on his instrumental prowess, featuring ten great Beatles moments in which Lennon showed his talents on guitar and keyboards.

"All My Loving," Recorded July 30, 1963

One need only look at this date for evidence of the furious pace at which the Beatles were expected to record. On a day when they also spent several afternoon hours recording a BBC session, the Fabs recorded *four*—count 'em, four—classic tracks for the *With the Beatles* LP.

The last song recorded on this thirteen-hour day was "All My Loving," a country-and-western-inspired McCartney original written on piano during the group's summer 1963 tour. The group's arrangement omitted keyboards altogether, calling instead for a rhythmic underpinning of Ringo's brisk drum tempo and Paul's walking bass line.

Harrison took the tricky lead guitar, leaving Lennon with his most difficult part yet—a strumming pattern of rhythmic "triplets," or chords played quickly at waltz tempo. Lennon handled this difficult part, on his Rickenbacker, with aplomb, saying years later that he "played a mean guitar in back."

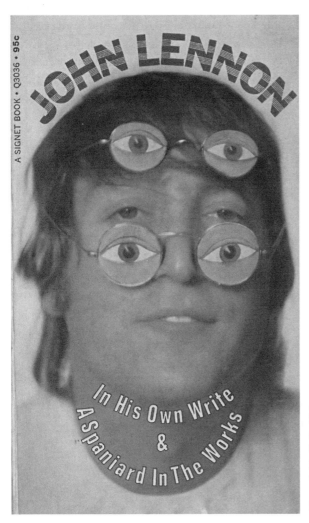

As Beatlemania crested in 1964 and 1965, two collections of John's Carroll-esque stories and poems were published to critical acclaim. This 1968 edition collated both titles.

"You Can't Do That," Recorded February 25, 1964

On George Harrison's twenty-first birthday, the Beatles recorded for six hours. The only completed song of the day was "You Can't Do That," a soulful Lennon shouter featuring George playing the riff on his new twelve-string Rickenbacker electric—which he was using for just the second time on a session.

With George creating the ringing tones, Lennon ripped into the rhythm part with barely contained ferocity, tearing off huge chords to drive the song. Then, to make things even more exciting, John for the first time manned the guitar solo. Rather than carefully plucking out his part, Lennon threw himself fully into the song, hurling a cascade of roaring notes, some sloppy, some perfectly realized, but all powerful. Despite its raw character, Lennon's solo on "You Can't Do That" is one of the greatest on any Beatles record.

Certainly no white group was doing music like this—four-on-the-floor, driving rock and roll with adventurous sounds and unbridled energy—in early 1964.

"I Call Your Name," Recorded March 3, 1964

One of John Lennon's first songs, "I Call Your Name" began as a blues, but by the time the Beatles recorded it, it had turned into laid-back, almost Caribbean R&B.

Once again using Harrison's ringing twelve-string guitar as the lead instrument, the Beatles launched into this funky number with Ringo playing the offbeat, Paul holding down the fort, and John again playing almost unbelievably raw, driving chords.

The American mixes of many early Beatles songs added a lot of echo. (Check out the original British mixes of this song, "She's a Woman," and "You Can't Do That," in particular, to hear the differences.) That extra bit of reverberation often made Lennon's rhythm guitar sound even more raucous.

What's amazing about Lennon's rock playing during the early Beatle days—both in the studio and onstage—is that he was able to get such monster sounds out of a teeny little Rickenbacker 325 guitar. The Rick, which Lennon made his primary electric through mid-1965, was a three-quarter-sized model with small frets and a thin neck. Most other guitarists to use the model played the 325 for its jangle, or just enjoyed its look.

But Lennon somehow was able to coax a harder sound from the guitar while maintaining precise chord fingering. Perhaps the Rick's small neck and frets allowed him to overpower the guitar's design and produce his own sound.

"I'm Down," Recorded June 14, 1965

"Plastic soul, man, plastic soul," Paul intoned between takes of this song, his rewrite/homage to Little Richard. But on this cut, taped on a day when the band also recorded two other Macca classics ("I've Just Seen a Face" and "Yesterday"), the Beatles showed plenty of soul of the flesh-and-blood variety.

"I'm Down" features one of McCartney's great rock-and-roll vocals, and is matched by Lennon's furious organ playing. John had added keyboards to a couple of previous Beatles numbers during these *Help!* sessions, including "The Night Before," "Dizzy Miss Lizzy," and "Bad Boy," and was clearly feeling his oats by June 14.

After accompanying the rest of the band, adding seventh chords to accent the soulfulness of the track, Lennon then let loose with a raucous Vox organ solo. Playing high inversions, and making some goofy runs up and down the keys with his elbow, Lennon played damned well for someone who had, previously, hidden his light (as a keyboardist, anyway) under a bushel.

"Norwegian Wood (This Bird Has Flown)," Recorded October 21, 1965

Lennon's matchless melody for "Norwegian Wood" allowed the Beatles to try various recordings of the song with different introductions.

In an early version, George played the melody of the "She asked me to stay" portion of the verse on the sitar. When the Fabs remade the tune, however, Lennon chose to open the song with an instrumental lick from the *beginning* of the verse.

Using a capo on the second fret of the guitar, he negotiated the tricky opening melody, providing the song's only instrument for nearly ten seconds. This was something Lennon had not yet done on a record—build the sound around his acoustic guitar—and it worked perfectly. When Harrison came in, doubling the melody on the sitar, the ground was laid for one of the group's greatest songs.

The difficulty of the guitar part, especially for someone occasionally self-conscious about his playing, was shown clearly at the end of the recording. On bootlegs, you can clearly hear a defiant Lennon saying, after the final chord, "I showed ya!"

"Baby, You're a Rich Man," Recorded May 11, 1967

A rare session away from Abbey Road saw the Fabs record this number, eventually a B-side to "All You Need Is Love," in six hours. (Olympic Studios head Keith Grant told Mark Lewisohn that "The Beatles said that this was the fastest record they'd ever made." This is a somewhat fanciful claim, but the session *was* quite compact.)

John and Paul stapled this song together from two distinct, individually penned sections, but the final product shone with typical Beatles inspiration. Ringo's shuffling drums and Paul's funky bass provided the foundation. Both John and Paul played piano parts, and with George laying back on guitar, John added the odd instrumental touch—this time on a keyboard called a Clavioline.

This odd electric instrument, which features thirty-six keys and a finger-operated strip that produces vibrations, was first introduced to popular audiences on the Tornadoes' 1962 recording "Telstar," the first British rock song to hit #1 on the American charts.

The Clavioline can play just one note at a time, making its applicability somewhat limited, but the Beatles made good use of it on "Baby, You're a Rich Man." Lennon formed wild Eastern-sounding intervals that gave their newest confection just the right amount of *de rigeur* psychedelic frosting.

"I Am the Walrus," Recorded September 5, 6, and 27, 1967

John's intake of psychedelics had altered his moods enough that he began to occasionally suffer from paranoia. One such attack, said to have taken place in a New York City hotel, eventually led Lennon to want to duplicate the frightening sounds of a police siren on a keyboard.

Later, on two separate acid trips, Lennon turned his visions into a song, turning that siren into a riveting two-note motif. Choosing a particularly fuzzy—almost distorted—electric piano sound made perfect sense, lending "I Am the Walrus" much of its discomfiting feel. Though an untrained keyboard player, Lennon knew just how much to add and how much to leave out of his parts, and his typical underplaying style is well in evidence here.

Background singers, orchestral overdubs, and Shakespearean radio play turned "I Am the Walrus" into a full-blown bad trip, but the spare, September 5–6 original recording of the song stands on its own as a supremely intense group performance, all four Beatles chugging along with the two-note rhythm to help fulfill Lennon's original vision.

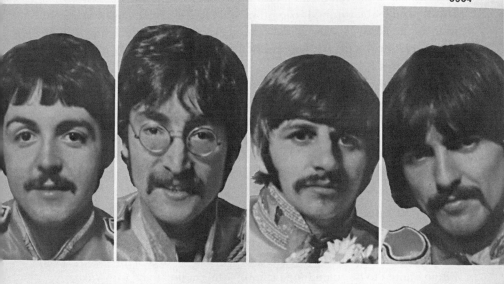

The BEATLES
Baby, You're a Rich Man
All You Need Is Love

Capitol RECORDS

5964

Released as the B-side to "All You Need Is Love," "Baby, You're a Rich Man" offered an increasingly rare true Lennon-McCartney composition: John's verses wedded to Paul's chorus.

"Across the Universe," Recorded February 4 and 8, 1968

Rarely has such a beautiful song emerged from such a tough time.

John Lennon, falling in love with Yoko Ono and struggling to deal with the heartbreak this would cause, left his bed one night after an argument with Cynthia. He sat down and wrote out his thoughts, the words "flowing out like endless rain into a paper cup," and eventually produced one of his greatest songs, which featured a lilting, beautiful melody.

Unfortunately, the Beatles never got it right. At first it seemed that the song would center around Lennon's crystal-clear acoustic guitar—it had been a couple of years since he had added this kind of acoustic work to a Beatles song—and the Eastern atmospherics of George's tamboura, along with the "whoosh" of flanging and the delicate plucking of what sounds like a zither or autoharp. Neither Ringo nor Paul had made significant contributions.

Unfortunately, the inexplicable decision to bring in female backing vocalists led to the recruitment of two thoroughly untrained fans from the crowd outside the studio. Lizzie Bravo and Gayleen Pease obviously meant well, but their poor vocals helped destroy the recording, which was deemed unsuitable for the Beatles and was only released later on a World Wildlife Fund charity LP.

When Phil Spector needed another song for *Let It Be*, he dusted off this recording, drowned it in sentimental strings, and threw a choir on top just to ram home the entire package. The original beauty of the song was lost until various bootleggers made earlier sessions public. The *Anthology* project finally gave take two of the song a good home in 1995, allowing us to hear John's playing.

"For You Blue," Recorded January 25, 1969

When the Beatles decided to undertake the "Get Back" project, they had no unified grand plan. Paul wanted to perform; George wanted to record; Ringo wanted to do something positive; John wanted to be with Yoko.

Little was accomplished during the dismal filmed rehearsals at Twickenham, which went for two weeks beginning on January 2. But after relocating to their newly installed recording facility at Apple, the Fabs got down to serious business, proving they could still knock out good records quickly.

On this day, the Beatles worked on a song of George's called, at that point, "George's Blues." Featuring a simple twelve-bar pattern in D, the light-hearted little number was nothing special, but did feature a fine Lennon performance on yet another different instrument.

During this time, Lennon—in thrall to Yoko and various chemicals—was having a hard time keeping focused, but on this song used a small "lap steel" guitar (which actually fits in one's lap) to play slide-guitar runs in the background. He also delivered a simple, delicate solo that summed up just what George was trying for. John's very lack of formal training allowed him to play a simple but innovative lead line.

And while George's "Go, Johnny, go" and "Elmore James got nothin' on *this*" exhortations may sound strained, especially in the context of the distressing "Get Back" / *Let It Be* project, Harrison *added* his commentary when cutting his final vocal one year later. He didn't have to if he didn't mean it.

"Get Back," Recorded January 28, 1969

John and Paul worked together writing this song, intended as a stab at British racism, before eventually deciding to err on the side of caution and not use any lyrics that could be misunderstood.

But "Get Back" remained a solid rock-and-roll song nonetheless, and an eventual #1 single when released in April. This record gave the world a positive picture of the group in early 1969, ironically when the Beatles' tempers were high and enthusiasms low. Perhaps Billy Preston, brought along to play with the group, had everyone on his best behavior—but for whatever reason, "Get Back" was one of those rare moments of clarity in early 1969.

One key to this session going off well was the understanding that John needed something to *do*. "Get Back" featured a rare Lennon turn on lead guitar, with Harrison keeping the rock-solid rhythm. John laid down a tricky guitar solo that spoke volumes about his rock-and-roll soul. Technically raw, but as solid and tasteful as anything coming from the "guitar heroes" of the time, Lennon proved his mettle once again.

Help Me If You Can

Outsiders on the Inside

A s their recordings became more ambitious in scope, the Beatles looked for more creative ways of broadening their musical palette. Recording studio innovations were one method, while enlisting outside voices and instrumentals became another.

The guest musicians on Beatles recordings ranged from masters of their craft to rank amateurs, from old friends to present and future spouses. One thing can be said of the Fabs: when in pursuit of a sound, they were remarkably eclectic.

Their position in the pop world made the inclusion of other musicians a win-win situation. It meant that the top talent at any given instrument was at their disposal, while their "magic touch" meant that anyone anointed as recording-worthy was suddenly elevated, no matter how modest his or her musical gifts.

Here is a roll call of figures who, regardless of their accomplishments, acquired a certain immortality from their association with the Beatles that would ever after color their lives.

Alan Civil, French Horn on "For No One" and "A Day in the Life"

Though not the first outside musician hired to play a solo on a Beatles record (that distinction belongs to John Scott, the flutist who performs on "You've Got to Hide Your Love Away"), Alan Civil was among the first to be credited by name. Beyond whatever musician's scale he was paid, Civil was rewarded with overnight pop notoriety, his name becoming familiar to an entirely different audience than the one he'd been accustomed to.

One of Britain's leading classical brass players, Civil in 1966 was first horn with the Philharmonia. His acquaintance with George Martin went back many years, to the days when he had supplemented his income by doing freelance session work.

Summoned to EMI, he was at first confused by the sight of what he described as an infestation of "bobbysoxers" surrounding the studio. Once inside, his puzzlement deepened when he was presented with a score sheet that he presumed to be for a symphony, captioned in shorthand "For no. (number) one."

But the Beatles, and Martin, soon clued him in to the actual assignment. Civil's work was complicated, first by the fact that the song's backing lay somewhere between the keys of B-flat and B major (due to the band's current penchant for varying the recording speed), and second by the band's having no clear idea of his exact part.

Ever the professional, Civil recorded a series of Baroque obbligatos, each pass wiped until the ideal result had been achieved. He would later describe the gig—an experience virtually guaranteeing that the Falstaffian musician would never have to pay for a drink again—as "interesting." He would later return to the Fabs' service as part of the forty-piece ensemble gathered to play on *Sgt. Pepper's* "A Day in the Life" in 1967.

David Mason, Piccolo Trumpet on "Penny Lane" and "All You Need Is Love," Trumpet on "A Day in the Life," "Magical Mystery Tour," and "It's All Too Much"

Not to be confused with the co-founder of Traffic, this David Mason was a distinguished trumpet player alongside Alan Civil in the Philharmonia. Another Martin acquaintance, certainly his best-remembered moment is the faux-Bach solo in "Penny Lane." Despite the producer's misgivings, Mason brilliantly knocked off the desired part on a notoriously difficult instrument.

Unlike the experience with Civil, the Fabs actually had a part on "Penny Lane" worked out for Mason: hummed by Paul, transcribed by George Martin. An attempt to repeat this process on "Magical Mystery Tour" went less smoothly, resulting in four very frustrated horn players. Trumpeter Gary Howarth ended up composing his own part, his ideas becoming key to the final arrangement.

Mason's work on the even more freewheeling "It's All Too Much" further underscored the chaotic nature of the band's approach to using professional musicians. Expecting everyone to be as committed as he to achieving the desired results, Harrison led a session that ran from 8:00 P.M. to 2:00 A.M., three hours past its allotted time. Said Mason of George, "I don't think he really knew what he wanted."

Brian Jones, Saxophone on "You Know My Name (Look Up the Number)"

By 1967, Rolling Stones founder Brian Jones's musical and personal disintegration was under way. Displaced as the band's central figure and increasingly marginalized by Mick and Keith both on record and in private, Brian took refuge in drugs, resulting in several arrests. (Though Jagger and Richards had their own troubles with the law, their own hard-bitten psychological makeup enabled them to battle through their problems in a way that Jones' weakened psyche did not.)

Though considered a friend by the Beatles, Jones became what John described as "the kind of guy that you dread he'd come on the phone, because you knew it was trouble." At loose ends during the Summer of Love, Brian accepted a figurative lifeline tossed his way by the Beatles that enabled him to feel—momentarily at least—musically useful.

The occasion was the recording of their comedy number, "You Know My Name (Look Up My Number)." One week after the release of *Sgt. Pepper's*, Brian turned up, apparently at the Beatles' invitation, to add a lounge-like sax solo to the sprawling track's closing minute. His playing is suitably ragged, given the tossed-off nature of the recording, and must have satisfied the song's creators.

As for Jones, the December 1967 release of *Their Satanic Majesties Request* came as something of a last hurrah. Though it was critically panned, hindsight recognizes its bold (for the Stones) experimentation. Brian contributed the Mellotron "orchestration" to "Two Thousand Light Years from Home" and nearly all the exotic instrumentation on "Gomper." By the time of 1968's *Beggar's Banquet* sessions, Jones was incapacitated beyond redemption.

Ronnie Scott, Saxophone Solo on "Lady Madonna"

Nowhere was the Beatles' habit of expecting results on demand more amply illustrated than on the recording of this single, their last for Parlophone/Capitol. Coming toward the end of a rather lengthy one-song session, the group decided that they must have a real four-piece saxophone section to augment their vocal approximation of one— and *now*.

At 6:30 in the evening, the call went out to the first horn player on the list, Harry Klein, who recommended contacting Ronnie Scott, musician and owner of the London jazz club bearing his name.

Scott's career began during the war years. Signing onto service aboard the liner *Queen Mary*, his trips to New York allowed him to see American jazz

Saxophonist Ronnie Scott was a fixture in London's jazz scene since the 1950s. Long renowned for his Soho club, he died in 1996 from complications involving dental surgery.   *Photo by David Redfern/Redferns*

legends in their prime, including the immortal Charlie Parker, who became a huge influence. No less an authority than Charles Mingus offered Scott high praise for his soulful style.

Given his credits and standing in the jazz community, Scott was not a talent to take lightly. Upon arriving at EMI only to discover that no arrangement for the four horns had been written out, he went off on Macca for his "unprofessional" expectations.

Eventually, with input from the musicians, four sax parts were set up so as not to step on each other, but Scott's moment in the spotlight resulted in one of the most agitated-sounding sax solos in rock history.

Over the years, Scott would acknowledge his contribution to one of the Beatles' best-known songs, but not without noting: "They broke up shortly after that, I might tell you!"

Lizzie Bravo and Gayleen Pease, Vocals on "Across the Universe"

Despite the merit of John's singularly inspired composition, the songwriter's inability to articulate any sort of direction made capturing a usable take on tape seem an elusive goal indeed.

Certainly George Martin was a reliable source of suggestions, but John would later complain bitterly that his best songs invited "subconscious sabotage" from his fellow Beatles. Citing "Across the Universe" as an example, he argued that the experimental mood of certain recordings kept his most inspired tunes from rising to the heights of, say, "In My Life." Certainly, the case can be made in this instance that the group erred in bringing in a pair of young girls, selected virtually at random, to sing on a Beatles record.

Plucked from the flock of fans that gathered regularly just outside the Abbey Road recording facility were sixteen-year-old Brazilian Lizzie Bravo and seventeen-year-old Gayleen Pease. Both were regular visitors; Lizzie lived just over a mile away, while Gayleen trekked in from outside Ealing, nine miles away. (In fact, both girls had been photographed with the Fabs the year before, with Lizzie getting her copy of *Sgt. Pepper's* signed by all four Beatles.)

The girls were escorted into the number two studio, the Beatles' main work place. After getting over their initial shock, they were coached by Paul and George Martin to sing a falsetto "nothing's gonna change my world" with John on the song's refrain. Once a passable take was nailed, they were quietly escorted out again, with sincere thanks from the band.

They would have to wait nearly two years, until December 1969 and the release of the charity album *No One's Gonna Change Our World*, to hear the results of the evening's work. For anyone wondering, Lizzie and Gayleen eventually petitioned Apple for some compensation, and each received a modest stipend.

Nicky Hopkins, Electric Piano on "Revolution"

By the time he'd been called into EMI Studios to assist on this recording, keyboardist Nicky Hopkins had made a name for himself as one of the most sought-after session players in British rock. Few musicians could boast the distinction of having played on records by the Kinks, the Who, the Rolling Stones, and now the Beatles. But Hopkins was that rare musical everyman who possessed an innate understanding of what a track required, yet was egoless enough to keep a distance from the stars he served.

What kept a man of his talents from attaching himself more permanently to any of the company he kept? The main obstacle was poor health. Afflicted with Crohn's disease, a malady of the digestive tract, Hopkins gravitated toward session work as a less physically demanding task than touring with a band. That said, his Beatles work came between stints in the Jeff Beck Group and the San Francisco psychedelic jam band Quicksilver Messenger Service.

The Beatles laid down the basic tracks to the single version of "Revolution" minus Hopkins. He came in the following day and overdubbed a frenzied solo, reminiscent of some of the filler work he had done on the Who's first album, beneath the guitar break. Despite his fine contribution to this track and "Sour Milk Sea," recorded around the same time, Hopkins was never asked back to a Beatles session (although Paul later suggested him for the "Get Back" / *Let It Be* project).

Years later, after working with John on *Imagine* and George on *Living in the Material World*, Hopkins heard Lennon say he wished the Beatles had used him more. When he asked why they hadn't, John replied that they assumed he was too tied up with the Stones to be available.

Jackie Lomax, Vocals on "Dear Prudence"

Newly signed Apple artist and longtime Liverpool mate Jackie Lomax received some spirited support from nearly all the Beatles (except for John, who, though an admirer, was always diffident about lending his instrumental skills to other musicians). On this rare occasion, Lomax was on hand to return the favor, lending his voice to John's evocative tune composed during the Rishikesh sojourn.

He can be heard on the "look around 'round 'round, 'round 'round" backing parts and some of the wordless harmonies. Also present was Paul's cousin, John McCartney (not to be confused with the "millionaire Irish peer"), who likewise sang along.

The recording of this track, which took place during Ringo's walkout, typified the seismic shift in previously existing band paradigms. For the first time in the group's career, studio recording sessions took on the casual air of public rehearsals, with relatives and acquaintances seemingly given leave to come and go at will. Paul would have two significant others (Francie Schwartz and Linda Eastman) pass in and out of the "White Album" sessions, while John's liaison with Yoko marked the start of a presence that would remain for the band's duration.

Eric Clapton, Lead Guitar on "While My Guitar Gently Weeps"

George Harrison's influence with his fellow Beatles peaked with the trip to India to study meditation with the Maharishi. The sabbatical ended badly, with John publicly denouncing the yogi as a fraud, raking him over the coals by proxy in "Sexy Sadie."

Perhaps feeling that the others unconsciously held him responsible for their disillusionment, George composed "Not Guilty," asserting that he was not to blame for "leading you astray on the road to Mandalay." Whether this was true or not, one thing was certain: getting a fair hearing for his compositions was becoming increasingly difficult.

Not until nearly twenty years after Lennon's death did the public get a glimpse of his fabled performance of "Yer Blues" alongside Clapton and Keith Richards from the Rolling Stones' *Rock and Roll Circus* special.   *Photo courtesy of Photofest*

This was all too obvious when his fellow Fabs all but shrugged off what he felt to be a high-quality composition: "While My Guitar Gently Weeps." Stung by their apathy, George attempted to record the song without their support, accompanying himself on acoustic guitar, with Paul providing a subtle organ backing. Lovely as this subdued version (released on *Anthology 3*) is, the composer recognized that giving the song its due required shaking the band out of its collective stupor.

With considerable misgivings ("But *nobody* ever plays on the Beatles' records!"), guitar-slinger Eric Clapton agreed to take over George's normal role. His mere presence in the studio, as George correctly anticipated, immediately snapped the group into shape, with the Fabs now acting sweetly, as one always does when company calls.

After Clapton laid down a solo that could scarcely be bettered, George added his own touch to it, running the part through the ADT (automatic double tracking) device to add the requisite "wobble" that made it passably Beatley.

The results gave both George and Eric a lift when they needed it, coming during times of particular turmoil within their respective bands. The former repaid the favor later that year by cowriting and playing on Cream's "Badge."

Lennon was impressed enough by Eric's performance to pick him later that year to back him on "Yer Blues" for the Rolling Stones' *Rock and Roll Circus* television special. A month later, George stormed out of the "Get Back" sessions, apparently for good. Before his amp had even cooled down, John nominated Eric as his replacement.

The Beatle Wives: Pattie Harrison and Yoko Ono, Vocals on "Birthday"; Yoko Ono and Maureen Starkey, Vocals on "The Continuing Story of Bungalow Bill"; Yoko Ono, Vocals on "Revolution 9"; Linda McCartney, Vocals on "Let It Be"

A looser atmosphere in the recording studio meant that making use of whoever was around became a habit. In this way the "White Album" sessions contrasted greatly with every preceding album. Also a departure was the diminished input from George Martin, with the Beatles essentially producing themselves as Martin stood by to assist where needed. The decay in the Fabs' relationship with their producer led to an almost completely hands-off situation throughout the "Get Back" fiasco, with Paul at last begging Martin to resume his traditional role for *Abbey Road*.

In any event, much of *The Beatles* was recorded with outsiders present. (In fact, the original ending of "Dear Prudence" was punctuated by spontaneous applause; this was faded out on the record.) It was as though on a subconscious level the four understood that they were at their best before an audience, despite the strain of the touring years.

The airing of the 1957 jukebox musical *The Girl Can't Help It* on British television sparked the creation of the "White Album" favorite "Birthday." Long before the advent of DVDs, cable, or VCRs, the showing of a film unseen in theaters for a decade was an *event*. As such, the Beatles, accompanied by their spouses, adjourned their recording session to watch the film at Paul's nearby residence on Cavendish.

The film, which starred Jayne Mansfield, also included a host of rockers in peak form, including Little Richard, Gene Vincent, and Eddie Cochran. Duly inspired, the Fabs returned to the studio to lay down this energetic rocker. Helping along with the track's party atmosphere were Yoko Ono, fresh from her first exposure to vintage rock and roll, and Pattie Harrison. Each chirped along on the "Birthday!" backing vocals.

Years later, John would tell the story of how Yoko marked her first appearance at a Beatles recording session by taking the band to task for using the same rhythm all the time. (In his telling, the song in question was "Hey Bulldog"; this is surely a mistake, for that song was recorded months before the two officially hooked up in May 1968.) Yoko's comfort level when it came to telling the biggest band in the world what's what had now grown to the point where she had no qualms about delivering a line in an actual song.

John's black comedy number, "The Continuing Story of Bungalow Bill," featured, like "Birthday," two Beatle mates. But while Ringo's wife, Maureen, limited herself to the sing-along chorus, Yoko chimed in on "Not when he looked so fierce," underscoring which character was being quoted. There are fans to this day who believe the line is sung by one of the Beatles using a funny voice.

Yoko (and George) also contributed spoken passages to "Revolution 9," a composition that could more accurately be credited to Lennon-Ono than to Lennon-McCartney. Her delivery of the "if . . . you become naked" line would, in 1968, reinforce the public perception that the Witty Beatle was a born-again nudist, what with the release of *Two Virgins* around the same time.

As George Martin prepared "Let It Be" for proper commercial release as a single, it became clear that the spartan backing harmonies provided by John and George on "Let It Be" (as seen in the film) could use some punching up. So it was that Lovely Linda made her vocal debut on a composition of her husband's.

She might not have been pressed into service at all, had the original plan panned out. Apple chanteuse Mary Hopkin had been the intended singer, but the nineteen-year-old left the studio before her part was cut, forcing a serendipitous arrangement that previewed Linda's vocal contributions to *McCartney* and beyond. (Ironically, Paul would criticize Phil Spector's work on "The Long and Winding Road" for its use of choirs by declaring, somewhat disingenuously, that the Beatles would never use female voices on one of their records.)

Billy Preston, Electric Piano, "Get Back," "Don't Let Me Down," and "Let It Be"; Organ, "Something" and "I Want You (She's So Heavy)"

One could make the case that Ray Charles was responsible for the Beatles lasting another year. Had Billy Preston *not* been in London in January of 1969, having just completed a European tour with his mentor, George wouldn't have run into him while on the outs with the Fabs. Their re-acquaintance culminated with George again playing the special guest card, smoothing things over within the group for long enough to get them to wrap up a substandard product (*Let It Be*), which then necessitated an *Abbey Road* just to flush away the stench.

Preston's presence was just the tonic needed to buy the Beatles some more time. With an inoffensiveness rivaling Ringo's, but carrying talent aplenty that added to the band's musical identity without stepping on it, he was the perfect supporting player.

Another aspect that made Preston so essential was that an accomplished keyboardist was crucial to completing a project predicated on live takes with no overdubs. The Beatles were free to play as a band in their traditional roles, minimizing the need to shift someone to bass while Paul played keys. Had Billy shown up during say, the *Pepper* or *Revolver* sessions, it's doubtful that his help would have been needed.

With Preston brought in after the shift to Apple studios, ordinarily the highlight of his tenure would surely have been the rooftop performance immortalized in *Let It Be*. But the Beatles' largesse also included a credit on the label of the "Get Back" single, an unprecedented gesture that moved Billy deeply. Given his key contribution to both sides, the Fabs could scarcely have done otherwise.

The *Abbey Road* sessions began insidiously, with the recording of "I Want You (She's So Heavy)" in February of 1969. Billy's jazz licks on organ enhanced the atmosphere without drawing undue attention. His work on "Something" was likewise critical, yet subtle.

26

I Can Be Handy

The Beatles in Service of Their Label

B eing hands-on proprietors, the Beatles were not content with simply signing new talent to their record label, or even with calling the shots as producers. Instead, when they had the time, the Fabs proactively provided instrumental support.

Having each scored a film by this time, Paul and George were, predictably, the Fabs most in pursuit of a studio tan. Their practice of guesting on sessions that they produced continued well into the solo years, with George repeating the exercise on another custom label launch and talent search for his own Dark Horse Records.

Though responsible for creating some truly outstanding recordings, the Beatles had a varying track record in terms of sales. Unquestionably, the product they generated deserved more success than it achieved the first time round, but fortunately, most of it is readily available on remastered CDs, awaiting rediscovery by fans today.

"Sour Milk Sea" by Jackie Lomax, Released August 26, 1968

Apple couldn't have been given a more promising start than with this recording. To back Jackie Lomax on a song he'd written in India, demoed in Esher, but would never have taken further on his own, George rounded up two other Beatles (John couldn't be bothered with a Harrisong), Nicky Hopkins on piano, and, for extra guitar firepower, Eric Clapton. The super session took place at London's Trident studios, which unlike EMI had the benefit of an eight-track recording facility.

George's paean to the marvels of meditation is a powerful, gritty rocker, more suited to Lomax's gutsy singing style than to his own. The backing band thunders along magnificently, each musician accorded a moment to shine within the arrangement. Though most guitarists would not relish a side-by-side comparison with Clapton, George acquitted himself capably with an understated solo that outshone Slowhand's.

Yet this single with so much going for it went criminally ignored upon release. "Sour Milk Sea" did not chart, suffocated beneath the Apple focus on "Hey Jude" and "Those Were the Days" in late summer 1968. The subsequent *Is This What You Want?* LP, issued in March 1969, suffered a similar fate.

"Carolina in My Mind" by James Taylor, Released December 6, 1968

Despite his sister Jane having had her heart handed to her by a cheating dog of a fiancé, Peter Asher was quite prepared to maintain his professional relationship with Paul McCartney. As Apple's A&R, he demonstrated great aptitude for spotting talent, evidenced in his discovery of James Taylor.

Paul took a particular interest in the Yankee musician. As a purveyor of introspective yet tuneful songs, Taylor was unique, possessing a compelling presence as well as a pop sensibility that dovetailed with that of his Apple handlers. Taylor was also not averse to production innovation; the novelty of having the songs on his debut album bridged by little instrumental links was later advanced by his mentor on the second side of *Abbey Road*.

"Carolina in My Mind" was chosen as the debut single from the rich material that Taylor presented. Other songs included "Rainy Day Man," "Something in the Way She Moves" (a title that proved inspirational), and a melancholy number titled "Fire and Rain." An early take of the last tune still languishes in the Apple vaults.

With Paul contributing bass, guitar, and backing vocals, "Carolina in My Mind" was recorded, with subtle orchestral shading added later. (Taylor himself has claimed that George also contributed backing vocals, but Peter Asher disputes this.) Sadly, this song failed to chart, disappearing without a trace.

In 1970, after Taylor moved to Warner Brothers and scored with "Fire and Rain," "Carolina in My Mind" began receiving airplay, becoming a minor hit in some markets. With the Apple catalog tied up in litigation for many years, Taylor was compelled to re-record the song in 1976 for release on his greatest hits collection. Most fans are familiar with the remake, which runs slightly slower and features scaled-back production.

"Goodbye" by Mary Hopkin, Released March 28, 1969

Living up to the tremendous worldwide success of Mary Hopkin's first vinyl outing, "Those Were the Days," would have been tough for any artist, but the Welsh songbird wasn't exactly in a position to call her own shots. With

Apple's—and by extension, the Beatles'—prestige on the line, Paul wrote and demoed a follow-up for her, a song that Mary herself understood to be Paul's "farewell" to micromanaging her career.

By this time, Paul was effortlessly knocking out songs for others. Cilla Black, Badfinger (formerly the Iveys), and Mary received his gifts, though the latter chafed most under his direction. Paul selected Mary's material, often old standards or show tunes, while marketing her internationally via recordings issued in French, Spanish, and Italian. At heart a folkie, she gamely played along, enduring his efforts at recasting her into a pop chanteuse, all the while biding her time for the day when she would at last take control of her career.

That day wouldn't arrive until 1971's *Earth Song / Ocean Song* LP, by which time Mary was ready to start a family. Till then, she swallowed her objections and recorded everything placed before her. (Well, almost everything; years later, she expressed her profound regret at having turned down both "Your Song" and "You've Got a Friend.")

"Goodbye" at least was a pleasant, well-produced effort at meeting her halfway. Paul stuck close to his own demo and played acoustic guitar, bass, and thigh slaps on the track, which was augmented by a tasteful horn arrangement. It reached #2 in the U.K. and #13 in the States.

"Thumbing a Ride" by Jackie Lomax, Released May 2, 1969

The failure of Jackie Lomax's album and single to set the music charts on fire vexed the Beatles. Given its estimation of Jackie's talent, Apple was unwilling to swallow the bitter pill of public indifference.

In hindsight, a major flaw in their marketing strategy can be seen in the decision to pitch Lomax as a singles artist rather than, more properly, as an album artist. Expecting him to compete within the same segment of the population that was lapping up Mary Hopkin was decidedly unrealistic.

With the enormously successful "Those Were the Days" single under his belt, Paul must have felt that he alone possessed the production talent to unleash Jackie's latent gifts. On his wedding eve, Paul set to work laying down tracks on an old Coasters' tune, "Thumbing a Ride." George contributed guitar, while some sources placed Paul on drums. Following his nuptials (and George's dope bust) the next day, Paul characteristically continued working on the track until it was completed.

The song would emerge as the flip side to the single "New Day," produced by Mal Evans. But again the release was greeted with decided apathy in the marketplace. By now distracted by their own internal affairs, the

Beatles were at a loss to come up with a thoughtful new approach to presenting the artist.

George gave Jackie another go by producing "How the Web Was Woven" in the fall of 1969. Featuring instrumental backing provided entirely by sessionist/singer Leon Russell, this too failed to chart.

Not blind to the writing on the wall, Lomax followed the Apple exodus led by James Taylor, taking his act to Warner Brothers, as would Badfinger and George himself in years to come. Successes varied.

"That's the Way God Planned It" by Billy Preston, Released June 27, 1969

It is ironic that a man whose career began in gospel should have been moved to revisit the idiom after working on a gospel-esque composition written by a white Liverpudlian. But keyboardist/singer/songwriter Billy Preston often gave props to Paul's "Let It Be" for inspiring him to come up with this soulful yet dynamic showstopper.

Perhaps feeling that he owed Billy after the lift his presence had given the Beatles during the *Let It Be* sessions, George once again shouldered production duties for a comrade in arms, recruiting the "cream" of available sidemen (well, two-thirds, anyway: Eric Clapton and Ginger Baker). Additional support came from Keith Richards on bass; Billy would later record extensively with the Rolling Stones, beginning with "I Got the Blues" on 1971's *Sticky Fingers*.

Nineteen-sixty-nine saw a religious sensibility manifest itself within the pop community. The Edwin Hawkins Singers scored a fluke hit with the hymn "Oh Happy Day," opening the floodgates to thematically similar tunes the following year, such as Norman Greenbaum's "Spirit in the Sky," Pacific Gas and Electric's "Are You Ready?," and of course George's own "My Sweet Lord" (which Billy himself covered on the *Encouraging Words* LP).

Whatever was in the air, "That's the Way God Planned It" anticipated the mood completely, satisfying as rock and as spiritual celebration. Disappointingly, the single failed to click in the U.S. marketplace, but Billy's performance of it at the Concert for Bangla Desh was literally showstealing.

"Remember Love" by Plastic Ono Band, Released July 4, 1969

Yoko Ono has been stereotyped as, at best, a talentless screamer incapable of producing a tuneful sound, and at worst—well, we won't go there. This belief is belied by the fact that her nine solo albums have found an audience, albeit a small one, and that her groundbreaking work proved distinctly influential with the onset of New Wave.

As a classically trained pianist, Yoko was no slouch when it came to Western music. But pop and rock and roll were completely alien to her when she was first drawn into the madness that was John Lennon's world. John, in the rare position of teacher, would spend many years bringing her up to speed, so much so that by the time of 1980's *Double Fantasy*, she was at least on equal footing (if not, as many believe, the greater innovator).

The B-side to "Give Peace a Chance" was where it all began. Long accustomed to composing poems and free verse, Yoko offered in "Remember Love" her own statement on what the world needed, set to the gentle acoustic picking of her husband. It is a charming little piece, sung in an almost childlike voice. John's sympathetic production enhanced the innocence of her avowal, which offered listeners a rather tranquil counterpoint to the A-side's rousing sing-along.

"Hare Krishna Mantra" by the Radha Krishna Temple, Released August 29, 1969

George Harrison's devotion to the teachings of Lord Krishna at last coalesced with his professional capabilities in the recording of this single. As it happened, marrying the temple's devotional to a pop sensibility wasn't much of a stretch.

Though smitten with Indian music, culture, and spirituality since at least 1966, George did not actually come into direct contact with the Krishnas until 1969, when members arrived to open a London chapter. After meeting with them at Apple, the Beatle knew he wanted to further the church's reach. Heeding the suggestion of A. C. Bhaktivedanta Swami Prabhupada, their leader, he quickly recognized that his best service to the movement would come through song.

Abetted by Paul, George assumed production duties, also contributing instrumentally on guitar, bass, and harmonium. The resulting single, "Hare Krishna Mantra," stunned the pop world by reaching #12 in the U.K. (George would later consider the Krishnas' *four* appearances on *Top of the Pops* among the highlights of his life.)

Its success would pave the way for a follow-up single, "Govinda," in early 1970. To this day, the song is performed at morning services in ISKCON temples around the world.

"Rock of All Ages" by Badfinger, Released January 9, 1970

Commissioned once again to provide the music to a motion picture (in this instance, *The Magic Christian*, a Ringo vehicle starring Peter Sellers), Paul had completed one original tune before recognizing the opportunity to kill two birds with one stone.

An article in an English music journal quoted a member of the Iveys as saying that Apple had been neglecting them, choosing to kill the release of their *Maybe Tomorrow* album in America. Seizing the moment, Paul at once

Note that the marketing for *The Magic Christian* film's soundtrack album played up Paul McCartney's role at the expense of Badfinger's (who weren't even mentioned).

realized he could placate the boys *and* shed a commitment that he lacked the time to fulfill by simply getting the group—now dubbed Badfinger—to take over the gig.

He quickly demoed "Come and Get It" for the project. Then, assuming the producer's role, he auditioned the singers to see who should take the lead vocal on the tune. He also issued an edict to copy the demo to the letter, but thankfully the band sped up the tempo slightly. Recognizing that his directive was heavy-handed, if not condescending, McCartney assured the novice recording group that "this is the hit sound."

For the B-side, the band, doubtless with some input from Paul, composed "Rock of All Ages." This guitar- and piano-pounding screamer was also slated for inclusion in the film, along with the melodic "Carry On Till Tomorrow." (The latter song came in response to the film producers' request to compose a "Simon and Garfunkel–esque" tune for a particular scene.)

Relaxed by the successful capture of the A-side, Paul commandeered the keys for the flip, resurrecting his Little Richard impersonation by adding whoops and screams behind Tommy Evans's throat-ripping vocal. (Paul's presence is much more pronounced in the mix issued on the *Magic Christian* soundtrack album than on Badfinger's first Apple LP of same. The soundtrack mix also runs slightly longer than the LP track.)

"Who Has Seen the Wind" by Yoko Ono / Plastic Ono Band, Released February 6, 1970

In what was becoming customary procedure, John for the third time presented a musical showcase for Yoko on the B-side of his latest single. Though the Beatles were nominally together, as far as the public was concerned, "Instant Karma" did nothing to reassure those paying attention. For the second single in a row, John had dispensed with the "Lennon-McCartney" songwriting credit.

Recorded the day it was written, the single marked the beginning of a relationship with the renowned Phil Spector. His groundbreaking production work reassured both John and George (who was present for the session) that he was the man to sort out the "Get Back" / *Let It Be* mess.

"Who Has Seen the Wind" once again typified the mellow side of Yoko. Accompanying herself on flute, with John on acoustic guitar and John Barham on harpsichord, she laid down a song that would have fit well in an *Addams Family* soundtrack. (Some sources say that George, too, is on the track, but likely as not he had left the studio for an evening of pub crawling with the local Krishnas he had brought to the session for vocal support.)

YOKO ONO LENNON
WHO HAS SEEN THE WIND?

PRODUCED BY
JOHN LENNON

Manufactured by APPLE RECORDS INC. • 1700 Broadway, New York, N.Y. 10019 • Printed in U.S.A.

In what became established practice until 1971's *Imagine*, John's single B-sides featured his missus. The practice was revived for the "Happy Xmas" and "Woman Is the Nigger of the World" releases, but thereafter shelved until 1980's *Double Fantasy*.

"Ain't That Cute" by Doris Troy, Released February 13, 1970

American soul singer Doris Troy entered Apple's orbit via Billy Preston, a friend and songwriting partner. George took it upon himself to take charge of her Apple debut, enlisting his usual crew of stalwarts, including Billy, Ringo (though not on this track), Eric Clapton, and assorted future Dominoes, plus Leon Russell and Stephen Stills.

"Ain't That Cute," co-written by Doris and George, was a superb song choice to reintroduce the singer to the marketplace. Playing lead guitar on the song was twenty-year-old *wunderkind* Peter Frampton, formerly of the Herd and currently with the up-and-coming English boogie band Humble Pie. Frampton would go on to make an uncredited guest appearance on George's *All Things Must Pass* album that year. (After an unfortunate star turn in the 1978 box office turkey *Sgt. Pepper's Lonely Hearts Club Band*, Frampton redeemed himself Beatle-wise with his participation in the 1997–98 edition of Ringo's All-Starr Band.)

Though her signing was considered quite a feather in the cap, Apple seemed at a loss to promote and market Doris (or, for that matter, many of its other artists). Only after her album initially tanked was a sticker added to the cover announcing the star-cluttered line-up. But Doris had moved on, guesting on John's "Power to the People" single in 1971 before leaving Apple altogether.

27

Do You Need Anybody?

Assistance Rendered

A fter the Beatles had proven themselves in America in 1964, their
continued success was all but assured. Safely past the "flash in the
pan" stage (at least in their own minds), the Fabs soon found
themselves in a position to dispense a touch of magic to their friends and
acquaintances in the business. All too happy to toss spare tunes around
(albeit songs they'd already judged as lacking), the Fabs would also contribute directly to the recording sessions of other artists, usually those with
whom they had some sort of personal connection.

Despite the demands that their own success placed upon them, the
boys continued to help out throughout their career. But, in keeping with
the standard industry practice of the time, the Beatles were never credited
in a performing capacity on another artist's record. Mostly, their presence
would be rumored, rightly or wrongly. (For example, to this day, some oldies
radio DJs will erroneously identify George Harrison as contributing guitar
to Donovan's "Sunshine Superman." He didn't, although Paul sings on the
chorus of "Mellow Yellow.")

Eventually, the boys took to crediting themselves under outlandish pseud-
onyms, keeping fans in the know but the record labels to which they were
contractually bound in the dark. On some recordings, Beatle participation
can't be verified beyond an educated guess (Paul, for example, is believed to
be heard masticating all over the Beach Boys' "Vegetables" from *Smiley Smile*)
but on others, there is no question. Here is a rundown of notables who, to
varying degrees, benefited from the Beatles' largesse—or didn't.

Cilla Black, "It's for You," Recorded July 2, 1964

The former Priscilla White was probably the earliest and most successful
recipient of the Beatles' musical generosity. Given the multiple ties that

bound band and singer (performing history at the Cavern; shared manager and record producer), it was inevitable that their personal and professional relationships would overlap in the studio.

Just days before the London premiere of *A Hard Day's Night*, Paul took time out from a packed schedule to sit in on the recording of a Lennon-McCartney tune tailored specifically to Cilla. With George Martin in his familiar role at what had become their stomping grounds, Paul played piano on this unique jazz-waltz ballad.

Though the single would stall at #8 on the U.K. charts, "It's for You" would not be Paul's last musical gift to Cilla. Four years later, his "Step Inside Love" became a smash hit as well as the theme to her newly launched musical-comedy series on BBC television.

Rory Storm and the Hurricanes, "America," Recorded September 30, 1964

Despite the loss of his Starr drummer to the Beatles in August 1962, Rory Storm maintained cordial relations with the Fabs. Though seemingly everyone who had ever shared a stage with the Beatles was eventually signed to a recording contract and whisked away to London, fortune seemed to elude the band once regarded as their chief competition in the club circuit.

This may have been because the Hurricanes' chief appeal lay in their vigorous stage act rather than in the strength of their cover-heavy material. Without a strong writer among them, the band tended to rely on the same pool of shopworn chestnuts as every other Merseyside band.

Ringo never forgot his old bandmates and was anxious to see some them receive their due from the record-buying public. At last, Brian Epstein, who'd spurned earlier entreaties to manage the act, agreed to sit in as *producer* on a proper recording session. He chose *West Side Story*'s "America" as the vehicle with which to present them.

Taking a breather from the *Beatles for Sale* sessions, Ringo contributed maracas and tambourine, as well as backing vocals, to the track. But the added Starr-power was for naught, as the single failed to chart. Despite Ringo's offers to set up future recording dates, Rory returned to Liverpool, seemingly at peace with his role as the big fish in a small pond.

Alma Cogan, "I Knew Right Away," Recorded October 2, 1964

Starting in 1954 with "Bell Bottom Blues" (no, not the Eric Clapton song!), Alma Cogan became one of Britain's best-loved entertainers. Known as "the girl with the laugh in her voice" from her penchant for letting mirth color her delivery, she got her start with a series of novelty tunes before finding her niche as a purveyor of Doris Day–style pop.

She soon became a show-business institution, starring on television, radio, and stage. A firmly established star by the time she crossed paths with the Beatles on *Sunday Night at the London Palladium*, to her credit she embraced their sound and bonded easily with them, thanks in no small part to her equally absurdist sense of humor.

John Lennon, who had heretofore mocked the old-school singer, found himself smitten, igniting a mutual attraction that stopped just short of physical involvement (though Alma's sister, to this day, suggests otherwise). Brian Epstein, decidedly a member of the opposite team, also found Alma irresistible, prompting rumors of a pending engagement—although his fixation may have been more in a Judy Garland sense.

Two days after Ringo lent support to Rory Storm, at least two of the Beatles were on hand as Alma recorded a self-penned single, "It's You," published by Brian's JAEP Publishing. For the B-side, "I Knew Right Away," Paul contributed, somewhat coyly, a tambourine part (suggesting that at this stage he wasn't going to overstep his bounds).

Though they never got around to composing a song expressly for her, the Beatles remained in Alma's orbit for several years. Alma would record a slew of Lennon-McCartney songs, none better than her torch ballad reading of "Eight Days a Week." In October 1966, Alma tragically succumbed to cancer. She was thirty-four.

The Silkie, "You've Got to Hide Your Love Away," Recorded August 9, 1965

During a rare week off between the release of their *Help!* album and the start of their North American tour, three of the Beatles were dragooned into lending a hand to Brian Epstein's latest project. An English folk quartet by the name of the Silkie, newly signed to a management deal, had released their first single, "Blood Red River," to universal apathy. Now, armed with a Beatles song and Beatle support, the band and their manager hoped to put them on the map.

With John acting as producer, Paul played guitar while George handled tambourine and percussive duties. The resulting recording stuck close to the original arrangement, chiefly differing by the addition of a female vocal line. The resulting single peaked at #28 in the U.K. and #10 in America, providing the Silkie with their sole hit. Later they would record an album's worth of Bob Dylan songs before quietly disbanding.

The Rolling Stones, "We Love You," Recorded
June 12–13 / July 1967

Long pegged as deadly rivals, the Beatles and the Stones were actually quite friendly with each other, socializing in London's club scene during off-hours. In the years since the Stones had covered "I Wanna Be Your Man," they'd carved out their own brand and musical identity, marketing themselves as the "anti-Beatles." Though far more bourgeois than their Mersey peers—truth be told—they created a "bad boy" image that was taken seriously by more than just their teenage audience. In 1967, three of the

445-08191-125 $1.25

THE FAMOUS *ROLLING STONE* INTERVIEWS
—PLUS 59 RARE PHOTOGRAPHS

LENNON
REMEMBERS

Resentful of everything and everyone he associated with the Fab Four's heyday, John did much spewing in his infamous *Rolling Stone* interview. Not even the Rolling Stones escaped his venom.

band's members were stung by highly publicized drug busts that would keep them tied up in court throughout much of the year.

Once their legal issues were sorted out, the Stones went into the studio to record a gesture of thanks to the public for support throughout their ordeal. (Lest anyone miss the point, the song begins with the sounds of a creaking jail door and chains.) A few weeks after the basic track was laid down, John and Paul turned up to help finish the song, adding harmonies.

John would later assert bitterly that the Rolling Stones habitually ripped off the Beatles' musical ideas, citing the similarities between "As Tears Go By" and "Yesterday," "Paint It Black" and "Norwegian Wood," "We Love You" and "All You Need Is Love"—notwithstanding Mick Jagger's presence at the latter song's world premiere.

While the claim comes off as rather petty, if not specious, in the Beatles' heyday the two bands did seem to display mutual admiration: the Rolling Stones were found worthy of mention on the cover of *Sgt. Pepper's*, while the Beatles' faces appeared on the sleeve to *Their Satanic Majesties Request.*

The Remo Four, "In the First Place," Recorded December 1967

This quartet of Liverpudlians followed a career path paralleling that of the Fabs. They, too, honed their skills playing overseas, in their case at U.S. Air Force bases in France. Such was their local popularity that the Remo Four placed third (after Gerry and the Pacemakers) in the famous "Beatles Top Poll!" issue of *Mersey Beat.*

Their sound, a mix of vocal harmonies and Shadows-type instrumentals, showcased their versatility. But the absence of strong songwriters and a certain lack of personality relegated them, despite having signed with Brian Epstein's management agency, to also-ran status.

They found work as a backing band, chiefly behind Tommy Quickly and Billy J. Kramer (as the "new" Dakotas). By 1967, they were barely in existence, going on nearly two years without a record deal, when George Harrison gave them a last-minute reprieve from oblivion.

Commissioned to write a film score for *Wonderwall,* director Joe Massot's first film, George drafted the Remo Four to act as house band for the Western portion of his score, with Indian musicians performing on the Eastern half. Abetted by uncredited luminaries like Eric Clapton, Ringo, and the Monkees' Peter Tork, the group took the opportunity to cut an additional track that would be overlooked for decades.

"In the First Place" is at once a creature of its time and timeless. Penned by band members Colin Manley and Tony Ashton, the track includes vocals by George. Very much in the in the mold of "Blue Jay Way," it is moody and atmospheric.

But the song went unused in the film due to George's mistaken belief that Massot only required instrumental pieces. Meanwhile, the Remo Four disbanded, with two members forming Ashton, Gardner, and Dyke, who would score their only hit with 1971's "Resurrection Shuffle."

Only in 1998, when Massot requested the soundtrack masters from George in order to assemble a "director's cut" of *Wonderwall*, did the song's existence come to his attention. Massot would include the track in the revamped film, crediting George, per his instructions, solely as producer.

Paul Jones, "And the Sun Will Shine," Recorded February 1968

Although mostly remembered for their recording of "Doo Wah Diddy Diddy" in 1964, Manfred Mann was one of the most enduring chart acts of the British Invasion era, producing a stream of hits in Europe, including "5-4-3-2-1," the theme to ITV's pop showcase, *Ready Steady Go!*

Handling lead vocals during the band's first few years was Paul Jones, a veteran of Alexis Korner's Bluesbreakers. He left Manfred Mann after recording the U.K. #1 hit "Pretty Flamingo" in 1966. (Also departing around that time was bassist Jack Bruce, who left to form Cream. He was replaced by Beatle friend Klaus Voormann.)

After he and Gordon Waller had parted ways, Peter Asher sought to carve out a career as a producer. In early 1968, his first client was Paul Jones, who fronted what amounted to a supergroup for this single. Handling guitar and bass duties were two ex-Yardbirds, Jeff Beck and Paul Samwell-Smith. On keyboards was session player extraordinaire Nicky Hopkins, and on drums was none other than Paul McCartney. (For good measure, Peter brought in his father and sister—Claire, not Jane—to handle background vocals.)

The A-side of the single was written by the Bee Gees. For the B-side, the band cut a wild rocker titled "The Dog Presides," but sadly, neither song found an audience and the single flopped. It was only rediscovered during the CD era, turning up on a Paul Jones compilation.

The Bonzo Dog (Doo Dah) Band, "I'm the Urban Spaceman," Recorded July 1968

This musical-comedy outfit began as a jazz-oriented novelty group, covering 1920s obscurities with a satirical bent, before their own native anarchistic tendencies mutated them into a singular purveyor of twisted tunes. Even more perversely, they first achieved wide notice in Britain via a children's television show, *Do Not Adjust Your Set*, which included three future Monty Pythons in the cast.

To most Beatle fans, *Magical Mystery Tour* provides a fine opportunity to see the Bonzos in action. In the strip club scene, they perform "Death Cab for Cutie," inadvertently inspiring a band name for some U.S. popsters thirty-five years later.

As fans themselves, the Beatles were happy to boost the band at every opportunity. Months after the *MMT* film crashed and burned, Paul was ready to assist the Bonzos in a more practical way. He contributed ukulele and production to their single "I'm the Urban Spaceman," under the name of Apollo C. Vermouth. The song became a bona fide hit, but by 1970 the band had played out its string.

Drummer "Legs" Larry Smith managed to parlay his zany persona into a role as comic relief for other rockers, inspiring a song by George in 1975 on his *Extra Texture* LP. Singer/composer Vivian Stanshall was likewise a notable eccentric, often seen in the company of the Who's equally twisted drummer, Keith Moon. But composer/pianist Neil Innes is perhaps the best-known ex-Bonzo. As resident musician to the Pythons, he turned up in their projects frequently, with the relationship culminating in his 1978 collaboration with Eric Idle, *The Rutles*.

Cream, "Badge," Recorded Late 1968

Eric Clapton's contribution to "While My Guitar Gently Weeps" invited payback from George. Following the July 1968 announcement of Cream's impending demise, plans for a farewell tour and album were made. Upon the tour's finish, the band set to work on its final release, originally intended as a double set, half live and half studio. Eventually, this was pared down to a single record, *Goodbye*. For many, the album's highlight would be the elegant "Badge," the only compositional credit the two friends would ever share.

Actually, Ringo's input was equally key. Arriving at the writing session in a state of less than full sobriety, he tossed out a series of non sequiturs that made the final cut, including the bit about swans that lived in the park.

The origins of the song's title are equally incongruous. Eric, sitting opposite George as the latter scribbled down lyrics and mapped out the song's structure, looked quizzically at the upside-down tablet and asked, "What's 'badge'?" "That's 'bridge,' " George corrected him. In keeping with the mirthful spirit of the session, "Badge" the song became.

The song's rather subdued first section gives way to a glorious bridge, with George's arpeggioed guitar forecasting similar work on *Abbey Road* the following year. It's one of the most memorable moments in Cream's entire recorded output. Appearing on "Badge" as "L'Angelo Misterioso" (mysterious angel), George would reuse the *nom de plume* on May 11, 1969, playing guitar on "Never Tell Your Mother She's Out of Tune" for Jack Bruce's solo debut, *Songs for a Tailor*.

As for Clapton, the song remains a concert favorite, with an added coda that asks, "Where is my badge?"

Wonderwall Music By George Harrison    **Apple Records**

Wonderwall Music's Magritte-inspired cover art was altered by George (over the artist's objections) by removing a single brick, so as to give the bowler-hatted onlooker some "hope."

The Steve Miller Band, "My Dark Hour," Recorded May 9, 1969

The appearance of Paul on this Steve Miller track came about as a direct result of an ugly episode of Beatle infighting. With three Fabs pushing for Allen Klein to manage their affairs and Paul the lone holdout, a confrontation over the deadlock was held on a day scheduled for recording sessions, this time at London's Olympic studios. The four were unable to find common ground, and John, George, and Ringo stormed out, forcing the cancellation of the session. Paul, who had stayed behind, needed an outlet for his pent-up frustration.

Steve Miller was, at the time, a relative newcomer to the business. In London for some recording work on his third album, the band that bore his name specialized in psychedelicized blues, and featured Boz Scaggs on vocals. Happenstance placed him at hand just Paul was looking to vent. The two talked at length before Miller suggested that they jam. With Paul on drums, the two laid down a track that Miller would add lyrics to, calling it, fittingly enough, "My Dark Hour." Prior to leaving the session, Paul added bass and instructed Miller to credit his contributions to the *Brave New World* album as "Paul Ramon," a throwback to his Moondog days.

Though the two shared a label throughout the '70s, they would not collaborate again musically until Paul's 1997's *Flaming Pie*, wherein Miller played guitar on "Young Boy" as well as playing on and cowriting "Used to Be Bad."

I Believe in Yesterday

Ten Beatles Moldy Goldies

Growing up in Great Britain during the 1940s and 1950s, the four young Men Who Would Be Beatles were exposed to all sorts of music. Even though the Fabs didn't truly find their way until rock and roll rammed the big Island in the mid-'50s, they were well aware of music from earlier decades. Lennon liked old blues singers; McCartney had a passion for music hall and jazz. George and Ringo both enjoyed country and western.

The Beatles' well-rounded musical taste is one reason that their albums were as good as (and sometimes better than) their singles: capable of playing in many styles, the foursome had enough of a central identity to make everything they played their own.

In the early days of the group, on stage in Germany and the U.K., and while backing up singer Tony Sheridan, the Beatles had to mine the vast history of music in order to scare up enough numbers to fill their long stage shows. Hence some surprising selections made their way into the Fabs' repertoire, and some of those old, old, *old* oldies continued to pop up throughout their career.

"My Bonnie (Lies over the Ocean)"

The Beatles' first appearance on record came on this 1962 Decca 45, released in Germany, in which—billed as the "Beat Brothers"—they backed singer Tony Sheridan. You can hear Lennon and McCartney singing background in the chorus and adding some descending harmonies in the verse.

"My Bonnie Lies over the Ocean," a traditional Scottish folk song, has been sung since at least the early 1800s. Why would the Beatles, or any other rocker, have chosen this song? In the early days of rock and roll, before there was a canon of "classic rock," groups needed material. As a result, many of them, rather than write their own songs, chose instead to amp up old folk songs, waltzes, and even operatic airs.

In the '50s, Ray Charles recorded a swinging version for the Atlantic label that might have reached the ears of Sheridan or the Beatles, who were huge fans of the American pianist. The Sheridan/Beatles version, taped in June 1961, is the only "My Bonnie" to make the Top 100 in the rock era, reaching #25 when released in America amid the early-1964 insanity of Beatlemania.

"Sweet Georgia Brown"

Written in 1925 by Maceo Pinkard and Ken Casey, this catchy, swinging jazz standard was said to be about a Georgia-born African-American prostitute. Louis Armstrong, Django Reinhardt, and Ethel Waters all famously recorded the song, but Ben Bernie and His Orchestra had the first hit (which reached the #1 spot in 1925).

Tony Sheridan also recorded the song in 1961, backed by the Beatles (including Pete Best, but minus Stu Sutcliffe). It's not clear which recording of the song Sheridan and/or the Beatles had heard; perhaps they were familiar with the Coasters' version, recorded in 1957, or with one of two late-'40s Top 10 versions by Joe Liggins and the Honeydrippers and by Brother Bones and His Shadows.

Needless to say, when Tony Sheridan and the Beatles recorded it in Germany, the lyrics had been "sanitized." (The song would garner a second look from the record-buying public in early 1964 when Sheridan dusted off the 1961 recording, adding a newly written verse about Georgia Brown going to Liverpool and making unkind comments about the Beatles' haircuts.)

The deepest association many Americans have with "Sweet Georgia Brown" is not the Beatles or Louis Armstrong (or even Joe Liggins and the Honeydrippers) but rather the Harlem Globetrotters basketball team, which has used the song as its theme for more than fifty years.

"Ain't She Sweet"

Jack Yellen and Milton Ager, writers of many hit songs including "Happy Days Are Here Again" and "Hard-Hearted Hannah," penned this up-tempo ditty in 1927. The lyrics were written in honor of Ager's young daughter Shana, who decades later, as television commentator Shana Alexander, inspired the Beach Boys' 1969 recording "The Nearest Faraway Place" with one of her nature-themed observations.

"Ain't She Sweet" was first recorded by Frank Banta in 1927, but the biggest hit version came from Ben Bernie and His Orchestra, who struck #1 with

In the summer of 1964, this release from the Tony Sheridan sessions scraped into the American Top 20, battling newer material from the soundtrack to *A Hard Day's Night*.

the tune later that year. A competing version, by Gene Austin, hit #4, and around the same time Johnny Marvin also made the Top 20 with *his* disc.

Recorded many times, the song became an American standard. The Beatles played it onstage and committed it to wax on June 22–23, 1961, in Hamburg, Germany, at the same Bert Kaempfert–produced sessions that yielded "My Bonnie." John sang lead on "Ain't She Sweet," one of only two songs cut at the session without Tony Sheridan. (The other was the instrumental "Cry for a Shadow.")

Beatlemania led to the release of all sorts of pre-1963 Beatles material. Atco, the American rights holder to "Ain't She Sweet," released it on 45 in July 1964, and the song entered the *Billboard* Top 20. In Britain, imported copies pressed by German rights holders Polydor sold enough around the same time to reach #24 on the *Melody Maker* charts.

(Interestingly, the Beatles would revisit the song on July 24, 1969, the same day they recorded "Sun King" and "Mean Mr. Mustard" for *Abbey Road*.

As eventually released on *Anthology 3*, "Ain't She Sweet" shows John camping it up, throwing in the odd "moldy old dough" for period authenticity.)

"The Sheik of Araby"

When the Beatles auditioned for Decca Records of Britain on January 1, 1962, their repertoire included two odd chestnuts. One of them was "The Sheik of Araby," sung by George Harrison.

"Araby" was written in 1921, largely to capitalize on the time's fascination with all things exotic and Eastern. It remained a favorite of jazz players for several decades because it's a short song, with the melody played over a pattern that lends itself to soloing.

The Beatles' version, from the session that led to Decca's famous rejection of the band, can kindly be called "comedy." Perhaps new manager Brian Epstein thought the group needed a "novelty" recording to break up all of that dirty rock and roll. This arrangement apparently was based on a cover version by British rocker Joe Brown (later a close friend of George's).

With a goofy stop-and-start tempo, faux-Arabian guitar riffing, and some odd Lennon/McCartney "not 'arf'" (British slang for "for real!") vocal injections, "The Sheik of Araby" clearly was novel, if not particularly accomplished. George, at times, sounds as if he has something stuck in his throat.

Would *you* have signed this band?

"Besame Mucho"

"Besame Mucho" is one of the most romantic songs of all time, especially in its original Spanish version, written by Consuelo Velázquez. But the Beatles took a cover version by the Coasters well in hand when they recorded the song at EMI's London studios in an audition session during June 1962.

Shot full of brio and kicked off with a "cha-cha-boom" intro, "Besame Mucho" featured an almost-out-of-control, colon-contracting Paul McCartney vocal and a bridge held together by drum rolls.

At the time, Pete Best was still the group's drummer, but he wouldn't be for much longer following this session. George Martin, a staff producer for EMI/Parlophone, thought Best's drumming was stiff, unimaginative, and not precise enough for recordings. (Anyone doubting his successor's superior rhythm skills need only listen to their big-beat rendition of this song, captured live at the Star Club later that year.)

When it came time to record *Please Please Me*, the group's debut album, Martin chose to overlook "Besame Mucho." And there it sat, lost in Beatles history, until Paul jokingly revived it during 1969's "Get Back" / *Let It Be* sessions.

"Red Sails in the Sunset"

This longtime classic, written by Hugh Williams and Jimmy Kennedy, reached #1 twice in 1935, as recorded both by Bing Crosby and Guy Lombardo.

It's not clear which version of this the Beatles knew; perhaps it was Louis Armstrong's recording, or Nat King Cole's. They were known to have been playing the song on stage in spring 1960, before a version by the Platters (which reached the U.S. Top 40) was released.

Not that any of the previous recorded versions of "Red Sails" sounded *anything* like the rocked-up version that McCartney led the band through at the Star Club on December 31, 1962. With a rat-a-tat opening and two guitar solos, the Beatles obliterated all visions of Guy Lombardo, the Platters, and even Nat King Cole.

"Falling in Love Again"

Frederic Hollander and Sammy Lerner's lyric found its greatest success in the hands of German actress Marlene Dietrich, who sang it in the 1931 film *The Blue Angel*. The song was one of Dietrich's biggest hits as a recording artist, and it followed the bombshell around for much of her career.

Hard pressed for material to fill out their legendary nightlong gigs in Hamburg, the Beatles took songs from the entire spectrum of popular music, both of the current time and from the past. The December 1962 show, recorded and released years later as *The Beatles Live! at the Star Club in Hamburg, Germany, 1962*, featured a fairly faithful version of Dietrich's classic, which would—of course—have been familiar to the German audience.

Even back in the pre-Beatlemania days, McCartney sang many of the Beatles' more overtly romantic numbers. It's difficult to picture John Lennon singing, "My love is your love / forever and a day."

"Your Feet's Too Big"

Fats Waller, one of the great pianists in jazz, wrote or cowrote the classics "Ain't Misbehavin'," "Blue, Turning Gray over You," and "Honeysuckle Rose." But one of his most famous recordings, and one the Beatles covered onstage in Hamburg, was Fred Fisher and Ada Benson's "Your Feet's Too Big."

This sardonic boogie, in which Waller's girl's "pedal extremities" are literally too large for him to deal with ("I really *hates* ya cause your feet's too big!"), was a major hit in 1940, just three years before Waller passed away unexpectedly at age thirty-nine. Waller's recording peaked at #15 on the *Billboard* pop chart.

For Paul McCartney to sing a Fats Waller tune onstage made plenty of sense. As a budding pianist, growing up with musically minded parents, Macca had been exposed to a lot of different stuff—including good old boogie-woogie.

In later years, McCartney would bring his love of old-time stride piano to Beatles recordings like "Good Day Sunshine," "Hello Goodbye," and "Lovely

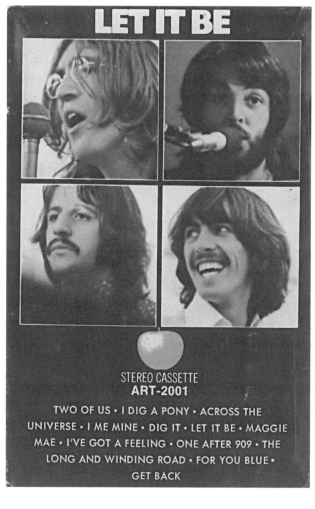

To capture the off-the-cuff flavor of the "Get Back" and *Let It Be* sessions, Phil Spector added "Maggie Mae," "Dig It," and snippets of dialogue to his mix. *Let It Be . . . Naked* summarily deleted these inclusions.

Rita" as well as solo flights, including "Venus and Mars" / "Rock Show" and "Flaming Pie."

"On Moonlight Bay"

When the Beatles took England by storm in 1963, Britons of all generations eventually embraced them—fulfilling the first piece of Brian Epstein's Plan for World Domination. Playing at the Royal Variety Performance, appearing on all the biggest television programs, and recording show tunes on their first two albums made the Beatles more than your usual scruffy rock and rollers.

Eric Morecambe and Ernie Wise were Britain's foremost comic team, with weekly programs on ITV from 1961–68 and 1978–83 as well as on the BBC from 1969–77. When they invited the Beatles on for the December 2, 1963, episode, the much-loved comedians had the Fab Four don old-fashioned straw boaters and striped jackets and join their hosts onstage.

After enduring some typically cheeky insults from the band about their age, Morecambe and Wise formed an "impromptu" six-man group with the Beatles—including Morecambe in a Beatle wig—to sing "On Moonlight Bay," penned in 1912 by Edward Madden and Percy Wenrich.

"Bay" had been repopularized by Doris Day in 1951 (in a film of the same name) and again by the Drifters in 1957. For the Beatles to sing it, along with their hosts, was a tactic aimed squarely at the middle of the British psyche—making gentle fun of the past while saluting it as well. It didn't hurt that the ones making light of the old lyrics were Morecambe and Wise themselves, representatives of the establishment and the older generation.

"Maggie Mae"

An old Liverpool street song about a local lady of the evening (a "Maggie") found its way into the "Get Back" / Let It Be recording sessions.

Lennon, during the January 24, 1969, sessions that produced "On Our Way Home" (the original title of "The Two of Us"), found himself thinking of the old days and laid into "Maggie Mae," singing as much of the Liverpool-lyricized folk song as he could recall while the others struggled to sing along.

"Maggie Mae" was an old favorite of the band's, from their long-gone days playing the Cavern, and the references to "Lime Street" must have been a little bittersweet for four grown-up-too-fast young men hundreds of miles from home.

Try Thinking More

The Original Titles of Beatles Songs

While many Beatles songs seemed to escape, almost perfectly, from the composers' pens in full stream of consciousness—"Across the Universe," written by Lennon in the middle of the night after being kept awake by his wife Cynthia's conversation, comes to mind—others took a while to finish.

And even with lyrics and music complete, some of the titles we now associate with Beatles classics didn't materialize until midway or late in the writing and recording process. Several songs, which we won't mention here, started off with the sobriquet "Untitled." Happily, in most instances, the Fabs eventually came up with titles at least as memorable as the songs.

(As an aside, would the Beatles' legacy seem different today had they used their working titles for the LPs? Would we revere *The Magic Circle* of 1965 for its warm, innovative mixture of folk and rock? Could 1966's *Beatles on Safari*, with its groundbreaking instrumentation and songcraft, still be thought by many to be the greatest album ever? What about the 1968 double LP *A Doll's House*? Or the band's last great collaboration, 1969's *Everest*?)

"Get You in the End"

Since the Fab Four's earliest compositions were fairly simple, song titles flowed fairly easily. Could "She Loves You" have been called anything else? Or "Please Please Me"?

In the case of the B-side to "She Loves You," though, the Beatles changed the early title of what was, admittedly, a failed single attempt. Recorded along with its A-side on a very productive July 1, 1963, "Get You in the End" is a perfectly obvious title given that the phrase makes up the key turnaround back to the song's "Oh, yeah, oh, yeah" hook.

But the group's penchant for using personal pronouns in their early songs made getting two of them, rather than just one, into the three-word title "I'll Get You" even more appropriate.

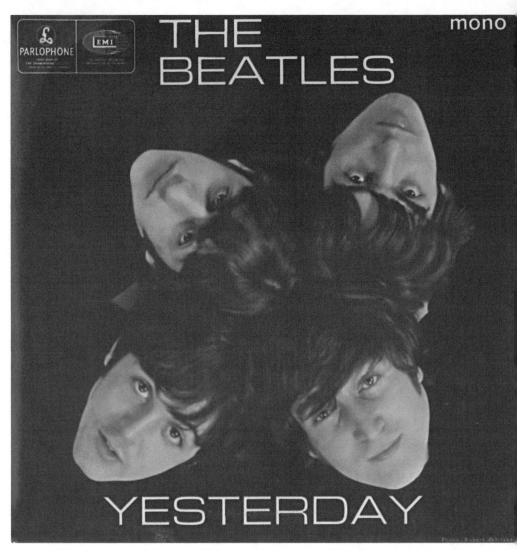

THE
BEATLES

PARLOPHONE

YESTERDAY

For a song regarded as special by everyone (not least its composer), it's surprising that the closest "Yesterday" came to release as a contemporary U.K. single was as the title track to this EP.

"Scrambled Egg"

McCartney had a knack for wrapping up good songs fairly quickly. But one special composition, which he began in early 1964 after hearing the melody in a dream, took more than a year to finish.

His new ballad sounded so good that Paul was sure he must have lifted the melody from another song. But nobody—not Dick James, George Martin, or Alma Cogan—could tell him what the song was, although everyone liked it. McCartney realized that he'd written a classic, a possible standard.

But while the melody and chords were polished, the words . . . well . . . Paul's placeholder lyric read, "Scrambled eggs . . . oh baby, how I love your legs." He knew the song deserved a better set of words. As he said years later, "Couldn't have that. Couldn't have 'scrambled egg.' "

So McCartney began the lyrics while on holiday with Jane Asher in Portugal, and finished them up on his return to London. The newly titled "Yesterday," first offered to singer Chris Farlowe (who rejected it) and then recorded by just Paul and a string quartet when the other Beatles felt they couldn't contribute much to it, was a #1 in America when issued as a single in 1965.

The group, however, could never agree to an English 45 release. Only in 1976, when issued as part of a mass singles re-release campaign, did "Yesterday" belatedly grace the British pop charts, peaking at #8.

"Auntie Gin's Theme"

Paul's bluegrass-influenced "I've Just Seen a Face," recorded, amazingly, the same day as "Yesterday" and "I'm Down," began its life as a piano-based instrumental that his father's sister, Aunt Gin (short for Virginia), enjoyed.

An oft-reproduced 1958 photo of George, John, and Paul playing guitars was taken at Auntie Gin's Liverpool house, apparently while the Quarry Men were playing at a family wedding reception. Gin's husband, Harry, is said to have built the original stage at the Cavern.

Paul also name-checked Gin in "Let 'Em In," his 1976 #1 smash recorded with Wings. (Macca also mentioned his "brother Michael" in the lyric.) Or perhaps he was singing about a different gin altogether—possibly the gin that left the doctor in "Rocky Raccoon" so stinking?

"That's a Nice Hat"

Lennon always disliked the *Help!* LP "It's Only Love" track because of its somewhat contrived lyrical pattern, although it was a pleasant recording. A version of this song, variously known early on as "That's a Nice Hat" and "That's a Nice Cap," was recorded by George Martin in 1965 for his third disc of Beatles instrumentals. (The first two came in 1964.)

The album, *George Martin and His Orchestra Play 'Help!'*, featured eleven songs from the Beatles' British soundtrack LP, including three with their original titles: "That's a Nice Cap," "Auntie Gin's Theme," and "Scrambled Egg." Martin would release one further album of Fabs interpretations, 1966's *The Beatle Girls*.

"Mark I"

When the Beatles began work on their landmark *Revolver* LP on April 6, 1966, the first song they tackled was an odd John Lennon number that sounded like nothing ever attempted in rock music.

Combining the somnambulant feel of old acoustic blues with a country-sounding lead guitar, then mixing in aquatic sound effects and an insistent drumbeat, "Mark I" began with Lennon intoning, "Turn off your mind, relax and float downstream." This was quite a departure from the group's last released recording, "Run for Your Life." (The initial "Mark I" recording eventually appeared on *Anthology 2*.)

Later, after layers of tape loops, backwards guitar, additional drum and cymbal parts, droning sitar, and heavily processed vocals had been laid onto the original recording, John—true to his surrealistic sense of humor—took a silly-sounding but rather deep Ringo Starr statement and applied it to his groundbreaking new song, making "Tomorrow Never Knows" the new title of one of rock music's greatest recordings.

"Granny Smith"

Given precious little time to record his songs, George Harrison—troubled by shyness and some buried resentment at what he perceived to be shabby treatment by John and Paul—didn't always have his songs finished, or even named, when his turn came up in the studio.

George jokingly named his first foray into Indian-influenced music after the crunchy green apple that two years later would become the logo of Apple Records. Recording began on April 11, and the song's title remained "Granny Smith" until sometime before the album was released on August 5.

In fact, the tune was still apply-named when mixed down and sequenced for the LP release. It's not known when Harrison chose "Love You To" as his new title.

"Laxton's Superb" / "I Don't Know"

The lyrics of George's final song for *Revolver* concerned the inability to express strong feelings either in writing or speech. Fittingly, Harrison had no title for the song as taping began.

Twenty-one-year-old recording engineer Geoff Emerick, humorously recalling George's earlier "Granny Smith" adventures, temporarily named the new song "Laxton's Superb" after another kind of apple grown in Great

Britain. Soon after, however, the song reverted to George's earliest admission when asked for the title—"I Don't Know"—which, given the song's lyrical concept, was thoroughly appropriate.

By June 6, however, George had given the new song its final title, "I Want to Tell You."

"Bad Finger Boogie"

Hunter Davies, in *The Beatles: An Authorized Biography*, spends several pages on a John-and-Paul songwriting session that produced "With a Little Help from My Friends," Ringo Starr's vocal from *Sgt. Pepper's Lonely Hearts Club Band*.

Most of the music had been completed when Davies attended the session at Paul's house (which, oddly, took place with both Cynthia Lennon and band friend Terry Doran in attendance), but the two songwriters were struggling with the lyrics.

On March 29, 1967, recording began for the song, which, according to Abbey Road records, was briefly known as "Bad Finger Boogie"—although Davies says that the final title was chosen before the song was completely written.

About a year and a half later, Lennon resurrected his digital reference and suggested that the Iveys, a four-man band signed to the Fabs' Apple label, rename themselves Badfinger, after his suggestion of "Prix" (pronounced phonetically) was met with an awkward silence.

"Too Much" / "You're Too Much"

This George Harrison song, originally called "Too Much," was recorded in May and June 1967, but not officially released until more than eighteen months later on the *Yellow Submarine* soundtrack.

Sounding positively anarchic for 1967 at over eight minutes (eventually cut to around six and a half for its release), "It's All Too Much" suffered from its time in hold, feeling in early 1969 slightly less groundbreaking and a little more reactionary to the psychedelic movement that the band itself had helped popularize.

George Harrison was never happy with "those damned trumpets," as he would later note, but Ringo Starr holds the song in particularly high regard.

For some reason, tapes of "It's All Too Much"— mixed in October 1967, but not included in the December *Magical Mystery Tour* TV film or soundtrack recording—leaked out to some American radio stations in early

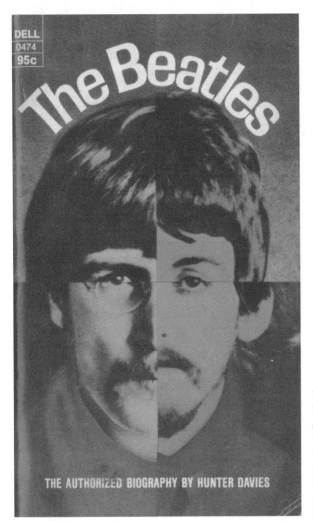

THE AUTHORIZED BIOGRAPHY BY HUNTER DAVIES

Unsurprisingly, John Lennon was dismissive of Hunter Davies's biography, calling it a "*Sunday Times*" (meaning toned down) version of their story. Still, for its time it was refreshingly frank.

1968. Rumored to be an upcoming single release, the mistitled "*You're* Too Much" clocked in at just under three minutes. The shorter mix differed from the released version, and certainly was one of the nuttier things on the airwaves at the time.

The proposed single never materialized. The tapes were pulled and the song forgotten until issued on the *Yellow Submarine* soundtrack—oddly, excluding a verse that was heard in the film. True to its tossed-off nature, the album didn't come out until January 1969, six months after the film's release.

"This Is Some Friendly"

In British football (i.e., soccer) parlance, a "friendly" is a game between international clubs played not as part of a tournament, but rather as a simple exhibition. It's not clear whether Ringo Starr was commenting on a particularly good game of footy when he came up with the song later known, when *The Beatles* hit the shops in late 1968, as "Don't Pass Me By," but it's as good an explanation as any.

Since Ringo just wasn't writing many songs, it is easy to forgive him for struggling to ideate a suitable title—although he had been working on this tune since *1963*. One assumes that the original lyrics to "Ringo's Tune," renamed ". . . Friendly" and then a few days later given its proper title, did not include mention of a soccer match.

Of course, the original mix of John's "Glass Onion" did include tape of a BBC soccer broadcast featuring play-by-play announcer Kenneth Wolstenholme. . . .

Please Lock Me Away

Unreleased, Until . . .

Despite releasing an impressive stretch of records in their lifespan—far more quickly than groups do these days—the Beatles had excellent quality control. Poor recordings rarely even made it to the overdub stage, and if one got that far, George Martin and the group usually vetoed the errant product. (Which makes the release of the frankly embarrassing "Hold Me Tight" that much stranger.)

All of these recordings were found, at the time, to be unworthy of release under the Beatles' name. That most of these recordings—outtakes only unearthed years later as historical documents for the *Anthology* series—would have been sufficient as A-list material for nearly every other band at the time merely points to the quality of the Fabs' output.

We didn't have space to list all the recordings that went unreleased until later. Some of the ones omitted (the electric version of "And I Love Her," "Mark I") are quite excellent, while others. . . .

"How Do You Do It?" Recorded September 4, 1962

The story of how the Beatles turned down Mitch Murray's future hit as their second single has become legend: the boys, showing tremendous brio, rejected the song outright in favor of their own "Please Please Me." Their confidence proved well placed as their song, benefiting from George Martin's arranging suggestions, reached #1.

But the legend leaves out the fact that the four actually recorded "How Do You Do It?"—the very same day they first attempted "Love Me Do" with Ringo. Even at this point, with little leverage, John and Paul insisted that their own songs were better than Murray's. Martin, for his part, somehow realized that the Beatles were at their best as a self-contained entity; he trusted their confidence and allowed them to release their own compositions as singles.

Featuring an atypically dispassionate Lennon vocal, the Beatles' unenthusiastic rendering of "How Do You Do It?" remained in the can for more

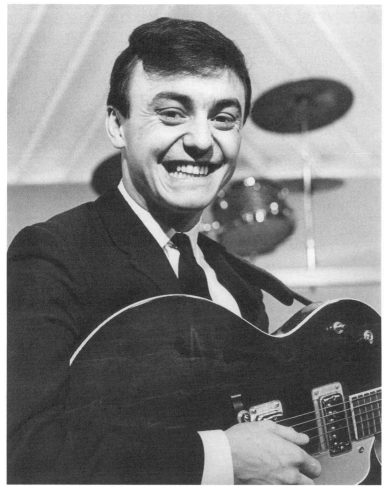

The Beatles' Liverpool mate Gerry Marsden benefited from the former's largesse when they decided to pass over "How Do You Do It?," effectively launching the Pacemakers' career.   *Photo by David Farrell/Redferns*

than three decades, only seeing official release on 1995's *Anthology I.* But by then the song had been featured on enough bootleg albums that most serious Beatle freaks were already familiar with it.

Bearing little resemblance to any other Beatles recording, "How Do You Do It?" is cast in the mold of the inoffensive, light British pop of the day. One can certainly see why the Fabs didn't particularly want to record it.

Given a much more spirited rendering by the charmingly clunky Gerry and the Pacemakers, "How Do You Do It?" did indeed reach #1 on the British charts and later hit it big in America as well.

"The One After 909, " Recorded March 5, 1963

The Fabs laid down this early Lennon-McCartney composition the same day they recorded their third 45, "From Me to You." Despite its somewhat strict structure, the Beatles' 1963 version of "909" featured a galloping tempo and an appealing harmony vocal from John and Paul.

The guitar break, however, proved to be the recording's undoing. George never got down a particularly good solo, and neither John nor Paul could decide what chords to play under Harrison's line. George's guitar also sounded distractingly like a rubber band.

Six years later, during the "Get Back" sessions, the band rescued the song and blew out the stops, turning the '50s-inspired chestnut into a full-on rock-and-roll revival. This time, Harrison's screaming, stinging solo elevated the reconstituted and retitled "One After 909" into a highlight of the *Let It Be* LP.

Like "How Do You Do It?," the band's original "909" recording could be heard for many years via the underground but did not come out officially until the 1990s.

"You Know What to Do, " Recorded June 3, 1964

George Harrison's first released composition, *With the Beatles'* "Don't Bother Me," showed a blooming talent at work. His second try was mid-1964's "You Know What to Do."

After a day of rehearsals for an upcoming Scandinavian and Australian tour (with Ringo ill with tonsillitis, temporary drummer Jimmy Nicol sat in), the Threetles laid down a demo of "You Know What to Do." While George's song featured an interesting descending bridge, the composer didn't quite get a hold on the vocal line.

Despite the song's pleasant qualities, neither Harrison nor the band could have been too impressed. When recording began for the next album, *Beatles for Sale*, George's new song was forgotten and he was handed, ignominiously, Carl Perkins's "Everybody's Trying to Be My Baby" instead. Better songs would soon flow from the Quiet One's pen.

"Leave My Kitten Alone," Recorded August 14, 1964

John rarely sounded as threatening as on this rip-roaring version of Little Willie John's warning to a would-be cuckolder, certainly the most passionate, intense recording ever to stay in the Beatle vaults.

Recorded in the same *three-hour* evening session that yielded "I'm a Loser" and "Mr. Moonlight" (let's hear it for economy!), "Kitten" for some reason did not pass muster and remained in the "unreleased" file until 1995.

The band's performance, outstanding all the way around, couldn't possibly account for the decision not to release the record. Perhaps "Leave My Kitten Alone" was judged too similar to the recently released Larry Williams rocker "Slow Down," which, like "Kitten," was a twelve-bar blues in the key of C that featured a prominent piano part.

"If You've Got Trouble," Recorded February 18, 1965

Written quickly, and expressly for Ringo, this appears to be the earliest "self-referential" Beatles number. "If You've Got Trouble," sung from a typically earnest point of view and twice mentioning rings, could only have worked for the bejeweled drummer.

While critics have heaped scorn on this number, hindsight reveals a few charms. Rarely did the group attempt a simple go-go dance number, but "If You've Got Trouble" is move-your-body R&B-influenced rock despite the silly lyric. The comical "Rock on, anybody," leading into a typically understated, twangy Harrison solo, adds further pathos to a lyric casting Ringo as a hapless foil to a domineering, greedy partner.

Four months later, the band got around to recording the Buck Owens standard "Act Naturally" to replace the failed "If You've Got Trouble" as the "Ringo track" for the *Help!* album.

"That Means a Lot," Recorded February 20 and March 30, 1965

Early in 1965, during the *Help!* sessions, McCartney brought in an odd new song with a complex lyric and some rather advanced chord changes more befitting a jazz ballad than a pop/rock number.

Unfortunately, despite the new composition's fascinating possibilities, the Beatles could never really get a hold of it. Slower and faster versions, and attempts in different keys and with different instrumentation, all failed to click. The February 20 version had more of a Phil Spector touch, while the later attempt is faster and poppier. The version appearing on *Anthology 2* is from the earlier session. No takes of this song reached the mixing stage.

Unlike most of the Beatles' rejected tracks, this one actually saw the light of day at the time—in a version recorded by Texas-born singer P. J. Proby, a far bigger name in Britain than in America. "We made a hash of it," Lennon said of the Beatles' decision to give the song to Proby.

With bootleggers upping the ante, EMI prepared to confront the issue with a collection of outtakes entitled *Sessions* in 1985. The project ended up aborted (and widely bootlegged, as seen here), but all the tracks eventually found release on the *Anthology* series.

"This Bird Has Flown," Recorded October 12, 1965

John Lennon's roundabout admission of an extramarital affair (perhaps the rumored tryst with reporter Maureen Cleave?) got the full exotic treatment on this, the first day of recording for what would be titled *Rubber Soul.*

Following an exhausting American tour, the Beatles took a short breather before hitting the studios again. They used the time to catch up with some new music, George in particular becoming besotted with the sitar, an Indian stringed instrument he had first encountered on the set of *Help!*

After a few lessons, George was able to play a Westernized, highly amateur set of sitar runs. John—jumping feet first into a love affair with interesting sounds—asked Harrison to play the song's riff on the venerable Indian instrument.

Adding to the Eastern-influenced, pot-hazy tone were Ringo's softly played cymbals and finger cymbals, an unusually compressed bass tone, and layered, shimmery acoustic guitars. Lennon's warm but slightly dispassionate vocals masked an intense lyric good enough to be anthologized separately as poetry (which it later was).

For some reason, the group decided to rerecord the song later, giving it less "wood and smoke" and more air. The released version became one of the Beatles' most loved songs; how great is it that *both* takes exist?

"I'm Looking Through You," Recorded October 24, 1965

A Sunday session, lasting eight hours, produced this recording, which the group nevertheless discarded two weeks later in favor of a remake.

Continuing the acoustic, folk-rock direction in which the band had been moving all year, Paul and the boys began this number with handclaps, maracas, and acoustic guitars. The verses and chorus continued in an acoustic vein, but a soul-influenced, electric organ–led instrumental section featured Harrison playing electric guitar leads high up the neck.

What this take of "I'm Looking Through You" *didn't* include was the bridge ("Why, tell me why did you not treat me right? / Love has a nasty habit of disappearing overnight"), which McCartney apparently hadn't yet written.

While on the final version the "instrumental section" was jettisoned in favor of the newly written bridge, the electric organ did appear, played by Ringo Starr. The Nose played a simple, rhythmic, slightly dissonant part at the end of each chorus.

Perhaps to reflect the song's downbeat lyric, the final version was more herky-jerky than the warmer original.

"Not Guilty," Recorded August 7, 9, and 12, 1968

Possibly the best song ever left off a Beatles album, George's somber-toned rocker hasn't dated, even with its contemporary references to upsetting the applecart and "making friends with every Sikh."

Perhaps "Not Guilty" was a random mix of images from George's time in India, or maybe he meant to express his despair that not everyone was learning the peace-and-love lessons of '67. The "applecart" line may reference his band's business entanglements.

Prior to the manic, all-night, last-minute album mastering session of October 16–17, 1968, "Not Guilty" was crowded off *The Beatles*. Harrison was only allowed four songs on the double album, and he or someone else apparently decided that "While My Guitar Gently Weeps," "Piggies," "Long Long Long," and "Savoy Truffle" were better.

Then again, Harrison may have submarined his own song by doing it to death. Clocking in at a massive 102 takes—only twenty-one of them complete—"Not Guilty" was remade enough times that it may have tired even its composer.

But to see this song left off the "White Album" in favor of such relative fluff as "Martha My Dear," "Rocky Raccoon," "Wild Honey Pie," "Honey Pie," and even "Revolution 9" may help one understand some of George Harrison's bitterness about his life as a Beatle.

George rerecorded this song, in laid-back fashion, for his 1978 *George Harrison* album.

"What's the New Mary Jane?" Recorded August 14, 1968

This is perhaps the best available evidence that not everything John Lennon recorded during the Beatle years shines with inspiration.

Apparently attempting to mix singsongy British psychedelia with genuine Yoko-inspired madness, Lennon hoped to include "Mary Jane" on *The Beatles*, but was outvoted. Perhaps Ringo and Paul felt that six minutes of John, George, Yoko, and Mal Evans banging on random instruments and letting out stoned, echoey cries wasn't particularly interesting or commercial.

At a later point, John wanted "What's the New Mary Jane?" as a Plastic Ono Band single and went to the trouble of remixing it for stereo in September 1969. But despite being scheduled to appear on 45 under the release number APPLES 1002, backed by "You Know My Name," the single never appeared—presumably because both sides were in actuality Beatles recordings, and the other three most likely didn't want to see the songs emerge in that form.

The mix left off the "White Album"—take 4—was eventually released on *Anthology 3*.

Don't Keep Me Waiting

A List of Releases We'd Like to See

D espite the release of the 1980 *Rarities* album, the three-volume double-CD *Anthology* series, and *Let It Be . . . Naked*, the EMI and Apple vaults still contain plenty of interesting and largely unheard Beatles tracks. Between the Beatles' 1960 home recordings, 1962 Decca auditions, unreleased BBC appearances, Hollywood Bowl and Shea Stadium concerts from 1964–65, alternate takes of released songs, film production acetates with different mixes, Fan Club Christmas records, 1968 acoustic demos for *The Beatles*, and sessions for what eventually became *Let It Be*, dozens of CDs' worth of Fab material is ripe for the picking.

Difficult as it is to take just ten from such a fruitful Apple orchard, here are some tracks we'd love to see released.

"Love of the Loved," Recorded January 1, 1962

When the Beatles auditioned for producer Mike Smith of the Decca record company on the first day of 1962, they sang twelve cover songs and three originals. Two of those originals, "Hello Little Girl" and "Like Dreamers Do," made their way onto *Anthology 1*, but the third Lennon-McCartney collaboration, "Love of the Loved," has never been officially released. (Most of the covers, too, have remained unissued.)

The Beatles never revisited "Love of the Loved" in the studio, instead giving it to Liverpool singer Cilla Black, who released it as her first 45 (produced by George Martin) in 1963. Paul McCartney did cut an acoustic demo of the song earlier that year, probably to give to Ms. Black; the audition record exists in a private collection.

Given the eventual longevity of her career, it's somewhat surprising that Cilla Black's vinyl debut, a cover of Lennon-McCartney's "Love of the Loved," barely scraped into the Top 40.   *Photo by David Redfern/Redferns*

"What You're Doing," Recorded September 30, 1964

The first attempt at this *Beatles for Sale* cut was played at a quicker pace than the released version, which the Fabs put to tape a month later. While take 11 uses a more conventional arrangement, it also rocks harder and changes keys at the guitar solo.

Without the stop-start opening, packing-case percussion, or acoustic guitars, but sporting sprightly singing and playing, this electrified attempt is an interesting and entertaining version of an underrated Beatles song.

"You're Gonna Lose That Girl," Recorded February 19, 1965

The process of making Beatles films involved synching the soundtrack songs to the movie, as well as deciding which songs should have scenes written for them in the first place. So the filmmakers needed versions of soundtrack tunes—even if they weren't quite finished. Therefore, during recording, EMI engineers cut acetates (seven-inch records that could be produced, almost instantly, in small quantities) of material intended for the films.

One curious thing about the nine *Help!* film production acetates is the inclusion of two songs ("Yes It Is" and "You Like Me Too Much") recorded around the same time as the soundtrack. This indicates that both were considered for the film, although "Yes It Is" was used as the B-side for "Ticket to Ride," while "You Like Me Too Much" wound up on the non-film side of the British *Help!* LP.

All nine songs for which there are production acetates differ, in some way, from the released versions; the acetates used rough (sometimes *very* rough) mixes. The most interesting variation is "You're Gonna Lose That Girl," which has an *entirely different* George Harrison guitar solo than any released version (backed by an electric piano, not audible on the final recording) and lacks both the bass and bongo overdubs.

According to Lewisohn's *Beatles Recording Sessions*, "You're Gonna Lose That Girl" was recorded in just one day, taking under three hours. So during that fairly short session, after the backing tracks were recorded but before the overdubs, engineers felt the need to cut an acetate. Talk about time pressure!

"And Your Bird Can Sing," Recorded April 20, 1966

Taking the folk-rock sound of 1965—twelve-string guitars and close-harmony vocals—and injecting more aggressive drums and a lot of sonic compression, the Beatles blasted through a terrific early version of this Lennon composition (which can be read as a jibe at Mick Jagger).

For some reason, *Anthology 2* uses the "jokey" mix of this song, in which John and Paul—knowing they've blown the take—end up laughing and whistling their way through it. An earlier mix, without the laughing, has found its way onto bootlegs. This is a great alternate version, one of their best, and a recording any other band in the world would have given its eyeteeth to have made.

"Penny Lane," Recorded January 12, 1967

Paul McCartney's intricate composition "Penny Lane," reflecting what writers Roy Carr and Tony Tyler called "Liverpool-on-a-sunny-hallucinogenic-afternoon," involved recording sessions on nine separate days.

The eighth session was an overdub of orchestral instruments in the song's solo section, including trumpets, oboes, and cor anglais (an oboe-like instrument, also known as an English horn, that produces deeper notes). These instrumental parts showed the influence of the Beach Boys' 1966 *Pet Sounds* album, which features several sumptuous orchestral settings.

This overdub was intended to complete "Penny Lane," and several hours were spent on a mix. While this January 12 version is beautiful and distinctive, Paul McCartney quickly found it wanting. After watching a performance of Bach's Brandenburg Concerto on television (and consulting with George

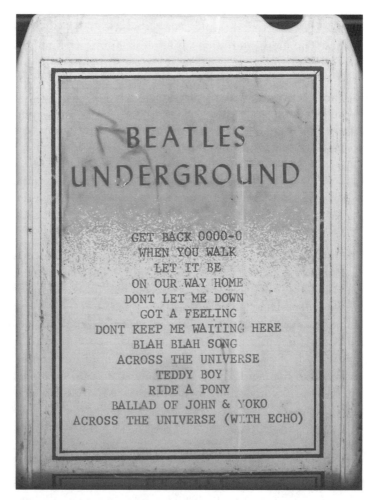

Much of the public's appetite for unreleased Beatle music was spurred by the appearance of illicit products like this eight-track tape, which featured the first draft of the *Get Back* album.

Martin, who explained what a piccolo trumpet was), Paul invited classical horn player David Mason to Abbey Road five days later to overdub a piccolo trumpet solo, wiping the oboes, cor anglais, and background horns from the middle section.

For McCartney, Mason's Baroque-style solo was the final piece of the puzzle. *Now* the song was ready for mixing.

"Carnival of Light," Recorded January 5, 1967

As a member in good standing of London's upper-class psychedelic underground, Paul McCartney was always up for tape experimentation. On January 5, following a "Penny Lane" overdub, he and the rest of the Beatles created a nearly fourteen-minute psychedelic noise/drone tape for an upcoming two-part multimedia electronic music concert/freakout at the Roundhouse Theater called the Million Volt Light and Sound Rave.

As described by Mark Lewisohn, this piece, which was mixed into stereo for full psychedelic benefit, contains drums, organ, guitar, percussion, voices (free-associating shouts of "Are you all right?" and "Barcelona!"), and lots of echo and other sound effects. While "Carnival of Light" is not a *song* as such, it would be exciting to hear the Beatles doing more of what they started on "Tomorrow Never Knows" and would repeat later with "Revolution 9."

This track, however, is one of the few unreleased Beatles numbers that has not yet been bootlegged, and George Harrison is said to have blocked its release on *Anthology 2*.

Several other psychedelic experiments remain in the can. A February 22, 1967, twenty-two-minute rhythm track called "Anything" has not been released, nor have jam sessions from May 9 and June 1, 1967. Another contender from this era is the full eight-minute "It's All Too Much," recorded in May 1967.

"Sour Milk Sea," Recorded May 1968

When the Beatles convened at George's home in Esher during May 1968 to record acoustic demos for what would become *The Beatles*, the four (well, three out of four) had a wealth of material. On their trip to India and in their off-time at home they had written more than twenty new compositions now being readied for the studio.

Most of these "Esher demos" were fleshed out and recorded for the "White Album"; others eventually saw the light of day on *Anthology 3*. Two George songs, however, "Sour Milk Sea" and "Circles," were left off both albums.

While George eventually recorded an altered version of "Circles" for his 1982 album, *Gone Troppo*, "Sour Milk Sea"—later given to Apple recording artist Jackie Lomax for his first single—has never been released with a George Harrison vocal.

"Helter Skelter," Recorded July 18, 1968

The Beatles attacked Paul's newly penned hard-rock opus, cutting three separate versions, all of which lasted more than ten minutes. While take two was released, in a highly edited form, on *Anthology 3*, the legendary third take, running an amazing twenty-seven minutes and eleven seconds, has yet to find its way onto a Beatles bootleg.

Following the five-hour session needed to record "Helter Skelter," the group let the song sit, not even bothering to mix or overdub it. Instead, a good six weeks later, on September 9, Paul and the boys undertook the recording of a new, shorter, and apparently more satisfactory version.

"Etcetera, " Recorded August 20, 1968

This acoustic number, which really does include the lyric "etcetera," was recorded by Paul alone on an evening when he also worked on two other "solo pieces" ("Mother Nature's Son" and "Wild Honey Pie") for the "White Album." According to Alan Brown, the technical engineer on hand, McCartney took the recording home that night from Abbey Road studios, and it has never resurfaced. Nobody seems to know just what this song is, or whether the general public will ever hear it.

"Suzy Parker," Recorded January 9, 1969

Several songs from the "Get Back" period deserve to be released: the full ten-minute "Dig It," John's raw but promising "Watching Rainbows," and Phil Spector's mix of Paul's "Teddy Boy," among others.

But if you're in the mood for some real Beatle spirit, "Suzy Parker" (jokingly named for a popular British model who took three husbands) is the one you want. Captured in the *Let It Be* film, this short but joyful rocker features a Dylanesque delivery by Lennon and some surrealistic lyrics.

Much of this day was spent on improvised songs with topical words. The group's performance is upbeat; it sounds like they're having a great time, countering the usual story that the "Get Back" sessions were nonstop misery. So why in the world hasn't this Lennon-McCartney-Harrison-Starkey performance been released?

What You Make for Us to Take

Ten Records That Directly Influenced the Beatles

ohn Lennon stated, years after the breakup, that the Beatles were essentially done as a band once they stopped trying to "better" their favorite 45s by other artists. Clearly, the Fab Four were great fans of all different kinds of music, from soul, R&B, and rock to pop, country, folk, and even classical.

The wide musical net cast by the Beatles helped make their own music much more varied, interesting, and universal than that of the competition. Here are some of the records that the Beatles listened to, dug, and tried to fold into their own work.

"Watch Your Step," Bobby Parker, 1961

John, Paul, George, and Ringo were among those stunned by Ray Charles's 1959 "What'd I Say." The erotic call-and-response vocals were set off by Charles's innovative use of the electric piano, an instrument almost completely unknown at the time.

Two years later, Louisiana bluesman Bobby Parker took Charles's electric piano riff, simplified it, adapted it to the guitar, then constructed a song around it. "Watch Your Step," a tremendously exciting R&B record on the small V-Tone label, reached #51 on the *Billboard* charts in summer 1961 and soon pricked Lennon's ears in Liverpool.

More than three years later, Lennon, pressed for time to write a new Beatles single, picked a variation of the "Watch Your Step" riff, penned some sprightly lyrics to match it, and instructed Ringo to play a drum pattern similar to the one on Parker's record. Thus "I Feel Fine," a #1 on both sides of the Atlantic, was born.

Though "Watch Your Step" was a minor hit for blues guitarist Bobby Parker in 1961, he passed an opportunity for bigger things years later, spurning an offer from Led Zeppelin's Jimmy Page to produce him.

During the 1960s, Lennon kept "Watch Your Step," along with thirty-nine other 45s, in his traveling jukebox, a record-playing contraption that he could pack up and take on the road with him in order to keep his favorite music at hand. Always happy to point out his influences, Lennon played Parker's record on his famous September 28, 1974, appearance on WNEW-FM in New York.

"Hey! Baby," Bruce Channel, 1962

Another oft-played choice on Lennon's jukebox, "Hey! Baby," was recorded in 1961 in Texas by the twenty-one-year-old Channel. Sounding as much like a traditional Cajun shuffle as it did like a pop record, "Hey! Baby" included a memorable harmonica line played by Delbert McClinton, a Texas bluesman renowned for his abilities in the Fort Worth club scene.

The record became a hit in early 1962, reaching #1 in America and #2 in Britain. On June 21, 1962, the Beatles appeared in New Brighton, Wallasey, supporting Channel on his British tour. John Lennon struck up a conversation with McClinton, who showed him some rudimentary harmonica licks, and Lennon took up the instrument with a passion, playing it on many Beatles records made between 1962 and 1964.

Some argue that McClinton actually taught Lennon the riff that graced "Love Me Do," the Beatles' first official release. Even if the harmonica part didn't come directly from Channel's harmonica man, the bluesy shuffle of "Love Me Do" owes much to "Hey! Baby."

In 1976, Ringo Starr would record a big-beat version of "Hey! Baby" for *Ringo's Rotogravure*, providing the album with one of its better moments.

The Freewheelin' Bob Dylan, 1963

Dylan's second album, released in February 1963, cemented his quickly growing reputation as America's foremost contemporary folk songwriter. Containing "Blowin' in the Wind" (his first British hit single), "Don't Think Twice, It's All Right," and "Girl from the North Country," among others, it was a seminal album in the history of pop music.

And in Bob Dylan the Beatles found a singer whose lyrics went deeper than moon/June/spoon. Lennon, in particular, was entranced by Dylan's combination of acoustic guitar, harmonica, cloth fisherman's cap, and skeptical but romantic lyricism, penning songs like "I'm a Loser," "You've Got to Hide Your Love Away," and "I'll Cry Instead" in response to the influence of the rising American star.

After initially rejecting the Beatles as a "bubblegum" band, Dylan was prodded by friends (including Joan Baez) to listen more deeply. While he never cottoned to McCartney's work, he did enjoy Lennon's songwriting and singing. The Beatles, the Animals, and the Rolling Stones all influenced Dylan to revisit his early love of Chuck Berry and fuse folk's lyricism and urgency with the gritty rhythms of rock and R&B.

While Dylan would remain close with Lennon, his most realized relationship with a Beatle was with George Harrison. The two collaborated on "I'd Have You Anytime," the leadoff track on *All Things Must Pass;* Dylan performed at the Concert for Bangla Desh; and many years later, the two played together in the Traveling Wilburys.

Dylan's influence was more than musical; on the night of August 28, 1964, following the Beatles' concert at Forest Hills in suburban New York

THE FREEWHEELIN'
BOB DYLAN

COLUMBIA

Blowin' in the Wind
Girl From the North Country
Masters of War
Down the Highway
Bob Dylan's Blues
A Hard Rain's A-Gonna Fall

Don't Think Twice, It's All Right
Bob Dylan's Dream
Oxford Town
Talkin' World War III Blues
Corrina, Corrina
Honey, Just Allow Me One More Chance
I Shall Be Free

First pressings of *Freewheelin'* are extremely rare; the album having been withdrawn and revised after Bob Dylan declared that it didn't contain enough "finger-pointing" songs.

City, he and his entourage showed up at the Delmonico Hotel and introduced three of the Fab Four to marijuana (John had already partaken at least once), thus helping to usher in the Beatles' greatest creative era.

"I Put a Spell on You," Nina Simone, 1965

Always more appreciated overseas than in America, soulful folk/blues singer/pianist Nina Simone had a surprise British hit single in 1965 with her slowed-down, mournful version of Screamin' Jay Hawkins's 1956 R&B waltz "I Put a Spell on You," one of the most famous twentieth-century songs never to be a Top 100 *Billboard* hit.

Simone's desperate, yearning scat vocals during the song's bridge ("I love *you* . . . I love *you* . . . I love *you* anyhow") stuck in the minds of both Lennon and McCartney, already Simone fans.

When the time came, late in 1965, to record Paul's charming French-lite ballad, "Michelle," Lennon suggested that Paul heavy up the composition by getting a little bluesy, advising him to stress the word "love" in that song's bridge ("I *love* you, I *love* you, I *love* you"), mirroring Simone's effect without directly ripping it off.

That mix of Lennonesque tension and McCartney beauty—an alchemy possible only for those artists who knew each had a contribution to make to the other—led to dozens of classic songs.

"Bells of Rhymney," the Byrds, 1965

By 1965, George Harrison was already an ardent fan of many of the top American R&B groups of the day, such as the Miracles and the Shirelles. But when Dylan and the Byrds came along, Harrison fell hard for American folk rock.

While the Byrds were heavily influenced by the Fabs—Roger McGuinn only got his twelve-string Rickenbacker guitar after seeing Harrison playing one in *A Hard Day's Night*—the Beatles in turn described the Byrds as their favorite American group, even after a disastrous 1965 tour of Britain in which the heavily hyped Byrds failed to please the fickle U.K. music press.

The circular guitar figure with which McGuinn anchored "Bells of Rhymney" (an old Welsh folk song about a coal-mining disaster), as well as the Byrds' trademark plangent three-part harmonies, played a large part in the construction of George's "If I Needed Someone," the penultimate track on *Rubber Soul* in late 1965. Starting with a twelve-string lick that's more than a little McGuinn-like, the song is Byrdsian from the get-go. (In 2004, McGuinn would himself record the tune, bringing things full circle.)

"Daydream," the Lovin' Spoonful, 1966

John and Paul were both big fans of John Sebastian and the Spoonful. This particular hit, another that resided in Lennon's traveling jukebox, was a key inspiration for Paul's lovely "Good Day Sunshine," the first track on side two of *Revolver*.

McCartney, as usual, wasn't content just to ape the Spoonful's record; he added his own piece to the puzzle, with a rolling, good-time piano part that also placed the song neatly in the tradition of British music hall.

Paul's love of bouncy, old-time material, a genre that also influenced Ray Davies of the Kinks ("Dandy" and "Mr. Pleasant" being but two examples), showed in other Beatles songs as well. But in "Good Day Sunshine," the paired British and American influences, plus the matchless three-part harmonies on the chorus and especially the fade, created a mélange that outshone everyone else in the field.

Pet Sounds, the Beach Boys, 1966

The Beach Boys were already big favorites of the British record-buying public, and the Beatles glommed on to them pretty early—especially Paul, who constructed the harmonies of 1966's "Paperback Writer" as an homage to Brian Wilson and crew.

Wilson had been blown away by the American release in late 1965 of *Rubber Soul*, which seemed to him to have no filler, only truly essential tracks. Always spurred to compete with his Capitol Records labelmates, Brian felt that the Beach Boys' next album should be as good, or better.

And *Pet Sounds* was that good—or better. Using strings, percussion, and vocals in unprecedented ways, Wilson created swirling instrumental pieces that fell as close to art song as to pop rock. Tony Asher wrote lyrics for eight of the album's thirteen numbers, capturing the rush, confusion, and heartbreak of life in one's early twenties.

McCartney, in particular, was stunned by the album, and especially by "God Only Knows," which he later called "the greatest song ever written." Later he admitted that *Pet Sounds* was a key influence on 1967's *Sgt. Pepper's Lonely Hearts Club Band*.

Throughout the rest of 1966 and 1967, McCartney tried to outdo Brian Wilson, plumbing his mind for deeper lyrics and music. *Revolver*'s "Here, There, and Everywhere" is a fairly straightforward Beach Boys–influenced ballad. "Penny Lane," with its Baroque arrangement (especially in an earlier, unreleased mix that included oboe), certainly owes much to *Pet Sounds*, as do the backing vocals of *Sgt. Pepper* numbers "Fixing a Hole," "She's Leaving Home," and "With a Little Help from My Friends."

The Mellotron Demo Disk, 1966

Mellotronics, Ltd., manufacturers of a keyboard instrument bearing the company's name, played a small but significant part in the Beatles' recorded history. To hype their new product, Mellotronics created a demo disc of the keyboard's sounds that they sent around to various London record studios in

1966. The Beatles, always hip to the possibilities of new sonic palettes, heard the Mellotron in action and had to have one for themselves.

A descendent of an earlier instrument called a Chamberlain, the Mellotron was played with keys that triggered the playing of small tapes placed inside the machine. The tapes contained sounds of various other instruments, allowing a musician to theoretically "play" a trumpet, a violin, or a flute with a keyboard.

The natural sounds contained on the tapes always came out sounding a little bit strange, which just made the effect of the Mellotron that much more interesting. In "Strawberry Fields Forever," its otherworldly flutelike intro sounds like nothing before ever played on a pop record.

Other contemporary bands, such as the Bee Gees, Traffic, and Moody Blues, also used the Mellotron to great effect. Within a year, of course, the instrument was felt to be horribly dated, but these days, any contemporary artist who wants to create an authentic '60s effect will use a Mellotron to transport the listener back in time.

Freak Out, the Mothers of Invention, 1966

When Paul McCartney—who is more adventurous than he is usually given credit for being—heard the Mothers of Invention's first album, he was intrigued by the political message, the lyrical and instrumental experimentation, and the overall weirdness of the whole package (despite the fact that Zappa and Co. would soon get even stranger).

Hence the Beatles' next album, *Sgt. Pepper's Lonely Hearts Club Band*, turned out to be, at least in concept, a fusion of *Pet Sounds* and Zappa sounds. With George contributing but one song, John struggling to write quality material, and Ringo not writing anything, much of the project was Paul's anyway, and—digesting Zappa's ideas as well as those of other American West Coast bands—he came up with the idea of altering the Beatles' identity. The lyrics of "She's Leaving Home" are a clear follow-up to the youth alienation present in nearly every number both of *Pet Sounds* and *Freak Out*.

The loose concept helped give *Sgt. Pepper* its own particular ambience, although Lennon would later point out that the "concept" of the LP fell apart after only a few songs. Zappa, for his part, repaid the Beatles by parodying the *Sgt. Pepper* cover for his "flower power sucks" response LP, *We're Only in It for the Money*.

When Zappa came up with the idea for the parody cover, he phoned McCartney in England to ask permission. Loath to discuss business arrangements over the phone, however, Macca referred him to lawyers, and a frustrated Zappa ended up putting the scathing *Pepper* takeoff on the his album's inner foldout, rather than the outer sleeve.

Music from Big Pink, the Band, 1968

Following the psychedelic excesses of 1967, many English musicians backed off from experimentation. The Beatles, the Rolling Stones, the Who, and Traffic went "back to basics," eschewing Eastern and Asian trappings for what people now call a "roots-based" feel, grounded in folk, acoustic blues, and early rock and roll.

The record that perhaps best encapsulated what these British rockers were after came out in 1968, recorded by Bob Dylan's former backing group. Called simply the Band, this quintet, which had come together in the early 1960s as the backing group for singer Ronnie Hawkins, consisted for the most part of transplanted Canadians who soon became fascinated with American folk mythology and songs.

Playing with Dylan led these musicians to rent a house together (called "Big Pink") in Woodstock, New York, and Capitol Records released their first album in 1968. Harkening back in time, lyrically bizarre, and obviously played with abandon and joy, *Music from Big Pink* was a revelation to English (and American) musicians who felt that "far out" had gone a little bit too far.

George Harrison, already a fan of Dylan, was greatly enamored of the Band's album and soon began to adopt a more American folk-based style of singing, playing, and dress. Pulling away from his instrument of choice in 1966–67, the sitar, he instead concentrated on improving his technique on his native instrument, adding slide guitar to his arsenal. In addition, he began to write songs ("For You Blue," "Old Brown Shoe") reflecting a simpler, rootsier Band influence.

No One's Frightened of Playing It

Ten Beatles "Singles" That Never Were (Until Done by Others)

Each original Beatles album had at least one song—and often many—that was commercial enough have been a hit single, but wasn't released on 45. So someone else tried to have a hit with it. Some of these covers were hits, and others, big flops.

Oddly enough, two songs expressly written by Lennon and McCartney for star British singers ("Misery" for Helen Shapiro and "No Reply" for Tommy Quickly) were rejected by their record companies despite the fact that the Beatles were already proven hit-makers; just ask Cilla Black, Peter and Gordon, and Billy J. Kramer.

"All My Loving," the Hollyridge Strings, 1964

"Hmm," said record executives in 1964. "How can we deal with this new long-haired rock music?" "I know! Let's make it beautiful!"

The first attempt at Mantovani-izing the Fab Four to hit the charts appeared in summer 1964, when the Hollyridge Strings, an L.A. group of session players, recorded an instrumental arrangement of Paul's appealing *With the Beatles* rocker. The aggregation recorded several albums' worth of Fab Four songs, all drenched in orchestral treacle.

While the first Hollyridge Strings LP, *The Beatles Song Book*, reached the Top 10, the "All My Loving" single hit #93 on the *Billboard* charts on July 6, 1964, then promptly disappeared. Orchestra leader Stu Phillips went on, two years later, to write much of the incidental music used as background in episodes of NBC-TV's *The Monkees*.

"Michelle," David and Jonathan, 1966

Singers Roger Cook and Roger Greenaway left the Kestrels in 1965 to start a duo, renaming themselves David and Jonathan. Their early 1966 cover of "Michelle," from *Rubber Soul*, featured production by George Martin and a release on the Capitol label. This almost made it an "officially endorsed" cover, like the 1965 version of "You've Got to Hide Your Love Away" by the Silkie.

David and Jonathan's lightweight, string-heavy version of "Michelle" reached #19 on the *Billboard* charts; it was the duo's only American hit. Cook and Greenaway went on to further success, however, Cook as a member of Blue Mink, which had several U.K. hits, and Greenaway with the Pipkins, who scored with "Gimme Dat Ding."

Together and with other collaborators, Cook and Greenaway wrote many other successful songs, including their joint effort "I'd Like to Teach the World to Sing," which later became a Coca-Cola commercial.

"Things We Said Today," Cliff Richard, 1966

The significance of Cliff Richard cutting a Beatles composition is difficult to miss.

Richard was England's biggest rock-and-roll star prior to the rise of Beatles, but saw his star eclipsed at home by the mid-'60s Beat boom. He had enjoyed seven British #1 hits through 1963, but scored only two during the remainder of the decade. Finally, in the mid-1970s, Richard broke out in America with several adult contemporary radio hits.

Just trying to keep up, Cliff covered McCartney's *Hard Day's Night* album cut for his 1966 "La La La La La" EP. The four-song record, which also included a cover version of Neil Diamond's "Solitary Man," failed to chart.

"You're Gonna Lose That Girl," the Cryan' Shames, 1966

A six-man aggregation from Oak Park, Illinois, the Cryan' Shames early in 1966 earned a chance at a recording contract with producers Bob Monaco and Jim Golden. Using their strengths—three-part vocal harmony, a fine lead guitarist in Jim Fairs, and a tight rhythm section—the band cut a song from the *Help!* soundtrack.

While charming in retrospect, the recording was deemed unfit for release, and the group instead turned to a song they had heard on a 45 by the Searchers. Hence "Sugar and Spice" became the Cryan' Shames' first record for the small Destination label; it reached #49 on the *Billboard* charts and led to a three-album deal from Columbia Records.

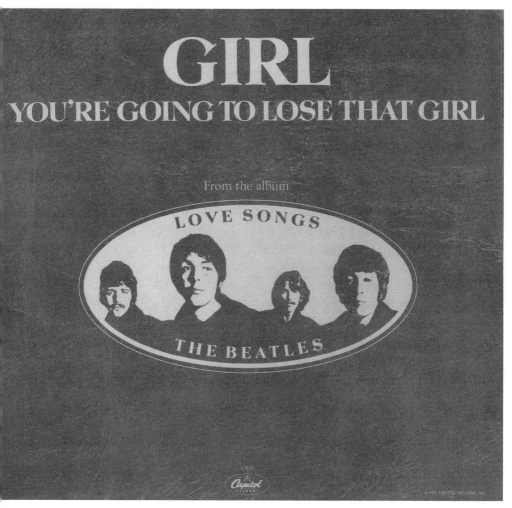

Hoping to repeat the success of "Got to Get You into My Life" as a chart single one year earlier, plans to issue "Girl" from the *Love Songs* set in 1977 were quashed, though not before sleeves were printed.

"If I Needed Someone," the Kingsmen, 1966

Three years after "Louie Louie"—which was just beginning its slide down the charts when Beatlemania hit the States in early 1964—the Kingsmen were unsure of their direction. Frat rock wasn't quite the draw it had been, and even hard R&B bands like this quintet from the Northwest needed to grow and change.

Therefore, the Kingsmen recorded George Harrison's "If I Needed Someone," which had come out in the U.K. late in 1965 on *Rubber Soul* but wouldn't see U.S. release until mid-1966 on *Yesterday . . . and Today*. A sensitive treatment featuring chiming guitars, the Kingsmen's version is a prototypically American response to British folk rock. The harmonies don't quite make it, but the track is interesting nonetheless.

It wasn't a hit.

"And Your Bird Can Sing," Spanky and Our Gang, 1966

Starting as a three-piece jug band in 1965, the group, featuring vocalist Elaine "Spanky" McFarlane, grew and eventually went on to enjoy five American Top 40 hits in 1967–68, including "Like to Get to Know You," "Lazy Day," and "Sunday Will Never Be the Same."

Their first 45, however, failed. A fairly wooden version of "And Your Bird Can Sing," which had been released in the U.K. on *Revolver* and in the U.S. on *Yesterday . . . and Today*, stalled before even making the *Billboard* Hot 100. While the vocals and backing were competent enough, the instrumentation couldn't match up to that of the Beatles' version.

In addition, Spanky and Our Gang were not really made for singing rock music, and the concept of having one woman and two men singing together about a "bird" may have been a little too strange.

"Good Day Sunshine," Claudine Longet, 1967

With beauty-queen looks and a voice lighter than helium, the French-born Longet gained a contract with A&M in 1966, singing soft, sometimes samba-inspired versions of current hits.

Like many other entertainers of the day, the songstress sank her lovely white teeth into several Lennon-McCartney compositions. A fluffy take on "Here, There, and Everywhere," from her first album (*Claudine Longet*), stalled out at #126 on *Billboard*'s "bubbling under" chart in spring 1967, while her second album, *The Look of Love*, contained two Fab Four tracks.

"Good Day Sunshine," bouncy and smiley, reached exactly the #100 spot on the charts for one week in August 1967, while her take on "When I'm Sixty-Four" was used twice as a B-side.

While Ms. Longet's singing has its charm, she is better known for the company she kept, starring with Peter Sellers in *The Party*, marrying Andy Williams, and fatally shooting her lover, skier Spider Sabich, in 1976. The death was ruled accidental.

"With a Little Help from My Friends," Joe Cocker, 1968

Perhaps the most commercial song on *Sgt. Pepper* was never a single for the Beatles, but British blues/soul shouter Joe Cocker took it to #1 on the U.K. singles lists in late 1968.

"With a Little Help from My Friends," featuring full gospel backing and a lead guitar part courtesy of then–session man Jimmy Page, also broke Cocker through in America, reaching #68 in *Billboard*.

Cocker's first single, back in 1964, had been a version of "I'll Cry Instead." Much more successful was his 1969 version of *Abbey Road*'s "She Came in Through the Bathroom Window." The characteristically histrionic performance gave Cocker his first U.S. Top 40 single.

Sheffield shouter Joe Cocker covered the Beatles early and often. Though scoring with well-known tracks from *Sgt. Pepper's* and *Abbey Road*, his first single, "I'll Cry Instead," stiffed in 1964.

Photo by Richard Upper/Redferns

"Ob-la-di, Ob-la-da," Arthur Conley, 1968

In America, the most successful of several competing covers of this "White Album" McCartney cut came from soul singer Arthur Conley, who had had his biggest hit, "Sweet Soul Music," in spring 1967.

Since then, Conley had enjoyed two more Top 40 hits ("Shake, Rattle, and Roll" and "Funky Street") without ever establishing himself as a star. Conley was a workmanlike singer with grit, but lacked the depth of his mentor and producer, Otis Redding. His version of "Ob-La-Di, Ob-La-Da," which stalled at #51 in America in early 1969, is not particularly memorable; the band doesn't quite get reggae, and Conley's delivery is rather wooden.

In the British Isles, a version by Marmalade was more successful, but the Scottish band didn't hit the American charts until spring 1970, when the very Beatlesque "Reflections of My Life" cracked the Top 10.

"Birthday," Underground Sunshine, 1969

Meaning no personal insult to anyone involved, this ranks as one of the worst Beatles cover versions ever to be a hit. A vacuous arrangement, nasal vocals, and a complete lack of rock dynamics sink this song for a serious fan—but this take of "Birthday" was pleasant and sugary enough to crack the Top 30 in summer 1969.

Despite an album (*Let There Be Light*) and a cover of "Don't Shut Me Out," written by David Gates, Underground Sunshine enjoyed no further chart success. Some of the Wisconsin quartet's own material was far better than this version of "Birthday."

That Is Confusing Things

Ten Odd Covers of Beatles Songs

Since 1963, various groups and solo artists, impressed by the new Biggest Thing in Show Biz, have been covering Beatles songs in hopes that some of the Lennon-McCartney (and, later, Harrison) fairy dust would sparkle on them as well.

"Legacy artists" like Nina Simone, Junior Parker, Rosanne Cash, Smokey Robinson, Brian Eno, Al Green, and others have lent their skills to Fab Four classics, and in the last few years a passel of newer acts like Sufjan Stephens, Chin Up Chin Up, and Ben Kweller have added twists to the catalog.

As for these others, well . . . entire CDs have been released of celebrities butchering Beatles songs. William Shatner destroying "Lucy in the Sky with Diamonds" is already a universal metaphor for "bad," but let's dig a bit deeper.

"We Can Work It Out," the Brothers Four (1966)

The Brothers Four, a folksy vocal quartet formed at the University of Washington, presented the nonthreatening side of 1960s folk: nonpolitical, clean-cut, and seemingly devoted to pinning and mounting acoustic music as one would a dead butterfly.

Their smooth version of "Greenfields" reached #2 in 1960, in the middle of the collegiate folk revival, but the foursome never hit the Top 20 again. Devotees of folk music as a museum piece, the Brothers Four approached the Beatles as they approached the rest of their material: cleanly, bloodlessly, and apparently without passion.

Their LP *A Beatles' Songbook* contained eleven dull arrangements guaranteed to incite torpor. Their takes on "Help!" and "All My Loving" are miserable, but perhaps the most ridiculous is "We Can Work It Out," with its echoey, out-of-place harmonica and a reading of the lyrics that sounds as if the Brothers Four had never heard the original version in the first place.

Which is entirely possible.

"Day Tripper," Mae West (1966)

Tower Records, a label that released records by some whacked-out singers and bands like the Standells, the Chocolate Watchband, and Syd Barrett's Pink Floyd, really went out there with this 1966 release.

Backed by a bunch of anonymous half-talents, appropriately named Nobody's Children, the aging sexpot growled her way rather uncomfortably through the Fabs' guitar-laden raveup. Neither the 45 or the album that followed (*Way Out West*) did much for the vamp's legacy.

Ms. West declined to be pictured on the *Sgt. Pepper* cover the following year ("What would *I* be doing in a lonely hearts club?" she is said to have asked, with some reason), but did expand her Beatle credentials with her final film, 1978's *Sextette*, in which Ringo Starr appeared.

"Rocky Raccoon," Lena Horne (1968)

This 1968 single, backed by the much more appropriate adult standard "Watch What Happens," is, to be frank, cringe-worthy.

Ms. Horne, a quality jazz and standards singer with a bluesy touch, tries to give "Rocky Raccoon" a sultry, down-home sort of swagger . . . and it doesn't work at all. Part of the problem is the song itself—few would argue that "Rocky" is much more than a cute novelty—but in addition, Lena's "Rocky" illustrates a key point: the Beatles were as good at *performing* their own songs as they were at *writing* them. "Rocky Raccoon," with its old-time tack piano, harmonica, and overall attention to detail, is a better *production*, a better *recording*, than it is a song, and as such probably cannot be improved, even by a star like Ms. Horne.

Lena Horne was a great singer of classics, but Beatles songs, even the mediocre ones, exist as completed entities with their own fully formed context. It's a real risk to interpret them in one's own style. Especially if the song ain't good enough to survive alone.

"Hey Jude," Bing Crosby (1969)

Bing Crosby: crooner, cool jazz singer, film comic . . . hippie? Well, not exactly.

For a singer whose career began back in the 1930s, singer-actress Lena Horne deserves props for at least attempting to stay relevant during the tumultuous 1960s.

Releasing versions of Beatles songs by aging former stars was, as we've already seen in this chapter, a familiar record company tactic by the late 1960s. And McCartney's piano-led, gospel-flavored paean to optimism would seem to be a good fit for Der Bingle's relaxed baritone.

In fact, Crosby acquits himself fairly well, giving the lyrics a bit of a swing, even though he can't bring any more meaning to "the movement you need is on your shoulder" than McCartney could. The real problem with this version lies at the end. A massive buildup toward the song's climax leads to Crosby intoning, "Pum . . . pum, pum, pum pum pum pum . . . pum pum pum pum . . . Hey, Jude."

Perhaps he thought he was cutting a new version of "The Little Drummer Boy." Maybe he was incapable, at this stage of his career, of letting loose or improvising. Or Crosby may have thought so little of the song that he simply chose to make fun of it. Whatever the reason, the delivery during what, on the Beatles' version, is a triumphant finish, makes Bing's record embarrassing.

"Every Little Thing," Yes (1969)

Given to recording songs that took up entire album sides, and changing keys and meters seemingly at random, Yes would seem to be the unlikeliest of bands to worship at the altar of the Beatles—and yet. . . .

Yes gained renown in the early '70s with complex arrangements of layered compositions, seemingly light years away from Beatles-style pop in general and this overlooked track in particular. But at the start of their career, perhaps as the result of an underlying Fab fixation, the prog-rockers took on this song, stretching it out to over five minutes in length and presenting it with their signature tempo shifts throughout. Whether this is a reasonable progression or completely unlistenable depends on your taste.

Though Yes cultivated a very different audience from that of the Beatles, some curious ties bind the two bands. Guitarist Steve Howe joined Yes after a stint in the U.K. psychedelic band Tomorrow, which covered "Strawberry Fields Forever" on its eponymous 1968 album. Howe's first release with Yes, *The Yes Album*, included the cut "I've Seen All Good People," which in addition to mentioning an "instant karma" in the lyric ends by quoting "give peace a chance."

Finally, Yes drummer Alan White made a name for himself in the business through his work with George on *All Things Must Pass*, and with John at the "Live Peace in Toronto" gig, on the 1970 Plastic Ono Band 45 "Instant Karma," and on the *Imagine* album.

"Give Peace a Chance," Mitch Miller and the Gang (1970)

This Plastic Ono Band 45, given a Lennon-McCartney writing credit even though John wrote it with Yoko, attracted what may be the most "out there" Beatles cover version *ever*.

Mitch Miller, the musical director of Columbia Records (and no friend of rock and roll), was also the star of *Sing Along with Mitch*, a popular 1960s TV series featuring "The Gang," a group of male singers in matching sweaters and buckskin shoes intoning old-timey hits. Their material relied more on the *1860s* than the 1960s, making the Gang's version of "Give Peace a Chance" still odder.

But even the most anti-rock artists found themselves going "current" to keep up with the times. Mitch and the Gang produced, in 1970, the *Peace*

Sing-Along LP, which, except for "Give Peace a Chance," could have been recorded in 1965, including as it does "Blowin' in the Wind," "Turn, Turn, Turn," and "Where Have All the Flowers Gone?"

Oddly enough, Miller had participated, on stage, in a Pete Seeger–led sing-along of "Give Peace a Chance" at a 1969 New York peace rally. Perhaps, then, his own version was sincere . . . but the Gang's cries of "Hassle the Man!" "Hassle the Congress!" and "Sing it to the Senate!" are just this side of insane.

If you want to hear this rather amazing rendition, it's found—as is Crosby's "Hey Jude"—on the CD *Golden Throats, Volume 2.*

"Because," the Percy Faith Strings (1970)

The genre called "beautiful music"—slow, relaxing, string-laden instrumentals that we now associate with elevators, retirement homes, and doctor's offices—was big business in the 1950s and 1960s, although it has almost completely disappeared from the cultural landscape.

Older folks, as well as many seeking calm amid the frantic pace of postwar life, enjoyed the soothing sounds of orchestras led by Andre Kostelanetz, Annunzio Mantovani, Frank Chacksfield, and Percy Faith.

The only way that such musicians could sell the Beatles' melodies to an older (or simply more sedentary) audience was to douse their songs—even their ballads—in treacly arrangements, ladle on the sentimentality, and serve lukewarm.

Percy Faith's version of "Because" is an especially snoozy example of this genre, meandering along for four-plus minutes and featuring a horn solo that invites mockery. Finally, after exhausting every possible option suggested by its dull arrangement, the song fades out in mid-verse, no one even bothering to tack on an ending.

"Let It Be," (Tony) Sandler and (Ralph) Young (1971)

During the 1960s and '70s, Sandler and Young carved out a career, which included several albums on Capitol, singing adult contemporary music. Standards, show tunes, and international folksongs (Sandler is Belgian and speaks several languages) were the key components of their repertoire.

Like other such singers, they struggled to adapt to rock. A version of Simon and Garfunkel's "The 59th Street Bridge Song (Feelin' Groovy)" was particularly embarrassing, with Sandler playfully counterpointing "Frère Jacques" as Young sang the second verse.

Their takes on Beatles songs were no better. "Blackbird," from 1970, is converted from a sensitive ballad into a brassy, fast-paced mover, barely giving Sandler and Young enough time to get the lyrics out. In addition, the arrangement calls for a particularly comical closing coda.

"Let It Be" is even worse. Again the song's tempo is completely altered, forcing the singers to rush through the lyrics, which they do very poorly. Worse, the faux-Elvis/soul/supper-club backing is barely competent.

SING AND PLAY ALONG
BEATLES KIT

LONDON
LL 3403

Kathleen Cuddihy

Featured on this record—the backgrounds to the BEATLES' biggest hits. Now for the first time YOU can sing the lyrics yourself. Words to all the songs included.

A HARD DAYS NIGHT • SHE LOVES YOU • I WANT TO HOLD YOUR HAND
LOVE ME DO • FROM ME TO YOU • DO YOU WANT TO KNOW A SECRET
TWIST AND SHOUT • ALL MY LOVING • I SAW HER STANDING THERE
THINGS WE SAID TODAY   PLEASE PLEASE ME • CAN'T BUY ME LOVE

Fans inspired to create their own Beatle covers were given license with this obscure release, which presaged the Beach Boys' 1968 do-it-yourself Karaoke disc, *Stack-O-Tracks.*

And once again, they can't get out of the song without dropping their pants; Young delivers a final "speaking words of wisdom, let it be" in a goofy low register as a ridiculous Benny Hill–style tenor sax tootles away.

"Maxwell's Silver Hammer," Steve Martin (1978)

One of the great things about comedian/banjoist Steve Martin, when he gained mass popularity in the 1970s, was how goofy he was to watch. His eyes, his odd body language, and his patented outrageous gestures made his material—already silly—that much funnier.

That said, his performance as Dr. Maxwell Edison in the celluloid fiasco *Sgt. Pepper's Lonely Hearts Club Band*—featuring the Bee Gees and Peter Frampton at their most embarrassing—is horrid. The Beatles' funny songs are funny when performed *by the Beatles;* they don't need anyone else to giggle them up. (Are you listening, Jim Carrey? Didn't think so.)

Unfortunately, Martin mugs his way through this interminable number in a cloying manner guaranteed to prompt even the most virulent hater of Paul's *Abbey Road* confection to wish for an endless loop of it, rather than have to hear this version even once more.

Among the worst of the worst on this benighted soundtrack are Alice Cooper's disgusting "Because," Paul Nicholas and Diane Steinberg's miserable "You Never Give Me Your Money," and Sandy Farina's flummoxing take on "Strawberry Fields Forever," which, if it is druggy at all, most resembles a fistful of downers.

"I'm Happy Just to Dance with You," Anne Murray (1980)

Canadian country/adult contemporary singer Anne Murray often tried her hand at the '60s songs she loved, and sometimes did a fine job—a somewhat funky 1974 cover of "You Won't See Me" was surprisingly good, and surprisingly successful. (About her follow-up attempt, "Day Tripper," featuring a slinky saxophone, the less said, the better.)

Her attempt at "I'm Happy Just to Dance With You," however, which careens from a sleep-inducing, senior-prom slow-dance tempo in the verse to a comical, muted oompah polka in the bridge, simply defies reason. The backing vocals are unwelcome, the instrumentation dull and lifeless, and Ms. Murray's singing a fading step ahead of narcolepsy. It may be the worst Beatle cover ever to dent the *Billboard* charts, happily only reaching #64.

The World Is Treating Me Bad

Ten Contemporary Songs About the Beatles

O nce the Beatles broke through stateside in early 1964, showbiz bottom-feeders began to chew the algae off the new superstars. Various artists, many of them second-rate, wrote and recorded songs on Beatle-related topics; the pre–"Dirty Water" Standells even sang a dreary twist titled "Come On and Ringo" in a 1965 episode of *The Munsters.*

While songs about the Fabs seemed to have died out in the metal/glam/ hippie/disco '70s (Mott the Hoople's 1972 "All the Young Dudes" noted scornfully that "my brother's back home with his Beatles and his Stones"), contemporary artists Daniel Johnston and Edwyn Collins, among others, have since taken on the myth and magic of the Beatles.

Here's a handful of songs written and recorded about the Beatles between 1964 and 1969, when their star shone brightest in America.

"We Love You Beatles," the Carefrees, 1964

"We Love You Beatles" is simply a rewrite of "We Love You Conrad," a fans' singsongy love lament (to teen idol Conrad Birdie) from the 1960 Michael Stewart/Lee Adams/Charles Strouse Broadway musical *Bye Bye Birdie.*

The Carefrees, a subgroup of an already popular Liverpool girl singing amalgamation, the Vernons Girls, offered scrubbed-up versions of American rock-and-roll songs.

Thousands of girls around the world adopted the record's jaunty chorus, "We love you Beatles, oh yes we do / We don't love anyone as much as you / When you're not with us, we're blue / Oh Beatles we love you," as a cry of devotion to their Fab favorites.

By 1964, *Bye Bye Birdie* had become a popular high school musical. As such, its "We Love You, Conrad!" was instantly recognizable to most teens and therefore readily adaptable to new allegiances.

Subsequent verses of the Carefrees' record alter the lyrics to individually address Ringo, John, Paul, and (last but not least) George.

Overly brilliant it wasn't, but catchy and successful it was, reaching #39 on the *Billboard* charts after its U.S. release in early spring 1964. A Carefrees album followed. The Vernons Girls, with different personnel, still exist today—they are, in fact, billed as the world's longest-running girl group.

"Ringo I Love You," Bonnie Jo Mason, 1964

Seventeen-year-old singer Cheryl Sarkisian LaPiere, who had already appeared in the background chorus of recordings such as the Ronettes' "Be My Baby" and the Crystals' epochal "Da Doo Ron Ron," released her first solo 45 in 1964, taking on the anodyne performing name of Bonnie Jo Mason.

This single, which stiffed completely when released, is now extremely hard to find. Why? Because the subject is the Beatles, the singer is actually Cher, and the song was cowritten and produced by Phil Spector. (One of the famous L.A. Svengali's cowriters is Vini Poncia, who many years later would actually work with Ringo Starr.) A store copy has sold for as much as $520 on eBay, while the promotional copies are nearly as difficult to get.

"A Letter to the Beatles," the Four Preps, 1964

This vocal-harmony foursome, formed at a California high school in the mid-1950s but now past its prime as a hit-making act, clearly saw the writing on the wall when the Beatles came along. This song, the Preps' last *Billboard*-charted record, only got up to #85 when released in March 1964.

Having already taken other acts to task in their novelty medleys "More Money for You and Me" and "The Big Draft," the Four Preps now cast a satirical eye upon the Fab Four's marketing machine.

The song itself is not a letter, but instead complains that each fan correspondence to the Beatles seems to generate a form letter demanding more money. "Twenty-five cents for an autographed picture," the Preps sing, noting at the end that for additional cash one can obtain "A lock of hair . . . from our Saint Bernard."

Oddly, one of the Preps, Ed Cobb, left a much more lasting mark on rock and roll than this record might indicate. Cobb wrote "Dirty Water" for the Standells, "Tainted Love," first made famous by Gloria Jones, and "Every Little Bit Hurts," Brenda Holloway's biggest hit. He also produced the West Coast psychedelic pioneers the Chocolate Watchband.

"Pop Hates the Beatles," Allan Sherman, 1964

Satirist Allan Sherman, of "Hello Muddah! Hello Fadduh!" fame, weighed in on the Fab Four with this late 1964 trifle based on the classic kids' melody "Pop Goes the Weasel."

On his fifth album in less than three years, Sherman took on the persona of a parent angry at how much money it was costing him to keep his Brit band–loving daughter supplied with records, souvenirs, and concert tickets. The tag line, "*I* hate the Beatles," was altered in the song's title, perhaps to cool down the sentiment somewhat.

Sherman's song parodies were big business in 1963–64, but you could sense in his lyrics the anger he felt about music being taken over by the young: "What is all the screaming about? / Fainting and swooning / Sounds to me like their guitars / could use a little tuning."

Additionally, Sherman advocates tossing the British Invaders into the Boston Harbor—after first taking them for haircuts. This single didn't make the Hot 100, but Sherman did reach #40 the next year with "Crazy Downtown," a parody of Petula Clark's "Downtown."

"Beatles Please Come Back," Gigi Parker and the Lonelies, 1964

While MGM records only had the rights to one Beatles record, "My Bonnie," they did test the market with this song, most likely released following the end of the group's first U.S. tour in late summer 1964.

The lyrics to this girl-group-meets-rock-band recording reference—with some wit—several Fabs songs, and the girls perform excellent three-part harmonies. Overall, this is a much better product than most Beatle-related novelties, despite the somewhat desperate tone of the lyric.

This beefy, rocking recording, which didn't trouble the *Billboard* charts, can be found on the compilations *Growing Up Too Fast* and *Beatlemaniacs*.

"Treat Him Tender Maureen (Now That Ringo Belongs to You)," Angie and the Chicklettes, 1965

By 1965, the "girl group" sound was past its peak and was on the way out; on the West Coast, the Ronettes' and the Crystals' hits had dried up, and back East, only the rough-and-tumble Shangri-Las could stand tall against the British Invasion.

Hence the Angels, known for 1963's chart-topping "My Boyfriend's Back," were no longer hot. To address this problem, the trio recorded under several different names, including the Powder Puffs. For this record, the Angels were joined by another singer, Jean Thomas, of the lesser-known Rag Dolls.

From the very beginning, Ringo was for many people the most identifiable Beatle for several reasons: his standout moniker, his place behind the drums, and his rather large nose. While few, if any, 1964–65 records specifically mentioned only John, George, or Paul, plenty of artists—the Bon-Bons, Christine Hunter, Garry Ferrier, Robin Garrett, Tina Ferra, the Tributes, the Rainbows, the Whippets (!), and the Starlettes, among others—focused on Ringo.

While Angie and the Chicklettes did not crack the national charts with "Treat Him Tender Maureen," the song of sad resignation did reach the lower rungs of the WABC (New York City) chart in March 1965.

"Beatle Boys," Rod Rogers, 196?

This incredibly rare record—there may not even be ten in existence—is a product of the "song-poem" (or, the "send us your lyrics and a fistful of money and we'll spend fifteen minutes recording a song for you") scam.

Many songs on this list could be found on this 1982 Rhino release, infamous due to the cover artist's decision to include John Lennon's murderer among the fans.

Most song-poem records are made cheaply, and "Beatle Boys" is no exception. Rogers (better known as Rodd Keith) was hired to play all the instrumental parts on a Chamberlain—an early predecessor to the Mellotron, which the Beatles themselves eventually used—rather than hire a full band. Still, Rogers's keyboard wizardry almost saves this ridiculous set of lyrics.

The poor protagonist of this song wants the Fabs to leave town because with all the girls flipping for the Beatles, he "don't get a chance . . . to take out the girl I love . . . have some fun and dance." He then wonders why "girls are favoring Beatle boys with their mandolins and swaying legs." (*Mandolins?!*)

By the end of this short but impossibly catchy number, our hero has decided that all he wants to do is attack the Fabs with "Beatle spray." Unfortunately, we do not know the name of the lyricist for this song of songs.

While this particular tune is not yet compiled on CD, two other Rodd Keith–sung, Beatles-inspired song-poems ("I Can't Decide" and "Great Fever") are available on volumes 3 and 4 of Carnage Press's highly recommended *MSR Madness* song-poem CDs.

"Beatle Bones 'n' Smokin' Stones," Captain Beefheart and the Magic Band, 1968

California blues/jazz/rock artist Captain Beefheart (born Don Van Vliet) made perhaps his most straightforward early LP, the disturbing, psychedelic *Strictly Personal*, in 1968. Beefheart claimed to be unhappy with Bob Krasnow's trendy, phasing-heavy production, although some reports have Beefheart okaying the sound and later retracting his approval.

By the next year's *Trout Mask Replica*, made in collaboration with Frank Zappa, Van Vliet had climbed over the transom into full-time weirdness.

One of Beefheart's Dadaist tone poems on *Strictly Personal* concerned the music of the Beatles and the Rolling Stones. In his Beatles verse, he free-associates, "The dry sands fall / the strawberry mouth / strawberry moth / strawberry caterpillar / Strawberry butterfly / strawberry fields / the winged eel slither on the heels of today's children / Strawberry feels forever."

Using Ry Cooder's bluesy guitar fills, a backward drum pattern, and his own gritty, blues-shouter voice, Beefheart created a brand of psychedelia resting somewhere between inspired parody of the English trip and outright rejection of same.

"John You Went Too Far This Time," Rainbo, 1968

John and Yoko's *Two Virgins* sparked plenty of outcry among Beatle fans, for its avant-garde content as well as the duo's decision to go naked on the record sleeve.

But nobody could have been prepared for the firestorm the album inspired from a seventeen-year-old Texan homecoming queen and drum majorette called Rainbo—a stage name for Mary Elizabeth Spacek, soon to be better known as Sissy.

"John, I love you," Rainbo sings weedily over a sunny, harpsichord-and-strings, folk-rock backing. Recalling the heady days of '67, she notes, "I recall you turned me on with *Pepper* / the tour we took with Lucy was a trip I won't forget."

Unfortunately, Rainbo—or, to be more precise, songwriter Artie Wayne—got in a twist over that *Two Virgins* sleeve. "But since that picture, I don't think my love will be the same." As Roy Carr and Tony Taylor wrote: "Such a big fuss over such a small thing."

Perhaps not too strangely, Rainbo's record, released on the Roulette label—whose founder, Mo Levy, would later sue Lennon in the '70s for crimes unrelated to open display of genitals—did not reach the *Billboard* charts.

"St. Paul," Terry Knight, 1969

In 1968, after splitting his commercially (and, most of the time, artistically) unsuccessful folk-rock group the Pack, Terry Knight told the *Detroit Free Press* that he would be heading to London to talk to Paul McCartney about joining Apple Records. It's not clear whether McCartney even knew who Knight was.

The next year, however, Knight secured a contract with the Beatles' U.S. record company, Capitol. Taking his cue from the "Paul is dead" rumors spread by Detroit disc jockey Russ Gibb, Knight wrote a grisly little piece of hagiography, "St. Paul," which Capitol released on a 45.

"While you and Sgt. Pepper saw the writing on the wall," Knight sang, "you knew it all along / something had gone wrong." Knight apparently was singing about the Beatles' plight and imminent breakup, but also was playing to the story that McCartney had died in 1966; this rumor had already spread to college and high school campuses by the record's release in the fall of '69.

While Knight's record wasn't successful in America, a singer named Shane from New Zealand recorded it, resulting in that country's biggest selling pop record of the entire 1960s.

It is interesting, viewing the six-year trail from "We Love You Beatles" to "St. Paul," to note the progress of tribute songs from unadulterated love to cynicism, envy, anger, yearning, disappointment, and, finally, death and dissolution.

There's People Standing 'Round

Friends and Acquaintances

As John and Paul offer encouragement, George seeks enlightenment, much to the delight of Jane Asher and Mal Evans. *Photo by Cummings Archives/Redferns*

Through Thick and Thin

The Beatles' Business Entourage

n the early years, their schedule crammed with recording, touring, interviews, and the like, the Beatles found they needed associates to help them navigate the red tape and complications of the "straight world." Beginning with manager Brian Epstein, a phalanx of characters—leaders, heroes, factotums—came in and out of the band's orbit.

Not all of the group's business associates are included; some are in the "friends" chapter, while others must be classified among the "villains" of the Beatle world. Among the others serving with dignity were press aide Brian Somerville, Beatles Fan Club secretary Freda Kelly ("Ann Collingham" was a fiction), chauffeur Alf Bicknell, Apple legal counsel Brian Lewis, concert promoter Sid Bernstein, and Apple press secretary Mavis Smith, as well as a host of EMI engineers: Norman Smith, Geoff Emerick, Ken Scott, Chris Thomas, John Kurlander, and Alan Parsons (yep, *the* Alan Parsons). All played their parts in helping to shape the phenomenon we celebrate to this day.

Brian Epstein

Brian's beginnings with the Beatles are described in chapter 3 of this book, and his tormented last months in chapter 46. In between were an amazing six years.

Brian Epstein came of age as a man out of place and out of time. Born in 1934 to a successful father and a doting mother, growing up Jewish in a northern England city, he was an outsider from birth. He lacked the talent, or perhaps the courage, to follow his dream of acting on the stage. His homosexuality led to heartbreak, blackmail, and beatings. A stint in the military did him no good. But still he persevered, waiting for that one thing that would change his life.

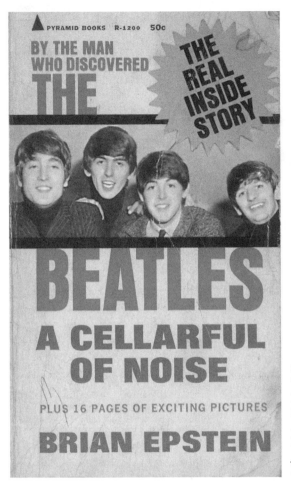

Ghost-written by Derek Taylor, the title of Brian Epstein's autobiography was mocked by John Lennon as *A Cellarful of Boys*—this after his earlier suggestion, "*Queer Jew*," reportedly reduced Epstein to tears.

In 1961, as Brian labored, successful but bored, as a record-store manager for his father's business, North End Music Stores (NEMS), that thing came in the form of the Beatles. From the first moment he saw and heard them, he loved their sound, their look, and the excitement they generated. His deep attraction to John Lennon—a lasting obsession—was admittedly a factor as well, but Epstein loved all of his charges and poured his heart and soul into their careers.

"Eppy" was the Beatles' father figure, their tireless champion, the one who introduced them to manners and high society, but also to the hard work and heartbreak of trying to make it in top-level show business. Yet no record-company rejection daunted the boys or their manager, because the dream of fame, fortune, and bright lights was one they all shared.

Brian longed to be among the cultured classes of show business, the moneyed elite who hobnobbed with the very wheels of the industry of human happiness. That this industry dealt in rock and roll was fine with Brian, even though the rest of his family found the art form crass and tasteless.

The time Brian spent on the Beatles caused a breach with his parents and brother, even when his efforts made the family wealthy beyond its greatest dreams. In fact, various financial dealings—some shady and some a result of ignorance—made Brian and his family rich at the expense of his four charges. The most obscene deal was an under-the-table agreement Epstein made with EMI that gave him 25% of all the Beatles' earnings, an agreement that his brother Clive—who did little, if anything, to help the Fabs along—claimed for himself following Brian's passing.

Brian was torn by guilt over family and finances, but the emotional strain was worth it to him; he loved the ride. Especially traveling with the Beatles on their endless tours from 1964–66, he apparently felt, despite being older, richer, and, certainly, gayer than they were, that he truly *belonged*. It was the concerts and their fast-paced, hectic preparations that made Brian feel useful, and when the band stopped touring, the mundane nature of the rest of the attendant NEMS business—which by this point encompassed an all-purpose entertainment booking and management firm—proved horribly boring.

Epstein found by 1967 that he was managing a staff of eighty, rather than the fifteen he'd overseen just three years previously. Artists like Cilla Black, Billy J. Kramer, and others he'd signed to NEMS in the early 1960s were taking far too much of his time. (This overcommitment, while financially rewarding from 1963–65, eventually led to Epstein's edge-of-nervous-breakdown decision to bring Robert Stigwood into NEMS.)

It can be argued that the great tragedy of Brian Epstein's life (and that of several other figures in the Beatles' orbit) is that he was never able to see his life in perspective. The go-go Beatle era sucked in its participants and spun them like clothes in a dryer, at great velocity and heat, demanding endless energy, providing stimulation both life-giving and soul-sucking, and, for some, stopping—just like *that*.

When the end of the cycle came for Brian, in 1967, his body was broken from drink, stress, and pills, his mind worn down by sexual, financial, and emotional stress. His death was shocking to many, but in retrospect seems hardly surprising, given his attempts at suicide, his amphetamine/depressant-induced rages, and his insane hours.

Brian's demise marked the end of the Beatles as a functioning business unit. Infighting, initially causing mere irritation, but later exacerbated by Allen Klein's maneuvering into full-blown fury, tore the band apart. While Epstein may have been a poor businessman in many ways, he was also in virgin territory; no popular act had ever made the Beatles' impact, or opened so many doors, doors that led both to triumph and grief.

Epstein, with his unshakeable belief, sophistication, and love for his charges, was just the manager the Beatles needed. In his wake, no combination of quality colleagues was able to do his job, or even come close.

Tony Barrow

The writers of this book owe Tony Barrow a debt of thanks, for in 1963 the professional scribe coined the term "Fab Four."

At the tender age of seventeen, Barrow began freelancing for the Liverpool *Echo* as a music reviewer (under the moniker "Disker"). Eventually he found work at Decca, writing copy on the back covers of albums. In 1961, Brian wrote to "Disker" to see if he couldn't interest the mysterious arbiter in writing a little something about the Beatles.

Disker wrote back, explaining that he only reviewed records, so until the Beatles released some vinyl, he was sorry but he couldn't help. Brian was intrigued, however, to learn that the writer he had thought was in Liverpool was actually in London, working at Decca. Never one to let an opportunity slip away, he asked Barrow to mention his fellow Liverpudlians to his employers.

Thus the Beatles came to Decca's attention, for better or worse, and Brian made the acquaintance of a real record company insider. For months after that, Brian picked Barrow's brain about labels, producers, and A&Rs.

Once "Love Me Do" came out later that year, Disker duly reviewed the record, but for Brian, this was just the beginning. His intense lobbying for tips on promotion led to the hiring of Decca underling Andrew Loog Oldham (future Rolling Stones manager) at NEMS, per Barrow's suggestion. Barrow struggled with the prospect of writing Beatles press releases while on Decca's dime, but Brian solved this moral dilemma by hiring him as the Beatles' first full-time press officer in May 1963.

Lennon, at least, was skeptical ("If you're not queer and you're not Jewish, why are you coming to work with Brian Epstein?"). But Barrow hit the ground running, utilizing his industry contacts to stir up interest. In October, things finally broke big, though, as Barrow observed, "I would love to say that it was my brilliant handouts which built the Beatles, but they didn't."

Around that time Barrow *did* have a brilliant idea to reward the loyal fans who had supported the group: an annual "Christmas message," pressed on a "flexi-disc" and sent out to members of the fan club. Though it took some persuading to get Brian to agree, the band couldn't wait to start. For the first three years, Barrow handwrote a set of talking points for the Beatles to

Surely Tony Barrow's most enduring legacy was his idea for the Beatles to issue annual holiday fan club recordings, seen here gathered in LP form in 1970.

work from, hoping these would allow the Fabs to follow their fancies while keeping things family-friendly. Sometimes this worked.

Barrow also continued in his former Decca role, penning hyped-up liner copy to the Beatles' releases. His notes on the back of the *Beatles' Hits* EP proved prophetic, inviting music fans to write him nasty letters in 1973 if the disc's contents weren't being discussed as "early examples of modern beat standards taken from The Lennon & McCartney Songbook."

Despite the effusive praise, Barrow's work didn't seem to have impressed the Beatles much, Lennon especially. Years later, during the poisonous post-breakup era, John compared *Let It Be*'s wretched "new phase" liner notes to Disker's work: ". . . written in the style of the great Barrow himself!"

As press officer, Barrow traveled with the band, adroitly handling reporters' demands. His job gave him a ringside seat at some of the Beatles' highest moments (such as the first Shea Stadium gig) as well as their lowest (essentially all of 1966). At their final show in San Francisco, Paul directed him to document the occasion by pointing his portable tape recorder at the stage. (Alas, the cassette ran out before the set ended.)

Barrow segued smoothly into the post-touring years, hyping *Sgt. Pepper's* in a style befitting its groundbreaking stature, as well as *Magical Mystery Tour*—about which, the less said the better.

He parted company with the Fabs just as Apple was launching, and was replaced by the inimitable Derek Taylor. Years later, he assembled his reminiscences into a book titled *John, Paul, George, Ringo and Me: The Real Beatles Story.* He also contributed some recollections to the *Hard Day's Night* DVD's bonus material.

Sir Joseph Lockwood

Arriving at EMI in 1954—with a background in, of all things, flour mills—Joseph Lockwood did a spectacular job of turning a loose aggregate of electronics manufacturers and record labels into an entertainment powerhouse. His gift for management and organization led to the company's preeminence throughout the 1960s, with a global reach as broad as the British Empire had been.

The same year he took over, Lockwood handed EMI's anemic Parlophone label over to a twenty-nine-year-old assistant in the classical department named George Martin, who shrewdly added a stable of comedy and rock artists to what had been primarily a jazz label. The youngest label head in the company's history, Martin made his mark with several high-quality recordings. (Alas, until good fortune arrived from Liverpool in 1962, sales never matched the level of Martin's efforts; had the Beatles not arrived, Parlophone would likely have been shut down.)

Lockwood had a simple motto: produce what sells. This the company did with a vengeance, even exporting a few acts that made a dent in the U.S. charts. Lockwood oversaw EMI's purchase of Capitol Records in 1955; thought to be a poor investment at the time, the gamble paid huge dividends down the road. With substantial TV and film holdings added to the mix, EMI's stunning revitalization earned Lockwood a knighthood in 1960.

Once the Beatles proved their mettle, "Sir Joe," as they called him, took a paternal interest in the boys despite having little use for their music. More importantly, he got on well with Brian Epstein, whose charm and politesse helped grease the Fabs' entry into the elite corporate world. (Epstein and Lockwood may have shared a sort of cultural solidarity: both were Jewish and gay. As Johnny Rogan pointed out in his 1988 book, *Starmakers and Svengalis*, an astonishingly high percentage of Britain's rock kingpins were homosexual, among them Robert Stigwood, Kit Lambert, Joe Meek, Larry Parnes, and Simon Napier-Bell.)

Perhaps Brian's biggest coup was convincing Lockwood to give the Fabs free studio time. In the band's first few recording years, given the boys' work ethic, EMI received plenty of bang for their buck. The Beatles cranked out million-selling records with astonishing ease, making efficient use of their precious recording dates.

But by the time of *Sgt. Pepper's*, Lockwood was nervously ruing his decision. With the meter running ceaselessly and no new product in sight, EMI's panicked president had a fiery exchange with Brian over the mounting expense. Two songs, "Strawberry Fields Forever" and "Penny Lane," were extracted from the work in progress to satiate the marketplace (and Lockwood), a move that George Martin regretted ever after.

The planned cover of the album also disquieted Lockwood, who found the inclusion of Indian national icon Mohandas K. Gandhi a bit too cheeky for his liking; unwilling to offend the former colony's populace, he made sure their fallen leader's visage was hidden.

So long as the Fabs delivered the goods, Sir Joe was willing to accept a certain amount of "eccentricity." Their use of illicit substances did not escape his notice, but he noted, "I never pursued it . . . largely because they were so successful." The Beatles' departure from convention even registered with the country's monarch: observed the Queen to Lockwood, "The Beatles are turning awfully funny, aren't they?"

Still, he gamely dealt with the headaches the Fabs threw at him, John and Yoko's *Two Virgins* being but one example. In fact, a measure of the mutual respect that had grown between the Beatles and EMI's president was evident when the struggle for control of the Beatles' publishing erupted in 1969. As a show of commitment, Lockwood offered an advance on their future royalties to support the Beatles' bid. In the end, though, the deal fell through.

Clive Epstein

The second of Queenie and Harry Epstein's two sons, Clive was born in 1937, three years after Brian.

Like Brian, Clive worked for the family business, NEMS; but unlike his brother he remained more a business acquaintance of the Beatles than a friend or confidant. The Fabs didn't particularly like or respect him, feeling that he didn't believe in them, and Clive himself later admitted that he did not share Brian's enthusiasm for the band. He continued, however, to work at NEMS in an administrative role as Brian and his charges climbed to international fame.

Following Brian's death in 1967, Clive and Queenie inherited the company. Clive became a director of NEMS (by now renamed Nemperor Holdings) but allegedly showed little interest in the day-to-day doings of the organization. He did, however, claim his 25% of the Beatles' income after Brian's management contract ran out in October 1967.

This infuriated the Beatles, who immediately sought ways to shake off Clive's control and influence. The setup of Apple was one attempt to extricate themselves from an organization that had come to include such unsympathetic careerists as Clive and Robert Stigwood.

It was apparently Clive's idea—since he was more interested in retail anyway—to invest some of the Beatles' money in a shop; this idea turned into the disaster known as the Apple Boutique. Once the store closed, John, Paul, George, and Ringo were truly done with Clive. The final straw came in February 1969 when Epstein sold Nemperor, against the band's wishes, to Triumph Investment Trust.

In the wake of this deal, the Beatles asked EMI not to pay any further royalties to Nemperor, an act that led Triumph to sue for its 25% of Beatle holdings. Shortly after, the group and Allen Klein made a seven-year deal with Triumph that removed them from all actual day-to-day control of the group in exchange for 25% of the Beatles' profits from 1969–71 and 5% from 1972–76. From 1976, Triumph would own nothing.

Clive Epstein died in 1988.

Walter Shenson

Born in 1919, Shenson served in the military in World War II, then started in the movie business in the late 1940s. After getting his feet wet in publicity, he moved to production and, by the 1960s, had made it big, producing the Beatles' first two movies, *A Hard Day's Night* and *Help!*

What does a movie producer do? In Shenson's case, he was responsible for securing the script, the director, and the rest of the cast; scouting out locations; and—most importantly—finding the necessary seed money to get the films made.

When United Artists asked Shenson to take hold of *AHDN* in early 1964, he had productions of several hit British films, such as *The Inner Sanctum*, *The Mouse That Roared*, and *A Matter of Who*, to his credit.

Shenson got along well with the Beatles and did a lot of things right in his time working with them: he hired Dick Lester to direct, he allowed the band to help in the selection of the screenwriter, and he respected the group's vision. In short, he helped make John, Paul, George, and Ringo comfortable enough to be satisfied participants in two very good films, ones that redefined the popular music celluloid genre.

The producer also oversaw the painstaking rereleases, on video and DVD, of the classic 1964 and 1965 films. Many of the negatives had deteriorated due to poor storage, and it took time and expense to fix the prints. Fortunately for Beatles fans, Paul Rutan and Triage Studios did an excellent job.

Shenson, who died in 2000, left a lasting legacy: the glorious *A Hard Day's Night*, the best rock-and-roll film ever made.

Robert Stigwood

By late 1966, Brian Epstein, stressed out by business, personal problems, and a troubling drug intake, was getting awfully tired of the daily grind of running NEMS, so he decided to take on a new partner.

In a move that surprised everyone but Brian, he eventually chose—in another one of his regrettable business decisions—to sell off every NEMS artist but Cilla Black and the Beatles. And he made the deal for just £500,000, just a few years after turning down a $20 million offer from an American syndicate.

Australian Robert Stigwood and his partner, David Shaw, were the beneficiaries of Epstein's largesse. Why in the world would Epstein bring on Stigwood, a man who had already established a reputation in the industry as a profligate spender? "Stiggy" had earlier bilked Sir Joe Lockwood and EMI out of at least £10,000 to help keep his company afloat—then skipped out on the debt.

To a certain extent, Epstein was simply desperate to sell out, go to Spain, and manage bullfighters. Brian had a personal bond with Stigwood and believed he could trust him, so he gave him and his partner until September 1967 to come up with the £500,000.

To be fair, Stigwood had been quite successful at managing groups like Cream and the nascent Bee Gees. He had also pioneered the "lend-lease" tape deal, in which he put up the money to produce songs, then leased the rights to release them to particular record companies, keeping control of the product himself.

By summer 1967, Stigwood had taken an office at NEMS. True to form, he upset Epstein by—surprise—overspending, unnecessarily renting a yacht for the Bee Gees.

Soon Brian began to regret his choice, and following Epstein's death NEMS withdrew the offer because Stigwood and Shaw hadn't come up with the money. The two left NEMS with a fairly small sum, but took with them all of the clients they had brought in.

Only after Brian Epstein had died were the four Beatles made aware of the plans to sell out the organization. The news hurt them deeply.

Denis O'Dell

The Beatles became aware of O'Dell, a film veteran, from his work with Dick Lester; he had been associate producer of *A Hard Day's Night* and later produced *How I Won the War*, in which John Lennon appeared. The band hired him in 1967 to produce *Magical Mystery Tour*.

After surviving that harrowing project, the forty-five-year-old O'Dell was named director of the new Apple Films in early 1968. O'Dell threw himself into his work, soliciting scripts and even bringing many of them for the Fabs to read on their meditation trip to Rishikesh that spring.

While the Beatles and O'Dell initially had grand plans for working on serious films (one early idea was *The Lord of the Rings*) with directors like Michelangelo Antonioni, the reality proved different. O'Dell was instead roped into another Beatle project—supervising the filming of early 1969 sessions for their newest album. This project eventually became *Let It Be*.

When Klein came aboard and it became clear that he was going to cut Apple's staff, O'Dell—who might well have been canned—resigned. He went on to produce *The Magic Christian* and continued his distinguished career into the 1990s. He also penned a memoir, *At the Apple's Core*.

In addition, O'Dell garnered a parodic mention in the song "You Know My Name (Look Up the Number)," recorded in 1967 but only released as the B-side to "Let It Be" three years later. Just prior to a jokingly nightclub-style vocal turn from Paul, John introduces "Dennis O'Bell."

Ken Mansfield

The Beatles, the Bible, and Bodega Bay: My Long and Winding Road possibly holds the distinction of being the most oddly titled memoir in the Beatles' literary canon. But its author, Ken Mansfield, can be said to have survived the madness of the longest cocktail party with his wits intact. Today Mansfield is what is commonly called "born again," a deeply spiritual but not-*too*-preachy survivor of both cancer and the '60s.

From hardscrabble origins on Nez Perce lands in Idaho, Mansfield began his musical career began as the leader of the Bay Area folk outfit the Town Criers (not to be confused with the group bearing the same name that included future Jefferson Airplane founder Marty Balin). Tiring of the limelight (and of the Limeliters, his folkie peers), Mansfield took an executive position at Capitol Records.

The job put him into regular contact with some formidable talents of the era: Stan Kenton, Peggy Lee, Al Martino, and Lou Rawls, among others. By the time the Beatles entered his whirl, he was beyond being starstruck; this decided lack of awe toward the Fabs made him stand out among the Capitol crowd, which included Stan Gortikov (president of Capitol industries), Alan Livingston (label head), and the infamous Dave Dexter Jr., who distinguished himself by *thrice* turning down the Beatles, mutilating their recordings with excessive reverb, and, working for *Billboard* years later, delivering a scathing "tribute" to John Lennon in the wake of his murder. Everyone in power at the label seemed anxious to make up for having ignored the act that would, by decade's end, account for *50%* of Capitol's business.

By 1968, however, the Fabs were not interested in settling scores; they were interested in seeing that Apple, their baby, received proper care and nurturing in the world's biggest market. For that reason, Paul made a surprise appearance at Capitol's annual convention in Los Angeles in June 1968 to suss out the situation. Pleased at what he saw, Paul approached Mansfield to head Apple's U.S. operations. Anxious to give the Beatles what they wanted, Capitol approved, while simultaneously extending Mansfield's duties to head all of their independent labels.

It is clear from Mansfield's book what a privileged position he held within the Beatles' inner circle. He describes being blindsided by the unexpected sight of the *Two Virgins* album art, which Paul had to "rescue" him from. Mansfield was present on the roof of Apple as the Beatles played together semi-publicly as a group for the last time. And he formed close a friendship with Ringo Starr that continues to this day.

Allen Klein's insinuation into Apple's affairs struck fear and loathing into longtime Beatle stalwarts. Unlike most of them, Mansfield was not a target of Klein's; in fact, when Mansfield turned in his resignation in late 1969 to take a position at MGM Records (feeling that with the Beatles' impending disintegration, his work was done), Klein refused to accept it.

Instead, a curious wager was placed. The tubby, out-of-shape but fiercely competitive Klein challenged Mansfield to a game of tennis: if he won, Mansfield would be on the first plane back to London: if Mansfield won, adios, Beatles. A score of 15 to 13 in Mansfield's favor settled things definitively.

Mansfield went on to further successes in the industry, sometimes as a producer (he was responsible for French chanteuse Claudine Longet's all-too-prophetic medley "Jealous Guy" / "Don't Let Me Down"). Mansfield also stayed in touch with the troubled Mal Evans, speaking with him by phone on the very day he was gunned down by L.A.'s finest.

Mansfield himself soon hit bottom as well. But, emerging from the darkness, he embraced Jesus and managed to strike a curious balance between celebrating his rock-and-roll past and spreading the word—gently—about his newfound faith. Today he is a regular on speaking tours.

Of all the insider tomes published, *The Beatles, the Bible, and Bodega Bay* manages to convey the tumultuous but exciting times the Fabs experienced during their latter days while sparing the reader sordid scandal-sheet anecdotes. Mansfield's portrait of the Beatles as human beings is loving and dignified (though some readers may chafe at the spiritual message).

Ron Kass

The Beatles hired Kass in May 1968 as president of the newly created Apple Records. He had previously run Liberty Records' British division.

One of his first duties, a month into his tenure, was to escort Paul McCartney to the Capitol Records convention in Los Angeles. When the Beatles decided to award Capitol—their existing label in the U.S.—the rights to distribute Apple product, Paul went over as an emissary.

Kass lobbied to have one of his favorite bands, the Modern Jazz Quartet, signed to Apple. The MJQ, a classically inspired jazz foursome, released two fine but tremendously unsuccessful LPs on the label before returning to Atlantic Records.

Felt by most at Apple to be loyal and trustworthy, Kass became close to several members of the staff. He was a good record man who knew his way around promotion and radio; as a result, Apple's record division was extremely successful—in fact, the only successful division of the company.

But when Allen Klein came aboard in 1969, Kass's days were numbered. Klein saw that Kass was honest as well as powerful, and could not be bullied or corrupted. Therefore he stood in the way of Klein's devious and dictatorial management strategy.

Peter Brown later claimed that Kass was eventually fired after Klein accused him—certainly spuriously—of stealing $1,250. Some of the urging to get rid of Kass also came, according to Tony Bramwell, from Yoko Ono.

Like many canned by Klein, Kass landed on his feet. He ended up marrying Joan Collins in 1972 (they stayed together for eleven years) and went on to work at both MGM and Warner Brothers Records prior to embarking on a successful second career in film production.

Kass passed away at 1985, just fifty years old, from cancer.

Neil Aspinall

Born in 1942 in Wales, where his Mersey-based mother had fled during the bombing raids on London, Aspinall grew up a school friend of George and Paul. Soon all three were hanging around with John Lennon and getting into all sorts of trouble.

But the straightforward, no-B.S. Aspinall was no musician, so in time he fell away from the Fabs a bit. He quit school in 1959, at age sixteen, to begin a career as an accountant. Renting a room in Mona Best's house (and eventually engaging in a clandestine affair with his lessor), he watched plenty of Beatles gigs, both in Mona's Casbah Club and elsewhere.

Soon it became clear that the Beatles were going somewhere—or they would be, if someone could drive them. Aspinall, who by this time was tired of accountancy, purchased a used van at the behest of Pete Best and, for a small fee, transported the Beatles and their equipment to gigs.

When the Beatles booted Best from the band in 1962, Aspinall was forced to choose between friends—with the added complication that his and Mona's son, Roag, had been born just a few weeks earlier.

At Pete's urging, Neil chose the Beatles, leaving Mona Best and his son behind and taking a job with Brian Epstein as the Beatles' road manager. It is unclear whether Aspinall was directed by Epstein, now his employer, to leave his "family."

Neil rode along with the Fab Four as they skyrocketed to international fame. As one of the Beatles' oldest friends, over time he gained the complete trust of all—even Paul, whom he often disagreed with. But one wonders just how much resentment and grief Aspinall buried.

After driving many thousands of miles between 1961 and 1963, through blizzards and rainstorms, in a series of used vans, Neil eventually became as much a paid companion as anything else—but continued to work very hard, even though Mal Evans was eventually hired to help out.

Like most people around the band during the '60s, he found that Beatledom was a full-time gig. Whether it was driving someone around, shopping for someone's wife or girlfriend, doing miscellaneous errands, or just being there, Neil did what the Beatles did, ate, drank, and smoked what they did, and dressed as they did, twenty-four hours a day. He also occasionally helped out with a song, banging a tambourine or singing in the background.

When the band set up Apple, Aspinall was hired as a managing director. He said he only wanted the job temporarily, and was thought by some to be the wrong man for the job, but ended up manning the helm for the next forty years.

He is alleged to have been one of the more reckless spenders during the 1968 "longest cocktail party," but when Allen Klein fired him, the Beatles stood up for their old friend (something they only did for a few others, such as Derek Taylor and Peter Brown).

Perhaps in exchange for this action, Aspinall's accountant tendencies reasserted themselves. He dedicated the next decade to helping sort out the company's files and finances, working particularly hard on the post-1972 lawsuits against their conniving former manager.

During the Beatles' end phase, Aspinall produced both the *Let It Be* film and the television special promoting Ringo Starr's first solo LP, *Sentimental Journey*. He also began to compile what was originally conceived as the band's next film—a compilation of its history, provisionally titled *The Long and Winding Road*, involving every single bit of Beatles film he could find.

This project fell apart, at least for the moment, leading Peter Brown to write that Aspinall's efforts were "pathetic." (One wonders whether Brown changed his mind in 1995 when this project, *The Beatles Anthology* TV special, was released.)

Continuing to soldier on for Apple Corps—long after most people believed it had ceased to exist—Aspinall shepherded the company through legal actions against EMI (for poor accounting) and Apple Computer (for trademark infringement).

But Aspinall, and Apple, truly reemerged in the 1990s and 2000s as the administrator of the group's work. *The Beatles Anthology*, a six-CD set paired with the exhaustive TV documentary, got the group back into the public consciousness in a major way in 1995.

With Aspinall providing much of the company's sweat, toil, and tears, Apple has built on the success of the Anthology with the best-selling *Yellow Submarine Songtrack*, *Beatles 1*, the American "mono" albums series, and *Beatles Love*. And in the near future, as a result of a long-awaited settlement between Apple Corps and Apple Computer, the Beatles' catalog will finally be made available for digital download.

Further tweaking of the Beatles' catalog is a certainty. Rumors have the band's original CDs being ultimately remastered and perhaps remixed, with improved packaging and bonus tracks. (And most fans would agree that it's about time.)

With Lennon, Harrison, Derek Taylor, Mal Evans, Brian Epstein, and Alistair Taylor, among others, having passed away, precious few of the true inner circle remain. For Neil Aspinall, the long and winding road came to an end on the very anniversary of Paul's announcement that he was leaving the Beatles. Forty-five years after buying a clapped-out old van, Aspinall unexpectedly announced he was stepping down in 2007. While the shocking announcement claimed the parting was amicable, insiders report pressure in the wake of the Apple Computer settlement.

One more down.

All These Friends . . .

The Beatles' Posse

In the wake of the Beatles' first unprecedented success in 1963, it became clear to everyone close to the band that plenty of business associates, "friends," politicians, and showbiz types wanted simply to exploit the Fabs' name, image, and position for their own gain.

Therefore, the boys reinforced their already strong pattern of closing ranks—hiring friends and trusted associates to serve as business partners, bodyguards, gofers, and travel companions. As such, an overlap exists between the Beatles' friends and business associates, but in this chapter we'll focus on those who were friends first. Left out, but worthy of mention, are Liverpool promoter Sam Leach and friend Terry Condon.

Pete Shotton

Perhaps John's best and oldest friend, Shotton also went to Quarry Bank High School. Like Lennon, Pete was tough, but not quite as hard as the Teddy boys who roamed the streets of Liverpool. The two pals often got into tough situations together, barely escaping with their lives.

Though Shotton had no musical ability, he was part of the gang, so he joined the Quarry Men, scraping away at the washboard.

By the time the Beatles got serious, Shotton had left music and tried a series of jobs with little success. John, who rarely forgot a friend in those days, bought a grocery store in Hampshire, at £20,000, for Pete and his wife to run—although Shotton would still journey to London to hang around. (He was at the "Eleanor Rigby" songwriting session, and years later offered pointed commentary dismissing Lennon's claim of an authorship role).

By 1968, Lennon had called Shotton to London to run the group's new Apple Boutique, making him again part of the band's circle. But despite Shotton's experience in running a successful store, the Apple Boutique was doomed to fail for a variety of reasons. Shotton resigned just before the shop folded, departing the scene (according to Peter Brown, anyway) in a company Jaguar.

After Shotton quit the boutique, Lennon hired him as a personal assistant and paid companion. He was at Lennon's house on the spring night in 1968 when John invited Yoko over and the couple created the *Two Virgins* album. Eventually, Pete parted ways with Lennon, when he and his betrothed crossed the line of friendship and took to ordering Shotton around as though he were their personal manservant.

Though they never again were as intimate as they'd been, Pete and John did not entirely lose contact. In his memoir, *John Lennon: In My Life* (coauthored by Nicholas Schaffner), published a few years after Lennon's death, Pete described coming to New York to see John the year before his murder.

Over dinner, the two talked over old times as Yoko sat, somewhat stiffly. Shotton would never forget the unmistakable impression that John seemed

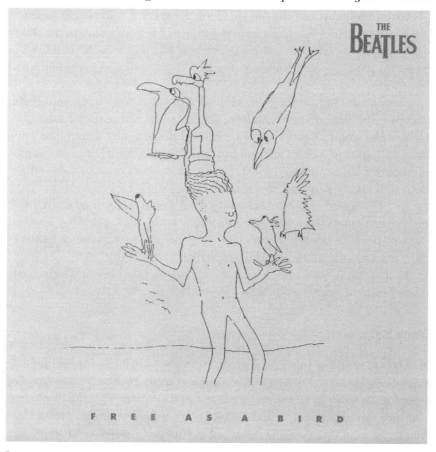

Lennon maintained his friendship with Pete Shotton for years, honoring him with this fanciful portrait published in *In His Own Write*; later used for the posthumous "Free as a Bird" single sleeve.

desperate to impart *something* to him, albeit somewhat guardedly. Ever after, he could only speculate as to what John was trying to tell him.

Ivan Vaughan

While it's possible that John Lennon and Paul McCartney might have teamed up eventually, Ivan Vaughan is responsible for introducing them.

Ivan was born the very same day as Paul McCartney, and the two went to school together. He also knew John Lennon, and joined the Quarry Men on tea-chest bass. A smart fellow who saw that both of his friends had uncommon talent and might do something if hooked together, Ivan convinced Paul to come see the Quarry Men play—and maybe pick up a girl—at the Woolton Garden Fête on July 6, 1957.

When Vaughan introduced the boys, Lennon was his usual sarcastic self, but McCartney made an impression with his guitar talent and ability to remember song lyrics, and eventually was asked to join the band. Years later, Vaughan would laconically observe, "I only brought great fellows to meet John."

Music wasn't in Ivan Vaughan's future. He settled down in the mid-1960s, marrying and fathering two children, but remained part of the band's circle. He took a memorable trip to California in 1968 with McCartney and Tony Bramwell, during which Paul and Linda fell in love. Vaughan also was part of Apple for a time, charged with coming up with ideas for alternative education. He ended up, in fact, as a teacher.

In 1977, Vaughan began suffering from Parkinson's disease. In 1984, he was the central figure in a BBC documentary about the disease. This was expanded into a book two years later, *Ivan: Living with Parkinson's Disease.* He passed away in 1994, at just fifty-two years old.

Paul would memorialize his friend in a poem, published in 2001 as part of his *Blackbird Singing* collection.

Tony Bramwell

A boyhood friend of John, Paul, and George, Bramwell was a rocker kid like the others. He tells the story in his autobiography, *Magical Mystery Tours,* of hopping on a bus in December 1960 to catch a ride to a local hall where a rock group was playing: "The Beatles, Direct from Hamburg." On the bus he ran into Harrison and was shocked to find out that his old friends *were* the group.

From that point, Bramwell and the Fabs became inseparable. He was honest with them, and the group trusted him. Hanging around the Cavern, carrying equipment, and eventually working for Brian Epstein at NEMS, Bramwell shared apartments, bar tabs, good times, and plenty of business ventures with the Beatles and ended up promoting their records on radio and to the press.

"Tone" soon found that a well-spoken, sharp dresser with friends like the Beatles could gain easy entrée to the mod London of the mid-1960s. He dated some famous women, including Mary Hopkin and Christine Keeler, a key figure in the Profumo scandal, and hung out with rock stars and TV presenters. Bramwell's man-about-town status helped make him even more successful in the record business. Later on, when the Beatles started Apple, he was a natural as director of promotion.

He is particularly proud of having promoted "Hey Jude," knowing as he walked around town distributing copies to DJs and writers that he had a very special record in his hands.

Mal Evans

When the twenty-six-year-old Evans first heard the Beatles playing at Liverpool's Cavern Club in 1962, he was working for the postal service. He began hanging round the Cavern more often and was soon hired as a bouncer thanks to his large frame and imposing appearance.

Eventually Brian Epstein brought the friendly, unpretentious Evans aboard as an employee of NEMS, his music managerial service. Shortly after, Mal was asked to help Neil Aspinall on the Beatles' road crew. Mal almost immediately became a trusted friend and confidant. He traveled with the Fabs, did errands, lugged equipment, appeared in *Help!* and *Magical Mystery Tour*, and hung around when any of the boys needed someone.

In addition, Evans was the gatekeeper to the boys' bedchambers on the road, sorting through various groupies and often sampling the offerings himself.

When the group needed a spare hand in the studio, Evans would bang away on a tambourine, blow a horn, or play a keyboard. (Though rhythmi-cally challenged, he was initially tapped for anvil work on "Maxwell's Silver Hammer," as shown in *Let It Be*. Eventually, Ringo's more capable talents prevailed.) When McCartney needed a few lyrics for "Fixing a Hole," Evans supplied them (for a one-time payoff), much to John Lennon's disgust.

Once the group founded Apple Corps, Evans tried his hand at talent scouting, enticing a young band, the Iveys, to sign with the company. After the group changed its name to Badfinger, Evans produced several tracks released on their *Magic Christian Music* album as well as their hit single

"No Matter What." Despite these successes, however, Mal was soon forced out of the picture by Badfinger's jealous manager, Bill Collins.

During the early '70s, exhausted and burned out by the whole Beatles marathon, Evans lost the plot, as did plenty of other '60s survivors. He moved to California, left his wife and kids, and became very involved with drugs, partying nonstop with some of rock's heaviest hitters, including Ringo, Keith Moon, and John Lennon.

Attempting to pull his life together, Evans was slated to return to the producer's chair for ex-Badfinger member Joey Molland's *Natural Gas* project. But ultimately his unhealthy habits proved too strong.

On January 5, 1976, Evans was so drugged out that his girlfriend, Francine Hughes, called the Los Angeles police for assistance. Greeted by a drunk and coked-out Evans waving a gun, which to this day nobody can prove was real, the cops opened fire and killed him instantly.

As a macabre footnote, Mal's cremated remains were lost en route back to England. When informed of this, John Lennon suggested that they check the dead letter office.

Klaus Voormann

When the Beatles were desperate for friends in Hamburg, Klaus Voormann turned up at just the right time.

Klaus, an art student from Berlin, heard the Beatles' nightclub act at the Kaiserkeller and was impressed. He dragged friends Jurgen Vollmer and Astrid Kirchherr along, and the three grew close to the band.

Hardly your usual rock-and-roll crowd, Klaus, Jurgen, and Astrid were all beatnik-influenced artists (or "exis," short for "existentialists," as the Beatles called them).

These three, and some other German friends, began hanging around this exciting bunch of raw British rock and rollers, feeling both fascinated and a bit scared by them. They fed off the Beatles' enthusiasm and goodwill, and the Fabs began to adopt some of the exis' style and social mores.

Though the Beatles left Germany for good in early 1963, only visiting again while on tour in 1966, Voormann kept up his relationship with the band, John and George especially, by relocating to London and insinuating himself into the local rock scene. He took up electric bass, joining forces with two friends to form the Brian Epstein–managed Paddy, Klaus, and Gibson.

After their breakup, he scored a higher-profile gig with hit-makers Manfred Mann before settling in as a session musician.

He also designed several record sleeves, including the classic black-and-white illustration for *Revolver* (which won a Grammy for cover design) and

His chance discovery of the Beatles in a seedy Hamburg rock club would prove life-changing for both Klaus Voormann and the group themselves.

Photo by Jurgen Vollmer/Redferns

the colorful collage wrapped around *Bee Gees 1st*. For the booklet accompanying Ringo's eponymous breakthrough album in 1973, Klaus produced an illustration for each song.

Following the Beatles' dissolution, Voormann played bass on various solo projects for John, Ringo, and George. Moving back to Germany in 1979, he produced the band Trio's world-famous "Da Da Da" but eventually returned to art. Klaus also designed the collage that graced the Beatles' *Anthology* series.

Today, the venerable Voormann occasionally turns up as a speaker at fan conventions, sometimes with Astrid. On occasion, he can even be coaxed into strapping on the bass guitar. (Exhort him to "Mach schau!" at your own risk.)

Astrid Kirchherr

The young blonde photographer was going out with Klaus Voormann when she met the Beatles, but soon she realized that her heart lay with the group's bass player, Stuart Sutcliffe. (Later she said it was "love at first sight.")

When she and her other friends started coming to see the Beatles play, they brought an artsier component to this cadre of young Brits searching for a new life far from home. In addition to taking some of the best pictures ever seen of the Fab Four, Astrid also led the group to a more bohemian style, even making them some clothes.

Kirchherr is often credited with suggesting that the Fabs get rid of their pompadour haircuts in favor of loose, free-hanging bangs, a style initially adopted by Stuart, with George close behind. Eventually John and Paul, who had ridiculed the style, succumbed to the inevitable in Paris, where "exi" Jurgen Vollmer did the honors, after pointing out that the style was in vogue among Parisian hipsters. Pete Best remained the lone holdout (though physiology may have played a part).

Sutcliffe decided to remain in Germany with Astrid in 1961, forcing McCartney to take over the bass guitar. The two lovers were engaged, and even took a trip to Liverpool together before returning to Hamburg. Sutcliffe, however, soon began suffering severe headaches, and died of a cerebral hemorrhage on April 10, 1962.

Astrid, "widowed" at age twenty-three, never moved to England as Klaus Voormann had done. She instead remained in Germany, eventually marrying Gibson Kemp from Klaus's old band. For a time she pursued photography (snapping George for the insert of his LP *Wonderwall Music* in 1968), but eventually wearied of the attention cast her way by fans and certain media figures who painted her as a tragic novelty. She gave up public life for many years.

Kirchherr had lost a lot of money by not looking after the copyrights to her Hamburg work with the Beatles. Eventually Genesis Publications remedied this, assembling three costly but beautiful folios of her work. Retiring from photography by the 1980s, she eventually resurfaced as an advisor to the 1994 Beatles biopic, *Backbeat.*

Bill Harry

A college friend and drinking buddy of Lennon's and Sutcliffe's, Harry in 1961 founded *Mersey Beat,* a Liverpool newspaper that covered the city's emerging rock music scene.

The first issue contained a satirical front-page story from Lennon purporting to describe how the Beatles had come by their name. A huge supporter of the group from the very beginning, Harry not only ran numerous items on the Fabs but also gave Lennon his own "Beatcomber" column, which John filled with witty nonsense and drawings.

McCartney, too, often contributed reports from Hamburg that Harry published in *Mersey Beat.* Staying close to everyone in the band, Harry even urged George to write songs, leading to "Don't Bother Me," Harrison's first self-composed number on a Beatles record.

Harry's paper was sold at Brian Epstein's NEMS record shops, and the urbane manager soon began to write his own *Mersey Beat* column. Eventually, after Beatlemania swept the nation and the group moved away from Liverpool, Harry moved into music publicity, later working for Fleetwood Mac, the Arrows, and Led Zeppelin, among other acts.

He also introduced a Cavern hanger-on, Priscilla White, to Lennon (mistakenly calling her "Cilla Black," which soon became her professional name), and the young redhead became a good friend of the Beatles; Paul gave her "Love of the Loved" and "It's for You" to sing.

Bill Harry has written more than twenty books, many about the Beatles, and currently works as a rock-and-roll memorabilia consultant.

Terry Doran

A Liverpool native who met Brian Epstein in late 1950s, Doran made his living as a car salesman. Brought into the Beatles' orbit by Epstein, he first won the boys' loyalty by getting them fancy cars at factory cost.

Eventually, Doran and Epstein set up an auto dealership, BryDor, in Middlesex. The business not only sold wheels to the Fabs but also vended vehicles to their famous and wealthy friends.

Gaining lasting Beatlesong fame as the "man from the motor trade" in Paul's "She's Leaving Home," Doran was a friend to the band, especially Harrison, from almost the very beginning of their time under Epstein's wing.

When John Lennon became stuck for a verb to describe the relationship between the four thousand holes and the Royal Albert Hall in the lyric to "A Day in the Life," it was Doran who achieved immortality by suggesting "fill."

In 1968, George hired Doran as his assistant. Terry held this position until being named, despite a lack of qualifications, managing director of Apple Music Publishing, in which role, unsurprisingly, he made several bad business decisions.

When transferred to the Records division, Doran signed the group Grapefruit to the label, but was soon made "redundant" by Allen Klein's budget cuts. By late 1969, Doran was again Harrison's assistant.

Derek Taylor

A Liverpool-born music journalist, Taylor was an early champion of the Beatles and soon helped ghostwrite George Harrison's column, which ran in the *Daily Express*.

In 1964, Brian Epstein hired Taylor away from newspapers and had him ghostwrite his memoir, *A Cellarful of Noise*. Taylor spent another several months working as the Beatles' press officer before eventually moving to California to open his own press agency.

As publicist for the Byrds and Paul Revere and the Raiders, among other bands, he enjoyed the California lifestyle and was much the man about L.A. Taylor was a key player in assembling talent for the Monterey Pop Festival and contributed liner notes to albums by Boyce and Hart and Harry Nilsson (whose career he boosted considerably by sending his first album to each of the Beatles).

Hired to run the Apple press office in 1968, Taylor moved back to London. Charming the local press with his mannerisms, and serving his employers well with an ability to get to the heart of a situation, Taylor was burning the candle at both ends, indulging heavily in drugs and drink.

When he was eventually forced out (by Lennon as much as by Allen Klein) in spring 1970, he returned to the U.S., joining Warner Brothers Records, where he stayed for the next eight years.

He penned a fine recap of the Summer of Love, *It Was Twenty Years Ago Today*, in 1987, and collaborated on George's autobiography, *I Me Mine*. He also found time to compose a pair of memoirs, *As Time Goes By* in 1973 and *Fifty Years Adrift in an Open-Necked Shirt* a decade later.

Taylor remained a close friend of the Threetles, especially Harrison, and in the 1990s helped relaunch the Fabs as a "new" commercial entity, doing yeoman work on the *Live at the BBC* and *Anthology* projects. A "beautiful man," in Paul McCartney's words, Taylor passed on at age sixty-five in 1997, leaving his devoted and beloved wife, Joan, and six children.

Alistair Taylor

A kind, engaging chap who worked for Brian Epstein at his Whitchapel Avenue, Liverpool NEMS store even before the Beatles came on the scene, Taylor was a favorite at Beatles fans conventions before his untimely death in 2004 at age sixty-eight.

One could argue that Taylor, who had accompanied Epstein when he decided to check out the Beatles at the Cavern, was Brian's most trusted aide. Smart and pleasant, he soon became known as "Mr. Fix-It" for his ability to work out particulars in tough situations. He not only got the Beatles out of trouble, but also *kept* them out of it.

Like some other Beatle friends, Taylor appears on one of their albums. The mysterious interlude on *The Beatles* between Paul's "Can you take me back?" fragment and "Revolution 9" is actually a conversation between Taylor and George Martin.

Taylor is apologizing to the producer for forgetting to bring him a promised bottle of claret. Martin agrees to forgive Taylor, then adds after a slight hesitation, "bitch."

Following Brian Epstein's death, Taylor ended up at Apple as office manager. Despite his abilities, he fell victim to Allen Klein's "cost-cutting" purge, which was really a power play to divide and conquer the Beatles' friends and supporters. First, Taylor was called on to cut expenses, then he himself was canned.

The Beatles knew about the firing, and John and Paul refused to take Taylor's calls that day, something that hurt "Mr. Fix-It" deeply. Later he wrote two books about his time with the group.

. . . And Lovers

Wives, Girlfriends, and One-Night Stands

During the Beatles' career, each of the four had wives, fiancées, steady girlfriends, affairs, dalliances, and flirtations. Some of the flirtations were harmless, many unconsummated, while others turned into emotionally devastating dramas.

Then there were the group's tours, wild bacchanalian festivals that Lennon famously described as being not unlike Fellini's film *Satyricon*.

It's not an excuse for the boys' behavior, but rather a partial explanation of it, to point out that more women threw themselves at the Beatles than, most likely, at anyone else in the world at the time. And the Beatles, as we now know, were very, very human.

Leaving out some deserving ladies, such as Bernadette Farrell, an early girlfriend of George's who ran the Liverpool Beatle City Museum for many years, here are ten women who meant a lot to one (or more) of the Fab Four during their years as a band.

Thelma Pickles

Introduced to Lennon in 1958, when she was seventeen and he eighteen, Thelma shared with John a broken home (both their fathers had left as youngsters) and a coarse sense of humor that belied the pain underneath. This brunette was something of a toughie, and as such nearly a match for John.

Unlike some of the other ladies in the often hardscrabble circle surrounding the Beatles, Thelma enjoyed Lennon's biting, often cruel wit. But Lennon proved too much, even for her. John's grief after losing his mother made him more abusive to everyone, including "Thel," and she—unlike some others in his life—didn't back down from his abuse.

They went out for about six months and remained friends until he left Liverpool. Recalling his early years, Lennon said with regret, "I will have to be a lot older before I can face in public how I treated women as a youngster."

Following a short dalliance with Paul, Thelma married beat poet Roger McGough, a member of the pop group Scaffold (which also included Mike McGear, Paul's brother). That marriage lasted through 1970. In later years, Thelma worked as a television producer.

Cynthia Powell Lennon

Pretty Cynthia Powell was studying at the Liverpool College of Art when she met fellow student John Lennon. The two were attracted to each other almost instantly, even though Lennon's latent insecurity—over Cynthia's posher background, for one thing—manifested itself in cruel ways: he'd cadge money off her, insult her, and a few times even hit her.

Everyone cared for Cynthia, because she was sweet, but she was shy. Wanting just to make John happy, she dyed her reddish-brown hair blonde because he was obsessed with French actress Brigitte Bardot.

But Powell effected a change in John as well; he became "artier" and less interested in rebelling for rebellion's sake. Having a real, serious girlfriend, someone he could be vulnerable with, helped him grow up some.

The two were married shotgun-style on August 23, 1962, just days after Cynthia learned she was pregnant. Lennon wanted to do what was right, both for Cynthia and for their unborn child, although from the start his heart wasn't in the marriage.

John's Aunt Mimi's heart wasn't in it, either; she refused even to attend the ceremony. Brian Epstein, worried about the bad publicity that either an out-of-wedlock child or a marriage could cause his new band of heartthrobs, took care of the details. Amid much nervous laughter, Cyn and John were wed and began a strange domestic life.

Julian was born on April 8, 1963. Tellingly, Lennon wasn't even around for the difficult birth; he was on tour and didn't see Julian until he was three days old. While Lennon was busy in London, Cynthia and the baby lived in near squalor in Liverpool until Epstein realized that if the press found out about *that*, it'd be curtains.

Though deeply in love with John, Powell knew fairly early on that it would be difficult—nigh on impossible—to keep him. She surmised that John was too much a searcher, too easily bored, too against the idea of routine, to be a good husband or father, and she was right. Lennon had dozens, maybe hundreds, of liaisons over the years.

But it wasn't so much the dalliances, flings, and affairs that made Cynthia aware that she'd eventually lose John. Despite a beautiful wife and son, and fame, Lennon was on a continuous search for deeper meaning, an often destructive quest that led him first to art, poetry, and rock and roll, and later, by the mid-'60s, to drugs, meditation, and the avant-garde.

Once Cynthia figured out the level of interest that artist Yoko Ono sparked in her husband, she knew the marriage was in deep trouble. After more than two years of serious doubts about her future with John, she came home from a holiday to Greece in May 1968 to find Lennon and Ono sitting together in bathrobes at the kitchen table.

Divorced soon afterward, Cynthia dropped out of the Beatles' circle, eventually marrying twice more and basically raising Julian by herself. She has written two books about her time with Lennon and comes across as a steady, intelligent, but in some ways tragic figure.

Dot Rhone

Quiet and shy, and coming from a difficult upbringing, including an abusive father, Dorothy "Dot" Rhone never thought she was attractive—but Paul McCartney did.

The two met in 1959. Aside from hooking up with Paul, Dot also became a close friend of Cynthia Powell's. Later that year, the two girls traveled to Hamburg to hang out with their boyfriends' band. Astrid Kirchherr became close to the two Liverpool lasses and took them around the mysterious German city.

Paul's slightly long hair and status as a rocker excited Dot, but along with his looks and talent came a controlling streak. He forbade her to see other boys when he was gone, and coerced Dot into dying her hair platinum blonde. (Later Paul remarked, "We got [Dot and Cynthia] to go blonde and wear miniskirts. It's terrible really. But that's the way it was.")

This aside, Dot loved spending time with Paul's close and very musical family. She recalls Paul writing "Love of the Loved" and "P.S. I Love You" for her during their time together.

Early in 1960, Dot became pregnant, and she and Paul planned to marry—a full two years before John and Cynthia would do so. But three months into the pregnancy she miscarried. Had she carried the baby to term, she and Paul would have married, and Beatles history would have been completely altered.

As the group became more and more popular, both in Liverpool and in Hamburg, Paul had more affairs—including an on-again, off-again, two-year fling with Iris Caldwell—although, typically, he still made Dot promise to be faithful. She wanted to be married, but Paul did not, and he broke up with her in 1963, shortly before the group found its way to America and eventually global success. Dot was shattered, but later came to see that the pressures that fame and fortune were to bring about would have been impossible for her to withstand.

Grieving but resigned, Dot moved to Canada in early 1964 and built a new life. At last word, she still resides in Ontario, and has been married to the same man for more than forty years.

Iris Caldwell

The sister of Liverpool rocker Rory Storm, Iris dated George in the late 1950s, when both were seemingly barely old enough to walk . . . but in 1961, at age seventeen, she became the nineteen-year-old Paul's girlfriend.

Working as a discotheque dancer on bills with the Beatles, she became familiar with them socially and professionally. She and Paul hit it off, dating on and off until Paul left for London at the beginning of Beatlemania. Eventually Paul met Jane Asher, which spelled the end of his relationship with Iris.

Left on her own, she soon rebounded, marrying Merseyside singer Shane Fenton (born Brian Jewry) of the Fentones. Years later, during the glam-rock 1970s, Fenton renamed himself Alvin Stardust and had several hit records, but he and Iris divorced soon afterward.

Jane Asher

For almost five years, beautiful red-haired starlet Jane Asher and Beatle Paul McCartney made the perfect trendy British pair.

The two met at a 1963 show at the Royal Albert Hall. Jane, at seventeen, was already a well-known actress who had appeared on the TV show *Juke Box Jury*, so the Beatles knew her, with Paul especially, and immediately, smitten.

Soon Paul was hanging out with Jane every chance he got, and the more time the band spent in London, the more chances he had. Getting on well with her family, he was eventually invited, in November 1963, to live in the attic room of the Ashers' London home.

Jane came from an interesting and artistic background. Her parents— Richard, an eminent physician, and Margaret, a music teacher—provided a solid background that Paul appreciated; the family gave the somewhat homesick young man some solace and grounding during his early days in London.

Paul became good friends with Jane's brother, Peter (later employing him at Apple), and younger sister, Claire, and enjoyed the comfortable family experience of a room of his own, communal meals, and intellectually stimulating conversation.

The press loved this appealing pair; Jane was cultured, well-mannered, and accomplished on the stage and on radio, while the handsome and talented McCartney was clearly in thrall to her—she was, as Cynthia Lennon later wrote, "a great prize." Hanging with actors, filmmakers, and musicians of all stripes, Jane and Paul were *the* "Swinging London" couple: the ravishing dolly-bird actress and the cute Beatle.

From the very beginning of his time at Jane's house, Paul found he could easily compose there, writing some of his most famous songs—"And I Love Her," "I've Just Seen a Face," and "Eleanor Rigby," among others—at a piano in the small music room. He and John had also penned "I Want to Hold Your Hand" at the Ashers' in 1963. Eventually Paul got a piano moved into his own room, where he wrote "Yesterday."

In 1965, Paul decided to buy a house, and eventually took possession of a fine mansion in St. John's Wood, not far from the Abbey Road studio.

Once Jane moved into Paul's Cavendish Avenue home, tensions grew. Paul, embracing a bohemian period in which he discovered pot, mysticism, underground film and music, and alternative literature, was diving into a life that Jane knew or cared little about. She was more used to hanging with theatrical types, whom Paul sometimes found fusty and stuffy. It seemed that Jane was most comfortable at dinner parties while Paul was just as happy with a singsong down the pub.

Jane's world of theater, concerts, and radio dramas was quite different from Paul's rock-and-roll lifestyle; he spent time learning about her interests, but Jane felt that the pop business was somewhat silly. In addition to these "artistic differences," Paul's and Jane's touring schedules kept them away from home much of the time, which didn't help the relationship; Paul took plenty of opportunities for secret liaisons, and Jane had other boyfriends as well. They spent holidays together, but ultimately both may have known that their futures lay elsewhere. Frustrated by Jane taking an important acting job in Bristol, Paul wrote "I'm Looking Through You."

The two took several trips together in 1967, hoping to rekindle some of what had made them fall in love. Jane even accompanied Paul to the Beatles' meditation weekend in Bangor. Perhaps hoping that making a commitment would help, they announced their engagement on Christmas Day.

But by early 1968, things were getting worse. Jane and Paul went to Rishikesh to study again with the Maharishi for five weeks, but despite enjoying meditation and writing plenty of songs, Paul did not feel the connection with Jane that he had hoped for.

In early July, so rumor has it, Jane came home from a job to Cavendish to find Paul in bed with another woman, and stormed out. On July 20, Jane appeared on Simon Dee's BBC-TV program, *Dee Time*, and announced to Britain that the engagement was over.

From this point on, Jane never publicly discussed her relationship with Paul. She instead continued her career as a critically acclaimed actress, joining the National Theatre in 1970. She met artist Gerald Scarfe (who did the artwork on Pink Floyd's *The Wall*) the following year, and they married in 1981, eventually raising three children. She expanded her career into writing (with more than fifteen books to her credit) and the domestic arts; in addition to her other doings, Ms. Asher is the proprietor of a successful cakes shop and baking supply house in London.

Maureen Cox Starkey

The teenaged Mo was an apprentice hairdresser in Liverpool who, for a while, dated Rory Storm's guitar player, Johnny Guitar. That all went out the window, though, when she laid eyes on Ringo in one of his first Cavern performances after joining the Beatles.

Despite being just sixteen and he twenty-two, the young lady (nicknamed "Micky") fell head over heels for the aggressive but sweet drummer. On a dare, she actually stole a kiss from Paul first, but it was the band's newest member who had clearly captured her heart.

Ringo was taken with the pretty, petite brunette as well, and before long they were—like any other down-to-earth Northern couple—feeling domestic and talking about settling down.

But being a Beatle's girlfriend carried a stigma. Other girls, jealous of Mo, would attack her in the streets, scratching her and pulling her hair. She stopped going to the Cavern, and Brian Epstein wanted to keep their relationship a secret anyway—it was bad business for *two* Beatles to be "unavailable."

As the group became more popular, spending less time in Liverpool, it was harder for Maureen to see her "Ritchie." By late 1963, though just seventeen, she was joining Ringo in London for the occasional weekend, and the next year she moved in with him.

The two sweethearts were married on February 11, 1965, at a ceremony attended by two other Beatles, Brian Epstein, and all four of the bride's and groom's parents. Their first child, Zak, was born seven months later.

Ringo and Maureen were clearly the most social of the four Beatle couples. They loved dancing, saw a lot of movies, and hung out with celebrities. They were fans of the swank gambling clubs and fancy restaurants of

London and overseas, and seemed—unlike the other Fabs—to have no problem with being wealthy after struggling so long just to make it.

Despite their free-spending ways, Mo and Rings were also in many ways quite grounded. They had little interest in the 1968 Rishikesh meditation excursion, leaving for Britain after just ten days. Maureen couldn't stand the flies and found the entire India experience rather unsavory.

Following the Beatles' breakup, the couple remained close to the others, especially George and Pattie. This produced a particularly strange episode in the early '70s when George, during a dinner at the Starkeys', professed—out of nowhere—his passion for Maureen. Later on, the two consummated a brief affair, the news of which was hurtful to both Pattie and Ringo.

Oddly, several years earlier, at the group's 1967 Christmas party, Maureen had stood up for George and Pattie, and for Cynthia, ripping John Lennon a new one for drunkenly flirting with Mrs. Harrison.

Ringo had several hit singles in the early and mid-1970s, but was drinking and jet-setting perhaps even more than before. Loving his celebrity, he saw that home life was not for him. After several dalliances, he finally split with Maureen in 1975, although she probably would have stayed married to him forever.

Despite her grief at the marriage's end (which reportedly led her to drive a motorcycle straight into a brick wall), she remained close to Ringo, partially for the sake of their kids but also because she genuinely loved and cared for him.

After nearly fifteen years of single life, Maureen married Isaac Tigrett, a successful restaurateur who helped found the Hard Rock Café chain, in 1989. But they had been married only a short time before she began suffering from leukemia.

The entire Beatles community mourned Maureen's passing in 1994. Ringo, although happily married to Barbara Bach, was with the Starkey children at Maureen's bedside when she passed away.

Paul McCartney wrote "Little Willow" after Mo's death; the lovely elegy appears on his 1997 *Flaming Pie* CD.

Pattie Boyd Harrison

Patricia Anne Boyd was born in England in 1944, but her father's career took the family to Kenya for a portion of Pattie's childhood and teen years. With her long blonde hair and her eyes of blue, Pattie blossomed into quite a head-turner. She parlayed her looks into a modeling career, taking a suggestion from an agent she met while working as a hairdresser.

Astrid Kircherr (left) stayed close with the boys after Stuart's death. Maureen Cox (center) married Ringo in early 1965, while Pattie Boyd tried unsuccessfully to keep her relationship with George secret before the press "outed" her.

Photo by Max Scheler/Redferns

A jet-setter by nineteen, Pattie frequently traveled between New York and Paris for assignments, gaining renown for her work on behalf of '60s fashion maven Mary Quant. Back in England, she landed a gig in a television advert for Smith's Crisps (a brand of potato chip, to you Yanks). She made an impression on the commercial's director, Richard Lester, who then cast her in a small role in *A Hard Day's Night*.

As "Jean" (though her name is never used), she played one of a pair uniformed schoolgirls traveling aboard the train taking the Beatles to London. On the first day of shooting, George and Pattie, to use the cinematic vernacular, "met cute."

Maybe it was familiarity from her crisps ad; maybe it was her acting chops ("Prisoners?" was her sole line). But George was smitten and wasn't shy about telegraphing his intentions: at first subtly, putting seven X's next to his name when he signed an autograph for her, and later with crude directness, by inviting the beauty to his on-set trailer.

Pattie, already engaged (to a fellow portentously named "Eric"), would have none of it. But Beatle charm worked wonders: first telling herself a dinner with George wouldn't hurt, then agreeing to go for a drive, Pattie eventually broke off her engagement and became an "item" with George.

Once their relationship became public, Pattie, like Maureen, found herself the recipient of much abuse from George partisans. Those "horrible little girls," as she called them, would physically attack her in public; when George attempted to cool the situation, fans would gape uncomprehendingly at him before resuming their tactics.

But, as with Jane Asher, it was hard to hate a potential role model. For many, Pattie, with her looks, style, and fashion sense, was the embodiment of the mid-'60s "Swinging London." She capitalized on her notoriety by penning a column for *16* magazine, "Pattie's Letter from London," which offered makeup tips while dispensing a nugget or two about life in the Beatles' inner circle.

Her place in the rock firmament was solidified in January 1966, when she and George wed. Paul was the only Beatle in attendance and Brian Epstein the best man. Though that year was his last on the road, George replaced his time on tour with long stretches in the studio. His demand that Pattie give up her career while accepting his long absences made him, by definition, a "Northern" husband to the core.

George's mandate that she also refrain from charitable work (since she was being "used" by people for her Beatle connection) was a harder pill to swallow. His virtual ban on a life outside their home seemed excessive, especially in light of his future altruism, but Pattie accepted the boundaries with good grace.

Despite these restrictions, Pattie managed to exert a powerful influence on George, and by extension, Western culture. In late 1966, the couple took a trip to India, ostensibly to further Harrison's sitar studies under Ravi Shankar. The sojourn also proved a catalyst for Pattie's growing interest in Indian spiritualism and Transcendental Meditation, which George eagerly embraced.

Despite this solidarity, the couple slowly began drifting apart. Having weathered the TM experience, acid trips, Pattie's predilection for the night-life (which Tony Bramwell asserts occasionally reduced George to tears), Rishikesh, a drug bust, and the eventual dissolution of the Beatles, Pattie's infertility sparked an unspoken but serious breach.

Furthermore, all Hare Krishna hoopla notwithstanding, George's serial infidelities rivaled Paul's. (Conversely, despite her taste for clubbing and her status as the object of many a rocker's lust—including John Lennon's—Pattie remained unwaveringly loyal.) Apparent devotion (as displayed in

"Something"—both the song and the video) aside, the reality was somewhat different.

In a desperate effort to spark some jealousy in her increasingly disinterested husband, Pattie flirted openly with George's friend Eric Clapton. The ploy backfired when George ignored the situation and Eric fell for her—hard. Pattie's sense of loyalty made her impervious to Clapton's entreaties, and the rejection is believed to have hastened his self-destructive plunge into heroin addiction.

George and Pattie's marriage ran on for a few more troubled years before the two finally called it quits in 1974. In 1979, Clapton and Pattie finally married, hosting a wedding reception that featured musical entertainment by Paul, Ringo, and George. The former couple remained friends, with George and Eric enjoying a singular connection as "husbands-in-law."

Yoko Ono Lennon

The circumstances of Yoko Ono's life, from her very infancy, ensured that she would never be a "normal" Japanese woman, or even a normal émigré.

Two weeks before her birth in Japan in 1933, her father—a powerful banker—was transferred to San Francisco. Yoko was soon brought to America, with the rest of the family, but returned to Tokyo at age four. Then, in 1940, she was moved again, this time to New York City, returning to Japan the next year.

Yoko was just twelve years old when she had to flee Tokyo during the bombings at the close of World War II. She and her family, formerly comfortable, were reduced to begging. It was at this time, she would later say, that she realized she was an outsider, and always would be, and that she would require tremendous strength to survive.

Following the war, she returned to Tokyo, where she graduated with a focus in philosophy from a private university. But in 1951, she moved back to New York, where her family again had settled, and enrolled at bohemian Sarah Lawrence College.

Carrying through her education to its natural conclusion, the young student began frequenting art happenings in New York City. By the mid-1950s, a strong avant-garde scene was developing, one that in its response—mocking, nonsensical, satirical, and strongly opposed to fusty convention—to World War II and 1950s America, mirrored in some ways the Dadaist response to World War I.

Yoko felt comfortable in this self-defined world, working in painting, film, photography, performance art, writing, music, and, most famously,

YOKO ONO
GRAPEFRUIT
Introductory drawings by John Lennon

It's revelatory to most fans that Yoko Ono had an artistic life well before meeting John Lennon. This book of "instructions," originally published in 1964, inspired no small part of the song "Imagine" years later.

installations, in which she would arrange her work in a particular setting. She was a well-known artist, especially in New York, by the early 1960s.

Her personal life was somewhat unfocused. An early marriage to Japanese composer Toshi Ichiyanagi ended in divorce, and a seven-year relationship with American artist Tony Cox (which produced a daughter, Kyoko) was riddled with violence, separation, and other drama by the time it ended in the mid-1960s.

How or why she decided to pursue John Lennon is something of a mystery, and one that gives Yoko-bashers plenty of fodder. She later claimed not to have known who the Beatles were when she met Lennon, a spurious claim refuted even by many of her friends. (Word is that *Paul*, a denizen of London's underground art scene, was her first mark, but things clicked with John first.)

Lennon first became aware of the artist when he visited an Ono exhibit in London on November 9, 1966. The humorous, conceptual quality of her work impressed him, but Ono might have become simply a forgotten infatuation had she not pursued him vigorously for more than a year.

She sent him letters and came to his home and business meetings to see him. She invited him to gallery openings and events. When the Beatles went to India, she wrote John long letters, oblivious to the fact that he was married with a child. (Such petty distinctions had never bothered Yoko in *her* domestic situations.)

Finally, convinced that Yoko was someone he could truly communicate with on an artistic and personal level, Lennon put things in motion. With Cynthia out of town in early 1968, he invited Yoko around to Kenwood for some recording, some acid, and, finally, a consummation of their affair.

When their relationship became known, the roof fell in on Lennon. Critics lashed out at him and his new girlfriend.

First, Lennon was divorcing his wife and leaving his child, bad business for any pop idol. Worse, it was in favor of a Japanese woman, a fact that would now seem a ridiculous reason for resentment. But in the late 1960s, with World War II just twenty-five years in the rearview mirror, many Westerners could not stomach anything reminding them of Japan.

In addition, Yoko Ono was anathema to many men (and, to be fair, women) because, despite her diminutive size, she didn't take crap from anyone. She was blessed with artistic talent, ambition, and a boundless drive to succeed on her own terms.

By her own admission, she had always seen men as "assistants" who knew "where the door was," but Ono fell for Lennon in a way she hadn't anticipated. And John was besotted with her (or, as Yoko's detractors would say, *addicted to* her.)

But the things that made John love Yoko—an unrelenting artistic spirit, a lack of interest in small talk, an assumption that she simply *belonged*—hardly endeared her to the rest of the Beatles, and most of their staff and colleagues, when she happened on the scene. Unlike other Beatle wives and lady friends, Ono was everywhere.

And she *didn't* belong, not in business meetings, where it had usually been just the four Beatles and an advisor or two, and certainly not in the recording studio. Yoko Ono had as much business telling Paul McCartney how to play bass guitar as Paul would have had advising Yoko on her next gallery show.

The fact that Ono simply acted as if she had business in the Beatles' orbit just made the situation more fractious, and seeing his mates struggle with this often proved amusing to a drugged-out, apathetic Lennon.

Lennon's insistence that things were *different*, that Yoko wasn't just a girlfriend, but simply *had* to be there, was breathtaking in its arrogance and shortsightedness, but it was true: things were different now. And as much as anything else, Lennon's habit of breaking old things for new ones led to the final dissolution of the Beatles.

Yoko Ono, in her new role as Lennon's woman, also began bossing around the folks at Apple. And, oddly enough, Lennon not only didn't stop it, but wondered aloud why everyone didn't love Yoko as much as he did.

Yoko and John lived through—*enjoyed* perhaps not being the right word—an eventful 1969, kicking heroin, getting on it again, kicking it again, traveling the world, creating the Plastic Ono Band, chasing Tony Cox (who had absconded with Kyoko), holding their famous "Bed-Ins," and spreading the word about peace.

The last is certainly one of Lennon and Ono's greatest achievements; they helped usher in an age in which popular entertainers could try to effect social change through their position. This phenomenon has its detractors, but it's hard to argue with peace activism, or to decry the money that has been raised for so many good causes in Yoko and John's wake.

To this day, many Beatles fans hold intense opinions about Yoko, either admiring her art, her pluck, and the fact that John loved her—or detesting her brusque nature and backstage machinations.

But just as many fans see that the truth about Yoko Ono is complex and impossible to explain in just a few sentences. Not all of her many facets are attractive, nor are all of them evil. In that regard, she's just like the rest of us, only she happens to be the widow of John Lennon.

Francie Schwartz

Despite not being a rock music fan—she actually preferred show tunes—the twenty-three-year-old Schwartz, having read about the Beatles' new company, traveled to London in 1968 from her native California to try and sell her screenplay to Apple.

Instead, she ended up personally meeting Paul, who soon invited her to move into his swanky home—this despite her professed interest in John Lennon.

(Many, including Peter Brown, have asserted that Jane's breakup with Paul occurred when she walked in on him and Francie, but this has not been confirmed. It could have been *anyone* that Jane walked in on Paul with.)

For Paul, Francie was a first—a real, live *American* girlfriend. Sure, Paul would bed anything carrying a handbag, and he'd already met Linda Eastman, but this was his first serious relationship following Jane—complete with the ups and downs experienced by any couple.

The ups? For Francie, hanging around with the Beatles, and Yoko, whom she adored, was a huge benefit. She worked at Apple with Derek Taylor, and also spent time in the recording studio during the stimulating but often difficult "White Album" sessions. She has great memories of being around while Paul wrote "Hey Jude" (which he told her at the time was "for her").

The downs? Dealing with Beatle tensions and stress. One day, for example, Paul was working on a difficult bass part when Schwartz popped her head into the studio. Angered and thrown off his concentration, Paul yelled, "Juden Raus!" ("Jews, out!" in German). Schwartz was deeply hurt, and Paul ashamed, so much so that the two never discussed the incident.

Eventually, the two parted in late summer 1968, Schwartz leaving London for her parents' home in New Jersey. She reentered the Beatles universe only with the publication of *Body Count*, her 1972 memoir including much Beatle trivia and a sometimes unflattering portrait of McCartney.

Demonized by some group insiders for this apparent lapse in protocol, Schwartz crafted a successful career as a magazine writer, and for several years has been attempting to find the right publisher for her new book, *The War on Sex, Drugs, and Rock and Roll*.

Linda Eastman McCartney

Born in New York City and raised in wealthy Scarsdale, Linda Eastman came of age during the fabulous '50s. Several months older than Paul McCartney, and an ocean away, she was drawn to the same music he was—R&B and rock and roll.

Her family, contrary to rumor, was not connected to the Eastman-Kodak photography business. Her dad was a lawyer, her mom an heiress who died in a 1962 plane accident.

Linda attended the University of Arizona, during which time she married, had a daughter (Heather), and got a divorce. Back to the single life, but with a child, she decided to take up photography, as more of a hobby than anything, since she had some family money to live on. Eventually she moved back to New York City in 1965.

Not knowing what else to do, she took an administrative job at *Town and Country* magazine. One day in spring 1966, while sorting the mail, she came across an announcement that the Rolling Stones would be holding a media event on June 24 in New York City on a private yacht.

Linda pocketed the invite, skipped work on the day in question, and brought her camera to the West 79th Street Marina.

Being an assertive, leggy blonde, Linda had an advantage over the rest of the press, and as a result was the only photog allowed on board. Taking full advantage of the situation, she snapped (and later sold) several good pictures of the Stones that day, and soon left the desk job for her own photography career.

Following her heart, she began hanging out with musicians on both coasts (and, according to rumors, becoming intimate with many of them). She was a nature lover and a sensitive photographer, and with rock and roll becoming a more accepted form of entertainment, there were plenty of opportunities for her to sell her work to magazines and record companies.

In spring 1967, she scored an advance to provide photographs for a rock-and-roll book and flew to London. At this point, Linda, without much money, stayed with friends, journeying through England on her assignment and photographing groups like the Animals, Traffic, and the Kinks.

The Lovely Linda first met Macca that May 15 at London's Bag O'Nails club, where both were watching a gig starring British R&B singer/keyboardist Georgie Fame. Paul introduced himself to Linda and invited her to accompany him and some friends for the rest of the evening. She accepted.

Four days later, the two ran into each other again at the *Sgt. Pepper's* press launch, and spent plenty of time chin-wagging, but Linda returned home to New York, and Heather, shortly afterward.

While Paul went back to trying to salvage his relationship with Jane Asher, Linda continued her life as a photographer in New York City. But the two met again on May 14, 1968, during John and Paul's trip to the Big Apple to launch Apple Records, and again on a sun-splashed June 20 in Los Angeles.

Before this last encounter, it had not been clear to either of them that this was anything more than a "let's get together when I'm in town" thing. When Linda met Paul the previous year, she most likely knew of his flirtatious ways; he was, after all, still living with Jane when he picked her up. (Ironically, as with Francie Schwartz, *John* was the one whom Linda told friends "excited" her, at least initially.)

Linda was no babe in the woods, and perhaps that's what Paul treasured about her. She was just as hip as he was, perhaps more so; she was grounded and mellow, cared about family, and, like Paul, apparently found little more thrilling than hanging out, listening to music, and smoking a great big joint. (In fact, she ran into legal problems due to pot more than once.)

Paul enjoyed Linda's bohemian but unpretentious life, spending a good deal of time in New York with her over the next several years.

In fall 1968, once his relationship with Francie Schwartz ended, Paul, realizing what he needed, invited Linda to London. The two were never apart again; Linda moved into Paul's home almost immediately. Several weeks later, the couple returned to New York to see five-year-old Heather, and the three became an instant family.

In late October 1968, Paul, Linda, and Heather moved to London, and eventually to Paul's farm in Scotland. Linda and Paul married in London on March 12, 1969. At the time, Linda was pregnant with Mary, their first child together.

The lengthy separations during Heather's first few years led Linda to realize that the thing she really wanted was a family, one that would stay together at all times. Eventually she and Paul raised four children; during the 1970s, following the Beatles' breakup, she traveled with Paul, playing keyboards in Wings and watching the kids.

While Linda took a lot of stick for not being a "professional" musician, Wings existed in part because she and Paul just wanted to be together—sort of like John and Yoko, but without the sandpaper edges. The occasionally anodyne, middle-class persona exuded by Paul and Linda sickened some people, but in the end, their very functionality, and that of their children, is a fitting tribute.

After expanding her career past photography and music to include animal rights activism and introducing a series of vegetarian frozen entrées, Linda passed away on April 17, 1998, after a long battle with cancer. Since Paul was knighted in 1997 by Queen Elizabeth, Linda died as a Lady.

All the Children Sing

Some Beatles offspring have been thrust into the limelight; some have chased it. Others have stayed as far as possible from the celebrity whirl. Leaving out any possible out-of-wedlock kids—which would be another kind of story altogether—here are brief sketches of each of the Beatles' ten children, whose births have, amazingly, spanned forty years.

Even in the lives of children, and even in the old days, you can find spin; concerns of perceived impropriety caused the Beatles camp to alter the birthdates of Julian Lennon and Zak Starkey so that nobody would realize the babies had been conceived before their parents were married. Zak was actually reported to have been born prematurely, although this wasn't so. Such were the social mores of the recent past.

John Charles Julian Lennon (Born April 8, 1963)

In the early 1960s in Britain, as well as in most of the rest of the world, if a woman became pregnant, she and the man responsible—assuming they were both single—were expected to marry in order to give the baby a stable home.

Unfortunately, Julian Lennon's world was anything but stable. John Lennon, who dutifully married Cynthia Powell on August 23, 1962, was not marriage material at this point. Indeed, he never settled comfortably into his relationship with Cynthia.

An admittedly less complex and not intellectually driven individual, Cynthia simply wanted to provide a good upbringing for Julian; John was busy being a young rock and roller, with all the drink, girls, and—later—drugs that such an occupation promised.

After spending Julian's first year in a cruddy Liverpool flat while John gallivanted about, Cynthia and her son moved with John to a London apartment, then to a mansion in suburban Weybridge, where they remained until the marriage dissolved in 1968.

Julian, who was on the bus in *Magical Mystery Tour* and triggered Paul's inspiration for "Hey Jude," was the first Beatle baby. But when John Lennon went off with Yoko Ono, Julian lost his dad and, understandably, grew up with a lot of resentment.

In the early 1980s, Julian became a singing star in his own right with a catchy if slickly produced debut album, *Valotte*, which featured three hit singles and bore more than a little resemblance to his father's band's work. The hits stopped coming soon enough, however, and the novelty of John Lennon's son as rock star wore as thin as his singing voice. Though gifted with name recognition and boundless public goodwill, the lack of a solid set of songs made him just another struggling musician.

Julian Lennon's 1984 debut single eerily, if superficially, evoked his father's sound. The remainder of *Valotte*'s bouncy pop more closely resembled Paul's work.

Since that time Julian has continued to ply his trade sporadically, but an unfortunate tendency to spew bitterness at every opportunity has marred his public image. It is easy to feel empathy for the deprivation he suffered in childhood thanks to his father's less-than-stellar parenting skills, but subsequent claims of financial double-dealing at the hands of his stepmother and the continued demonization of his dad at every opportunity (including on the twentieth anniversary of John's murder) have done little to elicit either sympathy or record sales.

Zak Starkey (Born September 13, 1965)

Ringo gave his firstborn son a rather unusual name, one that reminded him of the independent cowboys of the Old West. A lot of fans thought the name was horrid, but Ringo was unmoved.

Zak grew up in a fairly normal household, considering his father's fame, with mom Maureen providing a steadying influence. Ringo, an only child, had always wanted kids, and Zak was followed in the next five years by Jason and Lee. The Starkeys divorced in 1975, however, making Zak another Beatle baby from a broken home.

Zak Starkey's powerful, creative drumming has placed the low-key percussionist's services in high demand, despite his father's wishes that he had followed another career path.   *Photo by Bob King/Redferns.*

While Ringo said he never wanted his son to follow in his professional footsteps, the youngster loved music, particularly "Back in the U.S.S.R."—which, since Paul had contributed most of the drums on the song, may have caused Richard Starkey, M.B.E., some consternation—and eventually followed his father into rock and roll.

During the mid-1970s, Ringo was in full party mode, and not a particularly attentive father. Keith Moon—*Keith Moon*, for heaven's sake—helped fill the void, taking Zak under his wing and giving him at least one full drum kit. Later in his musical career, Zak Starkey would fill the Who's drum chair, made vacant in 1978 by Moon's untimely passing.

Zak was never interested in school, instead making a living playing rock music from his late teens onward; he drummed with Icicle Works and the Spencer Davis Group before permanently joining the Who.

A 1985 marriage soon produced a son, making Ringo the first Beatle grandfather. A longtime drinker, Zak gave up alcohol for good in the 1990s and has expanded his reach to play with the Lightning Seeds, Mike Scott, and even Oasis when not busy with the 'oo.

He donated bone marrow in 1994 in an attempt to save his mother's life, but Maureen passed away from leukemia that December.

Jason Starkey (Born August 19, 1967)

At the height of the summer of love, Maureen gave birth to Starkey #2. Jason grew up two years younger than Zak, but apparently far less ambitious.

While Jason is also a drummer, he has not enjoyed the success of his brother. Jason gave his first public performance in June 1987 at a pub in London as part of a pick-up six-piece known as Musty Jack Sponge and the Exploding Nudists. (Yes, really.) Brother Zak played guitar in the ensemble, and Ringo was said to have turned down an invitation to a twentieth-anniversary *Sgt. Pepper* celebration in order to see his sons jam instead.

Jason also backed Ringo in a 2002 appearance in Monte Carlo at a benefit for the Princess Grace Foundation, but his other musical activities—besides some work at Apple—have apparently escaped public notice.

Mary McCartney (Born August 28, 1969)

Conceived before Paul and Linda were married (March 12, 1969), Mary is the baby pictured inside Paul's jacket on the cover of 1970's *McCartney* album.

Mary already had a stepsister, Heather, born to Linda in 1962 from her first marriage to John See. Both children, along with baby Stella, were raised on the road, touring with Wings beginning in 1972. The McCartneys, rejecting the rules of most rock-and-roll stars, wanted their family to be together as much as possible.

Following her mother's artistic path, Mary chose a career in photography. She took, in 1998, the last photographs of Linda, and eventually worked as a photo editor in the publishing industry as well as specializing in portraits and fashion work (at times collaborating with her designer sister Stella).

Mary wed TV producer Alistair Donald in 1998 and has four children. She produced the documentary *Wingspan*, about Paul and Linda's band, and like her parents is an avowed vegetarian and animal rights advocate. In 2000, she was the official photographer for Madonna and Guy Ritchie's wedding.

Lee Parkin Starkey (Born November 17, 1970)

Maureen and Ringo's only daughter, Lee was five years old when her parents split up. Like many kids from broken homes, she turned to punk and goth to get her through the teenage years. During the 1980s and '90s, while Ringo toured with his All-Star bands, Lee adopted the rock-and-roll lifestyle in a big way. She was a major party figure and soon began designing clothes.

In 1991, she opened, with a friend, a London fashion boutique called Planet Alice. Lee relocated the shop to Los Angeles later that year, moving into a large house with her brothers, mother, stepfather (Isaac Tigrett, cofounder of the Hard Rock Café and House of Blues chains), and stepsister from Tigrett's earlier marriage.

Lee shuttled between L.A. and London in 1994, taking care of her mother during her final battle with leukemia. Then, in late August 1995, with Ringo's Third All-Star Band (including Zak on drums) near the end of a tour, Lee suffered a collapse in London, the result of a brain tumor. The rest of the tour was called off, and the next month Lee underwent a successful operation in Boston.

In late 2001, around the same time George Harrison suffered what would be his final illness, Lee was found to have another brain tumor, which was also removed. Since then, Lee, who lives in London, has remained a vibrant presence at fashion shows (often hanging with Stella McCartney) and charity events. Like many Beatle kids, she is an animal rights activist.

Stella Nina McCartney (Born September 13, 1971)

Enjoying the crazy lifestyle of her parents' rock band, Stella cottoned on pretty early to high fashion and celebrity. As a teenager she began to make her own clothes and interned with Christian Lacroix. At her 1995 graduation from design school, Stella's outfits were worn by some pretty fair models: Kate Moss, Yasmin LeBon, and Naomi Campbell. Nice to have friends in high places!

Early speculation that Stella's career owed more to celebrity than to talent, however, was disproven when critics and design houses gave solid approval to her work. She has designed clothes for singers and films and seen her product sold in high-end stores like Neiman-Marcus as well as less expensive ones like H&M. She has also entered the fragrance field.

Stella has never been afraid of the limelight. Madonna, a close friend, asked Stella to design the gown for her 2000 wedding to Guy Ritchie. In turn, Maddy (along with Pierce Brosnan, Liv Tyler, and other celebs) showed up for Stella's 2003 wedding to Alasdhair Willis. Their second child is due in 2007.

Outspoken in her anti-hunting and vegetarian views, Stella also caused a bit of a ruckus when she showed up at her father's March 15, 1999, induction as a solo artist into the Rock and Roll Hall of Fame wearing a tight-fitting white T-shirt covered with black letters reading "About Fucking Time!"

Ms. McCartney is also said to have converted Paris Hilton from wearing fur (and to vegetarianism) in 2006 by showing her a particularly shocking film of cruelty against animals.

Sean Taro Ono Lennon (Born October 9, 1975)

John and Yoko had tried for years to have a baby. They followed the diet and lifestyle advice of various doctors, but still couldn't conceive. Yoko began to wonder if she was too old to have a baby. Finally, following John's long "lost weekend," the two conceived in the winter of 1974–75.

Sean was born to a contented and peaceful household. John, basically retired from music, played the role of house husband while Yoko set about managing and developing the family finances. While the role of John as Superdad has certainly been overplayed, he does appear to have devoted a great deal of time and energy to doing correctly for Sean what he hadn't done for Julian.

Following John's murder, Sean came to rely more on his mother. Eventually he grew into his artistic heritage, learning to play a variety of instruments and moving into a professional music career. In 1995, he toured with Yoko in support of her *Rising* album.

His 1998 full-length debut, *Into the Sun*, drew plaudits for its stance: one foot in classic melodic pop, the other firmly entrenched in experimental music. Given his place in the public eye, it was no surprise that he became friendly with famous young singers and actresses such as Yuka Honda, the Beastie Boys, Lindsay Lohan, Lenny Kravitz, and Leelee Sobieski.

Following several remixes and guest appearances (many with hip-hoppers like Dan the Automator, Del Tha Funkee Homosapien, and Money Mark), Lennon went a long time without a record deal. Late in 2006, however, Lennon released a second album, *Friendly Fire*. Here's hoping he gets more ink for music than for his bloodlines.

James Louis McCartney (Born September 12, 1977)

With Wings still together until 1980, James Louis was a traveling baby. After the band's breakup, the McCartneys settled down for several years to give their kids some semblance of a normal life.

The youngest of the three children born to Paul and Linda, James is said to be the most devoted to the family unit—although they all remain close. James introduced his big sister Mary to her future husband, Alistair Donald, and sat right next to his dad at sister Stella's first big solo fashion show in 1999.

In addition to spending some time as a sculptor, James is the only one of the McCartney children to focus on playing music. James made his recorded debut on Paul's lovely "Heaven on a Sunday" (from *Flaming Pie*). While Paul took the acoustic guitar fills, James answered on electric—and did an impressive job. James also cowrote two songs on dad's *Driving Rain* album, but has largely managed to stay out of the limelight.

While he has often sported long, flowing blond hair that clearly comes from Linda's gene pool, James Louis has his dad's coy smile and baby face all the way.

Dhani Harrison (Born August 1, 1978)

George Harrison and Pattie Boyd did not produce a child. The quiet Beatle became a father for the first and only time in summer 1978, when Olivia Arias gave birth to Dhani. One month later, George and Olivia were married.

The young man has always looked like his father, but with his mother's skin tone. Dhani has also been blessed with musical talent. (After all, his name is a combination of two notes of the Indian music scale, "dha" and "ni.") Despite appearing to have inherited the laid-back personality of his parents, he has spoken of "hating" the *Yellow Submarine* film because class-mates deduced his parentage from it and mocked him unmercifully.

One of Dhani's first exposures as a young man to the great big Beatle world came on April 6, 1992, at his dad George's benefit concert for the Natural Law Party (a political arm of Maharishi Mahesh Yogi's organization). Talk about a Beatle family reunion: Zak Starkey played drums during Joe Walsh's opening set, and also on the scene were Julian Lennon, Lee and Jason Starkey, Ringo, Maureen, and Mary McCartney.

Dhani assisted with his father's landmark *All Things Must Pass* reissue in 2000, contributing backing vocals to the till-then unreleased "I Live for You." Following George's death, he worked with Jeff Lynne to prepare the unfinished *Brainwashed* for public consumption.

Appearing onstage in 2002 at the Concert for George, one year after his father's passing, Dhani impressed with his guitar ability. A fan of all sorts of music, pledging love for Leadbelly, Bob Dylan, and Air, he spent much of the decade lying low despite press reports linking him to famous British musicians.

Finally, Dhani and friend Oli Hecks announced that they had formed a group known as thenewno2 (a reference to the 1960s TV show *The Prisoner*). The duo released, in May 2006, a four-song EP that showed classic guitar sounds wedded to modern production and the floating vocals of guest Amanda Butterworth. In addition, a video for their song "Choose What You're Watching" showed a harder side.

Beatrice Milly McCartney (Born October 28, 2003)

The only child from Paul and Heather Mills's marriage, Beatrice is said to be the apple of her father's eye. Paul and Heather appropriately kept Beatrice out of the spotlight during her first couple of years, but that may change given the end of the McCartney-Mills union; one hopes that Beatrice does not become a pawn in a battle of what have become increasingly ugly divorce proceedings.

However Big You Think You Are

Various Celebrity-Beatle Connections

T he Beatles rubbed shoulders with plenty of showbiz celebrities during the swinging '60s and beyond. Most Beatles fans know, for example, that James Taylor released his first album on the group's label, Apple, before he took wing for greater stardom under manager Peter Asher.

The Fab Four hung out with Mike Love of the Beach Boys, actress Mia Farrow, and Donovan at Rishikesh in 1968. And their relationship with Peter Sellers went beyond professional (Ringo worked with him on *The Magic Christian*) and well into the personal. The group actually gave him a copy of rough mixes of *The Beatles* (the "White Album") for his personal perusal. These mixes have since shown up on bootlegs.

In the years after the Beatles' breakup, John, Paul, George, and Ringo hobnobbed with world-famous folks like Muhammad Ali, Jimmy Carter, Dustin Hoffman, Jerry Rubin, Joan Collins, Elvis Costello, Fred Astaire, Jack Ford (son of U.S. President Gerald Ford), Peggy Lee, and Marc Bolan of T.Rex . . . but all of that will have to wait for another book.

Here are ten other celebs that rubbed shoulders (or elbows, but probably nothing else) with various Beatles during the 1960s.

Her Majesty Queen Elizabeth

The idea of a bunch of rock-and-roll scruffs from northern England being in the same room as Queen Elizabeth, let alone meeting her, would have been absolutely unthinkable before the early 1960s. But the impact of Beatlemania, starting in late 1963, set an entirely new paradigm in Great Britain, as it soon would do in the United States.

That fall, the Beatles were asked to perform in the November 4, 1963, Royal Variety Performance, a spectacular featuring nineteen acts drawn from the whole spectrum of entertainment. The event, held at the Prince of Wales Theater in London, was, for many British entertainers, a career valedictory—whereas at this point Ringo, the eldest Beatle, was still just twenty-three.

This was the evening when John Lennon invited those in the cheap seats to clap along, and those in the royal boxes to "rattle your jewelry." Following the show, in which they played seventh but stole the honors, the Beatles met the Queen, as well as the Queen Mother and Princess Margaret, a great fan who later showed up at the premiere of *A Hard Day's Night.*

In June 1965, Prime Minister Harold Wilson announced that the Beatles, because of their status as entertainers and because of the attention, tax income, and tourism dollars they had brought to their homeland, would receive MBEs—awards given to Members of the British Empire. This is the lowest of five official "Orders of the British Empire." The group duly turned up on October 26 of that year at Buckingham Palace to receive their awards and crack a few more jokes with the royals.

When Apple Records first began pressing in 1968, the company boxed up its first four 45s—Mary Hopkin's "Those Were the Days," Jackie Lomax's "Sour Milk Sea," the Black Dyke Mills Band's "Thingumybob," and their very own Apple debut, "Hey Jude"—and sent them to Buckingham Palace.

The Queen, through a spokesman, thanked the Beatles for the gift, but did not issue any comments. It would have been fascinating to hear Elizabeth Windsor's opinion of Jackie Lomax's work.

Finally, John Lennon sent back his MBE to Buckingham Palace in 1969, citing Britain's support for America in the Vietnam War as his primary reason—and, as a joke, complaining that his solo single "Cold Turkey" was dropping in the charts. It's not clear whether the Queen went out and purchased a copy of "Cold Turkey" in response.

Trini Lopez

The Beatles went to Paris in January 1964—just as "I Want to Hold Your Hand" was breaking in America—hoping to turn the French into Beatlemaniacs. But *les Français,* at this moment, weren't having any.

On the other hand, the French *were* crazy about Trini Lopez, a guitarist/vocalist from Dallas who hit it big in 1963, at age twenty-six, singing electrified folk songs. A version of "If I Had a Hammer" hit #1 in twenty-five countries and #3 on the *Billboard* chart. Suave, handsome, a good singer, and showbiz to his polished teeth, Lopez became a favorite of the "old guard," recording for Frank Sinatra's Reprise label and hanging around with Dean Martin.

Lopez, the Beatles, and Sylvie Vartan—a pretty blonde French chanteuse—were the three biggest acts on an eighteen-day concert series held at the Olympia Theatre in Paris. Sometimes the nine acts on the bill played as many as three shows a day. (Ah, the good old days.)

Not surprisingly, the transplanted Texan hadn't heard of the Fabs before going to France, and even after meeting them and playing gigs in Paris, he told the British press he didn't think the Beatles would be as popular in America as the Beach Boys.

To the contrary, the Beatles-led rock renaissance ended the folk revival. Lopez couldn't—or wouldn't, or didn't—adjust to the new sound, although he'd been a rock and roller in the late 1950s. He had just one Top 40 record ("Lemon Tree") after "Hammer." Instead, he went into acting, continued to tour and record, and cultivated himself as an adult entertainer.

Davy Jones

Actually, the Beatles knew *two* Davy Joneses. The first, a black American singer, played some of the same bills as the Beatles in the early 1960s, and in fact was backed for two shows by John, Paul, George, and Pete on December 8, 1961.

Just over two years later, when the Beatles appeared for the first time on CBS-TV's *Ed Sullivan Show* on February 9, 1964, another D. Jones was in the wings. This Davy Jones, a smallish singer/dancer from Manchester who had just turned eighteen, was currently featured as the Artful Dodger in the Broadway production of *Oliver!*

Less than three years later, of course, this Davy Jones would be world famous as the heartthrob of the Monkees. Later, Jones recalled that he and Ringo Starr had exchanged pleasantries at the CBS studios the night of the Sullivan show, Jones jokingly offering to blow Ringo's nose when the Beatles drummer appeared to be suffering from the sniffles. ("I'm closer to it than you are.")

Oddly, Jones and Starr are the two Beatle/Monkee stars that didn't team up when the American band visited England in early 1967.

Years later, in 1975 to be exact, John Lennon would collaborate with a third David Jones, who only found success after renaming himself David Bowie. Lennon cowrote and played guitar on Bowie's #1 hit "Fame."

Phil Collins

Collins, born in 1951, was a typical early '60s British kid who loved music. He had a set of drums, dug the Beatles and R&B, and got on stage anywhere

Had the musical thing not panned out for the diminutive Englishman, Davy Jones's interest in becoming a professional jockey would likely have become a reality.

Photo by David Redfern/Redferns

he could. Like future Monkees singer Davy Jones, Collins played the role of the Artful Dodger in *Oliver!* on local stages.

Collins made his first Beatle connection by attending the Savoy Theatre, London, during the filming of the television special scenes in *A Hard Day's Night*. All of thirteen, Collins appears briefly in crowd reaction scenes during the film; thirty years later, he hosted a documentary, *The Making of* A Hard Day's Night.

During his teenage years, Collins became a mod, following British groups like the Action and the Small Faces as well as his beloved Motown. He also got into progressive rock in the late 1960s, joining a band called Flaming Youth.

In early 1970, with the Beatles still nominally together, Harrison began recording *All Things Must Pass*. One day Collins received a phone call asking if he'd like to come down to Abbey Road to play some percussion on George Harrison's record.

Several hours later, with the session over and his hands bleeding from playing the congas incessantly—parenthetically, he had *never played* congas before—Collins departed the studio. He wasn't even credited on the record, an error that Harrison bemusedly noted, and corrected, in his liner notes to *ATMP*'s deluxe CD reissue in 2001.

Bertrand Russell

Being a Beatle meant increased access to certain strata of the world heretofore unimaginable to a rock and roller. Paul McCartney, impressed with the writing and public speaking of Bertrand Russell, contacted the ninety-two-year-old, Welsh-born philosopher in 1964.

Russell, a mathematician, logician, and political writer and speaker, had recently been spoofed by Dr. Alan Bennett on the *Beyond the Fringe* comedy album, and was already a favorite of liberal intellectuals the world over by virtue of his work for peace and antinuclear causes as well as his nontraditional views on marriage and child-rearing.

Clearly Macca and Russell would not be discussing Euclidean geometry, electric bass playing, mathematical logic, Little Richard, or any of the other things they didn't have in common. Instead, Russell cannily used the opportunity to hip McCartney to an important concern—the Vietnam War. Russell had twice been imprisoned for peace campaigning, the first time in 1916 and the second in 1961, at age eighty-nine!

McCartney would later tell biographer Barry Miles, "I went in and had a little talk with him. Nothing earth-shattering. He just clued me in to the fact that Vietnam was a very bad war, it was an imperialist war and American vested interests were really all it was about."

Hayley Mills

While Paul McCartney had taken on "solo projects" writing songs for Peter and Gordon, many people consider the first true Beatle "solo projects" to have taken place in 1966, following the band's final tour.

During this time, John Lennon went off to Spain and Germany to make the film *How I Won the War*, George Harrison went to India, Ringo Starr planted a garden, and Paul McCartney wrote the score for Hayley Mills's newest film, *The Family Way*.

George Martin contracted an orchestra to perform the music, which was issued on a soundtrack LP (and later reissued on CD, although the sound quality is poor; the tracks were transferred to CD not from master tapes, but from a vinyl album).

Mills, who had become a star via such kid-oriented Disney films as *The Parent Trap* and *Pollyanna*, was nineteen years old in 1966, and her nude scene in *The Family Way* busted her child-star persona wide open. Surprisingly, given Mills's evergreen appeal, the presence of McCartney's music, and the general interest in all things swinging '60s, *The Family Way* still flies under the radar.

Mills and McCartney remained friendly over the years, and worked together in 2000 on an anti-duck-hunting campaign. Both are outspoken vegetarians and animal rights activists.

Michelangelo Antonioni

The director of such classic films as *L'Avventura*, *La Notte*, and *L'Eclisse* focused his lens on 1966 Swinging London for his first English-language film. *Blow-Up*, starring David Hemmings, Sarah Miles, and Vanessa Redgrave, was a spicy (for the time) exposé of a British fashion photographer—the character was based on David Bailey—and his crazy "sex, drugs, and rock and roll" existence. (Also appearing in a memorable cameo were the Yardbirds, featuring both Jeff Beck *and* Jimmy Page.)

When Antonioni spread word among the avant-garde that he was coming to London, Paul McCartney and his avant-garde/rock/art-scene friends, like Barry Miles, Robert Fraser, Christopher Gibbs, Keith Richards and Mick Jagger, Marianne Faithfull, John Dunbar, and the like, got a chance to hang around with the famous director—and show off.

One assumes that few people in the world have had the self-confidence to show home movies to Antonioni. Fortunately for Macca, he had the ego, the talent, and the charm to carry it off. McCartney had brought along some avant-garde silent films to screen for his friends one night at Fraser's place, and when Antonioni happened by, the films *definitely* went on.

McCartney claims that Antonioni enjoyed the films. It's not clear what McCartney thought of *Blow-Up*.

Frank Sinatra

By 1968, Frank Sinatra had recovered from a prolonged career slump and bounced back to the top of the charts with several hit songs that challenged rock music full on ("That's Life," "Strangers in the Night," "Somethin' Stupid") without succumbing to it or pandering. In addition, Sinatra always tried to keep on top of what was going on, even if he didn't like it at first, and was now prepared to allow the Beatles some access into his mental world.

Which is why he accepted a most interesting assignment that year: recording a song as a gift for Maureen (Cox) Starkey's twenty-second birthday, August 4, 1968. The cute Northern lass who had married Ringo in 1965 was a Sinatra fan, a fact well known within the Beatles camp.

Apple Records director Ron Kass phoned songwriter Sammy Cahn in America, who agreed to customize new lyrics for the classic "The Lady Is a Tramp." The new lyrics, of course, had a different message; the new recording was titled "The Lady is a *Champ*."

Sinatra was then enticed to sing the new, topical, humorous lyrics (backed only by a piano, which contradicts some Internet reports; the real story is in Tony Bramwell's *Magical Mystery Tours*). At press time, the file was accessible at music researcher and writer Phil Milstein's Web site: www.philxmilstein.com.

The record was the first ever to be pressed on the band's new Apple label, and only one copy was made. Probably by agreement with Sinatra, the master tapes were destroyed and the whereabouts of the one 45-rpm recording are unknown. Someone, obviously, made a dub, which ended up on Milstein's site.

A few years later, Sinatra would add *Abbey Road*'s "Something" to his stage set, calling it "the greatest love song of the past fifty years" (but mistakenly attributing it to Lennon-McCartney). He also solicited a song from Paul McCartney, but rejected Macca's submission—a tune called "Suicide"—out of hand. In fact, McCartney himself admitted, on reflection, that the song he'd submitted to the Chairman was horrible.

Andy Williams

American singing star Andy Williams, who had his first hit record in 1956 at age twenty-eight, spent the '60s starring in his own television show and releasing albums of middle-of-the-road pop. His occasional forays into chart music strayed far from rock and roll, settling instead into territory like "Music to Watch Girls By"—although he did record McCartney standards "Michelle" and "Yesterday."

Williams may have made a personal Beatle connection through his booking agent for British tours, Nemperor, an outgrowth of NEMS, the Beatles' financiers and management. He is also said to have nearly ended up in the 1969 film adaptation of Terry Southern's *The Magic Christian*, starring Peter Sellers and featuring Starr (in a part written specifically for him).

With all the drugs that went into creating this film, getting Williams involved might have been the most psychedelic thing of all. Too bad it didn't happen. (For more on *The Magic Christian* film, see chapter 12.)

Tommy Smothers

When the Beatles stopped touring, they took to using promotional films to publicize their new singles. In 1968, the Smothers Brothers, on CBS, had one of the hipper television series going, wedding a liberal viewpoint (at least more liberal than usually allowed on network shows) to edgy comedy and a wide spectrum of popular music.

Tommy Smothers lent instrumental support to the Plastic Ono Band's debut single. The supporting cast included acid guru Timothy Leary and his wife, as well as a host of local Krishnas.

As a result, the Beatles were happy to have the clips for their new single ("Hey Jude" and "Revolution") shown on *The Smothers Brothers Comedy Hour*. Each clip was played in its entirety on the shows of October 6 and 13. On November 17, George Harrison himself, resplendent in a frilly orange shirt, showed up to banter with Dickie and Tommy Smothers.

In spring 1969, CBS cancelled the Smothers Brothers. But this didn't end the Beatles' Smothersing. On June 1, 1969, with John Lennon and Yoko Ono in the middle of their "Bed-In" for peace at Montreal's Queen Elizabeth Hotel, Lennon decided to record a new song he had written for the global peace movement.

Lennon had an eight-track tape machine and a few mikes brought over from a local music shop. Tommy Smothers, already on hand visiting Lennon and Ono, accompanied John on acoustic guitar. Others who were there pounded on various objects and sang the chorus of "Give Peace a Chance."

While this decidedly low-fi recording, released on July 7, 1969, only reached #14 on the American charts, it has remained a much-loved and much-sung peace anthem.

Unfortunately, even *that* wasn't the end of Lennon's story with Tommy. During his "lost weekend" in 1974, Lennon and Harry Nilsson, bombed on Brandy Alexanders, heckled Tommy's older, bass-playing brother, Dickie, during the Smothers Brothers' performance at the Troubadour. The two drunken singers were thrown out of the club, but did send flowers as an apology the following day.

It Won't Be the Same Now That I'm with You

Other Acts Produced by George Martin

G iven their phenomenal success, it's easy to overlook the Beatles' incredible luck in blowing their Decca audition. Had they been picked up, they likely would have been assigned to an in-house staffer without a fraction of George Martin's vision.

The alchemy between Liverpool's favorite club band and the head of Parlophone Records could hardly have been improved upon. Under Martin's sympathetic direction, the Beatles' latent abilities were challenged and nurtured in ways that larger labels wouldn't have bothered to attempt. Martin was not only disciplined enough to enhance the commerciality of the band's raw material, but also secure enough to embrace experimentation, remaining flexible and open-minded as the boys' artistry grew by leaps and bounds.

Of course, the Beatles' ability to sustain a pop career for as many years as they did depended upon their own singular gifts and capacity for growth—rare qualities, then as now. But with Martin's involvement, they, and the following musicians, created excellent records that have stood the test of time, no mean feat for a product viewed as disposable.

Matt Monro

Known as "the Singing Bus Driver," the former Terence Parsons worked a variety of jobs while pursuing a singing career at night. Eventually, Munro scored—and passed—an audition at Decca, launching a career as a journeyman singer, recording everything from standards to commercial jingles.

His flexibility would pay dividends when he was enlisted to help out on a George Martin–Peter Sellers project. Though a talented mimic, Sellers was unable to do a creditable Frank Sinatra impersonation. Monro, credited as

"Fred Flange," did the honors for a reading of "You Keep Me Swingin' " on the *Songs for Swingin' Sellers* album in 1960, cementing a formidable a musical partnership between himself and Martin.

"Portrait of My Love," their second single, became a smash, as did the follow-up, "My Kind of Girl." (Ol' Blue Mouth himself recorded the latter tune in 1962, essentially imitating an imitation.)

Perhaps the height of Monro's career was recording the theme to the James Bond film *From Russia with Love*. (This represented the first of three 007 themes that Martin would produce.) Later Monro scored hits with "Born Free" and the Beatles' very own "Yesterday" in 1966.

The Vipers

Though linked with skiffle to the point of being its embodiment, Lonnie Donegan wasn't its only successful practitioner. The Vipers, originally called the Vipers Skiffle Group, were an outfit that for a time gave Donegan a run for his money. But Donegan's prominence, penchant for self-promotion, and habit of recording songs that the Vipers had discovered first eventually led to their eclipse and a change of direction.

Unlike the typical skiffle group of the day, the Vipers, fronted by Wally Whyton, were all accomplished musicians, accompanying themselves on guitar, banjo, stand-up bass, and dobro. This gave them a level of sophistication usually absent in the genre.

Signed to Parlophone in 1956, they scored a Top 10 hit with their second single, "Don't You Rock Me Daddy-O." "Cumberland Gap" followed, but as the Vipers' somewhat slick takes on these songs were superseded by Lonnie Donegan's more rustic versions, the Vipers drifted more into straight rock.

Of particular interest to Fab Four fans are a song and pair of B-sides recorded by the Vipers. "Cumberland Gap" (1957) was backed by the smutty "Maggie Mae," a tune most Beatles fans know from the abbreviated take performed on *Let It Be*. Another commonality was "My Bonnie Lies over the Ocean," recorded that same year, four years before Tony Sheridan's release.

One of their last singles was a rocked-up cover of George Jones's "Why Baby Why" (shortened to "Baby Why"). On the flip was a tune first recorded by Bobby "Jingle Bell Rock" Helms, called "No Other Baby." In the Vipers' hands, the tune was fairly standard late '50s rock and roll. But forty years later, Paul McCartney dusted it off and revived it as a slow dance number for his cathartic '50s homage, *Run Devil Run*, recorded after Linda McCartney's death. (He claimed to have never heard the Vipers' version.)

Rolf Harris

A self-invented instrument called a "wobble board" gave Australian children's television star Rolf Harris a novelty hit record in 1963. The goofy instrument produced "wobbly" sounds not unlike those of a functioning plunger.

Harris's deathless contribution to civilization, a ditty titled "Tie Me Kangaroo Down Sport," typified much of Martin's pre-Beatle work—catchy but out of left field (and marred by the inclusion of a slur derogatory to Aborigines, something Harris apologized for decades later).

Nonetheless, it hit #3 on the American charts, around the same time the Beatles were recording a song they couldn't give away in America: "She Loves You." Harris performed "Tie Me" on BBC radio with the Beatles later that year, customizing the lyrics for the occasion to include lines like "Don't ill-treat me pet dingo, Ringo."

Harris scored another Martin-produced hit, minus the wobble board, with "Sun Arise," a song later recorded by Alice Cooper as the finale to 1971's *Love It to Death* album.

Gerry and the Pacemakers

This Liverpool outfit, led by Gerry Marsden, was probably the Beatles' closest peer during their club days. Gerry and company followed the Fabs to London, becoming Brian Epstein's second signing and working with George Martin at EMI.

They proved their mettle early on by embracing "How Do You Do It," a tune scorned by the Beatles but recognized by Martin as a sure hit. His instincts were proved correct when the Pacemakers took it to the top of the charts in the spring of 1963, beating the Fabs to their first #1 in *Record Retailer.* "From Me to You" dislodged it in May, but GATP also enjoyed their second and third #1s before the Beatles with the Martin-produced "I Like It" and "You'll Never Walk Alone."

The latter tune, taken from Rogers and Hammerstein's musical *Carousel,* became an anthem to the Liverpool Football Club. The ritual of thousands of fans singing the song at Liverpool FC games continues to the present day.

Other hits—which followed as the British Invasion hit America's shores in 1964—included "Don't Let the Sun Catch You Crying" and the foursome's signature song, "Ferry Cross the Mersey."

But by the time the Beatles, evolving creatively, effectively moved the goalposts, many bands, including the Pacemakers, found it harder to keep up. They officially disbanded in 1966.

Billy J. Kramer and the Dakotas

It must be said that the former William Ashton was signed to a contract by Brian Epstein more out of a sense of marketability than in response to any actual talent. With charm, looks, and a passable singing voice, Billy (with the "J" inserted by John Lennon) scored his first hit with a pair of Lennon-McCartney compositions, "Do You Want to Know a Secret" b/w "I'll Be on My Way," in 1963.

Kramer teamed with another Martin-produced act, the Dakotas, for live and recording duties. Hailing from Manchester, the Dakotas had scored an instrumental hit ("The Cruel Sea," later remade by the Ventures as "The Cruel Surf") and continued to maintain a separate identity.

BJK and the Dakotas enjoyed their biggest success as part of the British Invasion. Another Lennon-McCartney tune, "Bad to Me," went to #1 in Britain and the Top 10 in the States. Unlike other Beatle tunes Kramer recorded, this one was written expressly with him in mind.

For a while, Kramer risked being charged with riding the Fabs' coattails, having recorded "I Call Your Name," "I'll Keep You Satisfied," and "From a Window," the latter his own personal favorite.

But he found his biggest hit outside the Lennon-McCartney catalog. "Little Children," a plea to his girl's younger siblings to make themselves scarce so he can have his way with her, reached #7, his highest-charting American release. "Trains and Boats and Planes," released in 1965, was Kramer's last significant single.

Cilla Black

Many people fantasize about becoming rich and famous one day. Some even envision their friends coming along for the ride. Whatever the Beatles' dreams were back in the Cavern days, few could have predicted that the girl who checked coats and sat in with them occasionally would one day also become a showbiz institution.

But Cilla Black did exactly that, abetted by Brian Epstein's astute guidance and George Martin's unerring musical instincts. Recognizing that for all her brassy bravado, she was at heart a pop singer specializing in torchy ballads, Martin chose her material accordingly.

Her first single was a reading of a Lennon-McCartney tune performed at their Decca audition, "Love of the Loved." Surprisingly, it barely squeaked into the Top 40 in England, but the follow-up, Bacharach-David's "Anyone Who Had a Heart," topped the U.K. chart.

Thus the formula was set: Cilla and Martin alternated between Beatles songs and tunes from the Bacharach-David catalog. Her covers of McCartney's "It's for You" and "Step Inside Love" hit the charts during the Beatle years, while "Alfie," "What the World Needs Now," and "Make It Easy on Yourself" competed in Britain with Dionne Warwick's mellower takes. (Bacharach himself, showing where his loyalty lay, called Cilla's voice, not inaccurately, "strident.")

Cilla's only American success came from neither songwriting team. An Italian song called "Il Mio Mondo" (better known as "You're My World") gave Cilla her only stateside hit, reaching #26 in 1964.

Cilla's girl-next-door persona and nonthreatening charm endeared her to the Brits in a way that eluded the American public. A musical-comedy series, *Cilla*, began airing in 1968 on BBC television, with Ringo Starr as her first guest. In one form or another, Cilla Black has been on English TV ever since.

Shirley Bassey

Born in Wales, this big-voiced alto went professional in 1953 at the age of sixteen, touring with bandleader Jack Hylton. She began recording solo in 1957, issuing a string of successful hit singles including "The Banana Boat Song."

Not until 1964—George Martin's banner year—did Ms. Bassey make a dent in America. That fall, her incomparable reading of the title theme to *Goldfinger* made her a household name (while also demonstrating George's knack for producing 007 music). As a team, the two also scored with "I (Who Have Nothing)."

It is interesting to note the versatility Martin showed, as well as the success he enjoyed, all over the musical map. Though enjoying his primary success with the Beatles, his own career was certainly rolling along nicely.

Though recorded without Martin's involvement, Bassey's 1970 take on "Something" charted higher in Britain than the original. She would go on to record two more James Bond themes: "Diamonds Are Forever" in 1971 and the forgettable "Moonraker" in 1979.

The Action

This well-regarded outfit was that rarest of things: a George Martin-produced recording act that failed to score a chart hit. Formed in 1963 as the Boys, this standard-issue beat group from Kentish Town had by 1965 gone completely mod, changing its name in the process.

Subsisting on covers of American R&B and soul, the Action built a solid following among mods, third only behind the Who and the Small Faces in popularity. When George Martin learned of them, he quickly steered the group to a Parlophone recording contract, though he himself was no longer connected with the company.

Stung by EMI's refusal to offer him a raise in pay after the millions he had helped generate for them, Martin had let his contract lapse, forming Associated Independent Recording (AIR) in August 1965. EMI, in turn, was shocked that the heretofore company man had so audaciously cut his ties. Not wishing to spoil a good thing, they had no choice but to pony up, probably paying Martin more to produce the Beatles as an independent contractor than it would have cost them to give him a simple raise.

In any event, the Action first covered Chris Kenner's "Land of a Thousand Dances." Typifying their approach to other people's material, their cover

Renowned for her worldwide smash hit, "Goldfinger," Shirley Bassey typified the musical diversity of George Martin's productions.   *Photo by EMI Archives/Redferns*

sounded nothing like the original (actually resembling a cross between Cannibal and the Headhunter's version and Wilson Pickett's, both of which were unreleased in England at the time.)

Despite critical accolades and a loyal fan base, the single went nowhere. Martin attempted to sharpen their sound, focusing on lead singer Reg King's brand of blue-eyed soul, dynamic backing vocals, and the chiming twelve-string Rickenbacker of Alan King. Still, subsequent Action singles inexplicably failed to click.

After EMI canceled their debut album in 1967, Reg King quit the group; the remaining Action figures recorded a pair of high-quality but rare albums under the moniker Mighty Baby before calling it a day.

Edwards Hand

As the unity of purpose that had defined the working relationship between the Fabs and their producer began to decay, Martin turned his attentions to other acts. With the Beatles essentially producing themselves for much of the "White Album," Martin, abetted by engineer Geoff Emerick, began making time with a duo sprung from the ashes of the English flower power band Picadilly Line.

Ron Edwards and Roger Hand were a pair of singer/songwriters specializing in breezy, harmony-infused pop. Their solitary Picadilly Line release, *The Huge World of Emily Small*, was a delightful nugget of ever-so-British period psychedelia. But the album was lost within the sea of similar sounds then in vogue. By 1968, Edwards and Hand were ready to leave the Summer of Love behind.

Now recording under their own names, Edwards and Hand began moving toward a more produced, orchestrated sound. Given George Martin's considerable expertise with both classical arrangements and pop productions, his enlistment for their eponymous debut album was a natural fit.

Edwards Hand emerged in early 1969 in America, but sadly was canceled in England due to the collapse of their record company. Evoking Love's *Forever Changes*, but with the addition of Hollies-like harmonies, the album is a lost masterpiece, having never truly found its audience.

A follow-up, *Stranded*, was released in 1970, again with the Martin-Emerick production team at the console. A thematic work culminating with the twelve-minute "Death of a Man" suite, *Stranded* was more in the mold of what became called "progressive" rock. (In fact, John Wetton, later of King Crimson and U.K., made his debut on this record.)

Adding to the inevitable Beatles comparison was the album's cover art: a black-and-white line drawing, courtesy of Klaus Voormann. The unflattering caricature of a pot-bellied Southern policeman was deep-sixed for U.S. release by RCA, which substituted a bizarre red, white, and blue gloved hand graphic.

Though largely unknown to anyone but hardcore English psychedelia aficionados, these two albums may yet be rediscovered through their recent CD reissue.

The George Martin Orchestra

As the Beatles' bitter breakup began in earnest at the close of 1970, John Lennon took a blowtorch to his Fab past in the pages of *Rolling Stone*. In an interview laden with bitter hyperbole, John raked over the coals the very vehicle that had afforded him a platform in the first place.

In particular, he took aim at George Martin for, according to John, believing that he had "made" the Beatles. He asked rhetorically, "What music has George Martin made?" It's a galling statement; not only did Martin's talents help turn John's unrealized inspirations into gold, but John himself had penned the liner notes to the first of three albums' worth of Beatle songs that George Martin had released during the group's lifetime: "Some of the sounds on the album may be new to you (and me), that's 'cause George has a great habit of matching unlikely instruments together (like a Jew's harp and a twelve-stringed finger) but the results are great and I think he should get a raise."

It might have astonished John to know that George Martin's solo career began (under a pseudonym) with an experimental electronic concoction back in 1962, at the same time the Fabs were coming to grips with "Love Me Do." "Time Beat," a collaboration with Italian electronic composer Maddalena Fagandini, was released as a single under the handle "Ray Cathode." Interestingly, the track presaged the Beatles' own forays into tape loops and backward voices that they would claim as their own three years later.

Though he wouldn't revisit *that* idiom again anytime soon, Martin eventually found a new audience for the Beatles' superlative melodies: folks who wouldn't give rock and roll the time of day. Tarted up with strings and brass, the first George Martin Orchestra album, *Off the Beatle Track*, was released in 1964. Using a title he had originally suggested for the Beatles' debut LP, Martin featured instrumental versions of some early Fabs singles and album tracks.

In 1964, the GMO was credited with the instrumental score to *A Hard Day's Night* (and nominated for an Academy Award for best score, losing out to *Mary Poppins*). The American soundtrack to the film, issued by United

Artists, was split between Beatle tracks and GMO instrumentals. Later, an album comprised entirely of Martin's AHDN instrumentals was issued (dubiously titled *By Popular Demand*).

Due to some uncharacteristic friction with the Beatles' film producers, George Martin was not accorded soundtrack duties for their second movie. Instead, honors went to Ken Thorne, who went on to perform similar duties for the Monkees' *Head* and Ringo's *Magic Christian* film.

Unmoved, Martin issued his own *Help!* soundtrack in 1965. To fill an album's worth of songs, his release featured an original track, "Bahama Sound," as well as three Beatles tunes that had yet to be released in America, two under their working titles: "That's a Nice Hat" and "Scrambled Eggs."

Between projects of exclusively Beatle material, the GMO released an album of current pop hits, titled *George Martin Scores*, in 1965. In addition to tunes like "Downtown" and "You've Lost That Lovin' Feelin'," Martin covered three Beatle favorites he'd heretofore overlooked. He followed it up

What might have been: the Action cut a series of fine R&B-flavored tracks under George Martin's supervision, but somehow, stardom eluded the Mod rockers.

Photo by Sylvia Pitcher/Redferns

with *London by George* two years later, featuring all-British material, including "Whiter Shade of Pale" and "I Am the Walrus."

Though he went to the well perhaps one time too many with 1966's *George Martin Instrumentally Salutes the Beatles Girls* (the concept of songs with girl's names in the title apparently wore thin too quickly, forcing him to record "And Your Bird Can Sing" and "Good Day Sunshine"), his best soundtrack work was yet to come.

Comprising the whole of side 2, Martin's score to *Yellow Submarine* was perhaps the GMO's finest half hour. His imaginative orchestration meshed perfectly with the innovative visuals on the big screen, making for pleasurable listening even without the film. Far from filler, Martin's "Pepperland Suite" borrowed from classic and stock cinema motifs to weave a musical tapestry befitting the film it supported. His work garnered him, along with John, Paul, and George, a Grammy nomination for 1969's Best Original Score, but Martin and the band lost out to Martin's old nemesis, Burt Bacharach.

So Let Me Introduce to You

Beatle Protégés at Apple

When the Beatles introduced their Apple Records label in 1968, they saw it as an opportunity not only to market their music in their own way, but also to give a break to singers and bands whom they thought deserved one.

Paul and George were the Fabs most interested in giving new artists that initial push; Ringo was happy to play on anyone's records, but John and Yoko, occupied as they were with their jet-setting peace campaign—and their dalliance with hard drugs—were barely interested in other artists.

The "kingmaking" (or, in some cases, queenmaking) effort at Apple led to several hit records, and, in a few cases, spectacular failures. Despite some big successes, the Beatles turned out to be much better recording artists than entrepreneurs; groups like Grapefruit, the Web, and the Aerovons were left in the dust of corporate mismanagement, broken promises, and failed hopes, while records by established artists Doris Troy, Ronnie Spector, and the Modern Jazz Quartet died on the vine.

Mary Hopkin

A three-time winner on British TV's "Opportunity Knocks," the waiflike seventeen-year-old Welsh chanteuse caught top model Twiggy's eye in early 1968. Twiggy then passed Hopkin's name to Paul McCartney.

Relishing the chance to move into production work, Paul called Hopkin to London for an audition and soon signed her to Apple. McCartney then selected a series of songs for her, choosing to first commit to tape "Those Were the Days," a catchy, minor-key Russian folk melody with English lyrics penned by Gene Raskin.

Apple released "Those Were the Days" along with records by the Iveys, the Black Dyke Mills Band, and Jackie Lomax, as part of a promotional push

Produced by PAUL McCARTNEY

APPLE RECORDS

1806

MARY HOPKIN

GOODBYE

SPARROW

Mary Hopkins' follow-up single to "Those Were the Days" was hardly anything to cry about, though Apple's mismanagement of her career certainly was.

titled "Our First Four." The most successful of the new label's initial releases was Ms. Hopkin's.

Beating Sandie Shaw's competing version up the charts, "Those Were the Days" knocked the Fabs' "Hey Jude" from the top spot on the English charts in early fall 1968 to become Apple's first #1 record. The dramatic production also made #2 on the U.S. charts.

Almost immediately Apple groomed Hopkin for international success, releasing "Those Were the Days" in French, German, Spanish, and Italian with positive results. Hopkin also often sang in her native Welsh.

McCartney also wrote and produced Hopkin's second hit single, "Goodbye," but after this the U.S. hits soon dried up. Hopkin was still successful in the U.K., however, reaching #2 with Britain's 1970 entry in the Eurovision song contest, "Knock, Knock, Who's There," and selling enough albums to make Apple happy.

Some out-and-out rockers, like Mick Jagger, criticized McCartney's willingness to push a seemingly middle-of-the-road singer like Mary Hopkin, but Paul never disguised his desire to appeal to all sections of the music-buying public.

In the early 1970s, management problems, confusion at Apple, and her own lack of clarity about exactly what kind of singer she wanted to be made Mary disenchanted with her career. Following her marriage to producer Tony Visconti in 1971, she dropped out for most of the next few years.

Jackie Lomax

Back in the early 1960s, Lomax played guitar in a Liverpool group called the Undertakers, who dressed in old-timey British undertakers' suits with top hats, boots, and ribbons. The Undertakers didn't make much of a splash, but they were admired by many other musicians for their tight playing and foot-stamping showmanship.

Lomax then went to America and led a group called the Lomax Alliance, which on the recommendation of Brian Epstein recorded for Columbia Records producer John Simon. When this came to nothing, Lomax reemerged on Apple—signed, in fact, before Mary Hopkin—under the auspices of George Harrison.

"Sour Milk Sea," a Harrison track demoed for *The Beatles*, instead became Lomax's first solo single, included in Apple's vaunted "First Four" series. The backing group on the 45 could hardly have been more celebrated, including as it did Harrison, McCartney, Starr, Eric Clapton, and Nicky Hopkins. But despite publicity and some airplay, "Sour Milk Sea" wasn't a hit, either in the U.K. or in the U.S.

Despite the single's failure, Harrison also produced the rest of Lomax's L.A.-recorded first album, *Is This What You Want?* Lomax penned twelve of the songs and played guitar. He was ably assisted by Los Angeles session musicians Hal Blaine, Joe Osborn, and Larry Knechtel of the legendary "Wrecking Crew."

Despite this heavy help, and the record's overall quality, Lomax's album didn't sell. Even a 1969 McCartney-led session, including sidemen Harrison and Billy Preston, of the Coasters' "Thumbin' a Ride," led only to a B-side.

Lomax left Apple in 1970 but to this day continues his career as a singer, guitarist, and recording artist.

The Black Dyke Mills Band

The official music group of John Foster's Black Dyke Mills (a northern England textile mill) has been in existence since 1816 and won several brass band competitions in the 1960s.

Paul McCartney, perhaps in one of his less lucid moments, thought it would be thoroughly appropriate for the world's most famous rock band to have a traditional brass band on its new label, and pushed for a recording of "Yellow Submarine," backed by a TV theme, "Thingumybob."

Despite being released as one of Apple's "First Four," neither side of the record really took off with the British public, and the Black Dyke Mills band returned to the world of brass band competition . . . except that Paul McCartney apparently never forgets. He hired the band to back him on "Love Awake," a cut from his 1979 *Back to the Egg* album.

Badfinger

The Iveys—Pete Ham, Tom Evans, Ron Griffiths, and Mike Gibbins—attracted the attention of Apple through persistence, sending demo reels to Beatles gofer Mal Evans until the right combination impressed Paul McCartney and others in the Fabs' camp.

Following a worldwide hit (everywhere but the U.K.) with the middling string-laden ballad "Maybe Tomorrow," the Iveys changed their name to Badfinger, after declining John Lennon's suggestion of the Prix (pronounced to rhyme with "sticks").

Seeing an opportunity to expand his reach and bring in bucks for his new label, Paul McCartney gave the band a demo of his new song, "Come and Get It," and advised them that if they simply redid his recording, they'd have a hit. The youngsters duly followed Macca's instructions and, with the single also serving as the theme to Ringo's film *The Magic Christian*, "Come and Get It" reached #7 in the American charts and the Top 10 in Britain as well.

From this point, Badfinger became Apple's most consistent seller and a virtual house band, playing on solo projects "It Don't Come Easy," *All Things Must Pass*, and *Imagine*, lending guitars to the Concert for Bangla Desh, and embarking on several successful tours.

Ron Griffiths left the band in fall 1969, to be replaced by Joey Molland, but Badfinger simply got stronger, rolling on with the *No Dice* (produced by

Mal) and *Straight Up* (some of which George Harrison produced) LPs and hit singles "No Matter What," "Day After Day," and "Baby Blue."

All was not well, however, at Apple. Allen Klein's hardball negotiating tactics compelled the band's management to look elsewhere, and Badfinger left even before its *Ass* LP died in the shops. The group went to Warner Brothers, recording two superb LPs (*Wish You Were Here* and *Badfinger*) that, oddly, failed to sell. Ham briefly quit, keyboardist Bob Jackson joined, and then Molland left amid intraband squabbling.

As lawsuits between band, label, and management flew, an increasingly despondent Ham committed suicide in April 1975. Troubled bassist Evans also took his own life in 1983, while Gibbins passed away in 2005.

Crooked management, bad timing, and a change in musical tastes are seen as the main villains in the Badfinger story, but at least all of their original albums—a clear precursor to the power-pop movement—are now available on CD for future generations to enjoy.

White Trash

Tony Meehan, manager of the Scottish group the Pathfinders, somehow got to Paul and George in late 1968 and impressed them with his band's recording of a Carole King song, "Road to Nowhere."

Richard DiLello, Apple's American-born "house hippie" and general gofer, named the hard-rocking new group White Trash. "Road to Nowhere," the band's first single, was the fifth 45 released by Apple. Hopes were high for the rip-roaring quintet.

Unfortunately, when Apple promo man Tony Bramwell took the record around to the BBC, he was informed that the band's name was too offensive for airplay. Not only did Brits chafe at the name, but Americans—especially Southerners—were also unlikely to enjoy the humor in it.

In order to get the record on the radio, then, Apple was forced rename the band Trash, recall copies of the single, and paste new labels atop the old ones, using the amended name.

Controversy aside, "Road to Nowhere" made little noise in either Britain or America, and a proposed album, set for June 1969 release, never made it to the shops. After one more single on Apple, a cover of *Abbey Road*'s "Golden Slumbers" that reached #35 on the British charts, Trash couldn't generate a follow-up, and Apple did not renew its option on the group.

Despite bright beginnings and a world of potential, Trash was soon consigned to rock and roll's circular file.

James Taylor

Boston-born guitarist Taylor joined New York's Flying Machine in 1966. The group made a few recordings, but was not a success. Taylor then went to London and juggled his new solo career as an acoustic troubadour with a growing dependence on heroin.

Peter Asher, still a good friend of McCartney's despite the dissolution of Paul's relationship with his sister Jane, was working at the time for Apple. Asher heard something he liked in Taylor's songs and had the twenty-year-old guitarist signed to the Fabs' new company. Paul produced Taylor's initial, folk-influenced album, *James Taylor*, released in Britain in December 1968 and in America shortly afterward.

Unfortunately, Taylor was in no shape to help promote the album, since he was still strung out. In an attempt to cure his addiction, he returned to America in early 1969, and successfully got the monkey off his back. He then, however, broke both his hands in a motorcycle accident.

When *James Taylor* was received as an unexceptional, but promising, debut, Taylor got impatient for the stardom he thought he deserved. Realizing that his label spent most of its time on the Beatles, he fled to California with Asher—who, since he was working both as an Apple employee and as Taylor's personal manager, could certainly be accused of not working in the company's best interests.

Settling in at the Warner Brothers label, Taylor gained the confidence he needed and hit it big in early 1970 with *Sweet Baby James*. He has since gone on to record a baker's dozen more top-selling, if unexceptional, albums.

Radha Krishna Temple

As a student of the Indian spiritual path, George Harrison learned in the mid-1960s about ISKCON (the International Society for Krishna Consciousness). In 1969, Harrison met Shayamasundara, leader of London's Radha Krishna Temple, and shortly afterward the Temple was signed as an Apple recording group.

Its first single, a chanted/sung version of the Hare Krishna mantra, made the Top 20 in Britain in 1969. Harrison, Paul and Linda McCartney, and Cream drummer Ginger Baker are said to be on the record. A music journalist suggested to one member of the group that their 45 would reach #1 on the charts. "Higher than that," was the famous reply.

A follow-up, "Govinda," was not as successful, reaching #23, but Apple still released the *Radha Krishna Temple* album in March 1970. Harrison sent out a personal message to the media and fans in promotion of the LP, printing the Hare Krishna chant ("Hare Krishna / Hare Krishna / Krishna Krishna / Hare Hare") as well as quoting "Give Peace a Chance" and "All You Need Is Love."

While Apple and the Temple soon parted ways, Harrison continued his association with ISKCON and for the rest of his life remained a devotee of Krishna Consciousness.

Billy Preston

A touring R&B musician since age fifteen, Preston had a long career as a recording artist, including 45s for famous labels Sar and Vee-Jay. In 1969, at age twenty-two, he entered the Beatles' circle when George Harrison asked him to come by Apple and jam with the group during the early days of its "Get Back" multimedia project.

Preston's electric piano flashes led to a co-credit on the "Get Back" 45 from early 1969, and his playing lent energy to often drab and, at times, even hostile Beatles recording and film sessions.

Such a talent could not remain as a sideman for long, and Preston signed with Apple as a recording artist. His first album, *That's the Way God Planned It*, provided the label with a British hit single in the title track. Following another Apple LP, *Encouraging Words*, Preston left for A&M Records and worldwide stardom with hit singles "Outa-Space," "Will It Go Round in Circles," "Space Race," and "Nothing from Nothing."

Preston would also record with Lennon, Starr, and Harrison in their solo work, and had a solo spot at 1971's Concert for Bangla Desh. He was in George's backing band for a 1974 American tour, and played with the Rolling Stones as well.

Years after his deep involvement with the band, Preston penned "You Are So Beautiful" for Joe Cocker, dueted with Syreeta Wright on "With You I'm Born Again," and worked with artists ranging from the Rolling Stones to Neil Diamond.

Remaining in the Beatles' orbit, Billy in the 1980s recorded a tribute to the Fabs, "John, Paul, George, and Ringo," and provided a solid contribution to 2002's Concert for George, a tribute to the recently departed Harrison. When the much-loved Preston himself passed away at age fifty-nine in 2006, it was like losing another Beatle.

Doris Troy

A New York–born respected soul artist most famous for "Just One Look," a Top 10 hit in 1963, Troy released two 45s on Apple in 1970. A mature artist among a roster of mostly kids—she was thirty-two when recruited—she had already been signed for more than six months before her first Apple single came out (an indication of the confused and screwy state of the label).

Despite sensitive production from George Harrison, a huge fan of Troy's, neither "Ain't That Cute" nor "Jacob's Ladder" was a hit. Troy did, however, find a career renaissance after relocating to England. She served as a backup

It's a shame that the thundering gospel-rock of Billy Preston's Apple debut didn't find its place in the commercial marketplace, but live, it remained a concert highlight.

singer on Ringo Starr's *Sentimental Journey* in early 1970, and then famously sang with Pink Floyd, Nick Drake, Harrison, and others.

Her one Apple LP, 1970's *Doris Troy*, was out of print for many years but has been reissued. With a cover fashioning her in an Earth Mother/Nina Simone mode, the album included her two Apple singles as well as songs by Stephen Stills and Joe South, and featured an all-star backing band of Harrison, Starr, Stills, Eric Clapton, and Peter Frampton. Troy passed away in 2004.

Modern Jazz Quartet

After recording more than thirty albums, the classically trained chamber-jazz quartet of pianist John Lewis, vibraphonist Milt Jackson, drummer Percy Heath, and bassist Connie Kay signed with Apple in 1968.

The pairing seems odd; the Fabs had never professed much love for modern jazz, especially if they tried to play it too darned fast. But Apple's Ron Kass, a huge jazz fan, recommended the band, and the label was nothing if not eclectic—recall that early plans called for a spoken-word label with records released weekly, like newspapers—and the MJQ were quite popular in the U.K.

As the only jazz act on the label, the MJQ were treated with almost complete neglect. Their *Under the Jasmin Tree* LP was released in late 1968, but unfortunately for all concerned did not sell; Apple had no experience promoting jazz records, and the rock audience wasn't biting.

A second album, the more experimental *Space*, appeared in 1969, but fared little better on the charts. The MJQ went back to Atlantic Records, home of much of their classic material, for 1971's *Plastic Dreams*.

The Movie's Gonna Make Me a Big Star

Cinematic Fellow Travelers

T he Beatles' first three films (1964's *A Hard Day's Night*, 1965's *Help!*, and *Magical Mystery Tour*, which could only have been made in 1967) featured not only the Fabs, but an assortment of veteran British comic actors hired to lend a familiar air to the proceedings—familiar, at least, to British audiences.

Most Americans would probably not have known any of the excellent actors listed below prior to their involvement in the Beatles' films. In fact, even today, the majority of these actors may be best known in this country expressly for their Beatles connection.

Victor Spinetti

Spinetti has enjoyed a varied career in Britain, occasionally gaining international notice as well.

The Welsh-born actor's involvement with the Beatles apparently began after one or more members of the group saw him in *Oh! What a Lovely War* in 1963. When the Fabs signed up to do their first film, they requested that Spinetti be cast. George Harrison, in particular, was said to be keen on his involvement, apparently because his mum was a big Spinetti fan.

And Spinetti nearly stole *A Hard Day's Night* from the stars, playing a nervous, micromanaging television director based on someone whom both director Dick Lester and writer Alun Owen knew. Already balding at age thirty-one, Spinetti made his TV man jumpy, egocentric, and scared: the visual equivalent of sticking one's finger in an electrical socket.

Given his outstanding job in *AHDN*, Spinetti—who bonded especially with Lennon—was a natural for *Help!* as well, playing the evil mad scientist who, because of lack of funds and lack of help, can't do anything right. Once again, he was spot-on, parodying British intellectual-speak with seeming ease.

Two years later, Lennon asked Victor to play a major role in the Fabs' 1967 TV film *Magical Mystery Tour*; Spinetti could have had his pick of Jolly Jimmy the courier or the slightly barmy coach rider who "*thinks* he's the courier" (later named "Buster Bloodvessel").

Unfortunately, Spinetti was already booked in another stage run of *Oh! What a Lovely War*, and as a result couldn't take on a key part. He did, however, volunteer to lend a hand one afternoon, playing a loony British sergeant and improvising a dialogue with "Major McCartney." The Pythonesque scene was one of the odd film's most enjoyable moments.

Spinetti also cowrote a stage adaptation of John's *In His Own Write* for the National Theater in 1968. The two remained close friends for years afterward, while Victor's brother Henry, a noted session drummer, recorded with George on 1982's *Gone Troppo* release.

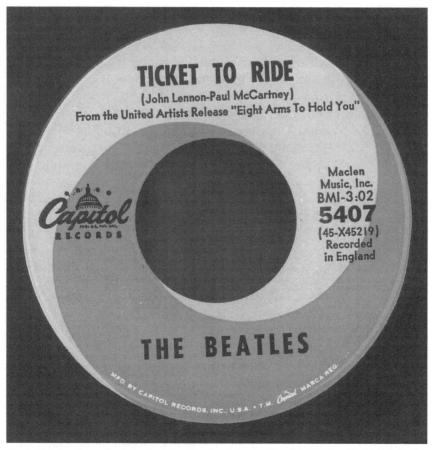

Capitol's penchant for jumping the gun is evidenced by the "Ticket To Ride" single, which attributed the song to a film that was never made.

John Junkin

Veteran comic actor Junkin (who described himself as "the bloke next door") was thirty-four when *A Hard Day's Night* director Dick Lester cast him as the Beatles' put-upon roadie, Shake, a sort of combination of Mal Evans and Neil Aspinall.

Junkin's performance is one of the underrated comic features of the film. His character is sweet and well-intentioned, but at the same time is treated almost as a doormat by both the Beatles and their manager Norm.

A former teacher, Junkin also wrote for British television and cinema, and in 1966 again appeared with Lennon in Lester's *How I Won the War*. He also upped his '60s "hip" quotient with two appearances in *The Avengers*. Following a late-career turn in the popular British program *East Enders*, he passed away at age seventy-six in 2006.

Norman Rossington

Liverpool-born Rossington made his mark as a slapstick actor in the *Carry On* films, a long-running series of clever, raunchy comedies. He also had a long career in television and, later in life, on the stage.

Rossington played Norm, the Beatles' manager, in *A Hard Day's Night*, but is nothing like our image of the refined and polite Brian Epstein; instead, Norm is gruff, dictatorial, fatherly, and unpleasant, whether berating road manager Shake or pushing the Beatles back into their confining little boxes.

Rossington adds wonderful comic tension to the film, with his nervous, moody finger-chewing and brassy standing up to Lennon. But one also can sense Norm's dedication to the boys.

Interestingly, Rossington is the only actor to appear with both the Beatles and Elvis Presley; he has a part in 1967's *Double Trouble*, in which the Pelvis tours England.

Wilfrid Brambell

Born in Dublin in 1912, Brambell was most famous for playing character roles, or rather *one* character role: that of an obstreperous Irish crank. After moving to England in the late 1940s, Brambell—a refined man not at all like most of his characters—settled into a solid British television and film career.

His most famous television role was as Old Steptoe in *Steptoe and Son* (which, many years later, was mined for American TV as *Sanford and Son*), which ran from 1962–74 and sparked two movie spinoffs. Brambell was often on the receiving line of his son's admonishment: "You dirty old man!"

That line made Brambell's role as Paul's grandfather (a "clean old man") in *A Hard Day's Night* that much funnier to the British audiences of the day. Amazingly, Brambell was just fifty-two when he played the part of Paul's grandfather; he easily passed for fifteen to twenty years older.

Perhaps the best-acted scene in the film is Brambell's comic turn in the TV station canteen, in which he tries to convince "poor Ringo" to live his life and not take kidding from the other three Beatles. Not only did Brambell give a fine performance, he also coaxed reactions from Ringo that the young drummer may not have known he possessed.

Leo McKern

Australian-born and possessed of a glass left eye (he lost the eye in an accident as a teenager), the bearish McKern moved to Britain after World War II and began his career on the stage.

He debuted in films by 1952 and by the mid-'60s was a well-known character actor, both on television and in the cinema, despite suffering from stage fright.

The forty-five-year-old McKern was perfect for the splashy *Help!*, playing to perfection the put-upon, moody, and psychopathic temple leader, Clang. Alternately droll, sympathetic, frightening, and just plain mean, Clang may be just a cartoon cutout, but McKern gives him unexpected depth with his ability to pull faces and infuse dialogue with real feeling.

The beloved McKern, excellent as both a comic and a dramatic actor, also played the role of Number Two on three separate episodes of *The Prisoner,* and spent much of his later years as the indefatigable, incorrigible barrister Horace Rumpole on the British TV series *Rumpole of the Bailey.*

Eleanor Bron

As Lieutenant Colonel Ahme in *Help!*, Bron—already a barrier-buster for being the first woman in the prestigious Cambridge Footlights society— played a part not written into any other Beatles film: that of an attractive female lead.

Beginning the film as a baddie, but soon feeling sympathy for poor Ringo and eventually protecting him from the evil Clang and his minions, Ahme dances with Paul and draws jealous looks from George. Bron got along best in real life, however, with John Lennon. (Very well indeed, as rumor has it.)

McCartney, who never forgot a good song source, kept the name "Eleanor" in his head and used it for one of his better-known songs the following year. Later, Paul worked with the Bonzo Dog Doo Dah Band (managed by Eleanor's brother Gerry), recruiting them to appear in *Magical Mystery Tour* and producing their hit "I'm the Urban Spaceman," using the pseudonym Apollo C. Vermouth.

Bron, who was twenty-seven in *Help!* but appeared much younger, has stayed busy on the big and small screens. Some of her movie roles have been closely connected with rock (*Bedazzled*, the Bee Gees' *Cucumber Castle*), and she also appeared in both *Doctor Who* and *Absolutely Fabulous* (as Patsy's mum).

Well known for her sharp wit and intellect, Ms. Bron has also contributed to several TV series as a writer.

Roy Kinnear

First famed for his work on the British TV series *That Was the Week That Was*, Kinnear signed on for *Help!* as Algernon, devoted assistant (and possibly lover?) to Victor Spinetti's mad scientist Dr. Foot.

Algernon is a comic stumblebum with evil undertones ("[Animals] trust me . . . I should have been in vivisection"), although his character is almost impossible to take seriously. Much of his humor in *Help!* is visual, making fun of his portly frame.

Kinnear, like Junkin, also appeared with Lennon in Lester's *How I Won the War* and in episodes of *The Avengers*. During the '70s, he reprised his stock stumbling fool character in films like *The Last Remake of Beau Geste*, *Sherlock Holmes' Smarter Brother*, and—most memorably—*Willie Wonka and the Chocolate Factory*, in which he portrayed Veruca Salt's beleaguered, blustery father.

Late in his career, he made comic appearances in two videos for Mike and the Mechanics songs: "Taken In" and "All I Need Is a Miracle." Unfortunately, in 1988, while filming *Return of the Musketeers* in Spain, Kinnear fell from a horse and bled to death from a broken pelvis. He was fifty-six.

Jeremy Lloyd

Six people appeared in both *A Hard Day's Night* and *Help!* Four of them, of course, were Beatles. The loveable Victor Spinetti was the fifth, and Jeremy Lloyd the sixth.

Actor Roy Kinnear, seen here alongside John in *How I Won the War*, is probably best known to audiences as Veruca Salt's indulgent father in 1972's *Willie Wonka and the Chocolate Factory.*

The tall, thin Lloyd, a onetime suit salesman, had made a mark writing for various British television shows of the late 1950s and early 1960s. Dick Lester hired Lloyd for the dance-club scene in *AHDN*, realizing that pairing him with the shorter Ringo would be quite amusing, especially when the pair began bouncing up and down. Lloyd then had a speaking part in the restaurant scene of *Help!* a year later. ("Rather a jolly place!")

Lloyd increased his Beatles connection with a part in *The Magic Christian*, and also appeared in the swinging London document *Smashing Time.* Lloyd's highest-profile role for American audiences came on NBC-TV's *Laugh-In* during 1969–70. Married for a time to actress Joanna Lumley, later a star of *Absolutely Fabulous*, he also cocreated and wrote two smash hit British series: *Are You Being Served?* and *Allo! Allo!*

American actress Sharon Tate, a friend, invited Lloyd to a gathering at her Hollywood mansion on August 8, 1969. Fortunately for Lloyd, he fell asleep on his couch and missed the party, which ended with Tate and several others being murdered by Charles Manson and his followers.

Ivor Cutler

For many years, Cutler's main gig was teaching drama to schoolchildren; he did this for more than twenty-five years following the end of World War II. A master of puns and jokes and an author of several books, Cutler also did comedy stage shows, appearing regularly as a guest on many BBC radio and television shows by the mid-1960s.

With his conservative dress, odd manner, and absentminded witticisms, Cutler seems an obvious choice as Buster Bloodvessel, the slightly deluded coach rider who ever so badly wants to be the trip's uniformed courier. Cutler only got the part, though, when Victor Spinetti, already booked, had to turn the Beatles down. (Cutler himself invented the name "Buster Bloodvessel" for the character.)

One of the nicer scenes in the film has Cutler, under a magic spell, fall in love with Ringo's large and outspoken Aunt Jessie (played by Jessie Robins). Oddly, BBC censors had problems with Buster's dream-sequence romance with Jessie, even though it was sweet and handled very cleanly. The censors in question almost certainly questioned the scene because they believed that nobody would want to see a fat person in love.

Known from his stage appearances as an accomplished harmonium player, Cutler followed up his *Magical Mystery Tour* gig with a George Martin-produced album, *Ludo*, released in 1968. Credited to the Ivor Cutler Trio, the boogie-woogie set led to his introduction to younger audiences via John Peel's long-running radio show.

Nat Jackley

Long a comic hero of Lennon's, Jackley had fashioned a career in music hall, and was asked to join the *Magical Mystery Tour* as "Happy Nat the Rubber Man."

Unfortunately, the experience turned out badly for all concerned. Jackley, a very traditional, very British performer with a cloth cap, Hitler mustache, and gawky walk, was expecting a real script. His style was in direct clash with the loose, druggy, surrealistic structure of the film, and Jackley resented the process as well as the final product; he famously ran down the TV film in the press.

One of the odder moments in the shooting had Jackley, in a dream sequence, chasing several bikini-clad girls around the Atlantic Hotel pool in Newquay. With temperatures hovering in the forties, the girls were turning bluer with each successive shot. Neither that scene nor one of Jackley chasing girls along a cliffside made the final cut.

The Only Difference Is You're Down There

Ten Acts that Opened for the Beatles

The Beatles as a performing band earned their spurs in the age of the package tour. During these extravaganzas, several big acts would travel cross-country, often sharing the same bus. As a result, John, Paul, George, and Ringo crossed paths with a wide range of popular musicians while traveling across England in the early 1960s.

When the Beatles headlined their own tours in 1964, 1965, and 1966, several support acts were hired to open the shows—at least some of them at the behest of the Beatles themselves. Most of these bands and singers had enjoyed big hits on their own.

The long parade of openers (during the 1966 U.S. tour, for instance, four different acts took the stage before the Beatles) allowed for the sale of more concessions and got the audience good and primed for the stars. But few fans were listening particularly hard.

Helen Shapiro, 1963

In 1961, when she was just fourteen, Ms. Shapiro signed with Columbia EMI in Britain. Her first 45, "Don't Treat Me Like a Child," reached a surprising #3 on the charts, and she enjoyed four more Top 10s through 1962. Fans voted her Britain's outstanding young female singer.

Ms. Shapiro's February 1962 tour featured, as the opener of a six-act bill, a young group from Liverpool called the Beatles. This was the Fabs' first national tour. When they learned they would be meeting and touring with the successful young chanteuse, John and Paul wrote the song "Misery" expressly for her to record.

Interestingly enough, Helen Shapiro hit the *Billboard* Hot 100 in America more than two years before the Beatles did, charting at exactly #100 for one week in December 1961 with "Walkin' Back to Happiness."

Unfortunately, this was Helen's only U.S. chart record, and the 1963–64 British beat boom helped wipe out middle-of-the road pop singers like Ms. Shapiro both in America and back home. She never enjoyed another Top 20 hit after 1962's "Little Miss Lonely."

John and Paul wrote the Beatles' third single, "From Me to You," on the bus traveling to a February 28, 1963, show on the Shapiro tour, and recorded it just a week later.

Touring as a supporting act to the big-voiced Helen Shapiro in 1963 afforded the Beatles their first real glimpse of what the big-time show business was like.

Photo by David Redfern/Redferns

In 1987, after two decades as a jazz singer, Ms. Shapiro committed her life to preaching the word of Christ. Since then she has done outreach and recorded several gospel albums.

Chris Montez, 1963

Nineteen-year-old Los Angeleno Chris Montez enjoyed a surprise smash with the organ-dominated hoofer "Let's Dance" in 1962. Along with fellow American singer Tommy Roe, Montez was booked on a British tour starting March 9, 1963, in London at the Granada Cinema.

Originally the Fab Four were to support the American acts, but "Please Please Me" had become a runaway hit in mid-February, and on the very first night of the tour, the Beatles were elevated to the top spot on the bill.

The tour continued through March 31, with shows nearly every day. John Lennon missed three days' worth of shows due to a cold, forcing the Beatles to perform as a three-piece. Paul McCartney remembered, years later, how hard the Fabs worked during these early years, and the early spring of 1963 proves it; during the Montez/Roe tour, the Beatles, over twenty-three days, played at least twenty-five shows and recorded three BBC radio broadcasts as well.

While the British invasion initially wiped out a lot of American acts, Montez reemerged in 1966 as a somewhat miscast middle-of-the-road singer on A&M Records, placing four records in the Top 40 in less than a year ("Call Me," "The More I See You," "There Will Never Be Another You," and "Time After Time"). While Montez's run of hits ended before he turned twenty-five, he continues to write, record, and tour, and has a place in rock history as one of the first Latino pop stars.

Tommy Roe, 1963

In February 1962, Roe recorded "Sheila," a Buddy Holly pastiche that soon shot to #1 on the American charts. Soon he was a hit in Europe as well. Booked on the early 1963 tour with the Beatles, he must have seen something he liked in England, because he moved there in the mid-'60s and remained until 1969.

Roe hit the U.S. Top 10 with "Everybody" in 1963, then again with "Sweet Pea" and "Hooray for Hazel" in 1966. (His "It's Now Winter's Day," also from '66, is an undiscovered baroque pop gem.) While, for example, Chris Montez's hits ended that year, Roe continued posting Top 40 records until after the Beatles split up, moving with the times and producing some of the more memorable "bubblegum" records of the late '60s and early '70s: "Dizzy," "Jam Up and Jelly Tight," and "Heather Honey."

The last Top 100 record on Roe's résumé? A May 1973 cover of John Lennon's "Working Class Hero."

Del Shannon, 1963

On April 14 and 18, 1963, the Beatles played on the same bill as Del Shannon, the headliner, who at that time had posted several American hits, including 1961's "Runaway" and "Hats Off to Larry," and 1962's "Hey! Little Girl" and "Little Town Flirt." Shannon was even bigger in Europe.

Born Charles Westover, Shannon liked what he heard from the Beatles. In June, he became the first act ever to chart in America with a Lennon-McCartney composition with his recording of "From Me to You," a smash Shannon had heard while in England. The Beatles weren't happy that

Though Del Shannon's take on "From Me to You" was not a hit, his own composition, the exquisite "I Go to Pieces," was successfully covered by Beatle buddies Peter and Gordon in 1965.

Photo by Harry Goodwin/ Redferns

Shannon (whose records they enjoyed) was covering their song, as they initially felt it would hurt their own chances of success.

Shannon—who was moving into record production and label ownership—wrote "I Go to Pieces," a 1965 hit for Beatle friends Peter and Gordon. In early 1967, while touring the U.K., Shannon went full-bore into Britpop, recording an album under the aegis of Rolling Stones Svengali Andrew Loog Oldham (who had previously worked for the Beatles). Despite the high quality of the musicians involved, the album was shelved after two singles failed to make noise in either England or America.

While Shannon remained a respected figure in music, he rarely enjoyed chart success after the mid-'60s. Shockingly, he committed suicide in 1990 despite having just finished recording an album with Jeff Lynne—and being under consideration as a replacement for the late Roy Orbison in the Traveling Wilburys.

Roy Orbison, 1963

The Beatles' third package tour of 1963 began on May 18 and lasted nearly three weeks. Roy Orbison, a genial Texan adored by British audiences, was the purported headliner of the tour, but despite his fame and long string of hit records, he ended up agreeing to close the first half of most shows, while the Beatles—who by this point had posted their first undisputed #1 with "From Me to You"—took over the top spot.

For the Fabs, topping a bill including such a presence as Orbison was mind-blowing—and it became even more so when Orbison showed his respect for them as peers. The Beatles and the Big O became friends, and would catch up when in the same locales. Orbison's "Oh, Pretty Woman" was an American response to the Beatles' aggressive guitar rock, and gave him a deserved #1 hit in 1964.

Personal tragedies and changing tastes laid Orbison low for much of the late 1960s and early 1970s, but he continued to have huge hits around the world. By the mid-1980s, Orbison was on the comeback trail, and, in a thoroughly unlikely setup, joined his producer Jeff Lynne and George Harrison, Bob Dylan, and Tom Petty in the makeshift band the Traveling Wilburys.

The fictional backstory of the group—they were supposedly a set of five brothers with Orbison as "Lefty"—underscored the friendly, unpretentious all-for-one setup of five famous stars happy to share a stage.

The band's artistically and commercially successful LP, *Volume I*, featured memorable Orbison performances on "Last Night," "Handle with Care," "End of the Line," and "Not Alone Any More." Unfortunately, Orbison's

Wilbury work ended there; on December 6, 1988, he passed away at age fifty-two of a heart attack.

The Exciters, 1964

The Beatles' first American tour began August 19, 1964, in San Francisco. On the bill were two acts whose biggest hits were yet to come (the Righteous Brothers and Jackie DeShannon), one whose best days were well behind (Bill Black's Combo), and one with a fairly recent smash (the Exciters).

"Tell Him" climbed to #4 on *Billboard* in early 1963. It was the only Top 40 record for the three-woman, one-man African-American quartet from Jamaica, New York, and a smash in England as well. Despite a lack of consistent chart success, the Exciters, spearheaded by dynamic vocalist Lillian Walker Moss, continued to make excellent R&B, soul, and even psychedelic records through the late 1960s.

As the only black group on the tour, the Exciters attracted some unwelcome attention for their skin color. Moss told *Mojo* magazine in 2004, "At Red Rocks [Colorado] when we came out onto the stage [some fans] booed and yelled, 'Niggers Go Home.' We cried and ran off. It was devastating for us." Implored by fellow group member Herb Rooney to get back onstage, the quartet went back out and won over the crowd.

Moss said, in retrospect, "The Beatles were very music savvy. Their favorite music was soul, R&B, and blues . . . but the fans were wack! They drove us all crazy. We never faced any racism among the people involved with the tour."

Sounds, Incorporated, 1964 and 1965

From October 9 through November 10, 1964, the Beatles undertook a twenty-seven-city tour through England, Scotland, Northern Ireland, and Wales. Motown star Mary Wells was the top support act, and the bill also included Michale Haslam, Tommy Quickly, the Rustiks, and Sounds, Incorporated, a six-piece group from Kent.

The saxophone-dominated Sounds, Incorporated enjoyed two U.K. Top 40 hits in 1964, instrumentals "The Spartan" and "Spanish Harlem." Often booked on British tours backing visiting American acts, the group was respected for its musicianship.

The sextet played in Hamburg, met the Beatles there, and soon signed to Brian Epstein's stable of artists. Sounds, Incorporated backed Cilla Black for many dates and also appeared on 1964's "Around the Beatles" TV special.

Sounds, Incorporated also went on the Beatles' 1965 American jaunt, becoming the only act to tour twice with the Fab Four. The first 1965 U.S. concert took place August 15 at New York's Shea Stadium, in front of a sell-out crowd of around 55,600. It's the largest crowd the Fabs ever played for.

For the opening acts—the King Curtis Combo, Brenda Holloway, and Sounds, Incorporated—it was almost futile to play, since the hyped-up crowd screamed endlessly, anticipating the arrival of the Beatles. The King Curtis Combo and Sounds Incorporated at least had the collective firepower of a group.

These shows didn't end Sounds Incorporated's Beatles connection. The sax section helped provide the beefy riffs to 1967's "Good Morning, Good Morning" (from *Sgt. Pepper*), though the horns, overdubbed well after the basic tracks, are noticeably sharp to the Beatles' vocals and instruments.

By 1967 the group changed its name to "Sounds, Inc.," but had no further British hits, and eventually broke up in 1971.

The Ronettes, 1966

What heterosexual male wasn't enthralled by the Ronettes in 1963? The star singing trio featured three pretty-but-tough females, led by lead singer Veronica "Ronnie" Bennett (who would marry their producer, Phil Spector, in 1968).

Spector's revolutionary "Wall of Sound" production influenced every record maker of the 1960s in some way—he produced "Da Doo Ron Ron," "You've Lost That Lovin' Feelin'," "He's a Rebel," and "Then He Kissed Me," as well as the Ronettes' biggest hits, "Be My Baby" and "Baby, I Love You."

In early 1964, the Ronettes, touring England, were introduced to the Beatles. When the Beatles then visited America in early February, the Ronettes (escorted by DJ Murray "The K" Kaufman) visited their New York hotel suite. Lennon and Ronnie Spector formed a mutual crush.

The two bands would meet again in 1966. Despite not having had a hit for a few years, the Ronettes went on directly before the Beatles during the Fabs' last-ever tour, which began August 12 in Chicago and ended August 29 in San Francisco. For this tour, however, Ronnie Spector was absent, with cousin Elaine stepping in.

Although the British Invasion knocked the Wall of Sound into dust, the Beatles would employ Phil Spector's services in 1970 for *Let It Be*. Spector would also produce much of John Lennon's solo work as well as George Harrison's *All Things Must Pass* triple album. Harrison returned the favor, writing and coproducing (with Phil Spector) "Try Some, Buy Some," a minor hit for Ronnie in 1971.

The Cyrkle, 1966

The Cyrkle was managed by Brian Epstein associate Nat Weiss, and apparently named by John Lennon. When the New York–based quartet scored big early in 1966 with "Red Rubber Ball" and "Turn-Down Day," it made perfect sense to include the band on the Beatles' upcoming American tour.

Going on two spots before the Beatles, and riding high on their hits, the Cyrkle enjoyed the tour, playing in front of huge crowds and playing cards and smoking joints backstage with the Fabs. "They weren't snooty to us at all," said Cyrkle guitarist Don Dannemann.

After Paul McCartney told the Cyrkle that he enjoyed the group's odd version of "Bony Moronie" (a track on their *Red Rubber Ball* LP), the band decided to record "I'm Happy Just to Dance with You" for their second album, *Neon*, which came out in 1967. The Cyrkle's rather nutty take on the 1964 Lennon-McCartney composition included strange key changes and a full-scale sitar solo.

Both Dannemann and Cyrkle bassist/guitarist Tom Dawes became successful jingle writers for the advertising industry. Dawes released, with his wife, a tribute record to John Lennon, "I Did It for You," in 1981.

The Remains, 1966

Playing support for a Beatles show appears to have been a thankless task, but nobody was turning down such opportunities in 1966. The Remains, a four-man R&B/rock act from Boston, are best remembered for their garage nugget "Don't Look Back." While never scoring a major hit, they were a powerful studio and live band with interesting material and a rip-roaring approach. They opened the shows on the tour.

The entourage (the Beatles, the Cyrkle, the Remains, the Ronettes, and Bobby Hebb) performed nineteen shows over an eighteen-day span that included four days off. Remains lead singer and guitarist Barry Tashian enjoyed the company of the Fabs and struck up a friendship with John Lennon. Following the tour, the Beatles went on to the rest of their lives, and Tashian to his. The Remains broke up soon after.

Barry Tashian would eventually write a book about the Beatles' final tour, *Ticket to Ride*, and his admittedly minor role in the Fabs' legacy. He spent ten years in Emmylou Harris's band, recording ten albums with the singer, and has also cut six bluegrass-influenced LPs with his wife, Holly.

I'd Rather See You Dead

A Rogue's Gallery

"You have to be a bastard to make it," John Lennon told *Rolling Stone* in 1970, "and the Beatles were the biggest bastards on earth." What he didn't say was that bastards also *attract* bastards.

Though largely surrounded by folks quite willing to abet their rise to the top, the Beatles also attracted a flock of opportunists who attempted to enrich themselves at the Fabs' expense. Then there were those especially vilifiable souls who, formerly on the inside, turned on their benefactors as soon as it became profitable to do so.

Here are a few of the villains in the Beatles' story, whose crimes range from poor judgment to exploitation to murder.

Bruno Koschmider

When the Beatles first went to Hamburg in 1960, they little realized that they were signing on to work for one of the Reeperbahn's toughest customers. Bruno Koschmider, a disabled former circus clown, had parlayed his show-business leanings into a string of nudie clubs and porn cinemas, but the Kaiserkeller was the jewel of his holdings.

Instead of becoming the star attraction of that venue, the Beatles were unceremoniously shuffled off to the Indra, a rundown strip joint that Koschmider hoped to turn into a second Kaiserkeller. If that wasn't dispiriting enough, the pre-Fabs found themselves lodged in squalor at one of Koschmider's other properties, the Bambi Kino—a derelict porno theater.

Koschmider didn't hold back when it came to working his employees. The Beatles were contracted to perform from 8:30 P.M. to 2:00 A.M. (with three half-hour breaks) seven days a week. Faced with so many hours to fill and their boss's constant exhortations to "mach schau," the boys soon learned to partake of the amphetamines that were freely available.

The Indra experience didn't last long, due to noise complaints from neighbors. Before long, the Beatles' wish to upgrade to the Kaiserkeller was granted. There they alternated sets with fellow Liverpudlians Rory Storm and the Hurricanes. A friendship between the two bands blossomed, as did a friendly competition to see who would be first to destroy Koschmider's jerry-rigged stage during a set. (Rory Storm won.)

These antics did not endear the Beatles to their taskmaster, but what really riled Koschmider was any hint of defection. Tony Sheridan, his biggest draw, had skipped out on him when Peter Eckhorn, Koschmider's nemesis, opened the Top Ten club in October 1960. Adding insult to the injury was Eckhorn's stealing away the Kaiserkeller's bouncer, Horst Fascher, for good measure.

Though contractually forbidden to perform at any venue within forty kilometers of Koschmider's club, the Beatles were happy to join Sheridan at the much more prestigious Top Ten, where customers were likewise flocking. Eckhorn took a shine to the boys; with the promise of decent accommodations, the die was cast for a showdown.

Koschmider, a man whose clientele included a good number of underworld types, was not one to take losing face lying down. For starters, he tipped off authorities to George's underage status, in itself grounds for immediate deportation.

John and Stuart, meanwhile, had moved into their lodgings above the Top Ten almost immediately; Paul and Pete, a little slower on the draw, had to return to the Bambi to retrieve their belongings. As a final act of defiance (and because Koschmider had cut off the power), the two nailed a condom to the cement-block wall and set it aflame. Though they only succeeded in scorching the wall, it was enough to enrage Koschmider, who immediately had them arrested for attempted arson. They, too, were soon deported.

Thus did the first Hamburg excursion end in disgrace. But the Beatles, having tasted the Reeperbahn's earthly pleasures, were anxious to book a return, this time for a residency at the Top Ten. Allan Williams and Peter Eckhorn managed to pull the appropriate strings with the authorities to smooth things over; as for Koschmider, he could only snarl impotently, given Fascher's pledge to protect the boys.

Dick Rowe

Winning the derision of Beatles fans and industry types alike, Decca Records representative Dick Rowe's decision to pass on signing the Fabs has long been pointed to as an example of one of history's great blunders. This presupposes that the band's talents would have been nurtured and allowed to blossom at Decca the way they were under George Martin's tutelage at Parlophone, which is by no means certain.

Rowe was head of A&R at Decca, with a string of successes under his belt. Anthony Newley, Tommy Steele, and Billy Fury established his bona fides as a man who could spot talent (or at least divine what would sell). But his second in command, Mike Smith, actually handled the Beatles from the start.

Decca dispatched Smith to Liverpool to catch the Fabs' act at the Cavern. Impressed by what he saw, he returned to London with a favorable report and scheduled an in-studio tryout on January 1, 1962.

The rest, as they say, is history. Hung over, nervous, and lacking the adrenaline-fueling incentive of an audience, the boys recorded an hour's worth of tunes spread all over the stylistic map. Despite their somewhat lackluster performance, Smith stayed positive, assuring the group and their manager that he would recommend they be signed.

Rowe was in America, being briefed by the parent company that some corporate belt-tightening was in order. Hearing Smith's breathless praise upon his return of both the Beatles and the London-based Brian Poole and the Tremoloes, Rowe informed him that they would only be able to sign one group.

With logistics one concern (since Liverpool was a long train trip away) and the unimpressive recording another, Rowe opted to sign the local boys, the Tremoloes, who in due course would enjoy a string of hit singles.

In fairness to Rowe, it should be noted that he did attempt to check out the Beatles' Cavern act himself in response to Smith's incessant lobbying. Keen on seeing whether something about them had eluded recording tape, Rowe arrived in Liverpool in the pouring rain; daunted by the long queues of fans awaiting entrance to the club, Rowe turned away, washing his hands of the whole matter.

After weeks of pestering from Brian Epstein, Rowe finally copped to his disinterest in the future Fabs. His deathless remark in justifying his decision earned him a place of infamy in the Hall of Bad Decisions: "Guitar groups are on the way out."

Of course, Rowe would rue his assessment within a year, but he was able to temper his self-flagellation after signing the Rolling Stones (recommended by none other than George Harrison), Them, Tom Jones, and Cat Stevens. He did pass, however, on the Yardbirds and Manfred Mann.

As a postscript, here's food for some interesting speculation: Rowe gave American-born producer Shel Talmy (the Kinks, the Who) his first break. Had Decca signed the Fabs and paired them with Talmy, who specialized in capturing a rough-and-ready sound, the world might have experienced a wholly different Beatles, one resembling on vinyl the raucous act that had won over audiences in Hamburg and Liverpool.

Dick James

Born Reginald Leon Vapnick, which doesn't exactly roll off the tongue, James first made a splash in the 1950s, recording the theme songs to *The Buccaneers* and *Robin Hood* (the latter was a hit, produced by George Martin).

As changing tastes curtailed his singing career, James stayed in the business as a music publisher, a lucrative branch of the industry little understood by most songwriters, much to their financial detriment.

Martin introduced James to Brian Epstein. Ardmore and Beechwood, the Beatles' first music publisher, had earned Brian's enmity with their apparent failure to make "Love Me Do" the hit that he felt it deserved to be. Upon hearing an acetate of "Please Please Me," James's eyes lit up with dollar signs. He immediately won Brian over by utilizing his extensive showbiz connections to get the Fabs booked on *Thank Your Lucky Stars*, a hot new televised music showcase.

The delighted Brian readily accepted James's proposal to set up Northern Songs, a company that Lennon and McCartney would partly own. Hardly expecting Brian to agree to his proposition unquestioningly, James had stipulated that he would receive half the royalties generated by Northern Songs, plus another 37% as an administration fee paid to Dick James Music, with 10% of the gross taken off the top for James's "management" fees.

The upshot of this deal was that small-timer James was now suddenly a player. Dick James Music would become the launching pad for Elton John's success in the next decade, but not without everlasting bitterness on the part of John and Paul; the latter complained bitterly that James' empire was "built on our backs."

But for the time being, it was a marriage of convenience between the Northern novices and the man with the connections. Though resentful that James was becoming a multimillionaire off their creativity, the Beatles were hardly in position to go elsewhere.

James earned the group's everlasting rancor in 1969, when business troubles brewed from every corner. As Allen Klein attempted delicate renegotiations with EMI on behalf of three enthusiastic Beatles and a reluctant Paul, Dick James and his partner, Charles Silver, did the unthinkable. Without giving the Beatles so much as a heads-up—much less a chance to buy out his stock—James sold his controlling shares of Northern Songs to entertainment conglomerate ATV, run by British mogul Sir Lew Grade.

Years before, when Brian had floated the trial balloon of selling NEMS to Lord Grade, Lennon had told him in no uncertain terms that if he did, the Beatles would disband and never produce a note of music again. That the Beatles' work was now controlled by the very embodiment of every record company executive who'd slammed the door in their faces on the way up seemed the ultimate betrayal.

Though not exactly friends, the Beatles and James had at least been cordial, acknowledging that they were on the same team. Despite James's attempt to explain his position to the Fabs personally, especially his alarm in recent months at their erratic behavior, this bridge was burned for good. James's action meant that the Beatles' best chance for getting control of their own music had slipped away.

Nicky Byrne

In 1963, rock-and-roll merchandising wasn't the well-defined field that it is nowadays. Bands with younger followings see merchandising as a cash cow, stirred by fans that will indiscriminately buy up anything marked with their idols' faces or names. Given Brian Epstein's shallow understanding of rock and roll in general, it's not surprising that the implications of licensing would elude him completely.

What he *did* know was that, with all he had on his plate, someone else would have to deal with the manufacturers clamoring to generate products with the Beatles' blessings. To that end, Brian charged his attorney, David Jacobs, with finding someone to handle this end of the business on NEMS's behalf. Already overworked and distracted, Jacobs fulfilled the task by assigning merchandising to Nicky Byrne, a hustler he'd met at a cocktail party.

Despite lacking any qualifications or appropriate experience, Byrne schmoozed Jacobs into hiring him as exactly the man for the task. With Brian agreeing to accept whomever Jacobs chose, negotiations over the terms of the deal were a con man's wet dream. Asked what he proposed the Beatles' slice of the merchandising pie to be, Byrne coolly told him, "10%." (The norm was in the neighborhood of 75%.)

Without flinching, Jacobs accepted. Byrne was well aware of the Beatles' obvious inexperience in such matters, but this proof of their solicitor's innocence left him gob-smacked. Later, he would say that he would have given them 90% if they had only asked.

Byrne set up Seltaeb ("Beatles" spelled backwards) as his agency for licensing merchandise throughout North America and everywhere outside of England. With literally hundreds of manufacturers clamoring to issue

Beatle-related novelties, Byrne had pulled off an extraordinary financial fleecing, making himself a millionaire virtually overnight.

Not until personally arriving in America in 1964 did Brian Epstein realize the full extent of the damage his lawyer had wrought. Instead of having Jacobs disbarred, as most would have done, Brian entered into talks with Byrne to settle up for something more realistic and fair. Byrne raised the Fabs' cut to 46% in August 1964, but Brian pressed ahead with litigation, attempting to recover some of the millions lost through sheer ineptitude.

The ongoing lawsuit caused major chains like Woolworth's to back out of retail deals. Worse yet, at the end of the day, a judge ruled in Byrne's favor, adding insult to injury when NEMS was ordered to pay a settlement.

The episode illustrated the costly naïveté typical of Brian Epstein's management. Though he was able to elevate the boys from their club-level status and present and package them in a way that was pleasing to the masses, efforts at maximizing their profitability were nothing less than pitiful.

David A. Noebel

While the Fabs certainly had their critics at the height of Beatlemania, few showed the tenacity and single-minded purpose of ordained minister and college professor David A. Noebel.

The Colorado native penned no fewer than three tomes taking the Beatles to task for their "negative" influence on youth: *Communism, Hypnotism, and the Beatles* (1965), *The Beatles: A Study in Drugs, Sex, and Religion* (1969), and 1982's *The Legacy of John Lennon: Charming or Harming a Generation?* For those seeking insight into the Fabs' unholy alliance with Stalin, these publications are not to be missed.

Among the mass-produced Beatle goodies that the band failed to profit from was this Hohner Harmonica, evoking their early signature sound. John dropped the "gimmick" by the end of 1964.

Noebel's alliterative study of rock and roll, 1966's *Rhythm, Riots, and Revolution*, was a painfully earnest screed that set the tone for his subsequent output. Positing that 1) rock music is a Communist plot to subvert our youth, and 2) the rhythm of the backbeat has the effect of relaxing a listener's inhibitions, Noebel believed that rock made listeners susceptible to their own libidinous drive while increasing receptivity to Communist doctrine.

If Noebel is correct, then this stands as rather an ill-conceived concept; if world domination is the ultimate Communist goal, then why incite aroused listeners to produce more Americans?

Recognizing the Beatles as the most influential rock act in the world, Noebel set his sights directly on them. Describing the Fabs as "four mop-headed anti-Christ Beatniks," Noebel concluded that these Members of the Order of the British Empire were essential cogs in the "Communist master music plan."

Interestingly, Noebel did win mainstream airing for his assertions despite writing decades before the founding of Fox News Channel. He offered *Newsweek* readers a glimpse into the Beatles' marching orders from Moscow: "(The Beatles) were propelling U.S. youngsters into an excited state in which they would do whatever they were told, and that when the revolution was ripe, the Communists would put the Beatles on television on order to hypnotize U.S. youth." (The less said about the Monkees, the better.)

Noebel offered explicit descriptions of the depravity inherent in the rock-and-roll lifestyle, occasionally making the whole business sound unwholesome. But it would be Paul that best rebutted Noebel's thesis: "How could we be Communists? We're the four biggest capitalists in the world!"

Yanni "Magic Alex" Mardas

In 1967, the Beatles made the acquaintance of a television repairman and electronics tinkerer by the name of Yanni Mardas, better known by his middle name, Alex. As the flatmate of Indica Gallery owner John Dunbar, Mardas soon came into close contact with the Fabs.

Mardas had been hired by the Rolling Stones to design a concert lighting rig that would change colors in rhythm with the music. Portentously, it did not work. This didn't faze John Lennon, who became enamored with an "invention" of Alex's called the "nothing box." This was a plastic cube laden with small lights that flashed in a random pattern; the beholder was expected to guess which light would blink next. Lennon was fascinated by the contraption.

Now dubbed "Magic Alex" by John, the young Greek held unfathomable sway with the group, urging them to consider buying a small Greek island as a communal retreat. The Fabs took him seriously enough to visit the island, even purchasing another cluster of islands, which they soon judged uninhabitable and sold at a profit.

The other Beatles ultimately saw through "Magic Alex's" cosmic malarkey but were bemused by his continued hold over John. Mardas spoke of ever more fanciful inventions, such as an invisible force field that would render studio soundproofing around Ringo's drums obsolete. He requisitioned the V-12 engines to John's and George's Rolls-Royces with the intent of building a flying saucer; he also promised to construct an artificial sun to light the nighttime sky over Baker Street in time for the opening of the Apple Boutique on December 8, 1967.

Needless to say, Mardas never realized any of his nonsensical claims. Oddly, this did not undermine his position among the Beatles; rather, they seemed to tolerate his benign company as an amusement.

Magic Alex accompanied the Beatles to Rishikesh, India, in early 1968. There he displayed a talent for intrigue by filling John up with tales of the Maharishi's alleged designs on some of the women of their camp, notably Mia Farrow. Playing Iago to John's Othello, Alex succeeded with his innuendo in getting the two remaining Beatles to pull up stakes.

Back in London, Mardas even injected himself into a domestic crisis. With John's blessing, he had accompanied Cynthia and Jennie Boyd to Greece for a brief holiday in May 1968. Upon their return, Cynthia walked into the Lennon's residence to discover John with Yoko (the latter wearing one of her dressing gowns). In shock, Cynthia fled to the flat shared by Alex and Jennie to collect herself.

Following an unresolved meeting with John to discuss their future, Cynthia flew to Rome for a change of scenery. While she was there, Magic Alex turned up to personally serve divorce papers from John, citing Cynthia for adultery. Further, Alex put her on notice that he was prepared to testify on John's behalf that he had been her partner.

Even after this distasteful episode, Magic Alex managed to captivate the Beatles into naming him head of Apple Electronics. In addition to whatever whimsical electronic gear he fancied he could produce, Mardas had repeatedly bragged he could turn Apple Studios into a state-of-the-art facility.

Suffice it to say that his spectacular failure to produce even a basic, functional setup cost money and time and left both George Martin and the Beatles disgusted. Not long afterward, Allen Klein gave him his walking papers; his subsequent whereabouts remain a mystery.

Charles Manson

Though not personally connected to the Beatles, mass murderer Charles Manson is, regrettably, intertwined with their story. This career petty criminal, who'd spent half of his life in lockup, was paroled in 1967 *against his expressed wishes*. Before long, he had assembled a group of followers, most of them emotionally vulnerable runaways.

By most accounts, the diminutive, unwashed leader of "the Family" was a charismatic figure unusually adept at bending others' will to his own. Manson preached a messianic gospel, featuring a rich sacrament including drugs, mysticism, and sex. Scripture—such as it was—came largely from songs on the "White Album." Manson had convinced his followers that the Beatles were communicating directly with him via their music.

Manson laid out his view of an upcoming apocalypse in the form of a race war between blacks and whites ("Helter Skelter"). Informed by verses of the Book of Revelation, chapter 9 (which speaks of angels with the hair of women and the faces of men), Manson invoked the Beatles, quickly drawing parallels to "Revolution #9," which he interpreted as the *sound* of the pending Armageddon.

Other suggestive tunes included "Blackbird," which, according to Manson, exhorted the black man to "arise"; "Piggies," George's attack on the bourgeois who clutch their "forks and knives to eat their bacon" (it's no accident that these very weapons were used on the hapless Leno and Rosemary LaBianca); and "Sexy Sadie." Manson thought this one, actually aimed at the Maharishi, was acknowledgement of his right-hand girl, "Sadie Mae Glutz," a.k.a. Susan Atkins. (History has not recorded Manson's take on John's "Give Peace a Chance," a chart single in the summer of 1969.)

Manson informed his ragtag group that in order to take their place at the head of the New World Order (following the "Helter Skelter" day of reckoning), they must first prompt the blacks to arise. Therefore the Family must kick off the battle with a series of killings that would appear to be racially motivated, leading the establishment to retaliate against African-Americans.

Though his twisted logic best resonated with the impressionable, an underlying method fueled his madness. Manson was a frustrated musician; a chance acquaintance with Beach Boys drummer Dennis Wilson led him to expect an easy time parlaying his connections into a recording contract.

But Wilson, recognizing the perils of the position he'd put himself in, fobbed Manson off on record producer Terry Melcher (the Byrds, Paul Revere and the Raiders). Melcher, the son of actress/singer Doris Day, was suitably unimpressed with Manson's efforts.

Manson took the hint and was now out for revenge. Though he knew that Melcher had moved, he sent his death squad to Melcher's former address, now occupied by film director Roman Polanski and his heavily pregnant wife, actress Sharon Tate. Manson knew that Melcher would get the message.

This is not the place to describe the horror that ensued, but suffice to say the Beatles-Manson connection became an ugly footnote to the year of the group's breakup. The Fabs themselves were beyond mystified as to how anyone would extrapolate a murderous message from a song about a playground slide.

Peter Brown

Beginning as an assistant to Brian Epstein at NEMS back in Liverpool, Peter Brown was the classic insider, witness to the Beatles' rise from lowly scruffs to worldwide superstars. Present at both Paul and John's 1969 weddings (serving as best man at the latter), Brown also had the distinction of being on a very short list of people mentioned by name in a Beatles song ("The Ballad of John and Yoko," of course).

It is therefore a tremendous disappointment that 1983's *The Love You Make*, Brown's collaboration with coauthor Steven Gaines, spins sordid (and often untrue) tales of sex, drug use, and all-around dissipation by the Fabs.

As an example, one photo depicts John lying on the floor, cutting the vocal to "Revolution." On this occasion, the writers breathlessly inform us, Lennon was too high to stand upright. Pure nonsense: as recounted by George Martin, John, ever dissatisfied with his vocals, was simply experimenting with a way to alter the sound of his voice.

Throughout the book, Brown recounts incidents that he could not possibly have been privy to while magnifying his own role and impact on the Fabs' career. While he goes easier on John than on the others, a thinly veiled contempt for all his subjects permeates the narrative. (Coauthor Gaines furthered his post-Beatles book career by penning a tome on the Beach Boys that gave more attention to Dennis Wilson's sex life than to the making of *Pet Sounds*.)

Brown and Gaines were clearly more interested in selling books than in presenting a balanced, accurate portrait of people that Brown was privileged to know. They thus produced a joyless chronicle revealing considerable disrespect for its subjects as well as its readers. Brown certainly would not have dared to present such salacious pap in John Lennon's lifetime and market it as an "insider's story."

The Love You Make is not recommended to anyone interested in the Beatles' music, history, or cultural context. Instead, it stands as highly embellished fiction worthy of Albert Goldman's oeuvre.

Allen Klein

It was not for no reason that Allen Klein's name stirred fear and loathing in the record industry. An accountant by trade, Klein specialized in hardball tactics that never failed to squeeze every last nickel from a deal. His first important score was Bobby Darin; offering to make Darin $100,000 without his having to do a thing, Klein made good on the boast through a top-to-bottom audit of Darin's record company.

His reputation for performing accounting miracles made him legendary by the early 1960s. Sam Cooke became Klein's first customer as personal business manager; not only did he pry overlooked royalties from Cooke's label, but he also established a custom imprint for Cooke. (Following Cooke's murder in 1964, Klein took ownership of the label, setting a pattern of acquiring the rights to the work of clients whose hit-making days were over.)

Klein extended his reach into the British Empire by adding Herman's Hermits and the Rolling Stones to his roster by the mid-1960s. His financial prowess with the latter did not escape the notice of the Fabs, who wondered aloud to Brian Epstein why the Stones, who sold far fewer records than they did, were raking in more cash.

Brian Epstein, for his part, viewed Klein as a crude, heavy-handed hustler and would have nothing to do with him. He rebuffed Klein's overtures to sign on as overseer of their business holdings, refusing even to see him. However, in late August 1967, Klein was in his car when word came over the radio that Brian Epstein was dead. As the story goes, Klein gleefully rubbed his hands together and said, "Now I've got 'em!"

He was further encouraged by the published report of John's ill-advised words to reporter Ray Coleman in early 1969, saying that if Apple continued on its current path, "we'll be broke in eighteen months." Like a shark smelling blood in the water, Klein zoomed into London, quickly arranging a meeting with John and Yoko.

Klein rehearsed his part well, treating Yoko Ono with respect, playing up his own working-class origins, and reciting chapter and verse of every song John had ever written. Immediately sold, John was easily able to cajole George and Ringo into standing with him against Paul's proposal to have his soon-to-be father-in-law, John Eastman (formerly Epstein), take the managerial reins.

This drove a wedge between Paul and the other three Beatles. Appalled by Klein's outward coarseness (and possibly heeding a warning from Mick Jagger, who had divined that Klein was trouble and was in litigation against him), Paul stood his ground and rejected any attempt to arm-twist him into adding his signature to *any* paper bearing Klein's name.

Unconcerned, Klein set to work with his usual methodology, quickly discovering hundreds of thousands of dollars of unpaid royalties owed the Fabs. (Even Paul was impressed.) Furthermore, he negotiated a raise in their royalty rate from EMI, giving them the highest wages in the recording industry.

But Klein's taking over Apple resulted in wild axe-swinging in the name of bringing expenses under control. People who had served the Beatles well from day one were summarily sacked (including "Mr. Fix-It," Alistair Taylor, who was stung by Paul's refusal to intercede on his behalf). All divisions of Apple deemed less than immediately profitable were shut down, including Apple Tailoring and Apple Electronics.

Recognizing that his "divide and conquer" strategy was paying dividends as far as his own interests were concerned, Klein did nothing to mollify Paul's concerns, in fact going out of his way to bait Paul at every opportunity.

But so pleased were the other three Beatles with Klein's efforts to right the sinking ship that they refused to second-guess his actions. Only years later, after learning of the full effects of his under-the-table chicanery, would John, Paul, and George sue Klein, a tacit admission that perhaps Paul had been right all along. (In the late 1970s, Klein served a prison term for failing to pay taxes on illegal profits generated from the sale of promotional copies of the *Concert for Bangla Desh* charity album.)

Phil Spector

Separating hype from fact is rather difficult with this mythic rock figure. Stories of Spector's over-the-top behavior, often involving gunplay, are legion, but it's doubtful that anyone could have predicted the horrific events that played out in early 2003, resulting in a first-degree murder charge.

Spector was already a legend by the time he first met the Beatles in 1964. No other rock producer had created such an instantly recognizable product, but Spector's "Wall of Sound"—densely arranged recordings of very simple tunes—proved hugely influential, especially on the Beach Boys' Brian Wilson. "Little symphonies for the kids," he called his work.

The producer had, coincidentally, flown over with the Beatles from London on their first trip to America. On the flight, Paul expressed his unease about the group's prospects in the States. But Spector's attuned ears knew that they had nothing to worry about.

Hits like Curtis Lee's "Pretty Little Angel Eyes," the Ronettes' "Be My Baby," and the Crystals' "He's a Rebel" had established Spector as a force. During the Beatles era, he scored with the Righteous Brothers, whose "You've Lost That Lovin' Feelin' " became one of the best-selling singles of all time. But the failure of Ike and Tina Turner's 1966 single "River Deep, Mountain High" unsettled Spector, who responded to its poor performance by going into seclusion.

After Spector produced a comeback single, 1969's "Black Pearl" by Sonny Charles and the Checkmates, Lennon tapped him in January 1970 to produce his insta-single, "Instant Karma." So taken was John with Spector's

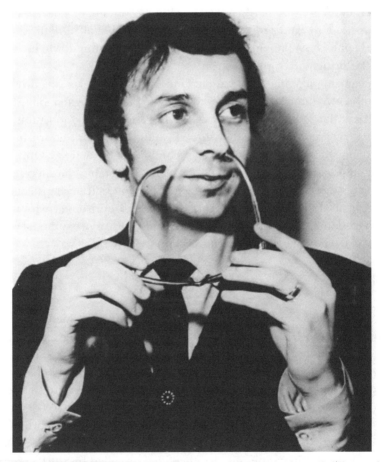

After scoring some musical successes with John and George in the early '70s, producer Phil Spector's tenuous connection with reality slowly began to deteriorate.

Photo by Gab Archives/Redferns

astonishing production that he suggested giving the eccentric American the moldering "Get Back" session tapes to see if he could make something out of them.

Allen Klein, only too glad to keep Paul out of the loop, quietly struck a deal with Spector after securing the tacit blessing of George and Ringo.

With less than top-flight Beatles material to work with, Spector was given leave to perform his magic and compile an album. His judicious editing and embellishments on the resulting *Let It Be* release are not entirely off the mark. Spector took George's slight "I Me Mine" and, through a repeated verse and bridge, lengthened it from just 1:34 to a sprawling 2:25. The clunky, out-of-tune intro and outro to "Dig a Pony" were excised, greatly streamlining the song.

Spector's work on "The Long and Winding Road" has drawn the most controversy. As originally laid down, Paul's tune was a spare piano ballad, with some subtle organ accenting for color. Spector thought the sound wasn't commercially viable; to his ears, this basic track cried out for embellishments.

And lay it on he did. Using the song as an excuse to revisit his "Wall of Sound" past, "The Long and Winding Road" emerged replete with strings and choirs, resembling the deliberately overbaked "Goodnight" from *The Beatles*. To be sure, "TLAWR" was a hit single accepted well enough by the masses at the time of its release. As produced by Phil Spector, it is a song most fans either love or hate.

But Paul never got over his outrage, claiming Spector (and by extension, Allen Klein) had deliberately sabotaged his work. The others said Paul had had a chance to sign off on the production before its release and had offered no objections at the time. But the heavy-handed syrup on the track stuck in Paul's craw enough to warrant the release of 2003's de-Spectorized retake on the album, *Let It Be . . . Naked*.

Never before in the history of rock had an entire album been reworked for the explicit purpose of spiting those responsible for its original production.

Life Is Very Short

Among the Dead

L ike most of us, the Beatles experienced the loss of loved ones—both family and friends—throughout their entire lives. Unlike most of us, however, they seemed to have experienced a lot of death firsthand, and in a relatively short time span—John especially.

Here are ten souls who touched the Fabs' lives and career in everlasting ways, directly and indirectly.

George Smith (Aunt Mimi's Husband): Died June 5, 1955

Overlooked by most biographers, George Smith was John Lennon's primary father figure through his mid-teens. Long before Julia Lennon turned the boy over to her older sister to raise, John looked forward to visiting Mimi at Mendips, where his kindly uncle doted on him. As life with Julia was by definition "unstable," George and Mimi's home provided consistency even before John moved in for good.

Smith had courted the oldest Stanley sister for ten years before she acquiesced and married him in 1939, two weeks after the Second World War broke out. Their marriage would be childless (and, according to one writer, unconsummated), but the two were happy to play surrogate parents to their nephew.

With Mimi staying true to her nature—flinty, strict, and rather dour— George played the good cop, softening Mimi's punishments by sneaking treats up to John's room. George took special pride in teaching the boy to read at four and a half, using the large type of newspaper headlines. (John remained a vociferous newspaper reader the rest of his life.)

In late spring 1955, while John was away on holiday, visiting Stanley relatives in Scotland, George suddenly took ill. Only fifty-two, he began vomiting blood and died soon after from a liver hemorrhage. Upon arriving home, fourteen-year-old John was devastated to learn that his beloved uncle was gone. It was the first such premature death to befall him, but sadly not the last.

Mary McCartney (Paul's Mother): Died October 31, 1956

Like John Lennon, the former Mary Mohin was raised by an auntie. Her own mother had died in childbirth; her father remarried, but she couldn't accept his new wife, and left, living with a maternal aunt as she began training for her life's work in medicine.

After entering nursing school at fourteen, Mary's devotion to her profession precluded many opportunities to meet men. Her time finally came at age thirty-one, when she crossed paths with forty-year-old ex-bandleader Jim McCartney.

Their relationship was cemented in, of all places, a bomb shelter during an air raid. Smitten by the happy-go-lucky Jim, Mary began making time with the war worker exempted from service on account of a ruptured eardrum.

After becoming pregnant with Paul, Mary left her job, not returning until after her second child, Michael, was born and Paul was five. Midwifery was an exalted profession during the postwar Baby Boom years, doctors being in short supply. Moreover, Mary's earnings were necessary to the household as Jim struggled to support the family as a cotton salesman.

Paul would recall his mother's cool professionalism as she packed her gear and left the house at all hours of the day and night, hopping on her bike without knowing when she would return. Being on twenty-four-hour call made life unpredictable, but as much as her job would allow, she ran a tight ship, keeping her close-knit family well scrubbed and provided with a good meal to begin and end each day.

At a time when few in the health care industry recognized the perils of cigarettes, Mary was a heavy smoker. By 1956, steadily increasing pain in her breasts became acute. For far too long, she denied or downplayed her symptoms, ascribing them to menopause.

But in October, after Jim's concerned pleas to see a doctor, Mary was diagnosed with breast cancer. An emergency mastectomy was performed, but the disease had spread and Mary died from an embolism soon afterward. Before she died, she expressed her regrets at not being able to see her boys grow up. Her lasting legacy was their drive to rise above the station into which they had been born.

Sons Paul and Michael had been kept completely in the dark about the dire nature of their mother's illness. When told she had passed, fourteen-year-old Paul immediately responded, "What are we going to do without her money?" (Sadly, it would not be his last outwardly inappropriate response to bereavement; twenty-four years later, he would tell reporters in the wake of John's assassination, "It's a drag, innit?")

Serious and hardworking, Mary aspired for her firstborn to become a teacher, and had she lived, it's extremely unlikely that Paul would have been a Beatle. Though far less open about his inner life than John, Paul would recount a vision he had of his late mother in a dream. In late 1968, he parlayed the visitation into a song, using her words of comfort as a starting point: "Let It Be."

Julia Lennon (John's Mother): Died July 15, 1958

Mary and Julia (born Judy) Stanley could not have been more opposite. Whereas eldest sister Mary (known as Mimi) was tightly wound, straitlaced, and severe, Julia was the free-spirited troublemaker of the five sisters, always out to provoke for a laugh. The one thing they did have in common was absolute adoration of Julia's son, John.

At fourteen, Julia found a kindred spirit in the equally puckish Alfred "Freddie" Lennon. The two shared a love of song and tomfoolery, completely lacking the capacity to take anything seriously. They married in 1938, eleven years after they met, but marriage did nothing to soften the Stanley family's attitude toward Freddie, who they felt was far beneath their social standing.

Freddie's irresponsible nature did not particularly faze Julia, but his time away from home as a merchant seaman did. Though he encouraged her (by letter) to go out and find some fun in his absence, little did he reckon on her becoming impregnated by a Welsh soldier. (The baby girl was quietly put up for adoption after her birth in 1945.) After spending some time in stir for some minor shenanigans, Freddie returned to Liverpool to find his wife pregnant and living with another man, John "Bobby" Dykins (later nicknamed "Twitchy" by John for his facial tic).

Attempts at reconciliation were rebuffed, but Freddie did not give up the prospect of raising his son until events forced his hand (as detailed in chapter 1). Thereafter, the still-married Lennons parted forever.

Julia gave birth to two more daughters, Julia and Jackie. John eventually formed a relationship with his erstwhile stepdad, who even gave him an allowance, while their flat became John's refuge when things became too intense at Mimi's.

Julia was only too happy to encourage John's nascent interest in music (doubtless as a way to spite her disapproving sister), letting Paul and George come over and rehearse with her son while she occasionally joined in or danced.

After George Smith died, Julia became more of a regular presence at Mendips, comforting her grieving sister. Following one of these visits, Julia was struck by a speeding, off-duty, intoxicated policeman.

Dead at forty-four, Julia Lennon is buried alone, in an unmarked grave.

Stuart Sutcliffe (Beatle): Died April 10, 1962

Popular folklore has John Lennon hauling friend and fellow art student Stuart Sutcliffe into the Beatles despite his utter lack of musical ability. In fact, while Sutcliffe's early musical experiences were rough as he got up to speed on his instrument, he eventually became competent if not brilliant, according to those who were there—including Pete Best and Klaus Voormann.

In fact, having stayed behind in Hamburg with Astrid Kirchherr after the Beatles returned to Liverpool, Stuart occasionally sat in with other bands.

As often happens with those who die young and ascend into mythology, much of Stuart's story has been embellished, when not fabricated outright. The film *Backbeat*, which purports to tell the story of his tenure in the Beatles and love affair with Astrid, is a melodramatic mess bearing little resemblance to actual events.

Stuart's sister, Pauline, has further spun tales, recently making an abrupt turn in her previous recounting of history by suddenly deciding to demonize John Lennon. She began by attributing her brother's premature death to a beating administered by an out-of-control Lennon, while intimating that the two were engaged in a homosexual relationship.

Even without the "lover's quarrel" angle, a substantial amount of Beatles literature maintains that a brawl following a gig resulted in Stuart sustaining a head injury that later killed him. Again, while reliable witnesses recall some sort of barney, there's no evidence of Stuart receiving a head injury of any sort, much less a lethal one.

The undisputed facts of Stuart's death are these: for some time before his death, possibly as long as a year, he complained of headaches. In February 1962, the headaches became increasingly severe, escalating to the point of what Astrid described as "fits." He saw doctors for treatment, but X-rays turned up nothing.

On April 10, 1962, two days before the Beatles were due to arrive in Hamburg, Astrid summoned an ambulance to rush Stuart to the hospital. (Word is that her mother called to tell her she was needed at home right away; Astrid found Stuart unconscious in bed.) In any event, he was still alive when loaded into the ambulance, but died en route, Astrid at his side.

The death certificate reported "cerebral paralysis due to bleeding into the right ventricle of the brain." Nothing about a head trauma, recent or otherwise.

Modern research into the symptoms Stuart exhibited points to two possible causes. The first: an aneurysm, which in lay terms is the bursting of a weak spot in an artery. Typically, the first sign of an aneurysm is a sudden, severe, and sometimes fatal headache, though occasionally there are smaller warning signs.

A more likely explanation is a cerebral arteriovenous malformation, or AVM. This malformation at the juncture of veins and arteries can result in cerebral hemorrhage, and the symptoms leading up to a large bleed match Stuart's much more closely than any other known disorder. (An AVM caused the hemorrhage, sometimes mistaken for a stroke, that befell South Dakota Senator Tim Johnson in December 2006.)

Both aneurysms and AVM are congenital conditions, present from birth and sometimes hereditary. As such, they need not be triggered by an external event, such as a beating.

Tara Browne (Guinness Heir): Died December 18, 1966

But for the fact of his tragic passing catching John Lennon's attention at a most propitious time, this scion of one of Britain's wealthiest families would scarcely be recalled by the public today.

While perusing a copy of the *Daily Mail*, Lennon noted the headline "Guinness Heir Saved Girl's Life in Crash." The article described the death of twenty-one-year-old Tara Browne, a London socialite most notable for making the scene with members of British rock's aristocracy, among them Paul McCartney.

Married at eighteen, Browne was the son of House of Lords member Dominick Browne and Oonagh Guinness, granddaughter of the brewery's founder. His brother Garech would later become the founding member of the Chieftains, a top Irish traditional band.

Already separated from his wife by 1966, Browne was dating nineteen-year-old model Suki Potier. Though he stood to inherit £1 million upon his twenty-fifth birthday, he lived and spent as though he'd already reached that landmark. Browne had, for example, flown American popsters the Lovin' Spoonful over to Ireland to perform at his birthday party. (Both McCartney brothers and Mick Jagger attended.)

On the final night of his life, Tara and Suki watched television at a friend's house. In the early morning hours, the couple got into his Lotus Elan and sped into the darkness.

Though largely embellished, Lennon's version of events in "A Day in the Life" did get a few details right. In his penultimate act, Browne ignored or "didn't notice that the lights had changed." Entering the intersection at great speed, a vehicle crossing his path posed an immediate threat. As his final action was described later, Browne veered the car to avoid injury to Suki, instead slamming into a parked truck. He was declared dead at the scene from multiple head trauma.

Whether or not a crowd of people stood and stared is unclear, but if they did, whispers of vague recognition may have speculated on whether the deceased might have been a member of the House of Lords, given the flash car he was driving and his last name. A photograph of the wreck indeed accompanied coverage of the story.

Suki did recover from her minor injuries, though she didn't seem to have much luck with boyfriends. Her next steady? Rolling Stones guitarist Brian Jones.

Joe Orton (Playwright): Died August 9, 1967

Had the Beatles agreed to work on the film they were pitched in 1967 (instead of *Magical Mystery Tour*), they might have created rock's most cutting-edge cinematic achievement, prior to Mick Jagger in *Performance* or David Bowie in *The Man Who Fell to Earth*.

Joe Orton's *Up Against It*, starring the Fabs, would have made *MMT* look like a Disney flick, and a rather poor one at that.

Orton was a daring choice to script a Beatles film, but a natural extension of the thought process that had landed them Alun Owen a few years earlier. Orton had gained renown as a purveyor of edgy black comedies that left audiences either enthralled or outraged. He had made a name for himself with *Loot*, a West End play revised several times (after being reviled) between 1964 and 1966. By sheer force of will, Orton had scored a minor hit.

Paul McCartney, driving the Beatles' artistic engine throughout much of 1966 and 1967, had been one of *Loot*'s backers. He suggested Orton to Brian Epstein as a possibility for scripting their elusive third United Artists picture. Epstein passed the information to producer Walter Shenson, who proffered a script they'd been considering to Orton, asking whether he felt he could punch it up.

Orton took receipt of the fanciful unnamed script in January 1967. It featured the Fabs playing, instead of four separate characters, four *aspects* of the same individual. (Whether Pete Townshend was inspired by this project or not, his *Quadrophenia*, written in 1973, mirrors its plot.) For the new script, now titled *Up Against It*, Orton reshaped ideas from some of his own earlier works, including a novel called *The Silver Bucket*, cowritten with his lover Ken Halliwell in 1953.

Paul had given Orton leave to do whatever he wanted "as long as it's good."

The refurbished screenplay was completed and delivered on February 25. Orton had every expectation that this draft would be rejected, and those expectations were met. As he described it, " . . . by page 25, they had committed adultery, murder, dressed in drag, been in prison, seduced the . . . niece of a priest, blown up a war memorial and all sorts of things like that. I can't really blame them (for rejecting it), but it would have been marvelous."

Epstein had sent an explanatory note with the rejection, saying in essence that given the Beatles' influence on the world's youth, he couldn't very well have them up on the big screen engaged in antisocial behavior. Paul McCartney offered a different, if less comprehensible take: "The reason we didn't do *Up Against It* wasn't because it was too far out or anything. We didn't do it because it was gay . . . Brian was gay . . . and so he and the gay crowd could appreciate it. [It's] just that we, the Beatles, *weren't* gay."

Orton apparently took the news with good grace, for on August 10 he was scheduled to meet again with the Fabs. A chauffeur was dispatched to the flat Orton shared with Halliwell, where he discovered the still-warm body of the thirty-four-year-old playwright. A doped-up Halliwell had bludgeoned him to death with a hammer.

Orton's favorite Beatle song, "A Day in the Life," was played at his funeral. Once the Beatles had passed on *Up Against It*, Dick Lester, slated to direct the film, had lined up Ian McKellan and Mick Jagger to star, but with Orton's death, the project was shelved.

Brian Epstein (Beatles Manager): Died August 27, 1967

The end of the Beatles' touring days, and the upcoming expiration of his contract with them, weighed heavily on Brian Epstein in the last year of his life. His personal vagaries were also catching up with him, including an ugly blackmailing attempt that kept him from witnessing the Beatles' final performance at Candlestick Park.

From the golden heights of that first trip to America two years earlier, Brian had seen his dreams realized, then dashed. The summer of '66 saw him turn from micromanaging the band's career trajectory to putting out fires around the world. Between the "butcher cover," the disaster in the Philippines, and the "bigger than Jesus" remark, Brian found himself spending much of the year doing damage control.

Late into their American tour, the Beatles let their manager in on their irrevocable decision to quit live performances at the conclusion of the current run. For Brian, who reveled in the logistical details of mounting a worldwide concert tour, this could only mean one thing: the Beatles, his boys, had outgrown him.

But what Brian perhaps didn't realize was that, whatever quarrels the Beatles had with his management decisions, he possessed one card that made him invaluable: they trusted him. As one of the select few in their business circle with whom their acquaintance predated fame, the Fabs knew that, if nothing else, Brian had their best interests at heart. Another singular quality that they perhaps underestimated at the time was his gift for keeping them focused and at peace with one another.

In any event, Brian responded to the onset of depression with a growing addiction to painkillers and a decided self-destructive tendency that put him in the company of those who could, if they wanted to, easily destroy him. A taste for "rough trade" sex, when homosexuality was still illegal in Britain, typified his dance with the devil.

But his own worst enemy was himself. Given his dramatic tendencies, high-strung personality, and generally manic-depressive nature, it was probably inevitable that Brian would make at least one carefully staged suicide attempt. It came one month after the Fabs played their last show.

Leaving a note that read "I can't deal with this anymore" and instructions for the disposal of his assets, Brian took an overdose of Nembutal. Though accustomed to his half-cocked impulses and periods of self-loathing, Brian's friends were stunned by the incident. After his stomach was pumped and he had spent two weeks in a rehab center, Brian spoke sheepishly of his "foolish accident."

In the months that followed, he seemed to right his course. Perhaps recognizing that his heart was no longer into the day-to-day details of running a business with so many interests, he struck a merger deal—without telling the Beatles—that brought Australian music mogul (and future Bee Gees manager) Robert Stigwood into the circle.

Though the Fabs were no longer receptive to his artistic input (Brian was adamantly against the extravagant album art for *Sgt. Pepper's*, even suggesting that it be packaged in a brown paper bag), there was no hint that the Beatles would not renew their personal management contract with NEMS in October 1967.

In fact, of late there had been an appreciable show of unity, with Brian coming to Paul's aid after a firestorm erupted with the latter's admission of LSD use. (Not only did Brian also publicly cop to taking acid, but he also added his name to a list of celebrities calling for the legalization of marijuana.)

He soon caught up with Transcendental Meditation, the Fabs' newest fancy. Enthralled by a London lecture by Maharishi Mahesh Yogi, the Beatles planned to attend a TM seminar in Bangor, Wales the next day. John invited Brian, who was expecting to hook up with friends that weekend, but agreed to meet up with them later.

It was not to be. After his plans fell through, Brian went home, but unexpectedly failed to make further contact. A concerned contingent of associates ventured to his Belgravia townhouse, only to discover Brian's moribund body in bed. He was thirty-two.

Given their experience with his "foolish accident" the year before, everyone in the Fabs' circle immediately saw Brian as having fulfilled his death wish. But this wasn't necessarily the case.

Brian's father had passed away just one month before. As the eldest son, Brian stepped up in taking on familial responsibilities, comforting his grieving mother and sorting out his father's affairs. Under these circumstances, it is extremely unlikely that he would deliberately inflict more hurt on his beloved mother.

Subconscious suicide was something else. The coroner reported findings of toxic levels of seconal (Carbitral) in his system. This barbiturate, incautiously ingested in immoderate amounts (and possibly mixed with alcohol), had risen to perilous levels. While the dose Brian took just before death was not in itself fatal, when added to the amount already in his blood, it was enough to kill him.

The Beatles, who were with the Maharishi in Wales, were stunned by the news. Assured by their guru that death was illusory, the Fabs returned home, but did not attend Brian's funeral (for fear of causing a spectacle).

David Jacobs (Brian Epstein's Lawyer): Died December 15, 1968

When the Beatles made their big move from Liverpool to London, Brian knew he would need the sharpest showbiz lawyer he could find to look after his (and the Beatles') professional interests. David Jacobs, flamboyant "lawyer to the stars," represented such diverse acts as Marlene Dietrich, Judy Garland, Liberace, and Diana Dors. Once the two men met, there was an immediate connection: both were Jewish, and, perhaps more significantly, both were gay (though Jacobs was not closeted).

Though possessing a big reputation and an outsized personality, Jacobs did the Beatles no favors in practically giving away their merchandising rights to Nicky Byrne, causing Brian countless headaches. Still, Brian sought Jacobs's counsel, granting him respect as he did with few others. Jacobs, for his part, seemed content to rest on his laurels, basking in the reflected glory of the entertainers he surrounded himself with.

By 1967, Jacobs's influence within the Beatles camp was waning, as was Brian's. Still, he was consulted after Brian was found dead to help "scrub" things before the authorities arrived.

By most accounts, including that of his close friend and client, actress Suzanna Leigh, Jacobs was content in his life, but others were less sure. According to Beatles biographer Philip Norman, Jacobs was extremely agitated and nervous in the final weeks of 1968, apparently contacting local police in Hove for protection.

What is known is that Jacobs was found hanging in his garage on December 15, 1968. Leigh, who had recently returned from a trip to the States, arrived home to learn of Jacobs's death from the newspaper, even as she held in her hand a just-delivered postcard from Jacobs, asking if she'd be available for lunch the following week.

Disturbed by the incongruity of a man apparently taking his life while making social plans, she imparted what she knew to the authorities. All agreed that the death was not what it seemed. Word was that the notoriously deadly Kray twins, Britain's most infamous psychopaths, had approached Jacobs to represent them on capital murder charges.

Frightened at being involved with such dodgy clients, Jacobs declined. But one said "no" to Reggie and Ronnie Kray at one's own risk. It is now believed that Jacobs paid the supreme price for spurning their request. But with the Krays going to trial in January 1969 on charges that would put them away for life, authorities felt that pursuing Jacobs's case was unnecessary.

The Lenono Babies: Died November 21, 1968, and October 12, 1969

With stunning hubris, John Lennon attempted to cut ties to Cynthia, the mother of his son, by filing for divorce in June 1968 on the grounds of adultery: *hers*. Mrs. Lennon answered this fiction with her own suit in August, but on somewhat more solid ground: *John's* adultery with Yoko Ono. Evidence for the assertion was growing within Ms. Ono's womb.

A divorce was granted to Cynthia on November 8, 1968, only days after Yoko was admitted to Queen Charlotte's Maternity Hospital for observation. With at least one abortion in her past and the extreme stress she'd suffered during their October 18 drug bust, Yoko's odds for carrying the baby (due in February) to full term were fair at best.

Yoko remained in the hospital for some time, with John continuously at her side. After the bed he slept in was removed to accommodate a patient, John camped out on the floor in a sleeping bag. (A photo documenting the event graced the cover of Zapple's debut LP release, *Unfinished Music No. 2:*

Life with the Lions, while a newspaper report of the story is *sung,* as "No Bed for Beatle John," on that same release.)

After almost three weeks of hospitalization, Yoko's doctors informed her that the five-month-old male fetus would not survive. John immediately sought to document the child's brief life by recording a segment of the baby's heartbeat on a portable tape recorder. Lengthened to five minutes through repeats, it was issued on the *Life with the Lions* album as "Baby's Heartbeat," followed immediately by "Two Minutes Silence."

As shown on this rare Apple cassette issue, Yoko's first miscarriage was commemorated on the cover to their second joint release.

Several sources report that the baby was christened John Ono Lennon II and given a proper burial in a tiny casket, somewhere in an undisclosed location. (Those privy have not talked.) What makes the assertion somewhat sketchy is that John did not change his *own* middle name to "Ono" until a Savile Row rooftop ceremony on April 22, 1969.

It is possible, however, that the child conceived in Ono's next pregnancy was given that name. A week after recording "Don't Worry Kyoko (Mummy's Only Looking for Her Hand in the Snow)," Yoko was admitted to London's King's College Hospital. Three days later, Yoko suffered a second miscarriage. Not until 1975, at the age of forty-two, would she successfully carry a baby Lennon to full term.

Brian Jones (Rolling Stones Founder): Died July 3, 1969

The "take-no-prisoners" competition between the Fabs and the Rolling Stones was manufactured by the media. The reality was more mundane; both bands were a part of the same social circle, shared some professional advisors and acquaintances, and were susceptible to some common influences.

Their association began in 1963. In one of their first conversations, Brian Jones, the Rolling Stones' founder and in-house multi-instrumentalist, asked John what kind of mouth organ he used on "Love Me Do." John and Paul then custom-tailored a relative throwaway called "I Wanna Be Your Man" into the Stones' second single.

From that point, the Stones took in a healthy Beatle influence and filtered in their own beat-inspired hard blues sensibility. The resulting records were cynical where the Beatles' were joyous, jaded where the Beatles' were romantic.

As their nominal leader, Jones's own influence ebbed with the ascent of the Jagger-Richards songwriting team. Though still a trendsetter in fashion, mores, and drug use, he eventually found a comfortable niche in being the go-to band member for adding musical shading to their recordings; he was a quick study on seemingly any instrument.

Outside the band, Jones was considered rock-and-roll royalty. The Beatles tapped him to play saxophone on their jokey lounge pastiche, "You Know My Name (Look Up My Number)." At 1967's landmark Monterey Pop Festival, he floated amid the crowd like a mystical vision, resplendent in full Summer of Love regalia, even introducing Jimi Hendrix to the assembled masses.

But the effects of drug use, arrests, and band politics precipitated a disintegrating mental state that accelerated Jones's downward skid. Though he was heavily involved in the making of 1967's *Their Satanic Majesties Request* (instrumentally, if not compositionally), the LP's perceived failure dashed any hopes for Jones's resurgence.

By the time 1968's *Beggars Banquet* sessions had begun, Jones was viewed by his bandmates as a needy, strung-out liability. Any input into an album that should have been up his alley—a return to the Stones' bluesy roots—was summarily shot down. The band completed the album with extensive help from guests like Traffic's Dave Mason and Eric Clapton.

To be fair, Brian's dissipated state hardly justified his presence on the recordings. Conversely, his efforts at relevance were often cruelly mocked by the others, who would allow him to play his heart out as they turned off his mic or disconnected his patch cords.

Frequently, he would phone John Lennon to commiserate. The latter, going through his own tribulations in 1968, admonished Jones to stop acting like a "little girl" and fight for his position in the group. Momentarily inspired, Jones relapsed when his moment of truth before Jagger and Richards came.

The *Rock and Roll Circus* television special marked his last meaningful appearance with the group. Push came to shove when the Stones recognized that Jones's drug convictions meant trouble securing a work visa for touring in America. On June 8, 1969, Jagger and Richards told Jones that his services in the band he had founded were no longer required.

Telling the press "I no longer see eye-to-eye with the others over the discs we are cutting," Jones seemed relieved by the dismissal. He immediately began making plans to assemble a new band, contacting original Stones pianist Ian Stewart and Jimi Hendrix Experience drummer Mitch Mitchell.

Friends said that Jones appeared happier and healthier than he had in some time, ensconced at Cotchford Farm, the former estate of *Winnie the Pooh* author A. A. Milne. Nearly a month after parting ways, things seemed to be on the upswing.

But it all ended around midnight on July 3, 1969. The official coroner's report ruled that Brian Jones's demise at the bottom of his swimming pool constituted "death by misadventure," legal jargon for self-inflicted irresponsibility. Both alcohol and drugs were detected in his body, but not at incapacitating levels. Jones was a strong swimmer, but also an asthmatic.

Several theories have been offered—in books and in the 2006 film *Stoned*—purporting to explain what *really* went down on Brian's last night. All point to his murder at the hands of Frank Thorogood, hired to remodel the house but fired that morning. Thorogood allegedly made a deathbed confession.

The sole variance in the stories concerns whether the death resulted from rough horseplay or a botched attempt to scare the hapless musician.

Brian Jones uncanny gift for quickly mastering virtually any instrument he touched helped the Rolling Stones keep up with the Beatles' musical experimentation.

Photo by Ivan Keeman/Redferns

What is known is that thousands of dollars' worth of expensive musical gear was stolen from the estate within hours of Jones's death, indicating   .

As for the Stones, a previously scheduled free concert in London's Hyde Park, intended to introduce twenty-year-old guitarist Mick Taylor, instead turned into a public memorial for Brian. It was, by all accounts, one of the worst gigs they ever played.

To this day, most who knew him well are of two minds over which Brian to remember: the errant man-child or the insufferable provocateur. Characteristically, George Harrison had the best summation: "There was nothing the matter with him that a little extra love wouldn't have cured."

It's Getting Very Near the End

Twilight of the Gods

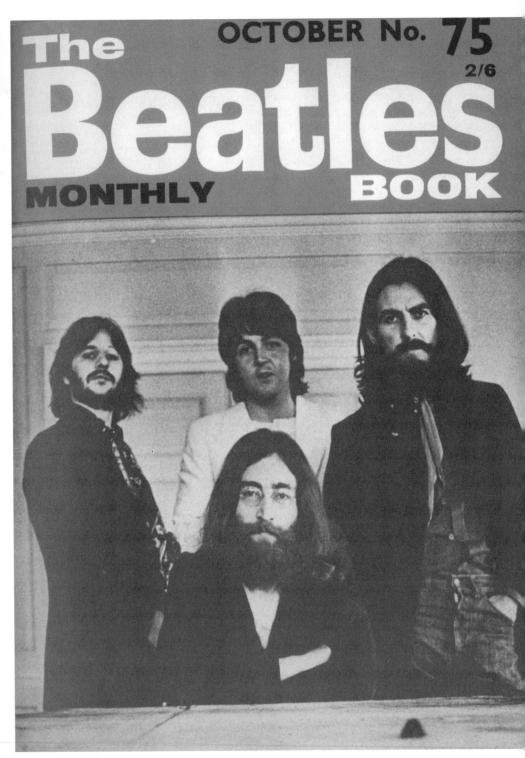

OCTOBER No. **75**

2/6

The Beatles

MONTHLY BOOK

As shown on one of the last issues of *Beatles Monthly Book*, the Fabs gathered for a final photo-shoot at John's newly purchased estate at Tittenhurst Park.

Half of What I Say Is Meaningless

Unexplained Beatle Trivia

In the thirty-seven years since the Beatles' breakup, their lives and music have been turned over like so much construction-site earth. But weird, hard-to-explain points of Beatledom remain, points that beg for analysis and, hopefully, some explanation.

"What Goes On (?)"

When this countrified Lennon-McCartney-Starkey composition, which had existed in some form since at least 1962, appeared on the late 1965 *Rubber Soul* LP, it felt a little out of place amid the glistening folk rock, exotic instrumentation, and period-rock experiments. With its clunky guitars, occasional background jokes, and odd harmonies, "What Goes On," in fact, just seemed weird.

Americans didn't hear the song until spring 1966, when it was debuted as the flip side of the single "Nowhere Man." It then appeared on the *Yesterday . . . and Today* album later that summer. By that time, the composition's title had acquired a question mark at the end, one obviously owing its existence to Capitol Records' typical sloppiness and disregard for the Beatles' work. "What Goes On?" indeed!

Why Are There All Those Mixes of "I'm Only Sleeping," and Other Mono/Stereo Questions

Since 1963, Capitol Records in the U.S. had been remixing Beatles tracks for American radio, believing that listeners on this side of the pond wouldn't appreciate the songs as recorded.

Therefore, American listeners at the time heard the Beatles' songs with extra echo and reverberation, added against the group's wishes by people who had nothing to do with the original conception of the group's music. In addition, the geniuses at Capitol would at times actually remix the songs themselves, changing the sounds to "Americanize" them.

Things reached a pinnacle of ridiculousness by 1966. Capitol regularly chopped up the British albums to make more product to sell in America, and in this case excised three Lennon numbers from the upcoming *Revolver* ("Dr. Robert," "And Your Bird Can Sing," and "I'm Only Sleeping"), added a few old and new singles and B-sides, and thereby conjured a new LP, *Yesterday . . . and Today*, out of thin air.

In their haste to release the new album, Capitol couldn't wait for the finished product, instead using rough mono mixes prepared in London. Therefore, *four* mixes of these songs exist for Beatles fans to wrap their frontal lobes around. Sonically, the most interesting song is "I'm Only Sleeping," with most of the variations involving subtle but significant differences in the amount of backwards guitar.

Annoyingly, Capitol couldn't wait for real stereo mixes of the three songs, putting "rechanneled stereo" mixes on the stereo *Y&T* album. (Rechanneled stereo is just mono with extra bass on one speaker and extra treble in another, and perhaps some delay between channels.) Only in the early 1970s did Capitol put true stereo issues of these songs on *Yesterday . . . and Today*. Other albums suffered this fate as well.

The story of the Beatles' mono and stereo releases is intriguing enough to fill an entire book on its own. While it has been impossible, for most people, to buy the Fabs' albums in any format but stereo since the late 1960s, the truth is that back in the golden decade, most fans in the U.K., the U.S., and around the world heard the Beatles music *in mono*—on the radio, on 45-rpm records (which weren't released in stereo until the late '60s), and on albums. Most people didn't even *have* stereo record players until the late 1960s and early 1970s.

The fact that the available Beatles CDs after *A Hard Day's Night* are all in stereo (except for the recent Capitol box sets of U.S. releases) ignores—in fact, papers over—the way the Beatles were perceived in their time. And a lot of the mono mixes (which were created, all the way through the "White Album," more carefully than their stereo counterparts) are better than the stereo anyway.

Who's Playing on "Fixing a Hole"?

The sessions for *Sgt. Pepper* saw several firsts, including the first outside arrangement of instruments on a Beatles number (the strings on "She's Leaving Home" were arranged by Mike Leander, rather than a previously booked George Martin) and the first British Beatles recording date held outside of EMI studios: for "Fixing a Hole," on February 9, 1967.

This new McCartney composition was taped just one day prior to the famous "Day in the Life" orchestral overdub session/party held at Abbey Road. The song was fairly simple, but still, by early 1967, the Beatles were rarely doing anything in just one night. The group finished the song two weeks later, adding some overdubs at Abbey Road.

"Hole" and the year's later "Baby You're a Rich Man," also recorded in one day, away from Abbey Road, showed that the Beatles could "jam econo" if they wanted to. Perhaps being away from their usual studio helped them get down to business.

Mark Lewisohn's *Beatles Recording Sessions* states that the bass and harpsichord on this track were played concurrently. Lewisohn throws up his hands and refuses to decide who played what, but, given the lack of supporting guitars on this song, it could well be Lennon playing the keyboard.

Or perhaps it was someone else. Visitors to Beatles sessions were becoming common by 1967. Lewisohn's book doesn't state that anyone joined the Beatles at Regent Studios on February 9, or for the overdubs on the 21st, but we know that the Abbey Road studios were full of visitors on February 10, and Lewisohn informs us that David Crosby of the Byrds came by to visit on the 22nd.

Given the way things were working by this time, is it outrageous to theorize that someone might have been helping the Beatles on "Fixing a Hole," either vocally or instrumentally? Listen for yourself, especially to the backing vocals.

"I Am the Walrus ('No You're Not!' Said Little Nicola)"

Lennon's "I Am the Walrus" provided a high point to a confused and somewhat thin *Magical Mystery Tour* soundtrack. Full of odd wordplay, acid-inspired visions, and even a BBC radio excerpt from Shakespeare's *King Lear*, "Walrus" is among the group's most disorienting but rewarding listens.

The track listing on *MMT* also provided intrigue. For some reason, the song is listed on the gatefold cover as "I Am the Walrus ('No You're Not!' Said Little Nicola)." This extended title isn't found on any 45 rpm release of the song, and no scene in the film includes a little child saying anything untoward to John Lennon concerning his pinnipedian identity.

Future reissues of the song, on LP and CD, omitted Nicola's "rejection" entirely, making the reference entirely dependent on one's willingness to suspend all sense of logic when dealing with matters surrounding *Magical Mystery Tour*. Which is probably a good thing.

1 a   "But I wonder where the MAGIC comes in?" thinks Paul.

IS
JS
IE
RE
he
e:
Y

12. Even as they dance THE MAGIC TAKES EFFECT and the bus is SPIRITED AWAY TO THE AMAZING MUSICAL LAND OF THE WALRUS! "I AM THE WALRUS" says John. "NO, YOU'RE NOT" cries Nicola, laughing at his funny feathery hat.

Whether replete with meaning or not, the subtitle given to "I Am the Walrus" on *Magical Mystery Tour*'s soundtrack attracted suspicion, following the spread of "Paul is dead" rumors in 1969.

Who Is "Big George Martin"?

For some reason, the credits on the *Magical Mystery Tour* album list the Beatles' producer as "Big George Martin." No such liberties with the dapper, dignified Martin had been taken before on an album sleeve, and it is difficult to envision the Beatles asking their producer's *permission* to make such a reference.

Perhaps this listing was just a further by-product of the group's hazy late 1967 collective state of mind, or maybe it served as a continuation of their general lack of formality.

Since becoming a completely recording-oriented group, the Fabs had begun having their way more often in the studio, asserting control in various areas that had been entirely the purview of Martin.

During the run-up to the summer 1967 "Our World" broadcast, Lennon can be heard (on bootleg recordings) making fun of Martin's advice that the Fabs be prepared for their cue. Stories told later by Abbey Road engineers and tape operators confirm that the group by then had begun to show progressively less respect to their esteemed producer.

"John Smells Like Shit!"

Even before the Beatles stopped touring, they began producing promotional films to hype their singles. The early 1968 "videos" for the "Hey Jude" / "Revolution" 45 featured two "performances" in which the Beatles sang live over previously taped instrumental backing. (The incongruity of this became apparent during "Revolution," when none of the four Beatles bothered to mime Nicky Hopkins's electric piano solo.)

A stranger story tells how one very raw vignette picked up by the cameras has since been entirely excised. During one of Lennon's verses, a red-sweatered George Harrison edges away from John and toward Paul, shouting to the latter that "John smells like shit!"

Perhaps the stage lights were especially hot that day, or maybe Lennon hadn't taken the time to properly shower. Either way, someone figured out, probably in the 1980s, what was going on and decided to sanitize history for John's protection. Another take of the performance shot by Michael Lindsay-Hogg has superseded the original, eliminating George's distasteful observation.

When this video was shown in the 1960s, 1970s, and early 1980s on television, at fan conventions, and in films, George's comment was visible. No longer.

"Yellow Submarine: Nothing Is Real"

Americans buying the soundtrack to the 1968 King Features film, which included the Beatles, took possession of a sleeve featuring Peter Max–style drawings of the Fabs. The group's name and "Yellow Submarine" were printed in op-art lettering.

On British copies of the LP, however, as well as those produced for other nations, the phrase "Nothing Is Real" is added in small, formal print lower on the cover.

The extra three words come from "Strawberry Fields Forever"—a song not even featured in the film. Obviously the extra phrase was intended to impart the fantastical quality the film's producers wished to convey. The reason Americans weren't trusted with the extra information is unknown.

Another inexplicable distinction between the releases can be found in the back cover notes. In America, a suitable essay on the film was included, presented as a tongue-in-cheek scholarly study tracing the film's mythology back to Beowulf. Across the pond, British listeners were treated instead to a laudatory review of *The Beatles* from the *London Observer*.

Who Are "Kevin and All at Number 9," as Credited on the "White Album" Poster?

The following people are credited on the poster included with *The Beatles*: George Martin, Chris Thomas, Ken Scott, Jeff [*sic*] Emerick, Barry Shefield, John Smith, Richard Hamilton, Gordon House, Jeremy Banks, John Kelly, Linda Eastman, Mal [Evans], and "Kevin and all at number 9."

Most of those folks are easy enough to identify . . . but who is Kevin, and what was number 9? The Beatles' Apple offices were at 3 Savile Row by this time; perhaps number 9 was a local address. Given the reportedly frosty relations between the Fabs and their more staid neighbors, however, this is not likely.

Perhaps Kevin and all at number 9 worked on the album's design, which featured an all-white cover, the aforementioned poster, and individual photos of John, Paul, George, and Ringo. Richard Hamilton, an influential and important British pop artist, was responsible for the overall package.

Another possibility is that the note refers to the red-haired chap named Kevin (seen on the rooftop in *Let It Be*, holding up "Dig a Pony"'s lyrics for Lennon to read) employed as John and Yoko's personal assistant during 1969.

Why Does the *Let It Be* Album Feature a Red, Not Green, Apple on the Label?

In Britain, *Let It Be* was originally sold as a costly box set with a book of Ethan Russell's photographs. This release featured a photo of a red apple on the box but the typical green apple on the record label. When the album was reissued in the U.K. a few months later as a standard release, minus the book, both the label and sleeve featured green apples.

In America, the album was issued in a standard gatefold jacket, without the book, by Apple Records. But because United Artists distributed the film of the same name, that company also held the rights to distribute the record in America. (EMI's subsidiary, Capitol, which held the Beatles' U.S. contract, had simultaneous rights to distribute the LP's songs on various singles and compilation albums, but not to issue the actual album itself.)

To indicate that *Let It Be* was *not* distributed by Capitol, the original record label in America sported a red apple, rather than the Beatles' signature Granny Smith.

(A side point: Why would a change in distributor mean that the record label had to be changed? It seems silly that a record label—a consumer product—should be designed with any consideration for the business side of things, which listeners certainly don't care about.)

Some argue fancifully that the apple was changed from green to red on the U.S. release to indicate that the band had "ripened" to its full maturity. (Or, perhaps, depending on your opinion of the album, that the Beatles were now overripe.)

In early 1976, when the Beatles' Apple contract expired, most of the group's catalog in the United States transferred from Apple to Capitol; *Let It Be*, however, was already out of print in America.

Some two years earlier, UA had lost its distribution rights for the *Let It Be* LP, and so the album disappeared from stores. As a result, wily bootleggers moved in and flooded the market with fake pressings. Since the bootleg versions must have been pressed from other LPs, and not the actual master tapes, the sound of the counterfeits was predictably inferior.

In the late 1970s, Capitol purchased United Artists Records, thus acquiring the rights to two Beatles albums previously distributed in the United States by United Artists: *Let It Be* and the *Hard Day's Night* soundtrack.

When Capitol finally acquired the rights to release the album, the company had inherited a bunch of original gatefold covers from UA. Capitol simply slapped new purple-labeled Capitol albums in the old UA covers and sold them to record chains at low prices in order to drive the bootlegs off the market.

And Why All the Secrets?

At this late date, with two Fabs passed on and the other two eligible for full-fledged AARP membership, far too many secrets, far too much intrigue, and far too many unanswered questions still fester in the Beatles camp.

One potential bombshell kept hidden for decades sheds some light on the reason for Pete Best's dismissal. In 2003, Best, of all people, revealed that the reason behind the successful Casbah Club's sudden closing in 1962 was the unexpected, adulterous pregnancy of Mona Best, his mother.

Roag Best was born three weeks before Pete was ousted. Perhaps the revelation that the father was none other than nineteen-year-old Neil Aspinall, then the Beatles' roadie (and Pete's best friend), would have been too scandalous a story to air publicly, carrying the potential to eclipse the Beatles and their music.

That's just one Beatle secret. There are many others. You probably have your own burning questions.

For instance, why isn't *Let It Be* out on video yet, after all these years?

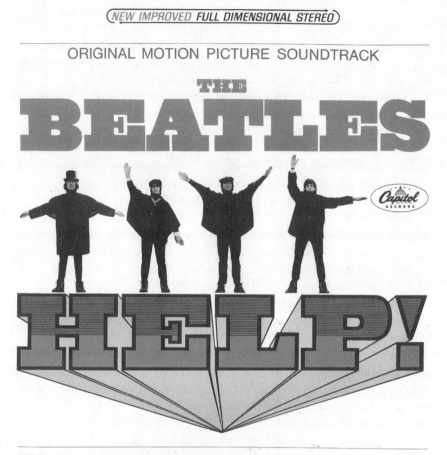

ORIGINAL MOTION PICTURE SOUNDTRACK

THE BEATLES

Capitol RECORDS

HELP!

HELP! · THE NIGHT BEFORE · YOU'VE GOT TO HIDE YOUR LOVE AWAY · I NEED YOU
ANOTHER GIRL · TICKET TO RIDE · YOU'RE GONNA LOSE THAT GIRL
And Exclusive Instrumental Music From the Picture's Soundtrack

Another trivial matter concerns the *Help!* cover, which features the Fabs spelling out not the LP's title in semaphore, but "NVUJ" (on the Capitol release) and "NUJV" (in Britain).

Why can't fans get the original British mono mixes of the group's mid-period classic albums? You know, the versions that the Beatles, their producer, and their engineers spent the most time on and thought were the most important?

And, on the other hand, why is *A Hard Day's Night*, which featured a perfectly good stereo mix when issued in 1964, not available in stereo now? (Unlike the first two Beatles albums, *AHDN* does not use amateurish "wide stereo" separation.)

Why did George Harrison veto the inclusion of "Carnival of Light," the 1967 experimental tape, on *Anthology 2*?

Why did Aspinall publicly deny the existence of the 1968 twenty-two-minute version of "Helter Skelter," one that author Marc Lewisohn had already confirmed in his book *Beatles Recording Sessions?*

And, while we're at it, why are certain important points omitted in Lewisohn's book? Given the author's access to the official records, it's odd and discomfiting that his otherwise fine session overview completely ignores legitimate questions about the taping of "She Said She Said" and "I'm Looking Through You."

That it fails to mention serious arguments and personality issues that affected the recordings is more understandable. Perhaps the Fabs and their representatives pulled rank on the author, prohibiting him from discussing certain facts.

But why at this point is anyone playing coy about assuming that Paul McCartney—already a mean hand on the drums—is playing on the *Anthology* demo of "No Reply"? Why no discussion of the dynamics around McCartney's frequent usurping of Harrison's lead guitar role from 1965 on?

There are so many unanswered questions, secrets, and obfuscations in the Beatles story that we might as well look to the Rutles' "All You Need Is Cash" mockumentary for veracity. Ouch!

Well, Well, Well, You're Feeling Fine!

The Fab "Medicine Cabinet"

F rom their very earliest days as a group, the Beatles formed relationships with various legal and illegal substances considered "drugs." Alcohol, tea, and cigarettes, legal pursuits all and staples of the British working class, helped the Beatles get to the top. But the long hours, impossible work schedules, and often crushing boredom of touring—starting in Hamburg—made the alternating use of stimulants and depressants easy and, at times, almost a requirement. Fame offered them access to the latest in psychedelics and, later, "harder" drugs.

All four Beatles went headlong into the drug culture of the 1960s, following jazz musicians, beatnik poets, impressionist painters, and other countercultural artists into exploration of the mind and body through chemistry. And while the Beatles didn't rot their brains on nineteenth-century absinthe, or engage in trepanning (despite John Lennon's hearty exhortations for Paul to do so), plenty of temptations, legal and otherwise, whirled around each of the Fabs. All four of them used various substances to forget their problems—sometimes creating entirely new ones.

Tobacco

Most Western teenagers experiment with tobacco, or at least are tempted to, and the young Beatles, most of whom grew up staunchly lower middle-class, were no exception. In the days before smoking was universally declared "hazardous to your health," cigarettes were part of life—in the bars, on the streets, in the concert halls. After starting out smoking foul-tasting discount "cotton wool" ciggies, such as Woodbines, John, Paul, George, and Ringo graduated to classier smokes as their fortunes improved.

Cigarettes were cheap, legal, socially acceptable, and could be smoked anywhere. Prior to the discovery of tobacco's addictive, harmful properties, the pleasure felt obvious; the nicotine provided a lift, and simply having something to do with one's hands helped many a musician—as well as a salesman, student, nurse, or soldier—deal with nervous tension.

Throughout their careers, all four members of the group lit up, and were frequently photographed, ciggies in hand. Years later, in the name of hazy political correctness, the offensive smokes were airbrushed out of the official record, Soviet-style. Casualties included the picture sleeve to the reissue of "I Want to Hold Your Hand," the Beatles' first Capitol 45; the sleeve to 1996's "Real Love" single, which sported a photo from 1965; and even the *Abbey Road* album cover.

The group continued smoking through the years, from their first photo session to their last and into their solo careers. Rationalized John Lennon in 1980, "Macrobiotics don't believe in the Big C."

Speed

When the Beatles first went to Hamburg, Germany, in fall 1960, their education began. (Lennon later averred that he grew up in Hamburg, not Liverpool.) The rigors of playing long shows at trashy clubs were such that as soon as the Beatles were introduced to speed—usually provided by waitstaff, German friends, or even club owners—they began to depend on it.

Preludin, in particular, was key. Used pharmaceutically to curb appetite and aid weight loss, "prellies" became a constant Hamburg companion. The boys would take a pill or three or four with beer, then stay up and remain focused for around twelve hours. As an added benefit, the boys—who didn't eat much as a result of the pills—remained lean and impossibly confident, in a "fake it 'til you make it" sort of way.

Later, back in England, the Fabs would hang with a crowd that took its speed in stronger appetite suppressants—amphetamines like Drinamyl (nicknamed "purple hearts") and Durophet. British mods ingested speed in order to stay up all night, or all weekend, dancing. Aside from its financing of mob-run drug rings, one problem with speed was that its ingestion also led to a need for sleeping pills in order to calm down.

With their Hamburg days over, the Fabs were no longer required to stay up all night six days a week, and saw no further need for such ridiculous drug-balancing, getting their kicks instead from coffee and tea. Britain banned most amphetamines from sale after various "Mod vs. Rocker" wars brought the use of said pills for recreational use into public view.

Speed remained a key part of the Beatle diet through 1964, when the boys amped up the pills to get them through the filming of *A Hard Day's Night*.

John, however, discovered another legal high on the legendary night when he went to see Liverpool beat poet Royston Ellis give a recital. Later that evening, Ellis and Lennon retired to a flat where they met (and enjoyed the pleasures of) a girl named Pam who was wrapped in polythene. Lennon turned the incident into a song some seven years later, but left out the part in which Ellis showed him how to get high from Vicks inhalers, which at the time contained strips soaked in Benzedrine.

Beer

German beer was inexpensive, powerful, and readily available in the Hamburg clubs, and the Beatles swilled anything sent up to the stage. Sometimes club owners, gangsters, or rough boys would send cases of beer (or even champagne) to the band and "ask" them—at knifepoint—to drink it all. So they did.

None of the Beatles became alcoholics in the traditional sense during the band's lifetime; there were always enough new temptations around to keep them from doing too much of any one drug. But none of them ever gave up alcohol, either, and during the '70s, at least one Beatle was drinking far too much for his own good.

Scotch and Coke

Strange as it may seem, the most sophisticated Beatle in the early days was . . . Ringo Starr. The eldest of the four by five months, Starr always lived large, perhaps feeling that given his early-life health problems, he didn't have long to stick around (how wrong he was!) and that he'd better see it all.

Despite being born into poverty, Starr learned about the high life, working hard and making money. Even before joining the Beatles, he was highly respected both for his drumming and for his *bon vivant* nature. Ringo had a beard, drove his own car, smoked the best cigarettes, and drank the most upscale alcoholic beverages.

A devotee of country music and the blues, he was "hard" in a way even Lennon had to admire, and introduced the rest of the Fabs to scotch and Coke, which soon became *the* Beatle beverage. Despite his taste for sophistication, Starr never appeared the least bit pretentious.

Marijuana

The prevailing Beatles myth has Bob Dylan and his entourage introducing the Beatles to pot in 1964 (see chapter 32), but evidence suggests that John

Lennon had tried the soul smoke some weeks or months earlier, with negative results.

By the end of summer 1964, however, the boys had taken the drug with a more positive set and setting. Pot soon became the new Beatle obsession. All four members found sweet relief in cannabis, which inspired them,

Sixties icon and future Traveling Wilbury Bob Dylan enjoyed a two-way influence relationship with the Fabs; the latter raised their lyrical game due to him while Dylan advanced beyond three chords and went electric.

Photo by Harry Goodwin/Redferns

freed their minds of stress, and simply made them laugh. It certainly was a welcome change from the rigors of speed.

While the initial fling, which manifested in the ridiculous excess of the *Help!* film's "smoking pot for breakfast" stage, soon subsided, all four Beatles continued, to varying degrees, to enjoy its effects long afterward, some for decades (despite Harrison's advice to his audience in 1974 to stop smoking "dirty reefers").

The Beatles rarely, if ever, were high in the studio during their most intense days of drug discovery, in 1965–66; they wanted to work "clean" and felt that not doing so would show lack of respect for the music, as well as for George Martin. In later days, when Martin wasn't always around, this Beatle policy would loosen.

Many of the group's middle-period songs were certainly influenced by a more open and bohemian lifestyle, of which pot was part but not parcel. The general loosening of social constraints in the mid-'60s led to discoveries—various spiritual paths, Eastern ethnic music, food, and clothing, electronics, ecology, and political philosophy—not heretofore the domain of popular entertainers. Some of the denizens of said areas were also into, or at least not judgmental about, recreational drug use, so different crowds connected in that way as well.

McCartney's love affair with the drug is well documented, foremost in song by "Got to Get You Into My Life" and also by his own actions. In the post-Beatle years, both he and future wife Linda were busted for possession, while post-Linda wife Heather Mills made much of her claim of having forced Paul to stop using pot. What Mills may not have realized—the marriage ended soon afterward—is that for some, marijuana is not only an enjoyable diversion, but also a *coping mechanism.*

Hashish

After marijuana, it was just a stone's throw to hashish, a product made of the pure THC resin from the cannabis plant, whose effect is slightly different from marijuana's—for some users it's more psychedelic, while other users experience feelings more associated with opiates. Hashish was often easier to find than pot in 1960s England, which helped spread its popularity.

One memorable Fab Four episode involving the drug occurred during a meeting at Apple involving the group's showcase band, Badfinger. The group wondered whether it could handle the pressure of a certain recording deadline. Harrison walked into the meeting, threw a huge chunk of hashish on the table, and said, "See if you can handle *this.*"

The future looked bright indeed for Badfinger with the addition of Liverpudlian Joey Molland in late 1969. His input steered the band from anachronistic pop into a harder rocking direction. *Photo by Harry Goodwin/Redferns*

In 1972, Paul and Linda McCartney were busted when Swedish police intercepted a package of hashish that had been sent to them.

LSD

Used initially as a therapeutic drug, LSD-25—discovered by Albert Hoffmann in 1943—soon hit the open market and, thanks to the efforts of such evangelists as Michael Hollingshead (in the U.K.) and Timothy Leary (in the U.S.), worked its way into the universe of musicians, actors, and artists by the early 1960s. Cary Grant and Groucho Marx were confirmed users, while the rumors spread surrounding Robert F. Kennedy and Marilyn Monroe. The drug wasn't ruled illegal in the U.S. until 1966.

Author Steve Turner recently ascertained that John Lennon and George Harrison were introduced to LSD, without their knowledge, at an April 1965 dinner party in London by "dentist to the stars" John Riley. While both Beatles were initially angry to have been "dosed," the experience was so transcendent for both that they soon became willing advocates. A California trip involving Lennon, the Byrds, Peter Fonda, and a few others resulted in the song "She Said, She Said."

Nobody really knew what it meant to be an "acid casualty" at this time, or how much was "too much"—the drug had only been in popular use for a few years—and many users ate it recklessly, therefore obscuring any possible positive effects the drug might have had.

Lennon later confessed to using it "hundreds of times" during a period of approximately two years. This careless, constant drug use drove a permanent wedge between John and his wife Cynthia, who found LSD terrifying and gave it up as quickly as she had tried it.

McCartney struggled with the idea of tripping, but eventually took his first dose in Lennon's presence. The experience was profound, but so intense that Macca largely eschewed the drug.

While McCartney's admission on British TV in spring 1967 that he'd tried the drug four times brought down a hailstorm of criticism, his use of LSD was actually more measured, well-considered, and sensible than that of many members of London's psychedelic underground, or the teenagers (mostly rich ones) hanging around the in-crowd. (Or of the "outraged" media members and upper-class hypocrites with alcohol problems, sexual addiction, or other nasty habits to hide.)

All four Beatles eventually found that the harrowing nature of acid was a good deterrent to overusing it.

STP

This psychedelic, said by most users to resemble a mix of LSD and amphetamines, freaked out more than one British rocker. Pete Townshend gave up hallucinogens completely after experiencing an especially bad STP trip on an airplane flight.

Meanwhile, Cass Elliot of the Mamas and the Papas apparently took it with the Beatles and some other folks at the Ad Lib club in London in late 1966. Elliot later told her friends, including some of the Monkees, that the drug was bad news. The unpredictable nature of STP, which led to bad trips all over the pop scene, led to its fairly quick decline.

Cocaine

Most observers believe that late 1966 marked cocaine's arrival into the British rock world. Immediately, the intense, ego-focused rush of cocaine added a certain daring and megalomania to the already riskily pretentious psychedelic scene, creating its own addictive base as well as helping to usher in the heroin age.

McCartney first snorted cocaine, brought to him by art dealer Robert Fraser, in late 1966 and then during the recording of *Sgt. Pepper*. He ended up using for about a year. Later McCartney would cite the harsh cocaine "mornings after" as the reason he stopped taking it.

While the image of the Beatles as a peace-love-and-LSD band carried through until 1968, the group had actually dropped most such "visionary" drugs months before, existing instead on a steady diet of pot and booze, some cocaine, and the (very) occasional psychedelic.

The emotional exhaustion created by acid, STP, and cocaine led everyone concerned to look for a deeper way. For the Beatles, meditation seemed to be that way. But, with the exception of George Harrison, none of the Fabs really found much salvation in meditation; instead of reaching a new level of consciousness, the Fabs just found new drugs to keep them busy through their long slow decline.

Heroin

It makes sense that Lennon, the Beatle most likely to do something far out (and self-destructive), would have fallen into the heroin trap. Already the province of jazz musicians in Britain, heroin found the Beatles and some of their friends by 1967.

Robert Fraser, part of McCartney's circle, was using, and some of the band's musician friends, such as Brian Jones of the Rolling Stones, had indulged as well. But while Macca was up for most things back then, he carefully held off from heroin despite the urging of its adherents—who, appearing skinny, hollow-cheeked, and pasty, hardly represented a positive endorsement.

Eventually, though, McCartney tried it once, in the company of Fraser and some of the Rolling Stones—but later claimed not to have known what he was smoking, simply inhaling what he was handed. When McCartney found out what he'd taken, he vowed never to use it again.

Lennon, who also wanted nothing to do with needles, became hooked during the early stages of his involvement with Yoko Ono, who like Lennon shared the desire to try anything and everything in the name of art. Ono, however, had dealt with tougher nuts, during her time in New York, than Lennon turned out to be.

JL's harrowing addiction, and even more harrowing withdrawal, are documented by his 1969 "Cold Turkey" 45. Lennon claimed to have finally gotten off the drug by locking himself in his room on an Atlantic sea voyage aboard the *Queen Mary* and literally sweating out his DTs. Tony Bramwell, however, notes that Lennon was booked at the London Clinic after this trip, and also asserts that John and Yoko didn't really get the monkeys off their backs until they'd undergone primal therapy with Arthur Janov in 1970.

The other two Beatles are not known to have indulged in King H.

Here's Another Clue for You All

Ten Reasons Why Paul *Must*'ve Been Dead!

Unquestionably *the* most bizarre chapter in all of Beatledom was the mass hysteria generated in the fall of 1969 by pervasive rumors of Paul McCartney's death, purported to have taken place *three years earlier.*

Apparently spawned on the campus of Ann Arbor's University of Michigan, the story was propagated by Detroit DJ Russ Gibb and supported by a host of "clues" gleaned from careful—and wacko—study of the group's albums and recordings.

Naturally, with the myth spurring sales of the Beatles' current release, *Abbey Road*, as well as their back catalog, no one connected with Apple's parent label was anxious to put out the fire. Not even after an intrepid reporter from *Life* magazine tracked down the reclusive McCartney at his Scottish farm for a statement did the rumors entirely die out (although Paul did let slip, in the same November 1969 article, four months before the story hit the headlines, that the Beatles were through).

The story itself went something like this: in November 1966, Paul died from head injuries sustained in a car wreck. Rather than allow the death of a key member to put an end to the band, the Beatles opted to soldier on, perhaps under pressure from their management and record company.

While tours were now out of the question, a stand-in would allow the band to maintain the ruse of the Beatles going about their daily lives. So, it was explained, the Beatles held a look-alike contest, the winner of which was never revealed. In fact, the story went, one William Campbell of Scotland was chosen on the basis of his uncanny resemblance to the deceased (and apparently, his singing and composing capabilities).

But, chafing under the directive to keep up the lie (it was said), the remaining Beatles decided to subtly tip their hand, letting fans in on the true

Though *Life* magazine's readers must've been relieved to know that Paul was alive, few caught his declaration that, "The Beatles thing is over."

story via an array of clues sprinkled throughout their songs and their album packaging. Soon, observant followers of the group were able to piece together the "real story" from fragments the surviving Fabs had thoughtfully provided.

Some cynics suggested that the Beatles themselves (or at least Allen Klein) were behind the fiction, considering the unexpected windfall that the story brought their way. All parties involved pointedly denied this; there's no reason to doubt them. Still, it was hard to accept, on the surface, any innocent explanation for John's declaration in "Glass Onion" that "the walrus was Paul."

Why such an obviously overblown conspiracy theory would take root in the first place may seem inexplicable on the surface, but given the tenor of the times, it was not. A generation that had revered the Beatles was reaching adulthood, at a time when cynicism and a sense of betrayal by authority figures was cresting. No less than three beloved leaders were slain during the decade, under murky circumstances and with less than compelling "official" explanations given.

Richard Nixon, the current president, had replaced a monumentally unpopular one, but was showing indications of deepening America's involvement in a despised foreign war. To a generation that had come of age feeling betrayed, the idea that they'd been fed one more lie and one more cover-up wasn't a hard sell.

Then there was this seeming mountain of evidence. Once people began looking, there was no end of hints to be found. (The fact that some of them actually *predated* Paul's alleged death didn't seem to faze anyone.)

Here, in reverse chronological order, is a rundown of some of the "evidence" that fueled the beliefs. Innocent explanations aside, it's easy to get caught up in the steady drumbeat of indicators.

Paul's Lowered Public Profile

Recognizing that the end of his beloved band was at hand, Paul uncharacteristically began to hole up at his Scottish retreat, near Mull of Kyntyre, in fall 1969. For the duration of the Beatles' career, Paul had been their most conspicuous face when it came to public pronouncements and general glad-handing of the press.

His apparent absence from the scene might have been enough to trigger suspicions. (This doesn't explain, however, all his public sightings from late 1966—when he is said to have died—through 1969.)

Paul began and ended the year sporting a heavy beard, a most uncharacteristic look for the heretofore fastidious Beatle. Furthermore, the fairy-tale romance between Jane Asher and Paul had ended—so that Paul could marry a *commoner*? Clearly, something was amiss. . . .

The *Abbey Road* Album Cover

The September 26, 1969, release of the last-recorded Beatle album marked a departure from the band's last couple of long players. No copy appeared on the jacket's front, nor were lyrics included. Still, the disc was chock full of terrific tunes, adroitly produced in a manner that bordered on slick.

The cover image itself was the embodiment of tasteful simplicity, certainly not as clever, ambitious, or artsy as others the Fabs had used before. But very soon this casual document of the Beatles at their workplace became one of most pored-over photos in history.

Once the Paul-is-dead story took off, the *Abbey Road* cover became Exhibit A as a depiction of his funeral procession. Leading the way was John, resplendent in white, as the preacher. Next, in a black suit coat, was Ringo, the undertaker.

As the departed, "Paul" was shown with eyes closed, in burial clothes, barefoot. The last characteristic was explained as depicting the supposedly prevalent practice of burying the dead minus footwear. To those looking for evidence of an imposter within the ranks, it was noted that "Paul" was holding a cigarette in his right hand; Beatle Paul was famously left-handed. Also, he is out of step.

Bringing up the rear, the denim-clad George represented the gravedigger in work clothes.

Another feature drawing attention was the presence of a Volkswagen Beetle bearing a license plate reading "LMW 28IF." The latter designation, it was pointed out, connoted that Paul would have been "twenty-eight, *if* alive." Although in fact Paul would have been (and was) twenty-seven, apologists noted that in Chinese culture, one year is added to a person's age at birth. Lastly, some explained that LMW stood for "Linda McCartney Weeps."

As a morbid footnote, a tangential connection exists between death and the Beatles in this photo. By the time the Beatles finished their work that August day, morning was breaking in Los Angeles. For actress Sharon Tate and several friends, their last day on earth had begun. By way of explaining the horrors inflicted on five adults and one near-full-term baby that bloody night, prosecutors pointed to "clues" of an apocalyptic race war found on the "White Album," as interpreted by sociopathic misfit Charlie Manson.

"Revolution 9"

Being a sound collage comprised of tape loops, dialogue, a Beatles rhythm track, and snippets of found sounds, this singular track contained enough stray elements to likely explain *anything* one wanted to. To "PID" buffs, the sonic onslaught conveyed nothing less than an enactment of Paul's fatal accident, complete with car horns and crash sounds.

A more readily accessible "clue" present on the track comes from the title sound bite itself. The phrase "Number 9," as uttered on this track, sounds something like "turn me on, dead man" when played backwards.

(Interestingly, it was Paul who had come up with the key tag line in "A Day in the Life": "I'd love to turn you on.")

"I'm So Tired"

This track from *The Beatles* is among the handful that, sonically and lyrically, were said to offer hints as to the state of things among the group. At the end of the song, John can be heard muttering a bit of gibberish that sounds like "Monsieur, monsieur, can I have another one?"

Once again, when the comment is played backwards, the ear of the beholder can detect a deeper meaning: the lament "Paul is a dead man. Miss him, miss him, miss him."

The *Magical Mystery Tour* Album Packaging

Going back to December 1967, thirteen months after the supposed fatal accident, the Beatles issued the *Magical Mystery Tour* soundtrack as a double EP set in England and as a full-blown album in America. Both releases contained a booklet of pictures depicting scenes from the film.

One image shows the band in performance mode, as seen in *Magical Mystery Tour*'s "I Am the Walrus" sequence. Ringo's bass drum head is sporting a new skin, a colorful design that appears to read "Love the 3 Beatles." Also, the "Paul" seen in the shot has removed his shoes; as some would have it, empty shoes denote "death" in some cultures.

Another picture shows the Beatles in white tuxes for the film's "Your Mother Should Know" finale. Three of the Fabs sport red carnations; the other's is black. Can you guess whose?

The "Beatles" name itself on the album cover is shown spelled out in stars. When read upside down (or in a mirror), a phone number is said to reveal itself. Calling the number (with the proper international prefix and London area code applied) will, according to the beliefs of some, lead to a voice detailing the particulars of Paul's end.

In fact, when dialed a certain way, the numbers reached a reporter for London's *Guardian* newspaper, who was being driven crackers by overseas calls at all hours featuring breathless foreigners seeking The Truth.

"I Am the Walrus"

Those unfamiliar with Lewis Carroll's poem "The Walrus and the Carpenter" were forced to invent their own explanations of the song's imagery. As explained by John, his own misreading of Carroll's work led him to identify with the wrong side in what some have read as an allegory on workers and capitalists. (Though he did point out that singing "I am the carpenter!" didn't scan well.)

Beatles mythologists instead contrived the explanation that in Scandinavian countries, a walrus is seen as a portent of death. (This is untrue, although some have asserted that a sailor spotting a dead walrus while headed out to sea may turn back.)

Muddying matters is the fact that while John obviously wrote and sang the song, and is indeed costumed as a walrus in the *Magical Mystery Tour* film, a subtitle to the tune appearing only on the MMT soundtrack reads " 'No you're not!' said Little Nicola."

Less than a year later, John would tell listeners in "Glass Onion" that "the walrus was Paul." Naturally (!) some took this to mean John was explicitly telling us that Paul was indeed deceased. (To believe this, one must accept that being a walrus equals death.)

But John explained in 1980's *Playboy* interview that the song was directed at overanalytical fans in general and that *that* line was a message to his bandmate in particular, declaring that he was abdicating his throne to Paul to be with Yoko, so "have this stroke, this crumb, because I'm leaving."

The final word on who *was* the walrus came in John's 1970 solo composition, "God." In it, he closes the door on his Beatles career with the words, "I was the walrus, but now I'm John."

As is noted elsewhere in this book, "I Am the Walrus" was augmented by the addition of a BBC radio feed, featuring a production of Shakespeare's *King Lear*. As serendipitous timing would have it, the scene being enacted, the slaying of Oswald, is replete with references to dying, including the gurgled line, "Oh! Untimely death!" Seconds later, the lines, "What, is he dead?" "Sit you down, father, rest you" are heard.

Simple Shakespearean coincidence, or an enactment of a priest arriving too late to administer last rites at the scene of Macca's accident?

The *Sgt. Pepper's* Album Cover

This elaborately packaged release proved to be rich with clues, at least to those looking for them. To begin with, it's beyond dispute that the party appears to be overlooking a grave, though it was likely intended as a farewell to the "old Beatles," seen in wax to the new Fabs' right.

A left-handed guitar made of yellow hyacinths is depicted in that grave, with three "strings"—signifying three Beatles? The "Paul" figure in the group is shown straight on, as if a cardboard cutout, while the other three are at an angle, as if propping him up.

Just above "Paul's" head is an open hand, read by some as a benediction for the dead. (Some "PIDers" aver that a hand above the head is a sign of death, in some culture or other. Though this belief appears unfounded, a similar hand-above-Paul's-head occurs, in cartoon form, on the cover of the *Yellow Submarine* soundtrack.)

Inside the gatefold, the four Beatles are posed in full Pepper regalia. On the "Paul" figure's shoulder, a military-looking sleeve patch appears with the apparent designation "O.P.D." This, the mythmakers told us, was police shorthand for how the late Mr. McCartney was tagged: "*Officially Pronounced Dead.*"

Actually, according to those who troubled themselves to do the research, it was a police patch received by the Beatles when they toured in Canada. The actual initials, O.P.*P.*, stand for "Ontario Provincial Police."

On the album's back cover, three Beatles are shown facing forward while the apparent Paul figure, dressed in blue, has his back to the camera. This in itself could raise suspicions of something untoward going on when added to all the other "evidence." Some have put forth the explanation that Mal Evans stood in for Paul, explaining that Macca may have been in America and therefore unavailable on the day of the shoot.

It would have made no sense for the Beatles to go to the expense of arranging such an important photo session when they weren't all in attendance. Other images recorded at the same time show all four Beatles facing forward, so it IS curious that Paul would avoid looking at the camera in a picture for an album that had his fingerprints all over it.

That same shot yielded further eyebrow-raising aspects. The band's photo was superimposed over the entire album's lyrics. George's finger appears to be pointing at the words "Wednesday morning at five o'clock" from "She's Leaving Home." Beatleologists assured us that this was the very hour Paul shuffled off this mortal coil.

Also, the head of the Paul figure appears next to the words "Without you" from the title of George's lone *Sgt. Pepper's* composition.

The "Strawberry Fields Forever" Single

Of all the Paul-is-dead clues, this one and the *Abbey Road* cover photo seemed to capture the public's imagination the most.

Until the advent of *Anthology 2*, which featured a stripped-down version of one of "SFF"'s numerous takes, it was rather hard to discern definitively John's mumbled words at the close of the recording. For fans sitting in front

The unearthly coda to this song unsettled many a close listener in the autumn of 1969.

of their stereo speakers in late 1969 with the sound turned up, there could be no doubt: Lennon was confessing, "I buried Paul."

Coupled with the otherworldly, Mellotron-generated flutes, tribal drumming, and stinging guitar, the experience was nothing less than spine-chilling.

The *Anthology* set's numerous bits of studio chatter and extended mixes gave the public insight into John's non-sequetic nature. Just about anything was liable to fall out of his mouth; in this instance, "Cranberry sauce."

The *Revolver* Cover

Though this album preceded the widely believed date of Paul's earthly departure, that didn't stop the fanatics from finding suspicious anomalies.

For starters, the "Paul" figure is distinguished by the fact that *he alone* is shown in profile. (When artist Klaus Voormann was asked about this, in all innocence, by a fan at a Chicago Beatles convention in recent years, he offered the bloodless rejoinder: "What you're saying is shit!")

To those bent on finding meaning, the lyrics were full of references to Paul's untimely death: "I was alone, I took a ride . . ." "I know what it's like to be dead . . ." "Long ago she knew someone, but now he's gone . . ." and, creatively, "*Paul* [*sic*] played the game, existence to the end. . . ."

The *Yesterday . . . and Today* Album Cover

This album's sleeve has received plenty of attention for other reasons, but so struck were the "PID" fans that they could not control themselves from including it for good measure.

Principally, it is claimed that the so-called "steamer trunk" cover, which replaced the infamous Bob Whitaker "butcher cover," is startlingly suspicious. The Fabs are shown, with palpable ennui, gathered around the oversized container; only Paul is actually inside it. When the image is given a ¼ clockwise turn, you can see the late Mr. McCartney in his coffin. *Was Paul forecasting his own death?*

And in the End

The Countdown to History

I t took years for the public to accept that the Beatles were finished as a group. For at least a decade after their last release, the drumbeat never ceased from fans, promoters, and SNL producer Lorne Michaels asking the Fabs to reunite. Only John Lennon's murder reduced those hopes, but even at that, calls soon came for Paul, George, and Ringo to get together with *Julian*.

What the public never suspected was the enormous toll that being a Beatle exacted on each member. Living in each other's back pocket for years, the pressures of sustaining an image, and the desire to be continually besting themselves—not to mention strains caused by business and personal issues—all ate away at the unity of purpose that had once buoyed them.

In the beginning, when so many expected the Beatles to be an overnight fancy, the eternal question was, "When will the bubble burst?" By the time critics and the public had come to accept the Fabs' staying power, cracks in the foundation were evident to anyone looking, including the group itself. Here are some of the stepping-stones that marked the path to disintegration by decade's end.

The Loss of Brian Epstein: August 27, 1967

Irrespective of his shortcomings as a human being and as a businessman, Brian Epstein was no less essential to the Beatles' success than George Martin. It was Brian's finely tuned sense of presentation, as well as an unshakable belief in the boys' greatness, that got them out of Liverpool and onto the world's stage at precisely the right moment in history.

He had set out to make them "bigger than Elvis" and succeeded beyond anyone's dreams. (In Brian's mind, everything that came after 1964 must have seemed anticlimactic.) Once the Beatles had arrived, Brian saw to it that they exploited every market through personal exposure, almost without break.

It was touring that sustained a rock-and-roll act in the 1960s; foregoing that path after 1966, the Beatles entered uncharted waters, but no less so than their manager, who now saw what he viewed as his primary duty rendered obsolete.

But had he lived, there is little doubt that Brian would by his very presence have kept the band from drifting too far into self-indulgence. Despite having long since written off his musical input, the Fabs respected Brian's uncanny capacity for seeing the big picture even when they could not—witness his last triumph, enlisting them for the *Our World* broadcast.

Epstein kept his charges buffered from any real nitty-gritty business concerns, and had he been around, Apple doubtless would have been run as the tight ship it needed to be. Indeed, the Fabs themselves realized this: conversations recorded during the *Let It Be* project reveal remarkable self-awareness, with George and Paul observing that Brian's death had left a void that they themselves were scarcely qualified to fill.

John amplified the theme in his 1970 *Rolling Stone* interview, telling Jann Wenner that he harbored no illusions about the Fabs' ability to do anything well other than make music: "I thought, 'We've fuckin' had it.' "

With Brian gone, a key component to their infrastructure went without replacement.

Paul vs. the Beatles, Round 1: Spring 1969

Until the insinuation of Allen Klein into the Beatles' business affairs in early 1969, the only real beef the other three Beatles had with Paul McCartney was his innate selfishness (according to George, Paul would happily work on one of your songs after you'd first recorded ten of his) and his propensity to push them harder than they were usually willing to work ("we're lazy fuckers," to quote John).

But given their complete fiscal disarray by the end of 1968, it was obvious that some sort of business overseer was essential to their financial survival. John first made overtures to Lord Richard Beeching, the railroad baron who gained renown, or everlasting infamy, for wielding the "Beeching Axe" in the mid-'60s, saving the British rail system by decimating it. He took one look at Apple's books before advising, "Lads, stick to music."

Another prospect came conveniently attached to Paul's betrothed. Linda Eastman, though known in rock circles as an accomplished photographer, was in no way connected to the Eastman-Kodak empire (except perhaps as a consumer). She was, however, the daughter of Lee Eastman, a powerful Manhattan show-business attorney. (Coincidentally, their family name before Anglicization had been *Epstein*; also, the pop standard "Linda" had

The closest that George and Eric Clapton came to being in a band together may have been while touring with Delaney and Bonnie in late 1969 throughout Europe.

Photo by Jan Persson/Redferns

been named in her honor by one of her father's clients, songwriter Jack Lawrence, when Linda was just five.)

At first, John, George, and Ringo were willing to accept Lee's fresh-out-of-law-school son John as general counsel for their affairs. The Eastmans were very big on artists owning their own publishing (or *other artists' publishing*, an idea Paul would eventually adopt with a vengeance). It made sense for the Beatles themselves to buy NEMS, secured by an advance against future royalties by EMI.

But Paul's coziness with the Eastmans never sat well with the others. It would be natural for Lee Eastman to place his son-in-law's interests before the others, if that's what it came down to, would it not? The other three were also put off by stylistic differences. Both father and son Eastman struck John as cultural wannabes; all their artsy-fartsy talk seemed unnatural and calculated to impress, at least to Lennon's ears.

On the other hand, the arrival of the politesse-immune Allen Klein on the scene signaled the beginning of the end of Beatle unity. Brash, rumpled, and impolite, Klein had no time for manners, except as an inconvenient means to an end, when absolutely necessary.

All working-class hero posturing by Lennon aside, Klein was the real deal, coming from a depressed background and raised by relatives. His personal background was irresistibly appealing to John and George especially, and with his arrival the Fabs would, at George's urging, at least see what Klein and Eastman could accomplish in tandem.

Unfortunately, it was not to be. Klein's Eddie Haskell–like manner of getting under people's skin while following the form, if not substance, of polite interactions paid off when he and John, already suspicious of the Eastmans, sandbagged Linda's father in a face-to-face meeting. After being baited mercilessly (Klein, among other things, calling him "Epstein"), the elder Eastman at last erupted with a torrent of verbal invective directed at Klein that burned all bridges for good. Klein's divide-and-conquer strategy was just beginning.

With Eastman permanently out of favor with one of the Beatles, Klein began to earn his keep with a thorough audit of the band's finances. What he discovered served to further splinter the up-until-recently Fab foursome.

Without telling the others, Paul had been buying up shares of the Beatles' publisher, Northern Songs, thus tipping the fragile equilibrium his way. When John was informed, he was outraged, and irrevocably so. "It was the first time one of us had gone behind the other's backs!" he later seethed. Whatever goodwill might have remained was quickly slipping away.

The Beatles were now separated into two camps: John, George, and Ringo in support of Allen Klein on one side, Paul and his in-laws on the other. Much of the spring of 1969 saw Team Klein do its utmost to get the contrarian bassist to come to the dark side and put his signature on the dotted line. Paul's understandable refusal would remain an open wound from this point on.

Live Peace in Toronto: September 13, 1969

Just over three weeks after the Beatles finished recording duties on *Abbey Road*, John, at his Apple office, took a phone call from Canadian concert promoter John Brower, who along with partner Ken Walker had scored a success with Toronto's first Pop Festival in June.

Now, three months later, their Rock and Roll Revival Festival, built around '50s legends Chuck Berry, Little Richard, and Jerry Lee Lewis, was headed for trouble.

The event, booked at the twenty-thousand-seat Varsity Stadium, was not even close to selling out. Contemporary artists, including the Doors and up-and-comers Alice Cooper and Chicago Transit Authority, were added to expand the appeal, but as Brower and Walker plotted ways to salvage the event, the notion that "only the Beatles could save us" took hold.

Brower seized the initiative and called John, recognizing the goodwill generated back in June when the second "Bed-In for Peace" resulted in "Give Peace a Chance" being recorded in Montreal. Hoping to draw at least one Beatle to his event, perhaps to MC, he gave the sweetest appeal he could muster.

Lennon, only half-listening, took the call as an invitation to perform and accepted. He told the nonplussed Brower that he could be there the next day, as soon as he got a band together.

Fresh out of Cream *and* Blind Faith, Eric Clapton was an easy choice for John, who had enjoyed playing with him at the *Rock and Roll Circus* the year before. Klaus Voormann, a confidant for nearly a decade, got the nod for bass. Rounding out the ad hoc Plastic Ono Band was drummer Alan White, fresh from the band Griffin (and later to join Yes).

Having assembled a band with relative ease, John now had to conjure a set list. On the transatlantic flight, the band rehearsed some rock-and-roll standards, sans drums and electricity. The songs traced a logical linear progression, from Carl Perkins's rockabilly "Blue Suede Shoes" through John's own free-verse anthem "Give Peace a Chance," with the as-yet-unrecorded "Cold Turkey" thrown in for good measure.

Once the reality of what he'd committed to hit him full force, Lennon spent much of his warm-up time vomiting backstage, in a combination of nerves and heroin withdrawal. But before a roaring crowd for the first time in three years, he quickly regained his nonchalant, cocky form: "We're just gonna do numbers that we know, ya know, 'cause we've never played together before. . . ."

The band settled into a groove, cranking out the tunes like the professionals they were. To the extent that a performer feeds off of the energy projected by his audience (who had greeted the POB by holding aloft their cigarette lighters), John and crew were in great shape.

Yoko followed with a pair of extended jams that resembled no music anyone in attendance had ever heard. After eighteen challenging minutes, the musicians exited the stage, leaving their live guitars against their amplifiers, causing some howling feedback mercifully cut short by Mal Evans, who shut the amps off.

Exhilarated by the reception and the buzz he'd generated, the *Live Peace in Toronto* gig (subsequently released as an album) gave John the motivational wherewithal to recognize that there was life after the Beatles. Though *Abbey Road* wasn't yet in stores, he began mentally laying the groundwork for the next phase of his artistic existence, in a future that didn't include sharing the spotlight with anyone he wasn't—literally—married to.

"Cold Turkey" Snubbed: September 1969

Having proved he could cut it without Paul, George, and Ringo, John nonetheless vacillated on the question of whether or not to carry on as a Beatle. Though inwardly torn between playing the game a little longer and cutting ties to the group that had given him an identity, furthering the status quo seemed to be the way for each Beatle to deal with his misgivings.

To that end, John brought in a new song he'd been working on. Continuing to mine the vein of personal experiences he undergone that year, he presented "Cold Turkey" as the next Beatle single. This graphic depiction of the agonies he'd experienced in getting off junk (replete with bone-chilling howls of distress) would have made for a startling contrast with "Something," penciled in for release the following week.

But Paul, in a reversal of the stance he'd taken all year, would have none of it. To this point, he had been all too quick to support John in any fancy he cared to indulge in, so long as it meant perpetuating the Beatles. McCartney's willingness to record and release "The Ballad of John and Yoko," dubious as the circumstances were (e.g., two Beatles present, a single already in release), was a prime example, as was not challenging John on his regular flouting of band policy by including Yoko in discussions of business issues.

But the band had been sensing an ongoing musical divergence. As far back as the *Let It Be* sessions, Paul had pushed his bandmates past all understanding with his insistence on getting "Maxwell's Silver Hammer" to qualify as single material. Less than enamored of the song from day one, by the time the *Abbey Road* sessions had concluded, at least three of the Fabs were thoroughly sick of the "fruity" (George's word) song "for Grannies to dig" (John's characterization).

Thus at the twilight of their career together the two principal songwriters of the band were at utter cross-purposes, with John uninterested in anything that wasn't "real" and Paul merely wishing get listeners' toes a-tapping. After all the accommodation Paul had provided in 1969 to keep John engaged and the show running, this latest contribution was just too much, and Paul told him so.

"Bugger you, I'll put it out myself!" was John's response. Gathering up his Toronto bandmates, but substituting Ringo for Alan White, John laid down the harrowing track at Trident Studios one month after the Beatles finished *Abbey Road*. In one stroke, he effectively ended the Lennon-McCartney songwriting partnership (to whatever extent it still existed) by crediting himself alone, simultaneously all but proclaiming the Beatles' demise. In a further gesture of defiance, the single's label read in large type "PLAY LOUD."

It was around this time that things between John and Paul came to a head at Apple. In response to Paul's pushing a little too hard for a commitment over some proposal (possibly his ongoing pipe dream that the Beatles could play a series of unannounced club dates under an assumed name in an effort to reclaim their mojo), John snapped.

The standard telling has John ending the discussion—after first opining that Paul was daft—by declaring "I want a divorce." John afterward seemed to take an almost sadistic pleasure in describing his partner's shock. As the story goes, both Allen Klein and Paul pressured John to keep the decision secret lest ongoing business negotiations go south (as they had earlier that year, the last time Lennon shot off his mouth).

It's hard to know how the other Beatles read John's statement. Certainly no one was prepared to publicly second his motion. Each Fab stayed busy while waiting to see if John really meant it: George, by producing Doris Troy's Apple debut and Jackie Lomax's "How the Web Was Woven"; Ringo with his not-quite-the-train-wreck-it-would-appear-to-be-on-the-surface swing-era pop album, *Sentimental Journey*; and Paul, enjoying his Scotland farm, wife, and firstborn child while absenting himself from the limelight.

As for Lennon, he remained outwardly sanguine when asked about the Beatles' future. In interviews he gave between October and the following April, he kept all Beatle options open, while admitting to struggles of late, both business and creative.

He noted that their future album releases might have to be carved up equitably track-wise, given George's ascension as a writer (not even counting Ringo's newfound input). That said, he also pointed out that he could hardly be expected to commit himself to six months' work on a Beatle album, only to have two songs on the completed release.

The Beatles' Final Christmas Message: Fall 1969

One of the more joyful aspects of the holiday season during the Beatles years was the little treat that came to members in good standing of the Beatles Fan Club. From 1963 through 1969, Christmas was marked by the arrival of a seven-inch "flexi-disc," containing a "message" from the Fabs thanking fans for their support.

The idea behind this little bit of extra originated with press officer Tony Barrow. While Brian was concerned about the potential costs, the Beatles themselves jumped at the chance.

The performances were typically knocked out at the end of recording sessions; after enough usable tape was generated, they were edited down, pressed on flexible plastic, and mailed out in December. These highly coveted items usually came in unique sleeves; typical "pressings" didn't go much beyond fifty thousand copies.

By the fourth go-round, the annual gift had become an outlet for Fab ambitions beyond mere holiday mirth. Nineteen-sixty-six's *Pantomime: Everywhere It's Christmas* took on the trappings of a radio show, with fully enacted scenes, characterizations, songs, and production values. A year later, *Christmastime Is Here Again* built upon the radio show theme, coming as an exploration of the Beatles' inner *Goon Show* tendencies. (It even featured a cameo from special guest actor Victor Spinetti.)

Alas, 1967 represented the high point of the Fabs' *esprit de corps*. By the time the next Christmas duty arrived, the Beatles had been through the wringer, namely the acrimonious "White Album" sessions, the start-up of Apple, and the advent of Yoko Ono on the scene.

The Beatles' 1968 Christmas Record was assembled from bits each Beatle recorded separately. With tension running high between the Fabs, it's clear that no one was interested in getting together to maintain the five-year-old tradition; indeed, John contributed the pointedly bitter tale of "Jock and Yono," an unsubtle commentary on the hostility they faced as a couple: "They battled on against overwhelming oddities, including some of their beast friends."

Amidst ever increasing trauma and rancor in 1969, no one had any reason to expect another Beatles Christmas record, yet there it was: like its predecessor, *The Beatles' Seventh Christmas Record* was stitched together from solo contributions. This time, however, three of the Fabs were only barely involved.

George particularly sounds as though he's phoning it in: his terse "This is George Harrison saying Happy Christmas" was taken by editor (and BBC radio personality) Kenny Everett and cleverly reedited to sound like a holiday Krishna chant.

Ringo's contribution was only slightly longer (and seemingly contrived purely as promotion for the *Magic Christian* film), while Paul dutifully presented an acoustic holiday greeting. Ironically, the bulk of the Beatles' final fan club message is from John and Yoko, though Lennon had turned in his notice only weeks before.

It therefore begs the question: what was he on about? Though he was role-playing with Yoko throughout (their "Mother" and child act makes its first appearance here), his very appearance and dominant role in this final Beatles message speaks volumes about his capacity for hoodwinking the masses by suggesting that all was well in Beatleland.

As for the Christmas messages, 1970 saw all seven collated onto an Apple LP (issued as *From Then to You* in England and *The Beatles Christmas Album* in America) and presented as a farewell from the Beatles Fan Club. Authentic copies are extremely hard to come by, but the release has been widely bootlegged.

The Last Beatles Recording Session: January 3, 1970

As the *Let It Be* film and accompanying album were prepared for release, it became obvious that despite hundreds of hours of film shot and tape expended, the Beatles were still short on usable material. ("Don't Let Me Down," earmarked for the U.S.-only *Hey Jude* compilation, due out in February, was already off the table, despite being seen twice in the completed cut of the film.)

To this point, George had been represented on Glyn Johns's initial construction of releasable product by "For You Blue," unquestionably the weakest of the songs he had offered. (Other far worthier tunes included "All Things Must Pass," "Let It Down," "Isn't It a Pity," and "Hear Me Lord," all of which ended up on George's first proper solo album, and "Old Brown Shoe," "Something," and "I Me Mine." The Fabs saw fit to revisit only two of them by the end of the *Abbey Road* sessions.)

One of the film's most memorable sequences included George's Twickenham Studio introduction of "I Me Mine," portentously played by what one day would be called the "Threetles" while John and Yoko performed a crude approximation of a waltz. It made sense to include the song on the album, but since the Beatles never picked it up again (John, in particular, rudely dismissing it), no multitrack recording existed.

It therefore became necessary for the Beatles, such as they existed, to return to the studio to tidy up loose ends and cut one last original tune.

By this time, Paul and Ringo had begun working on *their* debut solo releases. George, while producing others, had been writing at a furious pace but had not as yet laid down any tracks. His future producer at this time was a mere Spector on the horizon.

George Martin did the honors, capturing a rather unadorned arrangement of an uncharacteristically brief performance. Absent was John Lennon, on holiday in Denmark. Since he had quit the group back in September, it's doubtful that anyone expected him, but even if he hadn't left, George Harrison compositions remained somewhat low on John's priority list.

As if to commemorate this most auspicious occasion, George kicked off the session with a tongue-in-cheek announcement: "You all will have read that Dave Dee is no longer with us, but Mickey and Tich and I have decided to carry on the good work that's always gone down in #2" (referring to EMI's #2 studio).

He was referencing the English rock band Dave Dee, Dozy, Beaky, Mick and Tich. The outfit behind this unwieldy name had, commencing in 1966, scored a string of hit singles ("The Legend of Xanadu" the biggest), but remained unknown in America. Dave Dee had left for a solo career, also in September 1969.

Adding further lightheartedness to the session was an instrumental jam recorded between takes, as well as a run-through of Buddy Holly's posthumous hit, "Peggy Sue Got Married."

On the following day, the three returned to the studio to lay down overdubs on the album's title track. The next time Paul, George, and Ringo would record together in a studio was in 1994, for the "Free as a Bird" *Anthology* single. (Though all three would appear on George's tribute to John, "All Those Years Ago" in 1981, their parts were recorded separately.)

If there were any reflections or reminiscences among the folks present at the "I Me Mine" session, they've gone unrecorded. Surely the three Beatles and George Martin were under no delusions that they would ever work together as a unit again. It would have been interesting to know what they had to say before each went his separate way.

"Instant Karma!" Recorded January 27, 1970

Ever the instant gratification seeker, John Lennon had long aspired to release a record immediately after it was conceived and recorded. With this single, John achieved his goal, or at least came as close as anyone ever had.

No longer bound to offer material to his erstwhile bandmates, he nonetheless managed to make contact with George on this day. Freshly composed
tune in hand, by 4:00 P.M., the two met up at EMI's number 3 studio, along
with Billy Preston, Klaus Voormann, and Alan White as the core recording
unit. At George's suggestion, Phil Spector was recruited to run the session.

Requiring a platoon of singers to fire up the song's infectious chorus,
John dispatched Mal Evans and Billy Preston to recruit anyone with a voice
and a pulse. They returned with a number of patrons from Hatchett's Pub,
who were duly deputized to provide vocals and handclaps.

The track itself was a production marvel. Without his usual slathering of
glockenspiels and timpani, Spector managed to concoct a sound that was
simultaneously cutting-edge and timeless. With a delay-heavy lead vocal and
rather basic chords, "Instant Karma!" evoked nothing less than John's glory
days at the Top Ten in Hamburg.

Though recording a song the day it was composed was possible, pressing
and distributing it was not. It took nearly two weeks for the record to make it

John appeared twice on *Top of the Pops* in England to promote "Instant Karma." In
one performance, a blindfolded Yoko held up instructional cue cards to the audience; in the other, she sat and knit.   *Photo by Ron Howard/Redferns*

to the shops, where it went to #5 in England and #3 in America, the highest charting to date of any Beatle spin-off release.

Whatever else it proved, "Instant Karma!" must certainly have given John the confidence to proceed with a solo recording career, while doubtlessly stirring Paul's competitive instincts. As it happened, over a year passed before Paul released a single, 1971's "Another Day" (composed, at least in part, by early 1969). Though the single peaked at #5 in the States and #2 in the U.K., it received a lambasting from critics, especially coming on the heels of John's *Plastic Ono Band* LP and George's triumphant *All Things Must Pass.*

Let It Be: May 1970

Though a stream of solo singles from John may have given Beatles fans concern for the future of their beloved band, the March 1970 release of some "new" product must have reassured those not privy to the Fabs' in-house disarray.

Produced by George Martin, the "Let It Be" single at last found a public airing, some fourteen months after its initial recording. It followed Simon and Garfunkel's "Bridge over Troubled Water" to #1 in America, reaffirming the country's taste for piano-based gospel-style ballads. (S&G actually bested the Fabs, topping the U.S. charts for seven weeks, compared to "Let It Be," which lasted a mere three weeks at the top.)

But bigger issues brewed over the *Let It Be* album. The uproar over Phil Spector's production aside, another battle loomed over its proposed release. In scheduling an April 1970 drop date, the soundtrack collided head-on with *McCartney*, Paul's debut, and he was not amused.

Throughout their career, the Beatles had always been careful with release schedules, making certain to not bump heads directly with their biggest competitors, lest they compromise their sales potential. Certain that Allen Klein (Paul's self-interview for the solo album pointedly asserted that "he does not represent me in *any* way") was behind the chicanery, McCartney was livid. A note from the others suggesting that he push *McCartney* back to June assured Paul that it was "nothing personal." McCartney refused to budge.

Nearly overlooked amidst the bickering was Ringo's *Sentimental Journey* album, also ready to go. Perhaps recognizing that an LP's worth of "Good Night" was not likely to dent sales of *Let It Be* by much, it was rushed to market in late March to minimize any undue conflict.

At loggerheads with their estranged bassist, the remaining band members drew straws for the honor of heading over to Cavendish in an attempt to reason with him. Ringo "won" this thankless task, which went unappreciated by its recipient. Paul flew into a rage at Starkey, stopping just short of administering a physical beating as he unleashed a furious torrent of abuse upon the hapless peace emissary. The ugly incident ended with the drummer ordered to put on his coat and get out.

Though Paul was later to express his regret at having made Ringo the butt of his anger, the others ultimately relented and allowed Paul to keep his April 17 date, pushing *Let It Be* to May 8 in England and May 18 in the States. By the time both albums were released, Paul's infamous self-interview had made clear that the group was finished for all intents.

As for the film, the band first saw a rough cut on July 20, 1969, one day before laying down "Come Together." Not long after that, director Michael Lindsay-Hogg took a call from Peter Brown, who informed him that much of the John and Yoko footage would have to go. When the director protested, Brown told him, "Let me put it another way. I've had three phone calls this morning saying it ought to [be cut] out." (Can you guess whom the three calls were from?)

The end result ran eighty-one minutes long and was remarkable for what else was omitted. Nowhere was there a hint that George had walked out. Salacious material was removed completely, including anything hinting at drug use, Paul's complaints of "jock itch," unseemly language such as Paul calling Glyn Johns "fuck face," bizarre improvisations, like the one dubbed "Negro in Reserve," and even the racial satire that was the foundation for the original title song ("Don't dig no Pakistanis taking all the people's jobs—get *back*!").

On May 20, 1970, *Let It Be* made its long-delayed big screen debut. None of the Beatles attended. (In fact, George chose this night to begin work with Phil Spector on *All Things Must Pass.*) Though *Let It Be* went on to win an Academy Award *and* a Grammy for Best Original Score, the entire affair was joyless, as far as the Beatles were concerned.

Critics were equally underwhelmed, including Alan Smith of the *New Musical Express*. He succinctly expressed the disappointment felt by legions of fans in the album that would be the Beatles' swan song, calling it "a cheapskate epitaph, a cardboard tombstone."

The "Lennon Remembers" *Rolling Stone* Interview: December 1970

The final decade of John Lennon's life was bookended by lengthy magazine interviews. Nineteen-eighty saw the *Playboy* interview conducted by David Sheff (later published in book form under the titles *The Playboy Interviews* and *All We Are Saying*); ten years earlier, he had sat down with

Rolling Stone publisher Jann Wenner for an epic interview later released as *Lennon Remembers.*

The conversation was held in New York toward the end of 1970, some months after John and Yoko had undergone primal therapy under Dr. Arthur Janov, but just before Paul lobbed another bombshell at his former bandmates, this time in the form of a lawsuit to dissolve their partnership.

Given John's raw emotions regarding the year's events, as well as a lifetime's worth of deep-rooted pain from which therapy had recently ripped the scab, a high level of bile would have been expected in his recounting of life generally and the Beatle years specifically.

But it's doubtful that many fans were aware of the astonishing *level* of resentment that John Lennon had heretofore kept in check: anger at the price of being a Beatle, at those who despised Yoko, at every authority figure in his entire life, and, mostly, at Paul.

Though his scorched-earth venom spewed in all directions, stunning the public at large (but likely not anyone close to him), Lennon admitted years later to overstating, if not outright fabricating, much of what he had said in the interview. Still, his bitterness was real enough at the time, making *Lennon Remembers* an invaluable snapshot of the emotions stirred by the Beatles' breakup.

Paul vs. the Beatles (Round 2): December 31, 1970

Lennon Remembers and Paul's *McCartney* promotional interview notwithstanding, most of the 1970 Beatle commentary on whether the band would reunite was surprisingly open-ended. Each acknowledged generally that their lives had changed and they all needed a break from the Beatle thing as they followed individual pursuits, yet all seemed reluctant to rule out recording together again.

Even George, who could justifiably have walked away forever, given the grief of his Beatles existence, wisely pointed out that while working together entailed a personal sacrifice, the benefits outweighed the downside. Besides, he said, "I think it's very selfish if the Beatles don't record together."

All this changed dramatically with the lawsuit filed on the last day of 1970 by Paul in London's High Court of Justice.

As a partner in Apple, Paul had but one of four votes in matters taken up by the directors (i.e., themselves). In a 3-to-1 vote, Apple had become a company under the management of Allen Klein, or ABKCO. Though he never signed a piece of paper agreeing to this arrangement (while posing for pictures suggesting that he had), Paul was outvoted and thus subject to the rule of Klein, both as an Apple director *and* an Apple artist.

It galled Paul no end to discover that his *McCartney* record jacket bore the inscription "Apple Records—An ABKCO Managed Company"—and his temperature surely rose again when he discovered that Klein was billing for royalties on the release, viewing it as Beatles product rather than a solo effort, which would be outside his auspices.

To stem the flow of Macca royalties into the communal kitty, John Eastman requested that all monies be held by EMI, rather than paid to Apple. Until the mess was sorted out, Paul received no money from the sales of his own album.

Another concern was Inland Revenue's looming tax bill against Apple. The company's accounting was in complete disarray, even with Klein on board. Worse still, individual Beatles were long accustomed to tapping the partnership account as a personal piggy bank, John and Ringo being the worst offenders. Given their ongoing lack of self-control, the possibility that Apple would not be able to fulfill its tax obligations was quite real.

The only way for Paul to free himself from the tyranny of a manager he despised, and salvage Apple at the same time, was to file suit against the company, namely Lennon, Harrison, and Starkey. The remedies he sought were twofold: first, the appointment of a receiver to look after the business interests of Apple, which included himself. By definition, this would be someone with no vested interests or ties to any of the parties.

Second, he asked that an accounting of their collective finances be arranged by the receiver. David Hirst, Paul's attorney, argued that the assets of all of the Beatles were in jeopardy with Klein at the helm.

Despite Paul's warnings, as recently as October 1970, that something heavy would drop unless he was allowed to pull out of the Apple morass, the other Beatles appeared shocked at his petition. Said John in a postcard to Ringo: "Who'd have thought it would come to this?"

Depositions from each Beatle and Klein were duly filed and made public, airing the ex-Fabs' dirty laundry in a way at once unsettling and fascinating. Ringo revealed the scene at Paul's home when he had come to talk things out amicably, instead finding Macca "pointing his finger toward my face, shouting 'I'll finish you now!' and 'You'll pay!'"

George described the respect he'd been accorded in America in December 1968, hanging out and jamming with the Band and Bob Dylan. Still buzzing from the novelty of being treated like an equal, he returned to England, straight into the "Get Back" sessions, where he found "the same old Paul." Chafing at his second-class citizenship in his own band, George laid much of the blame at McCartney's feet. "I was fed up with him telling me how to play my own instruments."

In no position to describe abuse at the hands of his former songwriting partner, John instead simply softened the rhetoric he had used in his *Rolling*

Stone interview, telling the court of the divergent tastes within the band. "From our earliest days in Liverpool, George and I, on the one hand, and Paul, on the other, had different musical tastes. Paul preferred pop-type music, and we preferred what is now called underground."

It is hard to understand the point of airing these grievances, since the basis of Paul's action was to formalize an existing estrangement, not to curry favor as the maligned Beatle who wanted back in. The only real effect the depositions had was to badly tarnish the Beatles' image, giving an unseemly glimpse into the band's inner workings that most fans would have rather been kept in the dark about.

On the other hand, with the burden of proof upon them, Paul's legal team presented the court with a pattern of past and present deception in Allen Klein's dealings. (Klein's prior criminal conviction and SEC troubles made this an easy sell.) Furthermore, a series of business decisions enacted by the other three without his knowledge gave Paul a solid case for breach of partnership.

There was little doubt which way the High Court would rule. On March 12, 1971, the decision came down entirely in Paul's favor. But the court of public opinion was something else entirely. As far as the fans were concerned, Paul fully deserved the title of "Breaker-upper of the Beatles"—and their scorn.

As can be expected from any ugly public divorce, the public sniping between the former Fabs escalated. Given the character assassination John had unloaded on him in the *Rolling Stone* interview, Paul's desire to respond was completely understandable. But a head-on confrontation was not his style; instead, he inserted a few digs throughout his *Ram* album, released in May 1971.

The album's superb leadoff track, "Too Many People," spoke of "Too many people preaching practices / Don't let 'em tell you what you want to be," while also cautioning "That was your first mistake." "Dear Boy" spoke of regret over something lost, while "Back Seat of My Car" featured an emphatic refrain hammered home over and over again, "We believe that we can't be wrong."

Less anyone miss the point, the cover art depicted a pair of beetles in the act of copulation.

John Lennon rarely missed much of anything, real or imagined. Abetted by some stinging Harrison guitar, he retorted with the infamous "How Do You Sleep?" on his *Imagine* album, released in the fall of 1971. Rather than lay his invective between the lines, John launched a full frontal assault, presenting a laundry list of Paul's "crimes" that included living with straights, creating "muzak," and being p-whipped ("jump when your mama tell you anything"), a curious charge coming from John Ono Lennon.

For added measure, the release included a postcard photo depicting John parodying Paul's fondling of a ram, substituting a pig.

George would comment obliquely with his "Sue Me, Sue You Blues" on 1973's *Living in the Material World*. Rather than singling out any one Beatle for criticism, Harrison simply moaned about how awful the entire legal process between the band had become.

After his wistful "Early 1970," the B-side to "It Don't Come Easy," Ringo also got subtle, throwing a few barbs Paul's way in his 1972 single, "Back Off Boogaloo." Amplifying his negative take on Paul's recorded output, Ringo urged, "Don't pretend that you are dead . . . Get yourself together now and give me something tasty / Everything you try to do, you know, it sure sounds wasted." It was an observation that, until Paul's 1973 *Band on the Run* album, the critics concurred with.

As for Klein, he soon fell from favor with his clients. Reports of ill-gotten profits surfaced soon after George's charitable Concert for Bangla Desh in the summer of 1971. Upon the expiration of their contract with ABKCO in 1973, the three Beatles opted not to renew, instead launching a suit against Klein (which he met with a countersuit), representing a veritable goldmine to the legal profession for years to come.

In the end, Paul's views on Klein were vindicated, and each of his fellow Beatles eventually came around to accept this. But the cost of the battle in terms of goodwill, both with each other and the public, was enormous. Perhaps calls for the band to reunite stemmed less from a desire to hear more Beatles music than from the fans' childlike wish that their parents just stop fighting.

Nowadays, taking a long break between group activities and working on solo projects is considered pretty standard for a band with some longevity. Had matters not been exacerbated by the Apple fiasco and the Klein vs. Eastman battle, it is not unreasonable to expect that the Beatles would have worked together again, as Beatles.

The story of the Beatles and their end is replete with what-ifs. What if Brian had lived? What if John hadn't become distracted with a heroin habit? What if John and Paul, and George Martin, for that matter, had been more generous in their attitude toward George's songs?

One of the most striking ironies in the Beatles' story is this: after the meditation trip to Rishikesh in 1968, instead of divesting themselves of their hang-ups and selfishness, the Fabs became *more* infused with their own individual greatness and less disposed toward reaping the rewards of the collective. The very notion of finding peace of mind from within seems to have completely eluded them.

Afterword by Jackie Lomax

I was born in 1944 in Wallasey. The "wall of sea," we used to call it. That's across the Mersey from Liverpool, but it's pretty much the same. Nigel Olsson was from there; so was Eric Idle. Anyway, there was extreme poverty after the war. I remember as a kid only one car on the whole block. It was all broke down and rusted, but we thought that was high living.

I left home at three and went to live with my auntie—just like John Lennon. They couldn't handle me, I guess. I didn't do bad things—I just wanted to go to the beach and stuff. Like kids do. Where I grew up, it was rows of adjacent houses. A concrete canyon.

Music didn't hit me until Elvis. Then that was it. The first record I ever bought was that great first album of his: those guitars—that sound. Scotty Moore and James Burton. Of course, the parents hated it. It didn't sound like a dance band.

I was messing around with Dee and the Dynamites. We used to play the New Brighton Pier, places like that. We didn't play Elvis songs.

I first saw the Beatles at the Grosvenor Ballroom. Twice. Even then, this was before Ringo joined, they were fascinating. They were just back from Germany. I never saw a group before that sounded just like the record—better than the record. Those harmonies!

They were playing a lot of Buddy Holly, Everly Brothers, that sort of thing. Mostly, I remember seeing Stuart Sutcliffe, and Astrid. They were dressed exactly the same—lots of black.

My first gig with the Beatles was at Hambleton Hall. It was an audition, really. Here we are, we had to take a bus, then a boat, then another bus. We had one amp, and four of us plugged into it, including the lead singer. It was awful.

The Beatles were the main attraction, of course. Just before they came on, they had a musical cue. The *William Tell* overture, and then—boom—there they were.

Later on, I joined the Undertakers. We didn't compete with the Beatles—we were doing our own thing. Straight soul—R&B, whatever you wanna call it. We had a saxophone player. Never had a keyboard player, but I wished we did.

We got to know each other by playing the same clubs. Like I said, we never tried to compete with anyone, especially the Beatles. We did our thing—if anyone else did a song we were doing, that was it.

After things started to take off and we were going down to London, we found these boots made by Annello and David. We get back to Liverpool and we see the Beatles are already wearing 'em. We thought they were our discovery.

Once the Beatles got a record deal and left their stomping grounds, things really started happening for the Undertakers. Some German guys came to Liverpool, looking for bands. They were asking around to see who was worth checking out. We were playing at Litherland Town Hall. I guess they liked us; they made us an offer to play nine weeks in Hamburg, at the Star Club. Usually, a contract was only four weeks.

Now I had to give up my day job. I was at the Mersey Docks, spending three furious days a week working on balancing sheets—the rest of the time hanging out with the dock gateman. It was a solid job when full-time employment was scarce. When I quit to go to Hamburg, my dad was upset, to say the least. He wouldn't speak to me for three years.

So we went to Hamburg. I was living at Astrid's then—I think I reminded her of Stuart. Cheekbones, maybe. When we went back home, we got a record deal and recorded some singles for Pye. Brian Epstein had approached us, but I think we were still too leery of riding the Beatles' coattails.

Well, we went to America and toured a bit, but things never really caught fire. By this time, my dad had seen us on *Thank Your Lucky Stars* and he was talking to me again. He thought I'd gone off and joined a gang. Now he knew—it was just show business.

We split up in '65. A couple of the guys and me stayed on in America. Eventually, two of us ended up playing with these American guys—they thought it was something to have a couple of guys from England in the band, like some sort of British Invasion magic would just rub off.

But I stayed in touch with the Beatles. I was at the Shea Stadium show, the second one. I was riding in their limousine and I got to see all the screaming fans. It was madness. By that time, they were some kind of phenomenon.

About a year later, Brian Epstein was putting a record deal together for me—the Lomax Alliance. We played the Saville Theatre back in London. But before the album was finished, Brian died, so that fell apart.

The next year, after they got back from India, Apple was getting started. I was signed to Apple Publishing as a songwriter, writing for other people.

But George approached me and said he wanted to produce me. So I said, "Okay," playing it cool, but inside I'm like, "Yeah!"

He would invite me down to the Abbey Road studio, and Trident. "We're having a session, man, why don't you come down?" After the Beatles finished up, George and me would start laying down some tracks.

I was fascinated watching them record. But you could feel the tension then, especially after Yoko started hanging around. Chicks were banned from the studio until then. How would you feel if someone said to you, "This is how it is"?

The one time I'm sitting in the control room, just listening and watching. Then one of them goes, "Hey, Jackie, get down here and sing!" What could I do? Kick John off the microphone? Tell Paul to get back to his bass? They were doing "Dear Prudence," with that great three-part harmony. So I just added a fourth, that bottom part.

Apple was a lot of fun that first year. But after Allen Klein entered the scene, it was miserable. I stuck it out as long as I could, but eventually I just soured on the whole thing.

It was a great scene but I think the whole experience might have been too much. George was a very calm, deliberate guy, but at the end it was a trauma. For John, too, I think. The crowds, the hangers-on. Ringo was very happy-go-lucky—I guess that's how he handled it.

I had a great time. I feel like I accomplished a lot. But I was always a satellite, never a star—you know what I mean? But the Beatles were great. It's hard to think of yourself as a viable artist. But they believed in me. If not for George. . . .

Everything sprang from that.

Jackie Lomax
Ojai, California
May 2007

Jackie Lomax was the lead singer of the Liverpool band the Undertakers. He was also the first artist signed to Apple Records. Through the years, he's recorded with many artists, among them Allen Toussaint, Jeff Beck, Tony Kaye, and Bonnie Raitt. His latest album, The Ballad of Liverpool Slim, *can be found at his Web site, www.jackielomax.com. He also appears regularly at the Hub in Ojai.*

Selected Bibliography

In addition to loads of period magazines and ephemeral material, a wide array of books were consulted in the researching of this volume. Many were highlighted in Chapter 13. For those interested in further reading, here are some recommendations. (Books listed are in their latest editions, not their original publication dates.)

General History

The Beatles. *The Beatles Anthology*. New York: Chronicle Books, 2000.

Schaffner, Nicholas. *The Beatles Forever*. New York: Fine Communications, 1997.

Stark, Steven D. *Meet The Beatles: A Cultural History of the Band That Shook Youth, Gender, and the World*. New York: Harper Entertainment, 2005.

Trynka, Paul, ed., from Mojo magazine. *The Beatles: Ten Years That Shook the World*. London: DK Adult Books, 2004.

In-depth Biographies

Davies, Hunter. *The Beatles: An Authorized Biography*. New York: W.W. Norton, 2006.
> *An updated edition of the classic 1968 biography.*

Norman, Philip. *Shout! The Beatles in Their Generation*. New York: Fireside Books, 2003.
> *Reader beware: the author is an unabashed Lennon partisan.*

Spitz, Bob. *The Beatles: The Biography*. New York, Little: Brown, & Co., 2005.
> *This book, though hyped as a publishing landmark, is riddled with factual errors; as such, it is a good read, but take its veracity with a grain of salt.*

John Lennon

John has always warranted special attention from writers. These tomes are the most worthy:

Coleman, Ray. *Lennon.* London: Pan MacMillan, 2000.

Lennon, Cynthia. *John.* New York: Three Rivers Press, 2006.

Sheff, David. *All We Are Saying.* London: Pan MacMillan, 2001.

Shotton, Pete, with Nicholas Schaffner. *John Lennon: In My Life.* New York: Stein & Day, 1987.

Wenner, Jann. *Lennon Remembers.* New York: W.W. Norton, 2001.

Paul McCartney

McCartney, Paul, with Barry Miles. *Many Years from Now.* New York, Owl Books, 1998.

Sandford, Christopher. *McCartney.* New York, Carroll & Graf, 2006.

George Harrison

Harrison, George. *I Me Mine.* New York: Chronicle Books, 2007.

Leng, Simon. *The Music of George Harrison: While My Guitar Gently Weeps.* New York: Hal Leonard, 2006.

The Early Days

Best, Pete, Roag Best, and Rory Best. *The Beatles: The True Beginnings.* New York: St. Martin's Griffin, 2006.

Pawloski, Gareth L. *How They Became the Beatles.* New York: E.P. Dutton, 1989.

Williams, Allan, and William Marshall. *The Man Who Gave the Beatles Away.* New York: Ballantine Books, 1977.

The Later Days

DiLello, Richard. *The Longest Cocktail Party.* Edinburgh: Canongate Books, 2005.

Granados, Stefan. *Those Were the Days.* London: Cherry Red Books, 2004.

McCabe, Peter. *Apple to the Core*. New York: Pocket Books, 1976.

Sulpy, Doug. *Get Back: The Unauthorized Chronicle of the Beatles' 'Let It Be' Disaster*. New York: St. Martin's Griffin, 1999.

Their Recordings

Carr, Roy, and Tony Tyler. *The Beatles: An Illustrated Record*. New York: Crown Publishing, 1984.

Hertsgaard, Mark. *A Day in the Life: The Music and Artistry of the Beatles*. Peaslake Surrey, England: Delta Publishing, 1996.

Lewisohn, Mark. *The Beatles Recording Sessions*. London: EMI Records, 2006.

MacDonald, Ian. *Revolution in the Head*. London: Pimlico, 2005.

Riley, Tim. *Tell Me Why*. Cambridge, MA: Da Capo Press, 2002.

Reference

Babiuk, Andy. *Beatles Gear*. San Francisco: Backbeat Books, 2002.

Castleman, Harry, and Walter J. Podrazik. *All Together Now*. Ann Arbor, MI: Pierian Press, 1976.

Engelhardt, Kristofer. *Beatles Undercover*. Burlington, ON, Canada: Collector's Guide Publishing, 1998.

Lewisohn, Mark. *The Complete Beatles Chronicle*. London: Hamlyn, 2006.

McCoy, William, and Mitchell McGeary. *Every Little Thing*. Ann Arbor, MI: Popular Culture Ink, 1990.

Miles, Barry. *Beatles Diary*. London: Omnibus Press, 2002.

Spizer, Bruce. *The Beatles Are Coming!* New Orleans, LA: 498 Productions, 2003.

Spizer, Bruce. *The Beatles on Capitol Records (Parts 1 and 2)*. New Orleans, LA: 498 Productions, 2000.

Spizer, Bruce. *The Beatles on Apple Records*. New Orleans, LA: 498 Productions, 2003.

   Spizer's volumes are mostly meant for completists, but are quite fun to read.

Unterberger, Richie. *The Unreleased Beatles*. San Francisco, Backbeat Books, 2006.

Photography

Benson, Harry. *The Beatles: Now and Then*. New York: Universe Publishing, 1998.

Freeman, Robert. *The Beatles: A Private View*. New York: Big Tent Entertainment, 2003.

Freeman, Robert. *Yesterday: The Beatles 1963–65*. New York: Henry Holt, 1984.

Marchbank, Pearce, ed. *With the Beatles: The Photography of Dezo Hoffman*. New York, Putnam, 1983.

McCartney, Linda. *Linda McCartney's Sixties: Portrait of an Era*. New York: Bulfinch, 1993.

Russell, Ethan. *Dear Mr. Fantasy: Diary of a Decade*. New York: Houghton Mifflin, 1986.

Whitaker, Robert. *The Unseen Beatles*. San Francisco: Collins Publishers San Francisco, 1991.

Reminiscences

Bramwell, Tony, and Rosemary Kingsland. *Magical Mystery Tours*. New York: Thomas Dunne Books, 2006.

Emerick, Geoff and Howard Massey. *Here, There, and Everywhere*. New York: Gotham Books, 2006.

Martin, George and Jeremy Hornsby. *All You Need Is Ears*. New York: St. Martin's Griffin, 1994.

Taylor, Derek. *It Was Twenty Years Ago Today*. New York: Fireside Books, 1987.
    An insider's exploration of 1960s popular culture and how it was changed by the Beatles and the Summer of Love.

Humor (Deliberate and Otherwise)

Shipper, Mark. *Paperback Writer*. New York: Sunridge Press, 1978.

Schaumburg, Ron. *Growing Up with the Beatles*. New York: Harcourt Brace Jovanovich, 1978.
    This book details the Beatles' career from the perspective of a Midwesterner coming of age during the '60s. Its charm comes from Schaumburg's earnest, quaint prose, e.g., "I made a rotten hippie," "Heavens to Betsy, Yoko."

Collecting

Cox, Perry, and Frank Daniels. *Price Guide for the Beatles American Records*, 6th ed. New Orleans, LA: 498 Productions, 2007.

Some Outstanding Web Links

http://www.whatgoeson.com/
http://www.dmbeatles.com/index.php
http://www.beatlesource.com/savage/main.html
http://www.columbia.edu/~brennan/beatles/
http://www.pootle.demon.co.uk/wgo.htm
http://www.fabfourfaq.com